MW00900438

ch

LEARNING TO REJOICE IN THE MIDDLE OF ...!

LEARNING TO REJOICE IN THE MIDDLE OF ...!

MARY L. KLINE

iUniverse®

LEARNING TO REJOICE IN THE MIDDLE OF ...!

iUniverse books may be ordered through booksellers or by contacting:

iUniverse
1663 Liberty Drive
Bloomington, IN 47403
www.iuniverse.com
1-800-Authors (1-800-288-4677)

ISBN: 978-1-4917-8104-3 (sc)
ISBN: 978-1-4917-8105-0 (hc)
ISBN: 978-1-4917-8124-1 (e)

Library of Congress Control Number: 2015917522

Print information available on the last page.

iUniverse rev. date: 12/04/2015

"Rejoice in the Lord always..." Philippians 4:4
This is the story of how God prepared us individually,
brought us together, and led us to Africa.
He gave us a wonderful family, and supplied all of our needs.
Praise the Lord!

The picture of Lake Kivu on the cover is from a painting by Rev. Frank Adamson who gave it to Phil Kline in 1956. This painting has always been treasured by our family. Frank and Hazel were pioneer missionaries in Rwanda, Africa and founded the Kibogora Free Methodist Mission in 1942. The mission was built on a high hill overlooking mile high Lake Kivu.

CONTENTS

DEDICATION

This book is dedicated to the memory of the **many** faithful years of loving missionary service given by Rev. Frank and Hazel Adamson and their family. They shared God's Love with the people of South Africa, Burundi, and Rwanda, in Central Africa.

Frank and Hazel were our neighbors in McPherson, Kansas, where they lived during their 1947 furlough. Their children, Myra and Merlin, were students at Central College in McPherson. The *Banyarwanda* people told Phil, "*Bgana* and *Madamo Adamsoni* loved us."

Rev. Frank and Hazel Adamson, in front of the large church that Frank was building at Kibogora Mission in Rwanda.

Mary L. Kline

I would also like to dedicate this book to the memory of my parents, Orval and Lois Heath, who poured so much of themselves into the lives of their children. Thank you, Mother, for saving all of the letters I wrote to you and Daddy from Africa. The pages in this book are mostly copied from those letters. Thank you too, for enriching our lives by your loving and sacrificial living.

All scripture quotations are taken from the King James version of the Bible.

ACKNOWLEDGEMENTS

Why were these pages written? In 2005, on my 81st birthday, Paul, my oldest son, asked me, "Well, Mom, what are your goals for this year?" So, I decided it was time to quit procrastinating, and I proceeded to continue copying onto our computer many of the letters I had written to my parents all through the years our family was in Africa, 1953 - 1968. My mother had saved all of them. Re-reading these letters convinced me I should somehow preserve all this family history, just for our family to have. I decided to include a brief history of our lives before we were married - Mary's Story and Phil's Story.

But in 2013, so many people told me, "**We** want to read your story." So, I am finally willing to allow these pages to go public, praying that God will receive praise and glory by our telling of all the amazing things He has done for us through the years.

I am deeply indebted to my youngest daughter, Janet Porrazzo, who with her computer skills, has spent many hours working with me and helping to put all these pages of family history and pictures together. As we have spent hours editing I have greatly enjoyed re-reading and re-living our wonderful years in Africa.

CHAPTER 1

Preparation

Mary's Story

I was born in 1924, Mary Lois, the first child of Orval and Lois Heath in Los Angeles, California. My parents had met at Los Angeles Seminary, and lived in a small community, called Hermon, nestled in the hills of Highland Park, a northeast suburb of Los Angeles. Hermon had been built up around Los Angeles Seminary and the Free Methodist Church. It was a wonderful place to live.

My father was born in 1898. His mother died when he was seven, but he vividly remembered his mother, as she lay on her death bed, asking him to promise her that he would give his heart to Jesus so that they could be together in Heaven. His father remarried, and sold the family farm his first wife had inherited. Because the step-brothers fought each other all the time, his father left his own sons, Orval and Harland, in the care of their uncle, and moved into the city with his new wife and her four sons.

My daddy wrote in his autobiography that he was a little devil on wheels. He did not think that anyone could love or care for him. He felt all they wanted was to get all the work out of him they could. But he said that when he gave his heart to the Lord, he was a totally different boy. He prayed and read his Bible and became a true follower of Christ. He began to grow in the Spirit with the Lord, taking great interest in the Bible. He felt God was calling him to be a preacher.

My father became a student at Huntington College, a Bible school for training preachers, working very hard to pay his way. He became ill and had to quit school. At the age of 23, he boarded a train for Modesto, California, where he had been offered a job as pastor of a small United Brethren Church at a salary of $1,000 a year. The bishop and the elders didn't appreciate his preaching on Sanctification as a definite second

1

work of Grace, so he resigned and started attending the Modesto Free Methodist Church.

A Free Methodist preacher, Rev. Archie Stevens invited him to accompany his family to the area of Ione, California, where he had just been appointed pastor of a circuit of four small churches. Rev. Stevens felt he needed Orval to assist him in his work. When my father realized he needed more education, he was able to enroll in Los Angeles Seminary, a Free Methodist school that gave him credit for his studies in Indiana. It was there that his prayers for a Christian wife, who loved children, were answered.

Orval Heath married Lois Grace McReynolds on August 20, 1923. Lois' family, her parents, Leven and Sarah McReynolds, and her grandparents, Daniel and Rebecca Gehres, had recently moved from Santa Ana, to Highland Park in Northeast Los Angeles, California. Her grandparents had sold their ranch near Santa Ana, and had purchased property near Los Angeles Seminary so Lois and her sister, Pauline, could attend a Christian high school while still living at home. My Grandpa, Leven McReynolds, had retired from his business of purchasing produce from surrounding farms and ranches in the Santa Ana area. He then had loaded the produce onto a wagon pulled by horses, to sell in town, like a traveling farmers' market! Grandpa Leven became our church maintenance man. Grandpa used to let us 'help' him ring the church bell by pulling on the big rope that hung from the tall belfry over the church entry hall. Grandpa's favorite Bible verse was Psalm 84:10. " …I had rather be a doorkeeper in the house of my God, than to dwell in the tents of wickedness."

We were told that our Grandfather McReynolds came from a very distinguished family. One of his relatives had been a personal friend of George Washington. A distant 'cousin', James Clark McReynolds, had been appointed Attorney General of the U.S. by President Wilson in 1913. He had also been a Judge on the U.S. Supreme Court from 1914 to 1941. Most of this information was gathered from an encyclopedia. I always thought he must have been nice, because when I was in about fourth grade, I wrote him a letter, telling him he was one of my relatives, and he answered with a nice letter, mailed to **me**! The poor man, who was very well off, never married, but had adopted thirty-three British children who had been orphaned, victims of the German bombing of London in 1940! The article I read stated that he was a **very** conservative Democrat, who strongly opposed President Roosevelt's New Deal.

I was the first child of Orval and Lois Heath, the first of eleven! Mother quit school after they were married, but Daddy continued attending school until he had to find full-time work to support his family. Throughout his lifetime, he ministered on many weekends, either preaching or teaching an adult Sunday School class. I remember that sometimes he traveled with a neighbor, Rev. George Swift's father, to hold meetings way out in the San Bernardino valley, near Covina and Corona.

Mother had always been keenly interested in missions, but had been told she wasn't physically strong enough to serve on a mission field. She passed on her interest and burden for missions to many children in our weekly Junior Missionary Society meetings. I still remember one of the missionary stories she told us about the smoke from a thousand villages where people had never heard the Good News of the Gospel of Jesus Christ. She had drawn pictures of African huts to help us remember the story. Since childhood, I have always been a voracious reader, and I always read everything I could find about Africa. My mother probably never imagined that one of her own daughters would someday be privileged to work as a missionary in Africa!

Mother and Daddy lived a couple blocks away from Grandma's house. In September of 1924, when my mother realized I would be born that day, she walked over to her grandparents' and parents' little house on Coleman Avenue for my birth.

Mother did love babies, and continued having them about every two years until after I was married! My siblings are Sarah Fern, Lily Ruth, Orlean Esther, Harland Daniel, Orval Joseph, David Lee, Grace Miriam, Paul Donald, Abilene May and John Timothy. There were eleven of us, and each one was given a carefully chosen Bible name.

Los Angeles was a great place to live in those days. The weather was mild, with mostly clear skies, and no smog. Some days the sky was a bit foggy with the coastal marine layer blowing into the area. Nights were always cool with a lovely sea breeze. Sometime after my birth, my father was given the job of custodian on the lower Seminary campus, which was also the church Conference campground. Los Angeles Seminary, which later became Los Angeles Pacific College and high school, and the Free Methodist church had built a large gymnasium/auditorium there. We lived in the custodian's house for several years. Every summer Free Methodists would gather from all over southern California to pitch their tents for the annual Camp Meeting on our campground. I loved those exciting days. Many beautiful Eucalyptus and Acacia trees grew all over the big square block, so there was lots of shade, and when all the people were gone, it was a wonderful place to play. Even though we grew up during the Great Depression, I don't remember ever being really hungry. Mother was a good cook, and they were good managers of their money. Tithing and offerings to the church were always my parents' first priority, and we were taught to tithe whatever money we had.

I remember one time when we still lived on the campground where there was too much shade for a good garden, mother went out to pull up an onion for our soup. The onion was rotten, and she cried. Mother then told us the story about the hobo who instead of just begging for a meal, offered to make 'stone soup' for the family that had agreed to give him a meal that evening. He always carried in his pocket, small, clean, smooth stones. He would pull one out of his pocket, and tell the lady, "Now, if you will just bring out some carrots, celery, onions, potatoes, and maybe a little bit of meat, I'll teach you how to make stone soup." So that evening we enjoyed a delicious stone soup, minus onions!

Mother sewed all our clothes, and when we out-grew them, they were handed down to the next in line. We were often recipients of 'hand-me-downs' from other families also. We would get new shoes only once a year, just before school started. When our shoes had holes in the soles, we put cardboard liners in them. It helped that we were always given permission in the early summer to go barefoot. It was never soon enough to suit me!

I vividly remember the terrible earthquake in the 1930's. We had just sat down to eat our evening meal, when our table started to dance around, and Daddy yelled, "Earthquake! Everybody run outside quick, and don't stand under the electric wire!" No damage was done to our house, but in the southwest part of Los Angeles County there was a lot of destruction of homes and schools. Daddy took us for a drive to that area the next day so we could see what earthquakes could do! He also took us to the warehouse where he worked, and we helped him clear up the mess the earthquake had left. It took me a **long** time to get over the trauma of that earthquake. Night after night Mother would softly sing to us, "Be not dismayed whate're betide, God will take care of you," as we felt the afterquakes, and then I could sleep.

I also remember something else traumatic that happened in 1933. On New Year's Eve Daddy drove Brother Lee, Sue, and me over to the Glendale United Brethren Church to attend their Watch Night service. In the summer there had been fires in the San Gabriel Mountains just north of Los Angeles. This week there was continuing unusually heavy rain. As we were driving home after the service, in what my father called 'raining cats and dogs', we were on San Fernando Road, on the bridge over a usually very small stream, when suddenly our car was engulfed with a torrent of water. The engine stopped. Daddy and Brother Lee jumped out of the car, and started pushing it. Daddy told me to climb into the driver's seat and steer while they pushed. I didn't know how to do that, and I was **terrified**! As I remember, they succeeded in getting the car pushed off San Fernando Road and up onto Chevy Chase Street that also had water rushing down it! Friends who lived nearby helped us dry off the spark plugs and the engine so the car was able to start again. God was answering Mother's prayers for our safety. She had been claiming the promises in Psalm 91. We praised the Lord for answered prayer. Some cars after ours were trapped by tons of sand which the flood had washed onto the bridge, but we were safe. Mother finally persuaded Daddy to return to the Free Methodist Church. We were very happy to be able to walk to church again instead of driving clear over to Glendale!

On long summer evenings all the neighborhood kids would play kick the can in the huge front yard just two houses down the street from us. What fun that was, especially when my boyfriend and I ended up hiding in the same place. He was three years older than me, and when

World War II started on Sunday, December 7, 1941, many lives were changed. He enlisted, and wanted to get married before he went into the Army. He asked me if I was ready to get married. I told him, "No." I felt I was too young to get married, and I was determined to finish college. After he married someone else, it took a very long time for me to get over losing my first love.

Most of the young men were drafted or enlisted. Many couples married earlier than they had planned to, and I, foolishly, became engaged to a young fellow student, my chemistry partner, who was enlisting in the Navy. That was probably the biggest mistake I ever made. I'm sure I **didn't** ask God for wisdom and guidance before I promised to marry him! He was a very nice young man from a lovely family, but he had told me he would never be willing to leave his family's cult.

Summers, during World War II, I was employed in the steno pool at Lockheed Aircraft Corporation in Burbank, typing huge sheets of numbers to be dittoed for the Engineering Department. After graduating from junior college in 1943, I was accepted at Seattle Pacific College. Esther Stites, a neighbor, and I, boarded a train in downtown Los Angeles with our trunks and suitcases. That was my first time away from California. I loved the green beauty of the chilly, rainy northwest. I found out the hard way that good grades came only to those who studied and read assignments daily. Cramming for exams no longer worked! Pop quizzes were often given without notice!

My interests were in science, and I chose pre-med classes, because I thought I might want to be a nurse. I took many classes of chemistry, bacteriology, parasitology, and anatomy classes, where we dissected cadavers. I was assigned to do an arm. I still remember the over-powering stench of formaldehyde and how difficult it was to eat lunch after that lab! When we were given the assignment to practice giving each other injections, I couldn't do it, and decided right then I would never be a nurse, and I knew I couldn't become a doctor!

Seattle Pacific had many great Christian professors, and I took all the Bible classes I could, partly because Prof. Helsel was my favorite teacher, never imagining that in years to come I would be forever thankful for the excellent training in Bible study. I even studied Systematic Theology with the ministerial students and a class where we learned a lot about many different religions. Because of what I learned in that class I decided that since I was a fourth generation Free Methodist, I never wanted to be anything else. A revival meeting in my senior year helped me reach the point of complete surrender to God's will, even more than the class I had taken on Bible Doctrine of Holiness. I wrote a letter to my boyfriend, breaking our engagement. He was then stationed in Pocatello, Idaho, studying to be an Ensign in the U.S. Navy. His reply was that people would be much wiser to confine their emotions to a person of the same sect! Of course, that is what my parents had thought all the time! I should have obeyed them.

Mary gets called to teach chemistry!

At last, in 1945 I was 20, a college graduate with a B.S. degree. I had a minor in chemistry and a major in zoology, with classes in bacteriology and parasitology, which I hoped would help me get a job as a lab technician! I turned twenty-one that September, but I was already into one of the most important adventures of my life! One morning in August, I was summoned up the hill to the president's office at Los Angeles Pacific College where I had spent my high school and junior college days. The recently appointed president of Central College in McPherson, Kansas, was having a hard time filling the faculty. World War II had seriously decimated the teaching staff in that small Christian college. His telephoned question to President C. Hoyt Watson of Seattle Pacific College was, "Do you have a recent graduate who would be qualified to teach college chemistry?" They looked through the records and found the name of Mary Heath, who had minored in chemistry. He called President C. Dorr Demaray of Los Angeles Pacific College, and requested that he contact me. Never in my wildest dreams had I ever planned on being a teacher! I had no teacher training. I was tired of being in school. I didn't think I could teach chemistry! But I knew I wanted to be in the center of God's will, so I told President Demaray I would pray about it and let him know my answer in a few days. So, I prayed, and finally with many qualms, I told the Lord that though I considered myself totally unable to fill that position, if this was really an appointment from Him, I would do my best. God gave me peace, and I knew the Lord would be going with me. I dug out my old college freshman chemistry book, and started reviewing. The hardest part was all the math! How could I possibly teach that?

Off to Kansas

September, 1945 found me telling my family goodbye, boarding a Santa Fe train bound for Kansas with my nose in my chemistry book. I had always crammed for exams. This was the ultimate in cramming! The trip was exciting. I had never been east of California. The changing geography was fascinating, but when we reached Texas, the telephone poles were no longer tall and straight like the ones I had seen all my life. They were short and crooked! **Where** was I going? I was used to seeing hills and mountains and tall pine and fir trees, and here there were none I could see, just miles and miles of flat or rolling fields, and many tumbleweeds blowing around.

At Central College, in McPherson, Kansas, I was assigned a room in one of the girls' residences, the Elms. My job was to try to teach college chemistry, high school general science and geometry! Surprisingly, classes went well that first semester. World War II had ended, and many young veterans had returned to school. It was challenging and fun to try to teach them! Most of them were older than me. At the end of first semester, in January 1946, I was walking across the campus with another teacher, when I saw across campus, the man of my dreams! Tall, dark, handsome, in an Army Air Corps uniform! I remember remarking in wonder, "Do you suppose **he** will be in school here?" That man was Phillip Stephen Kline, who had spent three years doing Air Corps ground crew service on South Pacific islands, during World War II. He was hoping to get a college education.

Phil's Story
(Written by Mary from Phil's memories)

Phillip was born near Agricola, Kansas in February, 1923, the twelfth child of a farming family. His parents were Charles Henry

Kline and Lydia Emaline Dugger Kline. They lived in a sturdy, two story farm house built by Phil's grandfather, Henry John Kline, a master carpenter. Phil's older sisters were Ruth, Marian, Lois, Esther, Jeanne and Jennie Louise. His older brothers were Henry, Bishop, Paul David-(P.D.), Raymond and Cecil. Then came Phil, Burton, and Betty. Phil weighed fourteen pounds at birth! He was always tall, husky and strong. He actually **was** born in the barn! His nickname was Buster, but they called him Bus. His older brothers loved to tease him, once telling him to pick up a horse fly (really a bumble bee) from the horse water trough, and they laughed when it stung him! Phil also remembered being held down in bed by his older brothers, with the covers held snugly over his nose. He panicked, and thought for sure he was going to suffocate! All his life he couldn't stand to have anything over his nose! The Kline kids rode a country bus to school, and when it rained, the dirt roads were slippery. One steep hill was especially bad, and everyone had to get off the bus and walk to the top. When Phil was seven, his father was digging a well in their back yard, and the dynamite failed to explode. He made the mistake of leaning over the well to investigate, when suddenly it exploded, and he fell to the bottom of the well. As he was climbing up out of the well, there was a second explosion, which injured him so severely he never regained his strength. He died at the age of fifty, leaving Lydia with fourteen children to raise. The older brothers and sisters helped take care of the younger ones. Most of the family moved to live with older brother Henry and his bride, Carrie, on a vegetable farm. On the bank of the nearby river was a big water tank, full of water pumped up from the river to use for irrigation of the fields of vegetables. Phil remembered how welcome the cold water felt on hot days when they jumped into the tank after shedding their overalls!

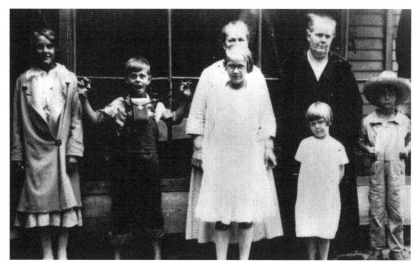

Jeanne, Phil, Aunt Jen, Phil's mom, Lydia, Louise, Betty, and Burton Kline

After a couple years, the family moved to live with older sister, Esther in the big city of Topeka, Kansas. She was employed as personal secretary to the County Superintendent of schools. Older brothers, Bish and Ray, had been working in a Molybdenum mine way up in the Colorado mountains near Leadville. P.D. later loaded up the family onto an old truck he had purchased to take them to Colorado where he was stationed at the Fort Logan U.S. Army Base. The truck was overloaded, and Phil remembered the tires kept blowing out. After the family got settled at Fort Logan, Burt and Phil would often walk up to the Commissary to get bread for the family. The baker told them that if they would sweep the floor, he would give them an extra loaf. They always devoured that right away before they got home!

Oldest sister, Ruth, and brother Bishop were living in the Colorado mountains near Climax, proving their homesteads. Phil and Burt went to live in Ruth's cabin for the summer. Some of Phil's best memories were of trout fishing with brother Burton in a nearby mountain stream with a stick for a fishing pole. At noon, they would build a fire, cook and eat the fish they had caught that morning, then fish for more to take home to Ruth. Coming down the mountains at the end of the summer while returning back to Fort Logan, Phil and Burt were riding on the open flat bed of the truck. Phil remembered being scared, looking down at the river as they rounded the curves, and shouting to P.D., "Slow down! All you care about is getting the front end of the truck around. You don't worry about us back here falling off into the river!"

Phil also worked with brothers, Cecil and Henry, irrigating on farms in Colorado, and later returned to Kansas to live with sister, Lois, her husband, Johnny Bryan, and their son, Robert, near Scranton. For several years Phil walked three miles to school, across the fields, even when it was snowing, with a scarf across his face to try to keep out the cold. He remembered bad leg aches after he had Rheumatic Fever. Phil helped with all of the farm chores; driving the tractor, even plowing in the moonlight, when it was cooler. While he was driving the tractor, he taught himself to whistle like a bird. He helped cut the hay, putting it into windrows, loading it into wagons, and putting it into hay stacks or bales for winter use. He also milked the cows, separated the cream, churned the butter, fed the hogs and chickens, gathered the eggs, chopped wood, and whatever else needed to be done. Phil finally finished eighth grade at the Highland School, Osage County, a one-room country school, and received his diploma on 5/25/39 at the age of sixteen. We have a picture of him with all of the thirteen students of that school. He was head and shoulders taller than anyone else, was the fastest runner, always winning the blue ribbons in competition. He never had the opportunity of going to high school. His days were filled with hard work. He joined the C.C.C.'s (Civilian Conservation Corps) in the late 1930's, and did a lot of trail and fire look-out tower building in the Colorado mountains. When World War II started, Phil joined sister, Jeanne and her husband, Glen Prevo in Inglewood, California, working in the Douglas Aircraft factory. They lived in a small home-made house trailer. Phil's job was doing sheet-metal work. When he returned to Wichita, Kansas, riding his Harley, he was again employed at an airplane manufacturing factory, doing sheet-metal work.

Phil joins the U.S. Army Air Corps

Phil joined the Army Air Corps in 1942, leaving the U.S. on a Liberty Ship from Camp Pendleton, California, and was horribly sea sick all the way across the Pacific Ocean. He lived for three and a half years on various islands in the South Pacific in tents under coconut trees, hoping not to get conked on the head by a falling coconut! He repaired shot-up airplanes, and saw tracer bullets blaze across the skies on dark nights. He was stationed on New Caledonia, the Solomon Islands, New Guinea, Guadalcanal, and Palawan in the Philippines. His Air Corps unit always arrived at an island after it had been freed from the Japanese by the Marines. In the Philippines he met two Free Methodist chaplains, Rev. Bob Warren and Rev. Bergen Birdsall. We have a letter that another chaplain sent to Phil's mother, telling her what a fine young man Phil was. He had fixed whatever needed fixing, and had faithfully attended all the worship services. Phil promised God that if He would keep him safe until the war was over, he would be willing to be a missionary somewhere if that's what God wanted. All the time Phil was in the Air Corps he had most of his income sent home to help support his mom and younger sister, Betty. At war's end in 1945, he returned to Wichita, Kansas, and was encouraged by Rev. Easterling, pastor of the Wichita Free Methodist Church, to further his education at Central College in McPherson, Kansas. Because Phil had never been able to go to high school or college, he was given the opportunity of taking a G.E.D. type test. Since he lacked knowledge in science, Phil ended up in my high school freshmen General Science class before he could start college.

Phil spent 3 years on South Pacific Islands, while in the Air
Corps, during World War II, living in tent barracks

Teacher has a boyfriend!

In January, 1946, when Phil enrolled at Central, he was assigned to my table for meals. For some reason, I found it very necessary to get up to go to breakfast, something I had not been doing before! Meal time became very interesting for both of us. We have joked many times about Central being a 'match factory'! Our first date was to a college basketball game, and we were greeted with calls of, "Teacher's got a boyfriend!" We had many things in common. We both came from very large families. We had both been raised in the Free Methodist Church, but he was a 'country boy' and I was a 'city girl'. However, he had never had the opportunity, until then, to go to college. Within three months we were engaged! In June, we drove to Los Angeles in Phil's '36 Ford, which had a leaky radiator! Phil poured water into it all the way to California! His Mom made the trip with us, so we were properly chaperoned! Phil had wanted to get married right away, but I insisted it took time to get ready for a wedding, and I wanted to make my own wedding gown! I worked in the office of the Los Angeles County dog licensing department, and Phil worked with his brother, P.D., who was a concrete contractor.

While I was working in that office, a lady suggested that Phil and I should try to get on a Hollywood radio program. So, we did. I think it was called Cupid's Couple. After all of the couples had told their romantic story, the audience would decide which couple was the winner. We were not chosen to be Cupid's Couple. However, we did receive a nice set of stainless steel flatware.

Phil added water to the radiator, all the way from Kansas to California

Phil and Mary get married!

We were married in Los Angeles in August, 1946, on the twenty-third wedding anniversary of my parents. Phil was twenty-three and I was twenty-one. Rev. Bob Warren, one of the chaplains Phil had met in the Philippines, was pastor of the Hermon Free Methodist Church where my family attended. He was delighted to see Phil again, and performed our wedding ceremony. We spent our honeymoon driving back to Kansas, stopping first to camp in Yosemite. We had a small tent, and I had nothing to cook on except Canned Heat! I didn't know how to cook on a camp fire! When I was almost in tears, after trying unsuccessfully to cook pancakes on Canned Heat at that altitude, a kind man, from the tent next to ours rescued us by selling us a small propane one burner camp stove for one dollar! They were packing up to leave for home that day. The pancakes tasted mighty good! We hiked up to the base of Bridal Veil Falls, and spent a wonderful day on the huge rocks at the edge of the big pool. Romantic! We took the Tioga Pass road out the east side of Yosemite. In those days it was just a steep, narrow, winding dirt road, full of rocks! We drove down into the Nevada desert, and Phil was planning that we would sleep that night in our little tent, but I was too afraid of rattlesnakes! I'm sure I slept in the car! When we got to Yellowstone Park, after driving around to see all the fabulous geysers, pools, and burping mud pots, we pitched our tent in a campground. We were awakened with the honking of our car horn. A big bear was trying to get in the window which we had forgotten to completely close! He had smelled the food we had stashed in the car. Phil scared him away and went out to close the window, but failed to get it completely rolled forward. The bear came back, and broke out a piece of the window! I was so terrified, I don't think I slept much that night, and I refused to stay in Yellowstone another night! I'm sure that by that time Phil was wondering, "What did I marry?!"

August, 1946, Phil and Mary were married

We arrive in McPherson with no place to live!

When we finally arrived in McPherson, Kansas we weren't sure where we were going to live! As I recall, we hadn't made any plans. Each of us previously had lived in school dorms. But now we were married! Some kind people rented us a small upstairs apartment. Later, Phil converted a friend's garage into an apartment. We purchased the empty lot next door, and Phil built us a cute little house in his spare time, in addition to going to school full time. The G.I. Bill gave Phil $100 per month for living expenses, as well as paying for all his school fees, tuition and books. I continued to teach college chemistry, high school general science and geometry at Central College.

In 1947 Phil said, "I think we'd better send for an application to the General Missionary Board." My first reaction was that we couldn't possibly do that! I couldn't think of a single thing we could do that would qualify us to be missionaries! Phil wasn't a preacher; I wasn't a nurse. What could we do? But Phil was sure that if God wanted us to be missionaries, He surely would have something for us to do. We finally decided many months after it had arrived that we would fill out the application, thinking that if we were accepted, God must want us to go somewhere, and if we weren't accepted, well, that would be a closed door. Of course, it had to be Africa. It had always fascinated me. I knew I would love to travel there! I had read everything I could get my hands on about the 'Dark Continent', full of savage tribes and lions and the mines of King Solomon, the Mountains of the Moon, and Mount Kilimanjaro!

The first little house Phil built for us

General Missionary Board said,
"Finish your education, Phil."

The answer came back from the General Missionary Board, "Thanks for your application, but we can't use you until you finish your education. Get your degree, Phil, and then contact us again. Keep in touch." Was I relieved! Phil continued going to college, and I continued to teach. Phil's favorite classes at Central were in the school shop. Howard Krober was his teacher. Phil made some beautiful furniture for us. He had a real talent for working with wood, and making things. Howard and Anita Krober had built a house close to ours. They were such good friends, and a big influence in our lives. A group of fellows, all recently returned from service in World War II, decided to form a construction company, even though they were all still going to college! Ed Pyle was president, since it was his idea in the first place. Ed, Mitch Allmon, Larry Clark and Phil formed the Pyle Construction Company, and they all did carpentry and concrete work. They built many homes and churches. All of them had also been students in my chemistry class! After he graduated from junior college, Phil worked with his partners for several years, helping to build more houses before going back to school to earn his B.S. degree from McPherson College.

Phil's sister, Jeanne, and husband, Glen Prevo had moved from Missouri to McPherson. She was teaching junior high math classes, and took an upholstery class with Phil at McPherson College. Phil and his friends later built us a nice little two bedroom house on the east side of town near our friends, Mitch and Joyce Allmon. We sold our first house to a newlywed couple for $10,000! I had taught at Central College for three years, and after taking education classes at McPherson College, and getting a Lifetime Kansas Elementary and High School Teacher's Certificate, I applied to teach in one of their country schools. I taught in two different country high schools, Canton and Roxbury, and then at Lone Tree School, a one room country grade school with all eight grades and sixteen students, in a Russian Mennonite farming community, very nice people, and really sweet kids. Again God must have been guiding me, because my work in Africa was mostly teaching, and I had discovered that I really enjoyed teaching!

Because I had farther to go, I always drove our car to work, and Phil drove to McPherson College on his little 'putt-putt' motor scooter. One day, in the middle of the winter, I was driving in the snow, way out in the country, to teach at the Roxbury High School. The snow turned into a blizzard, and I could hardly see through the swirling flakes where the road was. There must have been ice on the road, because all of a sudden, the car skidded completely around, and, amazingly backed up onto a tiny bridge over a deep ditch filed with snow, right up into the beginning of the driveway of a farm house! I thanked the Lord for his protection, and then drove safely on to school.

Lone Tree one room school, Mary, and her students

November 19, 1950, Sunday night, (A letter to my parents) It's cold! Just looked at the thermometer outside our kitchen window and it said twenty! To make it worse, there's a strong north wind. I shiver to think about school tomorrow.

Phil's mother and Betty will be here for Thanksgiving. I have to teach on Friday! I've caught up on housework! Phil is tired of holes in his pockets! Poor boy. He says I'm not teaching next year, but the only thing

I'd ever stop for is a baby! Phil is doing all right in school. Daddy, we are looking forward to your trip in the spring, too. I'm getting excited about it already.

I didn't know that in a few years I would be teaching my own children and children of other missionaries in Africa, and would be very thankful for that teaching experience! They invited me back to teach another year. I thanked them for their confidence in me, but I wouldn't be teaching another year, because I was very pregnant.

Our son is born!

Our first child, Paul Stephen, was born in July, 1951. We were so excited to be parents. After we had been married for over four years, and still had no children, I had prayed desperately that God would send us a son, and He did, exactly **nine** months later! Thank You, Lord! The next year, 1952, Phil graduated from McPherson College with a B.S. degree in Industrial Arts Education. He was accepted into the Master's Program at Oklahoma A & M College in Stillwater, Oklahoma. Our second house in McPherson that Phil and his friends had built for us, sold for $12,000, just the day before we were leaving town to move to Oklahoma! Isn't it amazing how God answers prayer, often just at the last moment?

Paul's first Sunday

Paul 11 months

The house that sold just before we left for Oklahoma

Letter to Mary's parents from Stillwater, Oklahoma

December 1952, I am hoping to write eleven letters this afternoon! I just finished our dinner dishes and Paul, (seventeen months old) was playing happily with my mops and brooms in the kitchen. Then, when he saw me bringing the typewriter into the living room, Paul came running. He is going in circles around me, trying to get his fingers in! At last, he changed his interest, but now he is messing with the radio. He turns the volume up real high, and scares himself, and then comes running, making cute sounds. I never saw a child who was so crazy about music. He keeps time almost perfectly, and tries to lead the singing in church. Other times he nods his head or sways back and forth in time to the music. He is really getting tall. He is 32 1/2" high, but still weighs only 24 1/2 pounds. He has had two pretty bad colds lately. Antibiotic snaps him out of it almost miraculously, but he is a mighty sick boy before it takes effect. He is completely over it this time, with not even a runny nose. I certainly hope he doesn't get sick again this winter. He was just about driving me batty trying to keep him out of things so I locked the baby gate to keep him in his room. As long as I stay there and play peek-a-boo with him or roll his tractor to him under the gate he is happy. Guess I'll set up my typewriter on a card table in front of his door. Poor little guy needs a brother! But no luck yet. One day I couldn't find Paul, so I looked outside, and there he was, climbing over the gate to run away!

Phil is home from school already. Paul has been asleep for quite a while, and at this rate I'll never get all 11 letters written! We will leave here Sunday afternoon and spend several days in McPherson with Mitch and Joyce Allmon, so Phil can work. We will go to Scranton the day before Christmas and will probably spend the weekend there. We will come back here, to Stillwater, on the third. School starts the fifth. Love to all. Have a very merry Christmas and a happy New Year. Wish we could see you. We'll be thinking about you! I think we will open your gifts tomorrow night before we leave for McPherson. We will pretend it is Christmas. It acts as if it might snow anytime. We had a good rain last night, and it is cold today.

CHAPTER 2
South Africa

We are asked to go teach in South Africa!

After Phil received his Master's Degree in Industrial Arts Education from Oklahoma A & M University in June of 1953, he had planned to teach wood shop classes in a junior high or high school. Phil had an appointment the next day, to sign a contract to teach in a Guthrie, Oklahoma junior high, when we received a phone call from Dr. Byron S. Lamson, General Missionary Secretary of the Free Methodist Church. He wanted to meet with us the next day. Dr. Lamson told us that a principal was needed at the Edwaleni (ed-wah-lay'-nee) Technical College for African boys in South Africa in January of 1954, "Would Phil consider taking the job?" Dr. Lamson told us that he felt that Phil was just the person they needed to fill that position.

Phil was immediately ready to say yes! But because he had forgotten to tell me about his promise to God before we were married, I struggled and prayed until I was willing to be obedient to the call. Then we both felt that God was really calling us through the Missionary Board. So, we agreed to go to South Africa after our second child was born, which would be in September, 1953. Phil had to take some Bible classes before we could leave for South Africa, so we traveled to Seattle, towing the little house trailer we had purchased from Barstow Hoffman. Phil enrolled at Seattle Pacific, my Alma Mater. Prof. Helsel let us park our little house trailer in their yard. Paul climbed over the fence one day and someone found him several blocks away, down a steep hill, and brought him back home! Thank You, Lord!

June, 1953, Dear Dr. Lamson, We have finally reached Seattle, and Phil is enrolled in all the Bible courses he can get in one summer. The letters you have written for us have been forwarded, and we have an appointment to get our physical exams next Tuesday. About filing an application for our passport, should we do so right away, or wait until our other child arrives? Our baby is due in early September. Summer school is out the last week in August and then we plan to leave immediately for Los Angeles.

We have seen the Ryffs, (former missionaries to South Africa), but haven't had much of a chance to talk with them yet. We are going to their house tomorrow evening. We still feel quite incapable of filling such a responsible position, but we do sense that the Lord is leading us, and we are trusting in Him to supply our needs and take care of our feelings of inadequacy.

Yours in His Service, Phil and Mary Kline

We travel to Los Angeles

And there were dozens and dozens of other letters, forms, instructions, and much work in preparing to travel to the other side of the world! I still have many of the original letters and I marvel at how immense and complicated the job was to get everything together, comply with all the pages of requirements, and purchase and pack everything. Makes me dizzy now to look back and think about it! Thank goodness we were young, healthy, enthusiastic, and rejoicing in doing what we knew God wanted us to do! We had been told it was extremely important that Phil be at Edwaleni when the new school year began in January, so we had to be ready to leave the States when our baby was just **four** months old! We had hurried to Los Angeles as soon as the summer quarter was over so I could be with my parents when our child was born. We were again pulling the little house trailer we had purchased from Barstow Hoffman, and I, foolishly, had insisted we drive down Highway 1, because I knew I would miss the beautiful Pacific Ocean when we got to Africa! I was surprised after we had arrived in South Africa, as we drove along the beautiful Indian Ocean coastline, it was every bit as beautiful as California's coastline!

1953, Mary and Phil with the Heath family, in Los Angeles

Our second child is born

Nancy Lyn was born in September, 1953, **five** days after we arrived in Los Angeles! What a joy it was to live so close to my parents, so they could get to know our son, Paul, and his baby sister, Nancy. We had parked our little house trailer on the vacant lot next door to my parents' house, so we could live in it while we visited them. When we were ready to leave, we just left it parked there for them to try to sell! There were two reasons why we had towed a little house trailer all the way from Oklahoma to Washington, and then to California. First, we figured moving would be much simpler and much less upsetting to our son if we could just take our house with us. Also, I wanted to give our washer to my mother, and we couldn't just carry it in our car! She was still using her old wringer washing machine. I knew wash day would be much easier for her with my little washer. She didn't want my dryer, because she enjoyed hanging wet clothes out to dry on her pulley clothes line.

Mary's parents, Orval and Lois Heath, and our
family, beside our little house trailer.

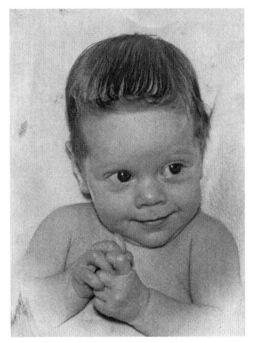

Nancy Lyn, 6 weeks

In December we started our journey to Africa, planning to visit Phil's family in the Midwest on the way. The following is a copy of the letter I sent to my parents from Scranton, Kansas after we had visited Phil's family in Colorado.

January 6, 1954, We are really tired. But probably will be more so! We arrived at Phil's Mom's house in Kansas yesterday afternoon. While Phil was in Oklahoma City, I finished up my shopping in McPherson. Virginia Hoffman did my washing in her washer/dryer combo. Sunday we saw all our friends in McPherson. The Lord is certainly taking care of us. It is only by His Grace that we are here at all!

Ice on the Million Dollar Highway in Colorado

In Colorado on the narrow 'Million Dollar Highway' between Durango and Montrose. It is the most beautiful highway I've ever seen, dizzy curves and steep grades, straight up above and straight down below! We didn't get in the San Juan Mountains until evening and I have never seen such a magnificent sight! Huge unbroken slopes of snow, deep and silent. Black stands of fir trees. Bright stars hanging low over the mountain peaks, a study in silver, blue, white and black. But when we started down, we hit ice and **slid**! By the time we stopped, the car was heading in the opposite direction! I was **so scared**! So was Phil, but he kept control and didn't show he was afraid. He was probably praying as hard as I was! Phil **finally** put on chains and we started off again. But we slid again on the next corner, so Phil got the wheels over next to the snow bank on the inside with the tires in the soft snow and we crept at ten miles per hour down the rest of the mountain. I was absolutely terrified. I held both of the kids tight and prayed hard, and shook from fear. We eventually got down and that was the end of the icy roads. But I was completely exhausted and felt almost sick. We stopped to thank the Lord for a safe descent, but I continued to shake from the danger we had faced. Phil's brother, Henry and his wife Carrie, were **horrified** we had even **tried** to come that way at night and in the middle of the **winter**! But we had never been on that road before, nor had we heard any of the horror stories about that beautiful highway. On the map it had looked like the best way to get to Montrose!

On our way to Kansas, on Sunday morning, we stopped in Colorado Springs, and attended the small Free Methodist church there. We were warmly greeted by several, and especially by two elderly people, Rev. and Mrs. William Hoffman, who years ago, beginning in 1919, had been missionaries stationed at Edwaleni in South Africa! They took us home for dinner, shared their Edwaleni experiences with us, and gave us a *Zulu* Bible! They were the parents of Estelle Orcutt, and Estelle was a cousin of Barstow Hoffman! Estelle and Paul Orcutt were later stationed at Kibogora (kee-boh-go'rah) Mission, in Rwanda, Africa! We would spend many wonderful days working with them in 1966-68.

After visiting Phil's relatives in Colorado, we then drove on to McPherson, Kansas to visit Phil's sister Jeanne Prevo and her family. We also were able to visit with Mitch and Joyce Allmon and many other friends from Central College days. We have had beautiful weather all the way. Sun every day, clear roads and no car trouble except when the car froze. But it was all right within an hour. We have to wait here, in McPherson, for our clergy certificates to get the reduced rate on the train. They should arrive tomorrow. (We left our car in Kansas, with Betty, Phil's sister, for her to use.) We won't have time to go both to Spring Arbor, Michigan and Winona Lake, unless we can get Eric Johnson to take us down to our general church headquarters in Winona Lake, Indiana. We hope Eric can take a family picture of us and arrange to have prayer cards made. We want them to say "So Send I You ..."

As far as we know now, we will leave the States about January 26. We will stay in a Missions Home in New York. I hope our freight is on its way by now.

Mary, Phil, Nancy and Paul on our way to New York

Off to Africa

Then we were again on our way to South Africa with a two and a half year old, and a four month old baby! (Most of these pages were copied from letters to my parents, which my Mother had saved!) In McPherson, Kansas we boarded a train to New York. Our visas had been granted in two months! An amazing answer to prayer!

Linguistic study in New York

January 14, 1954, Christian and Missionary Alliance (CMA) Home, in New York. Well, here we are in New York, and it's a nice place. Very easy to find your way around, and the snow is almost all trucked away. It looks as if it could snow some more any time. Nancy girl just woke up so I had to stop and change her diaper. Paul is still sleeping. He is adjusting very well, much better than I expected. Of course he **loved** the train and every time we stopped he would exclaim disgustedly, "My train stopped!" We have taken two lessons in linguistics from Dr. Cummings. A lady here at the CMA Home is taking care of the kids while we are in school.

Our train trip took fifteen hours. We had arrived in Jackson on Saturday afternoon, and were met by Polly and Eric Johnson. We stayed in Spring Arbor with them until Tuesday evening. Sunday morning after church, the Bishop ordained Phil, so he is now Rev. Kline. They combined the Deacon's and Elder's ordination service. He is now authorized to perform marriage, burial, and Sacrament ceremonies, but he can't be a member of an Annual Conference unless he completes the prescribed course of study. Phil's ordination had been requested by the South African Mission.

Well, both 'chickens' are awake now. Nancy is fed, and now she is fussing. Paul is entertaining himself by gazing down at the street. We are on the 5th floor. This home is like an apartment building. It was built for the CMA missionaries to stay in while in New York. Your letter was here waiting for us. Glad to hear people have been interested in the trailer.

Monday morning we borrowed Eric's car and drove down to Winona Lake, about 125 miles. We met everybody there in our church headquarters. Phil says it's time to eat now, so I'll stop for awhile. There is a nice restaurant on the corner, very reasonable. Phil took his first ride on the subway. He said it was really fast and it was only fifteen cents. He went to see about getting photographic supplies, thirty percent off! He loves bargains!

We are scheduled to fly from New York on the Dutch Air Line (KLM) on January 26th at noon. We have a three hour lay-over in Amsterdam the next day. We stop in Kano, Nigeria and then land in Johannesburg, South Africa the 28th! Paul has been dry all day today! He even told us tonight! He misses the trailer house and asks for it every now and then. He isn't nearly as upset as he was at first. Paul just now said, "Go back home, go Sunday School."

It's Sunday morning and Phil has gone downstairs to church. Paul is in his bed and Nancy is on my bed playing with a puppy toy that has a music box inside. Paul is coming down with chicken pox! Only he isn't breaking out, just runs a temp, but it has seemed like he feels OK most of the time. Today he isn't feeling so good. Phil just came back from lunch, so it's my turn now.

Just returned and I'm not quite thawed out yet! That cold wind is awful! It's coming from across the Hudson River which is full of ice.

We are just four blocks from the Hudson River, and the Seminary is just four blocks from the East River, only two blocks from the United Nations building. I think Paul may break out by tonight. He's been fairly quiet today. I got some carbolated vaseline to put on them. That's what Dr. Watterson told Joyce to get for her kids. Did I tell you that her kids broke out with chicken pox the day after Paul played with them? We are so glad they are both getting it now. This way they will be ready to leave on the 26th.

Friday, January 22, 1954, We hope we have everything filled out properly. Find out what all is necessary in order to sign the trailer over to you. That probably would be the wisest thing to do if it isn't sold soon. I am out in the hall writing. Everyone else is asleep. It's turning cold again here now, but they keep the building nice and warm. It's certainly nice to be able to stay here. Everyone is so friendly and helpful. Your package arrived just the day before our freight people were here to pick up our excess weight.

Everything is continuing to work out so marvelously! Even small little details that seemingly obstruct or delay are taken care of, usually at just the last minute! It's almost a temptation to worry sometimes, but each time the Lord works out something for us, our faith grows and we are better prepared to trust more fully the next time! It seems that the devil is trying his best to prevent us from getting to Edwaleni by the time school starts, but the Lord sweeps aside all obstructions, opens doors, and paves the way before us. Maybe He permits obstructions to loom up in front of us in order to help us grow by overcoming temptations to worry!

Miss Cummings at New York Biblical Seminary referred us to a Christian doctor. We made an appointment for this afternoon. She examined Paul and Nancy and said they would be non-contagious by Tuesday, so there will be no delay because of chicken pox! The medical office where we have to get clearance was almost positive we'd have to wait, but they hadn't seen the kids, so again the Lord has cleared our path! Psalm 37:5 seems to mean more and more. "Commit thy way unto the Lord: trust also in Him; and He shall bring it to pass."

Last night Nancy began to wheeze and cough. I thought it was just part of the chicken pox, so didn't think too much about it. But today when the doctor examined her, she said it was croup! She gave her penicillin, and said that by catching it so early she'd be OK to travel, especially by plane. Once more the Lord has worked things out! Even before we were aware that Nancy needed medical attention, He provided it! And the doctor didn't charge us a penny! Please pray that the kiddies' health may improve, that they won't be so susceptible to everything that comes along. Our constant prayer is that we may never hinder the workings of the Holy Spirit through our lives.

Our linguistics study is almost over. It's been fascinating and stimulating to be studying again! Miss Cummings has given us some excellent advice on how to proceed in learning a language. We don't feel at such a loss now. We know how to begin and we are learning how to plan our study for maximum effectiveness. She really knows how to teach! I thought that you'd like to know how God is working things out for us and that we **know** He is leading us.

Paul says thanks for the letters! He says, "Grandma Nanny" now, and then giggles! It is so cute the way Paul prays! He says, "Thank you, Jesus for Mommy, Grandma Nana, Grandpa, Abbie, John, Uncle Paul's train, choo-choo train track, help me. Amen." All we have to do is start him on "Thank you," and off he goes. Sunday we couldn't take the kids out, and Paul was begging to go to Sunday School, and of course, he insisted on "More songs, more stories, more pray, play Sunday School more."

Nancy is still 26" long, but is starting to get fat again. She weighs sixteen pounds now! The doctor said she is a very strong baby, all muscle. She sits up alone for about a minute, and fusses if you don't let her stand up. Today she rolled over, from her back to her tummy, and she got so mad because she couldn't pull her arm out from under her! It was funny! From Paul, "Thank you, Grandma Nana for my nice new shirt. I love you, Paul Stevie"

Flying to Africa

After taking two weeks of linguistic studies in New York, we boarded a four engine Constellation, made by Lockheed! As we were leaving America behind, two year old Paul looked out the window at the ocean and land far below, and sobbed, "Stop the plane, I want to get off!" We never dreamed that piloting airplanes would some day become part of his job and his special joy!

January 29, 1954, We've just landed in the neatest, most beautiful little country you ever saw, Holland. I love it! We had a nice trip, ten flying hours to Scotland, and two more to here. Nancy slept most of the way, and Paul slept good last night too. We have an hour or so here and then on to Africa! I still feel as though I were flying! We didn't fly up very high this last hop and then it was rather bumpy, but beautiful! We were above a billowy blanket of white clouds, and then we could see the ocean now and then with lots of white-caps.

There were some problems on that trip. To begin with, we didn't know that a baby wasn't allowed a free suitcase! But we felt we shouldn't pay the extra they wanted to charge! So we had to leave one to be sent to South Africa by ship! We didn't have much time to sort and choose, so we left most of Nancy's clothes behind, and ended up with not enough diapers! I ran out of diapers, had to rinse some out in the restroom on the airplane! Where to dry them? (This was before the days of Pampers!) And then the plane ran out of drinking water. I was nursing Nancy, and I needed to drink. By the time we arrived in Africa, I didn't have enough milk for the baby.

Quoting from a letter to prayer partners: The trip by plane to South Africa is one we will never forget. The ice of the winter morning in Scotland, the toy-town neatness of Holland from the air, the suspicion and tension felt in Germany, the magnificent beauty of the Alps, pink under the setting sun, the lights of Rome, sparkling like brilliantly colored jewels against the black velvet of the night. The absolute blackness of the night over northern Africa, with occasionally the orange glow of a fire only a tiny dot almost two miles below. The oppressive heat, humidity, and the flies in Kano, Nigeria, even at seven in the morning. The green carpet of the equatorial rain forests of Congo, with the red dirt of the roads standing out in bold relief. The broad rivers that wind their way across Central Africa. The enormous white billows of the clouds seething under us and around us as we came closer to Johannesburg in South Africa. We flew down white canyons and the cottony puffs towered over our heads. Then we were thrilled to see the lights of the big modern city of Johannesburg. Our long journey was almost over. After we taxied to a stop we saw people waving from the airport buildings, but never imagined any of them were waving at us. As we climbed up the stairway, after going through customs, we were pleasantly surprised to be greeted by five people! We recognized some of them from having seen their pictures. Rev. Wesley DeMille, Father Ryff, Helen Ryff, Mrs. Clemens, and Florence Carter, RN, were all there to meet us. Florence and I had been students at Seattle Pacific together!

We stayed all night with the DeMilles in Germiston and caught the plane for Durban early Friday morning. As we landed at the Durban airport, we saw a group of people waving enthusiastically, so we waved back just as wildly, hoping they were waving at us. Most of the South Africa missionaries were there, Mary Current, Gertrude Haight, Miss LaBarre, Warren and Jean Johnson, Dr. Rice and the Rileys. We felt just as though we were being welcomed into a big happy family. Our hearts were full to overflowing. When Gertie Haight reached out to hold Nancy, two year old Paul said, "No! You can't have her. She's **my** sister!" Nancy was just four months old. Gertie was the acting principal of Edwaleni Technical College, and was very glad to have a man finally arrive to relieve her of the job.

We arrive at Edwaleni Mission

After tea at Miss LaBarre's in Durban, we took off for Edwaleni, this time with Gertie driving the Dodge. We can't describe the thrill that was ours when we first saw the lights of Edwaleni shining brightly on a hilltop across a deep valley. Just a little farther on the narrow, winding, dirt road, we saw a big red welcome sign stretched across the nearly completed archway. We were **home**! This was our new home, and we breathed a prayer of thanksgiving. It was all so much bigger and nicer than what we had anticipated that it nearly took our breath away.

Mary and Phil at the entrance to the Edwaleni school campus

Our new home at Edwaleni Mission Station built
many years ago by Dr. Rice's father

School starts

Monday, January, 1954, Well, we're here, and are all rested up. We went today to Port Shepstone, about fifty miles over gravel roads, to get our permanent residence permits. We took Nancy with us, but left Edwaleni before Paul woke up this morning. When we got back home, about four this afternoon, Paul was playing happily with Clarabel. She is the most wonderful girl! She works for Gertrude, but she will be our cook when Gertie leaves. Clarabel is about thirty, is a marvelous cook and loves children, Paul is out in the kitchen talking with her now. When he woke up this morning he said, "Daddy gone, Mommy gone, Nancy gone, okay," and he proceeded to have a good time all day! So, you see, he is adjusting very rapidly. He was quite upset for about two days, but is all over it now. Nancy was the best little thing on the whole trip. Hardly a peep out of her!

We love it here. It really seems like home already! This is a nice house. The country is beautiful! High green hills all around. We are on top of one and can look down on the river way down in the valley from the upstairs verandah of Madgwick's house. It was built by Rev. Ghormley way back in the 1920's! Our house was built by Dr. Rice's father, many years ago. There is running water, electricity, and an **inside** bathroom, and a kitchen sink, all as modern as yours and the water tastes good! Of course, Clarabel and Celia, our two African helpers, keep the drinking water boiled and cooled. There are four big water collection tanks beside the house to store the rain water from our roof. We hardly can realize that we are in another country, to say nothing of being on the other side of the world! Many of the white people here speak both English and *Africaans*, which is similar to Dutch. We may be required to learn it. There have been some recent changes in the government here. I can't say more now, but please pray that the changes made by the government won't interfere with the Mission's efforts to teach the Gospel to the Africans. We are sadly in need of ways of training young pastors. Pray that God will work through us.

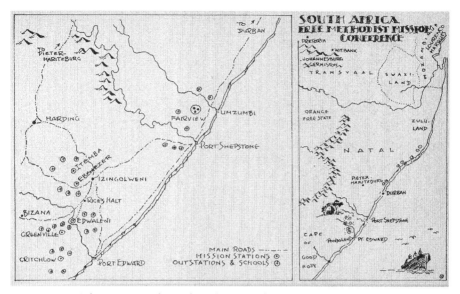

This map was drawn by Olive Teal for the book "Lights in
the World," written by Byron S. Lamson, 1951
Used with permission

Friday morning, February 5, 1954, I have a minute now to write. Nancy is asleep, and Clarabel is entertaining Paul in the kitchen. I have been helping out in the office for awhile this morning. It's difficult to understand our students, even though they speak English! We have 150 boys registered so far. Some are still waiting for their certificates of passing. The students are about 18 to 20 years old, nice looking young men. Wish we could speak Zulu! But we aren't allowed to use anything but English in the classroom. The boys have learned English in grade school. I haven't started to teach yet. Gertrude will teach until she leaves, then I will take over in four classes of English, Bible, and maybe music. Clarabel and Celia do all our cooking, dishes, house cleaning, ironing, washing, and even take care of the kids sometimes! But I still don't seem to have time to get everything done that I need to! Nancy has been very fussy lately, and takes quite a bit of time. I don't know how I'd ever get anything done without the girls! The new secretary is supposed to come tomorrow to see if she wants to work here. Hope she does, because then I won't have to worry about anything in the office, I'll just teach three hours a day and take care of my family. We have corn, tomatoes, cauliflower, green peppers, cucumbers, squash, green beans, radishes, all growing here in our garden. We can buy all sorts of fruit, watermelons, bananas, lemons, oranges, guavas, papayas, and pineapples, so we are really eating good. Paul is helping Celia set the table now. They are teaching him *Zulu* already! If I'm not careful he will learn *Zulu* before I do! Paul has gone to the office to get Phil for lunch now. All the Free Methodist and Brethren missionaries around here have a get-together every two weeks for Bible study and a social time. The Johnsons will be there and Mary Current, Mamie Larkan and all of us Edwaleni people. Nancy is sitting up alone now, with a support for 'just in case'. She is a little live wire! She turns over both ways so we really have to watch where we put her. Gertrude gave her a cute rubber monkey which she just loves!

March 4, 1954, Nancy is up rocking on all fours now, so it won't be much longer until she is crawling! Paul keeps talking about Uncle Paul's train, and says he wants to play with Abbie and John and Arthur. Today he kept talking about his cousins, Charles and Richard! He is very patiently waiting for his train to get here on the big boat, but of course he talks about it every day. He is some talker now, big long sentences, mixed with *Zulu* already! The girls talk *Zulu* to the kids all the time, so it will be interesting to see which Nancy learns first, English or *Zulu*.

I am teaching a half hour of Bible study every day right after chapel. All the students just stay for the class. We are studying the book of Mark now. Then on Mondays, Wednesdays and Fridays, I sit in on the music class for a half hour. On Tuesdays and Thursdays, I sit in on three classes of English, which will be mine in about two weeks. Gertie is feeling better. I told you, didn't I, that she fell and cracked a rib while playing Indians with Paul? Then a few days later she collapsed with a blood pressure problem, so she had to rest for several days. That's when I took over the Bible class. Tomorrow we are having 'World Day of Prayer'. (Looking back, I can see how God had led me, all my jobs while in school had been working in offices, preparing me to do secretarial work in Africa!)

Nancy slept all night last night, but Paul was very restless. We are going to ask Dr. Rice for some worm medicine Saturday. He shouldn't wake up so many times at night. We probably should have gotten some for him while we were in Seattle. Supper is almost ready. It's really a relief not to have to worry about getting meals, and doing dishes. The girls are so nice. Clarabel made Phil a raisin pie today. Was he ever happy. She made a birthday cake for him on his birthday too.

Phil says "Thank you" for the birthday card. Paul is outdoors ringing the little bell for his daddy to come and eat. He thinks that is a lot of fun. The boys here all think Paul is cute. He has especially taken a liking to Mason, the man in charge of the school food. I guess Mason is everyone's right hand man. Paul follows him around and 'helps' him fill the students' sugar cans. Guess where some of the sugar goes. Mason lets him play with the wagon they use for hauling milk cans. He thinks it is wonderful, but still wants his new wagon from the big boat. The student who works in our garden and takes care of the flowers is transplanting zinnias, petunias, nasturtiums, carnations, Canterbury bells, and asters now. I hope we get one more good rain after he is all through, so they will grow good. He waters them all every day with the waste wash water from the dormitories. We don't waste water here.

Yesterday afternoon LaVerna Madgwick, Miss Steele, Stella Hundly, and I visited a *kraal*, (a *Zulu* family dwelling). We had prayer and LaVerna read the Bible in *Zulu* in the hut of a Christian teacher. There was an old woman, and two heathen women there also, who lived in other huts in the *kraal*. One woman had twin girls, about one year old, and she fed them both at the same time during the little service. You should see the way they fix their hair, it's terrific! Gracie should try it! They make many tiny strands by twisting small bunches of their hair with red clay. This hangs like a fringe all around their heads, even over their eyes a little in front. I couldn't believe it was really hair at first. You can always tell a heathen woman from a Christian or an educated woman by her hairdo and dress. Bare shoulders aren't a new fashion. All the heathen women in South Africa have worn their clothes that way for years.

March 12, 1954, The school inspector has come and gone, leaving a good report. I have all of Gertie's classes now except the chorus class. She is rapidly turning over the office duties to Stella and Lily. Stella is a nice girl from Durban. Lily Steele has been working among the Indians in Durban, but couldn't agree with the doctrines of the church where she was working. After having spent several weeks here with us, resting, she has been lead of the Lord to remain with us! We had been praying that she would, if it were the Lord's will. Before we even said anything to her about how we would like for her to stay with us, she told us that the Lord had removed the burden of the Indian work from her and she felt that He would have her stay here and work with us. What a direct answer to prayer! She is a wonderful person, and will be a blessing to Edwaleni.

Last evening Lily held her first volunteer Bible class, and twenty-one boys came. We were all thrilled, and her face was just radiant after she was through. Stella doesn't know bookkeeping, but Lily does, and Lily can't type, but Stella can. Stella will have charge of the office and secretarial work while Lily will do the bookkeeping, and we will be free to teach and do evangelistic work. How the Lord does work things out! We are planning to send out groups of students from the school to visit and share God's Good News with the people who live in the surrounding heathen *kraals*. There are very few Christians in this area, and we are hoping and praying that soon there will be many more.

Tomorrow we go to District Quarterly Meeting at Emthini (ehm-tee'nee) Church. We saw in the newspaper that our ship was in port in Cape Town, which means that in about a week or less, our things will be in Durban. We have written for permission to take the school lorry in to Durban to get our stuff, but we'll have to wait and see. Everything is run by the government here. We can't take the lorry more than thirty miles away without permission from a government bureau, because no one is allowed to compete with the railroad. It is run by the government, too. But we aren't here to criticize the way the government is run, only to advance the Kingdom of the Lord. We are planning also for Conference which is to be held here during Easter vacation. We will have seventeen adults to feed, plus all their children, for a week! Am I ever glad Gertie is still here to organize things!

Phil is trying now to rig up a cable across the river so he can get sand to use in the building program. The river is high and you can't get across unless you go about ten miles out of the way. Phil and Dr. Rice are planning already on putting a bridge across the Umtamvuna River so we can have a shorter road to Greenville Mission in Pondoland, which would only be five miles instead of twenty-five miles! And that twenty-five miles seems like one hundred, all up and down and around and around hills, hills, hills! We went over to Rice's Wednesday evening for dinner. The hospital is built up to the first windows. It will really be nice when it is done. Dr. Rice has rigged up a rock crusher and they dig the rock from a nearby cliff, so all he has to buy is the cement, steel and wood.

Phil has taken Paul down to the river with him to see about the cable. I hope they don't run into any black or green *imamba*s (ee-mahm'bahs)! These snakes strike on a person's head, and you die in ten minutes! They run along on their tails, standing up higher than me, going about fifty miles an hour! I haven't seen any yet. I just keep my eyes open, because this is the season when they strike at anything. They will soon go into hibernation, so we won't have to be concerned about them except on hot, dry days. Paul wanders all over the campus, but stays on the paths. I don't worry about him, because he is in God's care, and what a restful, peaceful feeling that is. Sometimes I have a few moments worry and anxiously look for him, but then I breathe up a prayer of thanks and all is peaceful again.

In addition to my fear of lions, I had been afraid that we would have to use 'out houses' in Africa, but the house we were assigned to at Edwaleni was well built, spacious, with indoor plumbing! Part of our water supply came from the Umtamvuna River, which nearly circled our hill, way down in the valley. Our drinking water came from the huge tanks that stored the rain water from our galvanized iron roof. It had to be boiled before it was safe to drink. Phil took over as principal and taught carpentry as well. He was also in charge of the school farm, about 1,000 acres. Fortunately God had prepared him for that, because Phil had lived for many years on farms, so he was very knowledgeable about farm work! Also Phil was eventually put in charge of three outstation churches, Esangweni, (eh-sahn-gway'-nee) Mbodiya, (mm-boh-dee'yah) and Emthini. I worked as school secretary after Stella left, and taught Bible classes, English and chorus, using tonic sol-fa instead of notes. We were thankful Gertie Haight was able to stay with us for awhile, and the things she taught us made our transition much easier. School was scheduled to start February 4. There were two well trained *Zulu* girls living upstairs in our house who did the cooking, cleaning, washing, ironing, and babysitting. I was thankful that they were so helpful, but having someone else living with us was the most difficult thing I had to adjust to. Also difficult, was trying to learn the *Zulu* language. However, all teaching at our school was done in English! English is one of the national languages of South Africa.

March 22, 1954, Sunday we went over to Rice's at Greenville Mission in Pondoland for their District Quarterly Meeting. All of the Natal missionaries were there except the Rileys and Miss LaBarre. Rice's have an outside privy, and just a couple minutes after I left it, Warren Johnson went out, and as he opened the door a puff adder came slithering out! They are **very** poisonous! I am **so** glad I didn't see it! And the kids had been playing all around in the yard! Warren killed it and brought it up to the house and very calmly asked what they called this snake. Dr. Rice just as calmly answered, "Oh, that's a puff adder, very poisonous, you know." Believe me, I watched **very** carefully the rest of the evening! As far as snakes are concerned, all the missionaries believe in 'watching and praying'! And yet there is no anxious worrying about snakes. The Lord gives peace of mind, perfect rest, and a freedom from fear. But still, we are cautious. Our things from Los Angeles are in Durban, but not yet through customs. Phil is going to go get them tomorrow. I was going too, but Nancy has a cold, so I will stay here. Paul is so excited about his train, 'bicycle' (trike) and wagon being almost here now.

Only three weeks until time for Conference, and we will have about 500 African people on this hilltop, and at least fifteen missionaries to entertain in the two houses. LaVerna will feed the children at her house, and we will feed the missionaries here a half an hour later. Pray that the Lord will convict more of the people about this beer-grinding business. One circuit is sending a resolution to conference recommending that the church outlaw it entirely. Women on church membership probation are now permitted to grind beer for their heathen husbands, if they are forced to. Their beer, *utshwala*, (oot-shwah'-lah) is made from Kaffir corn. They make and consume it in huge quantities, especially on Saturday beer-drinks and at weddings.

These women who are grinding beer have been church members on probation for many years, and the more conscientious members are trying now to limit the probationary period. Well, those are just a few of the *izindaba* (eez-een-dah'-bah) (problems) that we hope will get settled at conference time. Pray with us that there may be a real revival. That will be the only permanent solution.

Nancy weighs seventeen pounds now and is twenty-nine inches long. She crawls a little, and will try to walk a little if you hold her hands. If you let go, she can stand alone for just a few seconds. She is the strongest baby I ever saw. She is now almost seven months and everybody loves her. We had dinner at Warren and Jean Johnson's Saturday evening. They are really nice people, our age, and were married just about ten days after we were! But they have three kids, ages four, five and six! They repaired the old dried mud block house that Miss Hartman used to live in at Ithemba (Ee-tem'-bah) Mission in the 1890's, but it isn't snake proof, or fly-proof. However, it looks nice and is cozy inside. They will probably move soon. They are in charge of nine outstations, and spend their time going from one to another! They are just finishing up a nice new church/school building at Emthini Mission. They only live about 35 miles from us, but it takes over an hour to get there, terrible roads.

Everyone is asleep now, but me. Phil leaves for Durban in the lorry at 4 a.m. I just finished his packing. He will go up to Pietermaritzburg tomorrow evening to take a tour of other industrial schools with the government inspector! Phil has just drawn up plans for a new building, with toilets, showers, ironing room and wash room for the students. He plans to make a new septic tank. The one they have now really needs to be replaced. Next on the list is a new shop building. Paul Stevie sends his kisses and love.

April 27, 1954, Conference is over, and we have had a week in which to recuperate! What a busy time that Conference week was! We had about 800 people in the Sunday morning service, a record for this Conference. They really swarmed all over the campus. Between the two mission houses, we entertained eighteen missionaries and Laverna fed the kids. (Laverna was also at Seattle Pacific College when I was!) We had Mission meetings Monday night and Tuesday, and then the Africans came on Wednesday. Conference began on Wednesday afternoon, and the Lord did meet with us! We all felt that the Lord definitely answered prayers during Conference time. No one could remember a more harmonious Conference. This year, there were no heated arguments, and we all felt it was because we met for special times of group prayer over the weekend! Whenever there arose a difficult problem to be solved, and a difference of opinion, we all prayed together, and asked God to give us wisdom, and He did. It was really wonderful! The Conference passed the resolution about church members not grinding beer, so the way is now open for the native church to grow spiritually. We trust that a new day for the South Africa Conference has begun.

Nancy crawls all over the house, really fast, and says, "Da-da" and "Ma-ma" and a lot of other jabbering. Paul has a terrific time trying to keep Nancy out of his toys, especially away from his train. Our things from New York are finally arriving. They should be in Durban tomorrow. A dock strike held them up in New York for six weeks. Gertie will sail for the States next week. We will all go to Durban to see her off, and we'll probably go before then to pick up our stuff.

We ladies are all in Gertie's room having a 'hen party'. She is working on new clothes to wear home. Laverna just finished a letter to her folks, Stella is knitting a sweater, and Gertie and Lily are sewing. Phil is in our room with the heat lamp on his legs. He says they hurt all the time. After Gertie leaves, I am going to put Paul in her room with all his toys. Nancy is already in the guest room. During conference we had them both in with us, and they woke each other up too much.

Zahnisers are gone now again. They are on their way to central Africa, holding conferences on the way. Their next one will be in Pretoria for Portuguese East, Southern Rhodesia, and the Transvaal Conferences.

Oh, I forgot to tell you that during Conference thirteen of our boys went to the altar, and some of them gave really good testimonies. Several of the women from other circuits prayed through to victory over beer grinding. Poor people, I guess they may be in for some severe beating by their husbands. The women are the property of their husbands. They buy them with cattle, even the Christians still 'buy' their wives!

It is beginning to get winter here now. It is chilly, and we get quite a bit of wind. All the hills surrounding us are higher than our hilltop. This is a beautiful spot. We had a picnic Saturday noon down by the Umtamvuna River. There is a lot of flat rock and sand by the river's edge, below where Phil is building the pump house. The Rileys, the Johnsons, the Madgwicks, and all of us went on the picnic together. We had a little farewell for Gertie.

May, 1954, We've just returned from a walk down to the river. We followed a good path down to the pump house and climbed back up along the pipe line. It's about a half mile down, and it is almost straight up and down in some places. The river is up about one and a half feet, and is very muddy. We just had two days of good rains. The rapids by the pump house are really roaring. You can hear them from the edge of the hilltop. What a beautiful place this is! On the hillsides under the trees grow wild carpets of ferns, sansevieria, moss, ivy, and many other wild plants that at home we coax along. And down by the river, bamboo! I brought some small shoots up to see if they'll grow up here where I can see them every day. However, the climb up was so rugged that I broke some of the ends off.

We finally have all our stuff, except the cement mixer, and it should arrive soon. Our latex foam mattresses are very comfortable. We're glad we brought them. And the washing machine is wonderful! You'd like the new wringer ones, Mother! The only thing, with the machine, I have to supervise every minute, but it's much easier on the clothes than the wash board. (On our travels, I got **so** tired of washing clothes by hand in bathtubs and on wash boards!) We wash Monday and Friday mornings after chapel and chorus. Nancy is finally asleep and I'm finishing this by candle light. She is usually such a good baby, but tonight she was fussy. I was sorting out things on my desk, and filing things in our filing cabinet, when Paul came and wanted to write a letter to Grandma Nana. So I helped him. The picture of our new home was his idea, also Paul, Mommy and Daddy at the windows! He is such a grown-up little guy now, and he goes to sleep in every church service. He takes his pillow along and always sleeps! What a relief! Nancy says "Bye-bye" now, and waves to everyone, even in church! Paul and Nancy play nicely together most of the time.

We are learning more *Zulu* all the time. This was in our last lesson: *Ake ungiphe isihlalo.* (Please give me a chair). *Umfazi yayi hlali emtonjeni.* (A woman sat on the well. - John 4). *Zulu* is coming quite easy to me, for which I am thankful. It's really cold here now. We've been shivering for two days. I am also thankful for my flannel p.j.'s. Phil even wishes he had let me make him a pair! We enjoy our fireplace. Phil fixed a screen to keep Paul and Nancy out of the fireplace. The wind is howling outside. Friday was the first day of winter and the Drakensburg Mountains, twenty miles from here, are covered with snow. And July is much colder! Brr! Love to all. My candle just burned out, so I'm using a flashlight now!

May, 1954, Paul's letter to his grandparents: Dear Grandma Nana, Grandpa, John, Abbie, Uncle Paul, Aunt Grace, and Uncle Harland, Hi! I like my new home at Edwaleni. I like to play with my train and my trucks. I pray every night and ask Jesus to help me be a good boy and be nice and not make Nancy cry. I pray for you too. Nancy has five teeth and when she bites me it hurts! I can say "*Sakubona*, (Hello), *Usaphila?*, (How do you do?) *unjani?*, (How are you?) and *Ngiyabonga*" (Thank you) in *Zulu*. We have a nice fireplace and the fire feels good because it's cold today! I wore my snowsuit outside. We have some bananas on our banana trees and tangerine and lemon trees. We have papaya trees,

47

avocado trees, mango trees, and pineapples in our garden. Bye. I love you. Paul Stevie

(He had me draw a picture of our new house with a big tree beside it and underneath his wagon and trike. And when his trike arrived from the ship, he put it all together by himself! He must have inherited some of his father's mechanical genes)

Paul, almost 4, putting his trike together

May 31, 1954, This is a cold, windy day. Had to stop awhile and go to faculty meeting. Nancy stood all alone about two minutes during dinner! She is almost nine months now, and weighs 22 pounds. She is wearing clothes that Paul wore at one year! Paul didn't take a nap today, so he is asleep already. He usually gets right up from the table at noon and goes to bed alone. He goes to the bathroom by himself most of the time now, and usually insists on no help.

Only one more month, and the first term will be over already! Seems impossible. Then we have a month's vacation before the second term begins. In the summer there is just a two month's vacation. In music class they are learning the "Lord's Prayer." They are doing pretty good, but they do better on songs like "Swing Low, Sweet Chariot." Of course I have a lot yet to learn about directing a men's chorus! Especially since they learn from tonic sol-fa instead of notes! (Like - do re mi fa so la ti do) Nancy is doing her best to grab this letter again. She is so strong.

Saturday we hiked about two miles to the prettiest little waterfall, and it falls about one hundred feet. This is the dry season so there was only a small amount of water, and we could walk right out on the rocks and look over. Made us dizzy to look down. We can see the falls from the campus. I brought back some plants that were growing wild near the falls. Hen & chickens & sansevieria. Need I tell you more to let you know that I love it here?

June 29, 1954, I started this letter five days ago and then began writing on our prayer letter, which I still don't have finished. This is our winter vacation, a whole month. After we saw the boys off Friday morning at 6:30 and settled the ending of school *izindaba*, we took off to see our good friends, the Johnsons at Ithemba Mission. We really enjoyed ourselves and our kids had a wonderful time playing. We've had a nice fire in the fireplace. Phil and Warren have gone hunting on Larkans' farm once or twice every day for guinea fowl. They've shot about a dozen. Delicious meat, as big as chickens.

Sunday we went to one of Johnson's out-stations, Mshiwe (mm-shee'-way), a little church on a hill about thirty miles from here. The church was jammed with people sitting on mats on the floor. It was a rally Sunday, and people had walked for miles from several different churches to be there. Then we were invited to eat dinner in one of the *kraals*. Our hostess was an old *Zulu* lady who had been raised by Miss Hartman, a missionary in South Africa in the early 1900's. We had a delicious dinner.

Friday morning, back at Edwaleni, we got up at 4 a.m. and went down to the chapel to sell the boys their bus tickets and give them their grade reports. Then the buses pulled in about 5:30. They were really excited to get to go home. Eight of the boys are staying for vacation at the school to work. In two weeks we are going to have Worker's Conference at Ebenezer Mission. Pray that the African church workers may really grow in their Christian experiences. The evening services will be evangelistic, and we are hoping a lot of heathen will attend

July, 1954, We are at Ebenezer Mission this week, having Worker's Conference. All the South Africa missionaries are here, and the kids are having lots of fun playing together. We brought Paul's trike and wagon and a pile of sand, and the Johnson children have their toys. This is such a nice place to play. There is a concrete porch, a wide one that completely surrounds this big house. Ebenezer Mission was Dr. Backenstoe's hospital. Mary Current, RN, lives here now and conducts a very busy clinic.

This year is only the second year for our Worker's Conference, and we can sense the presence of the Lord. Most of the African pastors and evangelists are here, as well as many of the women workers. I am teaching classes on tithing, and serving God. Rev. Ragsdale preached a sermon on that topic, and at the close of the service over twenty women came forward for prayer. I made some posters showing how we should tithe, one chicken out of ten belongs to the Lord, and the same with pumpkins and money. One old preacher who had never tithed, said he saw it so clearly now, and that he would tithe from now on. We have been having some good meetings. Many of the young people have been seeking the Lord. It's been so cold here we've all been wearing sweaters and heavy coats, and blankets around our legs in church. We are having services in the old stable because the church was too small. Warren enclosed the open side with corrugated iron. He even put doors and windows in. The holes are stuffed with long dry grass. The benches, with no backs, we brought from the Ithemba Mission church on the Edwaleni truck. We brought Riley's little 110 Volt electric plant, so we have electricity, and Warren Johnson shows film strips before the evening service. We have had crowds of children, dressed in ragged sweaters and coats and some wrapped in blankets, but even the very small ones sit very quietly and listen, their big brown eyes drinking in everything. They are such cute kids. I gave a Bible story in Sunday School on Sunday morning. This evening is our last service. We are praying for a good crowd, with more heathen in.

August 4, 1954, Edwaleni is a beautiful place; a large high hill, fairly flat on top, shaped like an ellipse, completely surrounded by deep valleys and higher hills. The Umtamvuna River is down in the valley about 500 feet from the top of the hill. It loops around our hill in almost a complete oval, separated only by a narrow ridge, over which our road is built. The sides of our hill are densely covered with brush, and several kinds of gazelles, birds, and snakes live there. Some Africans who were here to hunt several weeks ago killed a young python, eight feet long, in its hole at the bottom of a rocky precipice just below the top of our hill. We excitedly took pictures of it. The flat hilltop campus is approximately one block wide and two blocks long.

Snakes!

Before we left California, a retired missionary, Margaret Nickel, who had formerly worked at Edwaleni many years ago, had told us that she always prayed that no one would be bitten by a snake on the mission property, so that also became my prayer, and the Lord very graciously answered that prayer! There were many snakes in the area, pythons, *imambas*, puff adders, night adders, most of them very poisonous. Phil enjoyed being called to capture them. He put them into special boxes to put onto the train from Izingolweni (eh-zing-gohl-way'-nee) to Durban where they were used in the making of antivenin. *Imambas* were the most deadly, and could rise up on their tails to over head height! I always insisted Phil kill **them** with his gun and not even **try** to capture them! We had electricity every evening, but our refrigerator ran on kerosene, and our washing machine was gasoline powered. Two students, Robert Nxumalo and Seth Msweli worked as our gardeners, so we were able to grow lots of good fruit and vegetables all year long with water pumped up from the river. Both Robert and Seth eventually went to Bible school for ministerial training, and many years later Robert became the first African bishop of the Free Methodist Church in South Africa. Before the government took over African education, and our school had to close in 1958, Phil was led to counsel with several other students, and was able to lead them to surrender to the Lord's leading to train to become pastors if they felt God was calling them. This was a tremendous answer to prayer, since there had been practically no young men entering the ministry for many years.

Edwaleni students, Seth Msweli and Robert Nxumalo,
who became Free Methodist pastors

August, 1954, The Edwaleni farm includes two other high hills and all the valley in between. On the nearest hill is Esangweni Day School for African children, and on another hill is the Old Edwaleni Church. Including the school campus our Mission farm is approximately 1,000 acres, mostly steep hills and valleys! I came down to the river with Phil today. He has to change the oil in the pump and start it. The river is beautiful now, clear, but still rapid and deep, and cold. This is an ideal place for picnics. It is just like having a mountain resort almost in your back yard! There is nice sand and a long stretch of large flat rocks. The Lord is certainly good to us, letting us live in this beautiful place while serving Him.

Answered prayer!

September 12, 1954, This afternoon when I was talking with the women at Esangweni about prayer, I told them that we had just received an answer to a prayer we had been praying for a long time. Our house trailer is finally sold! Thank you, Mother and Daddy, for all your help. Lily and I go out to Esangweni School twice a week at 3 p.m. Class meeting is on Wednesday, and Women's meeting is on Friday. In order to attract the heathen women, and more of the younger church women, we are teaching them how to knit. Some are learning fast! We had about twenty altogether last Friday. This morning I walked back out again and taught Sunday School. Such sweet children! Both Edwaleni cars are being repaired so we walk these days. It's a long way off, over and around the hills to Esangweni. We walk it in about 45 minutes. Phil and Lily took two teams of boys out this afternoon in the lorry to do *kraal* (native home) visitation. Lily has divided her Bible class into four teams. They are anxious to do Christian work, especially since the revival meetings. The people are so appreciative of the fact that we are interested in them. One old man who had refused to have anything to do with Christianity actually left a beer drink to come and listen to the Gospel! Edwaleni has had a spiritual awakening! Praise the Lord! Many faces now glow that used to look like thunder clouds! We are so busy now, at night we just fall into bed and drop off to sleep. Pray for us that we will have the strength to do what needs to be done.

Lily Steele and Phil take volunteer students on Sunday afternoon *kraal* visitations

September 16, 1954, I'm sitting in the bathroom watching Paul and Nancy splash in the tub. They love to take baths, but I wish you could hear them scream when I wash their hair! I'm now in the office. The washing is finished. At least my part is. Celia cleans out the machine and hangs all the clothes, but I supervise and help run the machine.

We just put up all our nice new curtains. They really look nice! We are having District Quarterly Meeting here this weekend. The Johnsons, Rileys, and Mary Current will be here.

You asked for a list for Christmas. I can think of many things I wish we had! I'll type a list and put it in with this letter. Something else you can get for us, a large size plastic wading pool for the kiddies if it doesn't weigh too much to send. I hope it isn't too late in the year to get a good one. I'll enclose a check for $20.00 which should include postage. December will be the middle of our summer, and it really gets hot! The kids love to play in the water. Please send it right away if you can.

Patches' puppy is growing fast. He is as fat as Nancy! He and Nancy chase each other around in circles. You asked how long it took packages to arrive. It takes about eight weeks or a little more. So if you mail our package by the first of November, it will get here in time. Please don't send any packages air mail! It costs too much! Please also send a tube of cement that will mend plastic.

We plan to write a family letter, making carbon copies on air forms, so that we can give all our brothers and sisters the news at least every other month. Must get some typing done now.

Monday morning, Paul got up this morning, rode his trike into our room as usual and announced, "We're going to Jimmy's house today. My new home is sick. We must go to Jimmy's house." He misses playing with other kids so much! However, we do see either the Rices, (Audry is four), or the Johnsons two or three times a month. There are no native children living here on our hill, except Teacher Shembe's family, and they have been having whooping cough! Must get this letter in the post.

District Quarterly Meeting

September 27, 1954, One Sunday morning we went to Old Edwaleni, the third and highest hill on our mission farm. We took the car to where the old road begins that goes down to the cattle dip, and then we started walking down, down, down to the stream, crossed over, and started climbing up, up, up until one hour from the time we left the car, we were standing on top of the rocky hill called Old Edwaleni. Our District Superintendent and his wife were with us. This was DQM (District

Quarterly Meeting) for them. On the west side of the hill is a stretch of solid rock that is a sheer drop of 60 to 100 feet. Makes me dizzy to stand on the rocks and look down at the densely covered slopes below. The path we came up forms a long steep semi-circle to get around the cliff. Phil is continually wishing for a helicopter! The hilltop is mostly covered with trees, some garden space, several round mud and pole huts with thatched roofs, and a mud and wattle (Acacia) pole church with a galvanized iron roof with most of the window panes broken out. They get up during services and put burlap sacks over the openings if it gets cold, and it did! Church at the out-stations lasts from 10:30 a.m. to 2 or 3 p.m. There are no evening services, and no electricity!

We ate dinner at the pastor's house, a nicer than average African mud and pole house. It was rectangular, (most African huts are round), with floors smeared with cow dung, so it is level and looks almost like a smooth concrete floor. Chickens were running in and out while we ate. The family ate in the kitchen while we ate in the living room, (South Africa's Apartheid laws). The only pieces of furniture were a small table, several chairs, a bench and a cupboard. Mrs. Nyaose is a school teacher so they could afford a wood stove. Most rural *Zulus* cook their food outside in a big black iron pot over an open fire.

Phil was cold while we were waiting for dinner, so they brought in some fire on a piece of tin and put it on the floor. The fire felt good, but oh the smoke! Now our clothes smell of smoke just like many of the Africans do! Our dinner was delicious, roast chicken, curry gravy, white sweet potatoes, samp (dried corn kernels mixed with beans) juku beans, beef, and bananas. We had brought our own silverware and paper plates, but they had a nice tablecloth on the table. Of course we took our own drinking water. We are very careful and take no chances of eating anything that might give us dysentery. I was writing by candle light because Phil turned the electric plant off at 9:15. Phil just brought in a Coleman lantern. It is better than a candle. We are quite busy now. With Madgwicks gone, Phil has to teach David's building classes as well as his own. We will miss them. (LaVerna Madgwick, Mamie Larkan and I were all at Seattle Pacific together! But they came to South Africa as single lady missionaries and later married South African men). Dr.

Zahniser has also returned to the States and has left his 1953 Chevrolet for us to use. Dr. C.H. Zahniser was then the Africa Area Secretary and was in South Africa temporarily. His car is much more reliable than the old Dodge.

Friday, October 1. Lily and I go out to Esangweni School this afternoon again. The rains have come, so maybe the women will all be home hoeing their fields. They are fast learning to knit. Pray that our Gospel messages may sink deep into their hearts. The heathen women come with their red-mudded hair looking like yarn mops, their dirty blankets, sweet babies on their backs, and when we give them knitting needles and help them to begin knitting they giggle and laugh. But best of all, they listen intently to the Gospel.

Letter from former missionaries

October, 1954, We were encouraged to receive a long letter from former Edwaleni missionaries, Margaret Nickel and Mrs. Ghormley, the wife of the first principal of Edwaleni High School and Bible School, beginning in 1906, before it became an industrial school. They were excited to receive our prayer letters. (They both lived in Highland Park, Los Angeles, near my parents.) They assured us that they are still praying for the people here, and promised to continue praying for us. Miss Nickel said that when they were in South Africa in the early 1900's none of the missionaries had cars. They traveled by horseback, donkeys and wagons. We know that our work here depends on faithful people in the States who pray for us.

November 1, 1954, This is our morning for rest and relaxation. Paul and I have just had Sunday School. Even Nancy tries to sing now. Paul is sick again. He has been complaining of a tummy ache for several days, and now he has diarrhea, so I've put him on the medicine I give the school boys for dysentery. He'll probably be better tomorrow. It is very common here, but doesn't last long. I really need to be a nurse.

You should see the earthworms we have here! Fully two feet long, and as big around as your finger! Paul calls them "snakes." I hope sometime he doesn't think a snake is a worm! We saw a small green *imamba* down by the river one day. Speaking of the river, it is really full, and is out of its banks in many places. Hope it doesn't wash away the good sand deposit that the last flood brought us.

Sunday, December 13, 1954, Graduation Day was last Tuesday and the students left early Wednesday morning on four big buses and a lorry for their trunks. We gave out their grade reports, passes and concession forms. The boys were quiet and cooperative. They really like Phil, and he handles them as expertly as if he'd been teaching for years. Phil had turned the power plant on at 4 a.m., and then all bedlam broke loose in the dormitory as they did their last minute packing. Last week we worked from 6:30 a.m. to 11:30 p.m. every day. I still have much office correspondence to catch up on and government reports to complete. Now, I'm sitting out by the shop building, and the kids are playing in the sand, making mud pies. The Johnson kids are here. Warren and Jean are in Durban again. They should be back sometime today. I have been rather wary today. Mason, Phil's African right-hand man, killed a green snake, quite poisonous, not more than seventy feet from our back door! It was about two and a half feet long, but as thin as your finger, and fast. We had just been in the garden, picking cucumbers, and had walked right past where it was hiding in the grass! After Mason killed it, I took a picture of the kids holding it.

Paul and Nancy had so much fun playing in the little plastic wading pool you sent them. They were so excited. It came just before an almost unbearably hot day. Nancy screams when I take her out! We are in Durban. We left at five this morning and went to Pietermaritzburg for a meeting of principals and head teachers of African secondary schools, which lasted all morning. This afternoon we drove back down to Durban on a new super highway, four lanes, divided! When we are on it, we can hardly believe that we are in Africa. We are staying at the Concord Missionary Home. We left our kids with the Johnsons. Paul is undoubtedly very happy, he has been begging for weeks to go to Jimmy's house! This is first time we've left our children. Certainly seems strange not to have them with us.

(Excerpts from Paul's letter to Mother and Daddy, dated in January, 1955) Dear Grandma Nana and Grandpa and Abbie, Grace, Paul and John, I wrote Santa Claus a letter and he brought me everything that I wanted. Thank you, Uncle Orval, for my nice train. I like it very much. We are keeping it nice so it won't get broken. I like to wind it up and make it go. I like the tracing set too. Thank you, Auntie Grace. The car you gave me is nice. I like to make it go down a big board fast. Thank you, Grandma Nana and Grandpa, for the pretty red shirt. I like nice warm shirts to wear when it is chilly. Thank you for my farm book, Abbie. It will be lots of fun to cut and stick on. Thank you, John for the nice book you sent me. I like for Mommy to read me books about Jesus. I love Jesus. He helps me to be good and not fight. I pray for all of you. Love and kisses, Paul Stevie.

January 17, 1955, Have I written to you since Christmas? We are still having Christmas! We had another one today when your second package came. It took nearly two months to arrive. Must have just missed a boat. We are really relaxing. We spent two wonderful weeks with Jean and Warren Johnson, in Durban, really being lazy. We went to the beach twice. I certainly enjoyed swimming again. There is a pool at the beach which is hooked onto some big rocks that the water dashes over at high tide. It is a nice big pool, and on the far side you can feel the spray from the big breakers, and at the end they actually break into the pool. It's a beautiful beach, with big rocks and nice sand, but there are many sharks and jellyfish that sting. But they aren't in the pool, and beside the big pool is a small pool for children. They loved that! Even Paul stayed in the water for awhile.

Our Christmas would have been a terrifically homesick one if it hadn't been for Johnsons. We came back to Edwaleni with them for the day and went down by the river for a picnic. Janet Johnson fell in, but Jim fished her out by the leg before she went very far! Phil fell in Friday when he was trying to fix the valve on the end of the pump line. The river is rather high now, but not flooding. Paul thought it was very funny to see his daddy crawling out of the water. The river is fourteen feet deep in places and has some terrific rapids. We have taught Phil how to play tennis. He loves it now and has become a regular enthusiast! Mamie and John Larkan have a nice tennis court with a rolled 'ant hill' (termite) surface. John is a South African farmer. Every Saturday afternoon many of the Plymouth Brethren and Free Methodist missionaries get together for tennis at their place. It's nice. The kids play together and we relax. When you push yourself hard all week and feel exhausted, you have to get away and relax. Thank you for the dolls. We lost Paul's on the plane, so he is happy to have one again. Phil made Nancy a little doll bed and a wholesaler gave us some blanket samples so they have lots of fun playing house. Paul puts his babies to sleep and tries to make everyone be quiet. Then he gives them an 'ejection'. Poor kid, he's had so many shots! But he seems to be perfectly fine now. His tonsils are back to normal, and he never complains of his joints hurting any more. The doctor says that his heart is OK. So the Lord has answered prayer for him. (Tuesday morning) It's a terrifically hot day. Phil is laying block on an addition to an old building built by Mr. Ghormley, I think, out of stone and mud. It was one of the first buildings on the campus, probably built before 1910! But it is rather small and we needed more classroom space. Phil makes our own concrete blocks. The students are running the cement mixer today and are helping to make the blocks. Phil is going to be exhausted tonight. He isn't used to doing such hard work now. Paul wanted Nancy in his room, so we moved her out of the guest room, which is a good thing, because we've been having so much overnight company.

Lily Steele had told us that she had to make a trip back to England. Her aunt was dying and she felt she had to see her before she died. I wrote Lily a letter before she left:

Dear Lily, I haven't been able to tell you what I've wanted to because every time I even think about your leaving, I start to cry. It's been harder to say goodbye to you than to say goodbye to my own family. I'm so thankful that I have been permitted to know you. You have been to me what Granny Walshaw was to you, and like Elisha, I'm praying for a double portion of your spirit. I do want the Lord to be able to use me.

I know that God's way is perfect. I'm glad you will get so see your auntie again before she goes to meet her Lord. God bless you, Lily, and provide your every need, and bring you back 'home' to Edwaleni soon. And I gave her a poem I had written for her.

To Lily
God leadeth, but we cannot know
The why, or when, or where.
We only trust His tender love
To keep you in His care.
'Tis hard to say farewell to you.
We hope, we trust, we pray
That in God's matchless, perfect plan,
We'll meet again some day.
Our prayers, our thoughts will go with you
Across the restless sea.
And when you pray for me,
Pray that I'll spend more time alone with God.

Hungering and thirsting after righteousness

We had felt so privileged to have Lily Steele teaching the volunteer Bible study groups, personally praying with students as they came to seek the Lord, helping to lead the students as they went out to share God's love with those around us who were still living in darkness. And then I began to think, "What would happen to this ministry if Lily had to leave us? Would her responsibilities become mine? The early morning prayer meetings, the counseling, the Bible classes?" I felt totally inadequate, and so I asked the Lord that if she had to leave us, could He let a double portion of her spirit fall on me? He let me know that yes, He could do that, but only if I were more diligent about my prayer life. I began to see myself as God saw me, and it wasn't a nice picture. It was too difficult to get up early, I was too busy, my load was too heavy, and I was failing to cast my burdens on Him. I was trying to do things in my own strength instead of relying on the Lord. He began to convict me of my failure to make the time to drink from the Spring of Living Water.

I had become so busy 'doing missionary work' that I had neglected to give prayer and reading His Word first place in my daily life. I hadn't been keeping a sweet spirit. Sins of the spirit had crept in. Too many times I gave in to the temptation to think thoughts which I knew were not pleasing to the Lord. I had become too quick to criticize and find fault, and to talk behind the backs of my fellow missionaries. My love for others had diminished. I had lost many opportunities to witness. I was afraid no one could see Christ in me. But there were many people at home praying for us, interceding for us and the people we had come to win to the Lord. God was answering their prayers. I began to hunger and thirst after righteousness, and to seek the Lord with all my heart. I prayed that God would be merciful to me, a sinner, that He would forgive me, restore me, and fill me again with His Spirit. God led me to begin reading deeply spiritual books. Books by Tozer, Andrew Murray, Oswald Chambers, E. M. Bounds, and I read another book with a chapter on evil speaking: "Anything we say about another person in their absence that causes other people to think less of them is sin." The Lord reminded me of all the harm my tongue had done. "God … is a rewarder of those who diligently seek Him." Hebrews 11:6. He forgave me, restored me, and filled me fresh with His Spirit. Thank You, Lord!

Praise the Lord! Such a difference! I've found such peace and rest of soul. Pray now that I may really be used of God in the winning of souls here. The work here is extremely hard because of all the enforced racial prejudice. Pray that somehow there will be less prejudice and discrimination in South Africa, and that through it all more people will be saved. I wrote a poem about this time.

Holiness Found

So long the dark night of sin and despair
Hungry and thirsty, - Tempest within.
Then broken and humbled,
I bowed at His cross
My will bent to His, complete surrender.
Refined from all dross.
I live now rejoicing, in fellowship sweet

Walking with Jesus, His spirit within,
Peace overflowing, living for Jesus,
Others to win.
Now He can use me, a vessel made clean
Sanctified wholly, fit for His service
Doing His will.

(And I hadn't yet learned the secret of keeping filled with the Holy Spirit, continual surrender, and commitment to being obedient to God's Word!)

Warren and Jean Johnson are moving to Durban tomorrow. We will certainly miss them, but we will stay with them when we go to Durban. Did I tell you about the green *imamba* snake that Phil killed last week? He shot it in the head in the carpentry shop ceiling, and then when it dropped to the floor, he beat its head with a stick. Of course he had it pinned to the floor. We skinned it, 6' long. The Lord certainly protects us!

Jean, Warren, Janet, Julaine and Jim Johnson

Muddy roads!

February 20, 1955, We just returned this afternoon from the opening of the new Greenville Hospital building, and what a nightmare. Friday night it poured all night, but we were supposed to take a lot of food, so we put our chains on and started anyway. Our road was a little slippery, but not bad and the main road was good. But when we got down close to the Umtamvuna River bridge at Punzi Drift, what a sight! There must have been a cloudburst upstream. Pumpkins and cornstalks were tossing down the river. It was way out of its banks. We've never seen it like that before. The name Umtamvuna means 'the Reaper'. When we got to the Greenville road, what a mess! So soft that Phil put it in low and just gunned it up the hills. We slid all over, from one side to the other. We scraped the bank, and I was sure we'd swing back and go over the side, but the Lord helped Phil get control of the car and on we went, five more miles of hills and mud. We were the first car to get in. Only a few made it. Most of them couldn't make it up the worst hill and had to turn back. Dr. Rice took his lorry out to bring people in, but most of them had turned around and had gone back home, and then he couldn't get his lorry up the hill either. We decided not to try to go home that night, so we slept all night in the hospital! None of the important people who were supposed to give speeches were able to get there. It drizzled all day, but the African people were there by the hundreds. They ate three oxen. It's pouring rain again, and poor Dr. Rice is out taking his children back to school in Durban. Dr. Rice was born in South Africa. His parents were missionaries at Edwaleni, beginning in 1913!

February 27, 1955, Two kids sick today. Nancy has bronchitis, very nearly pneumonia even with penicillin, and Paul also has a temp. I'm keeping them both in bed. Hope they are better tomorrow. I've got work to do in the office, and I have classes to teach besides. Phil is getting another teacher, an African man who can teach English and Afrikaans. The main reason is that we are very nearly certain that we will have an addition to our family sometime in October! What a relief to have another teacher. I can do a better job now with my Bible class and Chorus, as well as keeping up with the correspondence in the school office. (Phil didn't think I should be teaching while obviously pregnant!)

The Umtamvuna River floods

March 16, 1955, I went down to the river today with Phil. He had to start the pump and what a mess the flood left! Nothing but sand and a few stalks across the river where some people had planted beautiful fields of corn. The water came up to within about ten feet of the pump house. It must have been fifteen feet higher than usual. It's still high, too high to cross with a horse, but it left a nice sloping, clean, sandy beach where there was only dirt and bushes before. Paul will like that!

They've been seeing a huge black *imamba* lately down by the *isibaya* (the cattle pen). The *imamba* is about twelve feet long and as big around as a man's arm! Almost time for lights out. Phil rigged up a wire today from the power house to our house so he can turn off the electric plant without going out there. I've gone out there at night to turn it off several times and when there is no moon, it's really dark and spooky! Gertie told us several years later, after we had left, that one dark night when she had gone out to turn off the plant, she met an *imamba* on the path. It had raised up on its tail! Only God's protection kept her from getting bitten! Gives me goose bumps to even think about it!

I am almost out of bandages made out of old sheets. Mother, if your Women's Missionary Society group would like a project, we could certainly use some more! There have been several new students with bad leg injuries. One boy was crossing a flooded river to get to school, fell in over his head, and a big rock gouged his leg open. He never did anything about it, until after he'd been here a week! It began to smell so bad one of the old boys brought him to me. What an infected mess! It is finally almost well, but it has taken a lot of bandages.

March 30, 1955, Nancy is asleep. I don't take her out much at night. She wants her own bed to go to sleep in. Usually she just lies right down and says, "Ta-ta," the South African way of saying good-bye. Paul still has to be patted and sung to! Lily and I went to a *kraal* this afternoon that we had to really climb to get to. (A *kraal* is a group of African family huts.) We drove out on the road to near Mrs. Hlope's, parked the car, and went down a steep, long hill, crossed the little stream that plunges into that beautiful little one hundred foot waterfall, and climbed up a terrifically steep hill nearly to the top. Our faces were red and we were gasping for breath when we arrived.

The headman of the *kraal* met us and took us into his hut. It was neat and clean. He gave us two chairs to sit on and rolled out a mat for Mrs. Hlope. (Africans prefer to sit on the floor). In the hut were an iron bed (a single cot), two plows, a planter, a rope up high on which the bright clothing of the heathen wife was folded, along with extra blankets. The rope was attached to sticks stuck into the grass roof just on top of the walls. Also there were her beadwork and many bracelets and anklets. He is industrious and well-to-do compared with many of the *Zulu* men, but he drinks too much, and is mean very often. Today he was nice and asked us to pray for him. He said he was still walking in darkness. He has two wives. One is a Christian and one is a heathen. His old mother is a Christian. About fifteen church women met us there and we had a good service. Three heathen men came and listened very attentively as Lily spoke. There were also five or six heathen women and about ten children. Oh, how our hearts long to help these people desire to come to the Lord. Last weekend we went to Durban. Phil went to two doctors about his leg aches. He found out that it is definitely not circulatory, but probably is muscular. They are worse now. Hot weather makes them worse, and they make him tired all the time. Saturday night we took the kids down to the amusement park at the Durban beach. Paul rode for the first time on little cars, a little train and a merry-go-round. He called it an "America-round!" He was thrilled silly! Tonight I asked him what a mommy was, and he said, "To read books to you.," and a daddy was, "To take care of you!"

April 26, 1955, Another day is nearly over and I feel more like dropping into bed than anything else. Nancy is sick again, kept us awake a lot last night, but she seems much better tonight. The kids are here playing on the living room carpet, making a general mess with Paul's tool set and wood that has been sawn up for the cook stove. Women, mostly heathen, come every Tuesday morning to chop firewood. They cut off branches from acacia trees down around the side of our hill, one bundle for themselves and one for the school. Then one of the men who works at the school cuts up the branches on the saw attached to the tractor. It's enough wood to keep the school kitchen and both mission houses in firewood. Friday one of the boys cut off the end of his finger, but it didn't bleed until about 9 o'clock at night! So Phil had to rush him to the Port Shepstone Hospital in the middle of the night. Dr. Rice was in Durban. I've had to dress it every afternoon. However, again, I realized I need to be a nurse.

Nancy can pedal her trike all over now. It's really fun to watch her. She's so tall for her age. Paul calls grasshoppers "hop-grassers." He caught one the other day, put it in a jar and fed it grass, but he brought it into our room the next day because he said it scared him at night!

Our school goes on strike!

May, 1955, The Lord has helped us to pass victoriously through dark days when the power of satan settled over the school like a cloud. The devil has tremendous power that can only be dispelled through prayer. In the midst of the conflict when the way looked the darkest, the Lord sent the assurance that He moves in a mysterious way to work His wonders. The next night some students burned the *rondavel* (ron-dah'vuhl), a round, stone-walled, thatched-roof hut, our prayer room, used for early morning prayer meetings and the voluntary Bible Study group. Our hearts are heavy because of the loss and because of the rebellious attitude against Christianity that has swept over the school. However, God answered our prayers and we were able to sort out the agitators in the strike. Thirty boys were sent home, and expelled. The Mission Executive Committee, the Inspector of Government schools, and the police were all called in to help settle the strike. Our enrollment is down to 137, but the spirit in the school is better now.

Later we discovered that two of the teachers had distributed anti-Christian propaganda literature throughout the student body. They were dismissed, and peace again prevailed, praise the Lord! We got hold of a couple copies of "The Student," which was what they had been reading. We could begin to see why attitudes had changed. One article denied that there was a God, another was written against Mission schools, and the rest contained some truth liberally sprinkled with lies, which most of the students believed! We also heard that submarines from Russia had been sighted off the coast of South Africa, taking young men on board to Russia to indoctrinate them. Our student body had averaged about 190 high school age boys. They could choose to learn tailoring, motor mechanics, leatherwork or carpentry. In addition, we had a daily chapel service, classes in English and Bible and Chorus, with church services on Sunday. Phil had also been appointed pastor of the Edwaleni circuit. We look back with disappointment at the results of our efforts, and think how terribly we have failed. However, on the very same day that we had contemplated closing Edwaleni, we learned that Fort Hare, a college of over 300, for Africans, had also closed down because of a similar school strike. But we had higher hopes for our Christian school than what has happened. Oh, how the darkness of satan can capture and paralyze the hearts and minds of mankind. May God help us to do our part in expelling this darkness, and bring peace to the hearts of men, and God's joy on earth. Everything seems to be back to normal now, the students have a completely changed attitude. They are cooperating nicely and are respectful like they were before the strike. We do praise the Lord for sustaining us during this nightmarish ordeal. We are so thankful that there was no further damage to mission property. We later learned that they had also planned to burn down the office, tailoring shop and the motor mechanics buildings!

May,1955, In Durban. Resting in bed after a day of fun. Jean Johnson and I took Paul, Nancy and their Janet to the beach on the bus. Julaine and Jim were in school. Warren has gone to Port Elizabeth on a ship to pick up his new car, and Phil is home at Edwaleni working. After our strike was settled, we all felt exhausted and had to get away for awhile. So Lily went with Mary Current to get her new car and then we came to Durban for a rest. Phil went home on Monday, but I stayed on with Jean to keep her company while Warren is gone. Paul was thrilled about riding the bus and train. The Durban beach is wonderful. Flat and smooth, clean sand, no rocks. It was low tide today, and the kids had so much fun in the water. I wish I could have gone swimming, but my suit would have been a wee bit too snug right now. I started wearing maternity clothes this week. It was so nice to be a full-time mother for a change instead of a part time one. Durban is so much like Seattle, it's hard to realize we are in Africa. It is hilly, built around the bay, and along the beach. You can even get good ice cream here! However, Jean doesn't have an African girl to help her, so we have been doing a lot of cooking and dish washing, and clothes washing. Only four more weeks until we have six weeks of winter vacation. They will be full of Worker's Conference, Youth Camps, Vacation Bible schools and missionary convention. So we won't be home much.

June, 1955, Nancy is nearly as big as Paul now. He will be four in July, and she will be two in September, but she climbs trees right after him and follows him around like his shadow. They love to walk down to the lower end of the campus to the *isibaya* and see the little calves and watch the African boys milk the cows. The school sow has nine little piglets, and the kiddies beg to go down to watch them. The Lord helped us find a young Christian man, Douglas Mthembu, who was qualified to teach English and Afrikaans. The government will soon enforce the requirement that Afrikaans be taught in all schools. I gladly turned my English classes over to him. So now my load isn't quite so heavy, but I still have plenty to do because the secretarial work in the school office is nearly a full-time job in itself, and I really need to spend more time with our children.

July 10, 1955, We took off for Johannesburg as soon as we could, on the day school was out. What a mad rush that was! We stayed with DeMilles in Germiston for several days until Johnsons sold their car. Then on Monday, nearly two weeks ago, we had planned to all come back to Durban when the doctors decided that Phil had to stay in the hospital there for a week or so for tests and observation, about his leg aches. So we came on to Durban without him and he had a nice rest and vacation in the hospital! I about died without him, but the separation has been good for us, because we've fallen in love all over again, better than ever before! They gave him ACTH and vitamin B12, but no change in his legs. All the tests they ran on him were perfectly normal, so they still don't know what the cause of his terrific leg aches is. He came back this morning on an airplane. We drove out and met him. Talk about excitement, the kids were really happy to see their daddy, and so was I!

Tomorrow we leave for Workers' Conference at Greenville Mission. Then a week at Ithemba Mission, and then back to Durban for another week to finish the remodeling that Phil was doing in Johnson's kitchen. That makes about six weeks living out of suitcases, and away from home, but we needed to be away from Edwaleni. We are so thankful for the prayers of the people at home who are praying for us. The Lord is helping us both spiritually. We feel that the Lord led us to Johannesburg. The DeMilles are such wonderful people. Just being with them a few days was an inspiration.

After six weeks of being away, we are finally really ready to live at home! I have things about packed and am just resting awhile before finishing the job. The way things look, we won't leave until tonight anyway! Phil and Warren have been putting in the built-ins Phil made for Johnson's house, doing the necessary plumbing, and installing an automatic hot water heater. This is what Phil had planned to do at the beginning of our vacation, but he spent ten days in the hospital at Joh'burg instead! Even though the doctors found nothing they could do for him, those ten days have made all the difference in the world to us! I should add that it was the association with the DeMilles, plus those ten days. The Lord has been so good to us. And, as if that weren't enough, just read this! The last Sunday night of Youth Camp at Ithemba Mission, Warren and Jean, Lily, Rev. and Mrs. Duma, and Phil and I, met together after the evening service in the Ithemba Mission house. Pastor Duma, an African Baptist preacher, who is a real man of God, was the evangelist for the camp. Many young people received help during the camp, and several dedicated their lives to the ministry. It was a good camp, with 84 in attendance. We had heard that there had been quite a number of people who had been healed after Pastor Duma prayed for them. So Phil asked him to pray for healing for his legs. We all realized that there was nothing doctors could do, only God could make him well again. So, Sunday night we had a healing service. Pastor Duma prayed, then others prayed. The burden lifted, we were all blessed and felt that God had answered prayer. And He did! Praise His name! Phil had been taking four pain pills that contain codeine, to relieve the pain in his legs so he could sleep! He hasn't taken a single pain pill for his legs since! They still ache a little, but even though he is on his feet all day long, it doesn't get bad. Phil is just like a different person. He feels ten years younger! Be happy with us. Thanks for your prayers.

August 21, 1955, Hope you had a happy anniversary yesterday. We did. (We shared the same anniversary.) Thanks so much for the nice card and the $5. You shouldn't have sent so much, but thanks. Paul got his package from Esther Stites Friday. Were the kids ever thrilled! The game for Paul is good. Nancy, of course, was excited over the adorable little doll with hair! Will write Esther soon. Did I ever thank you for the Bible school materials and Paul's shirt? They came quite a while before his birthday. That shirt is so nice and will fit him quite a while. He is growing out of and wearing out a lot of his clothes. Especially short pants, which he loves! He likes the elastic in the top! I have to force him into jeans when it is cold. Silly kid! We asked Phil's sister, Jeanne Prevo, in Kansas, to order a toy grader for Paul. It came, and we had a hard time keeping it until his birthday. The pastor who was supposed to move to Old Edwaleni last May, has decided not to come at all! That places a greater responsibility on Phil. He goes out and preaches in one of the three churches on our circuit every other week Thanks for praying for us.

September 7, 1955, Just came over to the office after my daily rest. Only today I feel very fine because I really relaxed and did my exercises! I am getting extremely impatient. Only 3 1/2 weeks to go! We washed and put away all the left over baby clothes, and blankets. I really have a lot of things. The only items I need are short sleeved undershirts, plastic pants, both small and medium, rattles, soft plastic toys, cotton knit gowns with draw-string in the bottom. Nancy is <u>finally</u> trained. Stays dry all day except when she sleeps. Goes by herself and empties and washes out her potty! Quite a surprise! Didn't think a two year old could do that! She has also abandoned her 'baby' bed and 'baby' chair. She is so proud of being a big girl, and she wanted a bed like Paul's, and insists on sitting in a big people's chair at the table. She is some character! So determined, but sweet and lovable.

Paul is thrilled about our having a new baby. He knows where it is now and takes great pride in helping mommy, sometimes! We are hoping for a boy, David Joseph (Davey Joe), but will be happy too if it is Patricia Anne (Patsy Anne). Paul wants both of them. He tells everyone he wants us to have twins! That would suit me fine! Because I do want four kids so much!

Mamie is expecting September 26, and has been confined to her house for months. I'll go to Greenville hospital probably October 2, if it doesn't come early! I expect this one to come fast!

September 20, 1955, A fresh, almost cool breeze has just come up, bringing relief from an oppressively hot day. Even the nights have been hot, very unusual for here. Makes you feel like wilted lettuce! I am sitting on the back steps watching the kids climb the tree and swing. Nancy can't open the back door and she is sitting here saying "*vula, vula*" (voo'lah), (open, open). She talks as much *Zulu* as she does English. Only twelve days to go. By the time you get this letter the time will be much less, maybe October 3. I have all the baby stuff packed and my suitcase nearly ready to go. I hope not to get caught unprepared this time with twenty miles of rough, almost mountainous road to cover. Should go over early, but I hate to be away from the kids any longer than I have to. I am feeling pretty good. No trouble so far. Still carrying it high. The kids played in the little pool today. They were so thrilled. They love water and have colds from getting wet on cold days! Thanks so much for Nancy's package. The dress is adorable. It's just a wee bit big, so it will last a long time. The panties came at just the right time. The ones she inherited from Paul were nearly worn out and she wouldn't keep them on. She loves these and calls them "pretty pants." She stays dry all day now, even uses her potty at night sometimes. This concrete step where I am sitting, is getting hard!

The Lord is continuing to work. Just last night another boy came to the office, and after talking with Lily, gave his heart to the Lord. That makes three this term. We feel revival is coming. Continue to pray. Well, the kids are washed and ready for bed and the house is cooling off. Keep praying for Phil. His legs are bad again, but he isn't taking codeine. Hope he won't have to.

Nancy and Paul in their tire swing in front of the
rain water storage tanks beside our house

September 27, 1955, Thank you for the lovely stockings. They arrived yesterday. This interminable waiting, I'm getting **so** tired of it. I'm sure this baby is going to either be huge or twins! I weigh 155, a gain of 30 pounds. Hope I lose it all! I may go over to Greenville Saturday. It's due next Monday. I don't want to get caught like Mamie did last Saturday. They arrived at the Harding hospital just forty-five minutes before the baby came! And such rough roads! Mary Current was along, just in case! But what a ride that must have been! They had another girl, and both are doing fine. I feel pretty good, but I rest a lot. My blood pressure is low and my pulse races once in a while, but no swelling.

Dr. Rice came over last Friday so I wouldn't have to go way over to Greenville Mission for my last check-up. He said the head was engaged and I could have it any time now. If Phil is there he will get to watch, and I'll get to have the baby with me all the time. Isn't that thrilling? When you get this letter you will be grandparents again! Ha! Don't you wish you knew if it is going to be Davey Joe or Patsy Anne? I'd like to know too. Well, I feel like going to bed again, but I guess I'll make myself go to the office instead. Got to keep things caught up so I won't be so far behind when I come back. Phil's legs are better again. He is taking some different medicine now, in addition to my pre-natal capsules. Ha! Pray that the Lord will help him to find some way to make them well.

Patricia Anne is born

Our Patricia Anne was born in September, 1955. We had hoped she could be born at Greenville Hospital just around the hills and over the river, but complications, (P.O.P. - face up), made that too risky. Phil and Mrs. Rice took me for a wild ride 50 miles to the nearest government hospital at Port Shepstone, where they did a forceps delivery. Dr. Rice had followed in their car. I was told that as I was recovering from the anesthesia, I was shouting, "Praise the Lord!" very loudly! Phil told me that they could hear me all over the hospital! Patsy Anne was born about 8 last night. It's after 9 a.m., the next day now, and Dr. Rice should be here any minute to take us back to Greenville Mission. It will be nicer there. Phil will get to visit oftener, and best of all, I'll have the baby right next to me instead of way away in the nursery!

Before we left the house this morning, Paul woke up, saw we were getting ready to leave, so he dressed himself and came out and said, "Let's go!" I told him we were going to go to the hospital to get our new baby and he said, "Oh, okay I'm going to sleep in my clothes," and so he crawled back into bed, perfectly satisfied. The kids will be happy. They both wanted a little sister. Dr. and Mrs. Rice took such good care of us. Wish you could see sweet little Patsy. She's such a good baby!

Phil holding Patsy, with Nancy and Paul

October 11, 1955, Home again. Patsy is sound asleep. The kids are out playing in the warm sunshine. The girls are getting ready to do the wash, and I am being lazy! Feel like going back to sleep. Patsy had to be fed at three this morning. She usually sleeps from 9:30 to 5:30! But she went to sleep too soon last night and I couldn't wake her up to eat more. We came home Saturday evening. Seems good to be home again. I haven't been to the office yet, don't think I'll even go over there until I get so I can bathe the baby in less than a half hour. Seems like it takes me forever to do anything! Marge Rice made me stay in bed **five** days! That is the way they do it here, and I didn't mind at all. I was so tired and sore all over. I'm feeling fine now, but I'll take it easy for a few days yet. The household runs itself without any supervision from me. We have three girls working for us now. It isn't as satisfactory as doing things yourself, but when you can't, you can't! I'd really like to stay home and take care of the kids and do my own cooking, but that isn't what I'm here for!

October 25, 1955, My, how time flies! Patricia Anne is three weeks old. She is growing fast and looks more like Nancy every day. She's sweet and cuddly. *Jabula*! (Joy). I'm losing a pound every day! When I came home I couldn't get into hardly anything except my maternity skirts. I feel starved, but I need to lose weight, Phil prefers a slender wife! We are accepting new students for 1956, and that is taking most of my time when I'm not busy with the baby. She is good most of the time, though, and sleeps the whole night through!

November 17, 1955, This is a warm sunny, windy day, the middle of our warm season. I am sitting with a student, who is taking a National J.C. exam in *Afrikaans*. (Similar to Dutch) It lasts three hours, and I just have to sit and make sure he doesn't cheat! Good opportunity to write letters! Only three weeks of school left. Seems impossible. I've had a good vacation, but I'm back at work full time, just taking off enough time to feed Patsy. I have to sleep about one or two afternoons a week to keep going. Patsy weighs eleven pounds now and is such a sweet, good baby. We haven't seen many snakes yet this season. Hope the *imamba*s stay away! The river is muddy, reddish brown. So much soil washing away to the ocean! The soil erosion in the native locations is terrible, great huge gullies and hills nearly bare in spots. Phil has had the African driver plow the ground down near the river. They've planted corn, beans, pumpkins, and I don't know what else. The crops should do well, it's rich ground.

We may go to Durban this weekend to hear Oswald Smith from Canada. We certainly miss hearing good sermons in English. Our garden is doing well, lots of tomatoes, lettuce, beets, peas, onions, peppers, cabbage, asparagus, carrots, chard, and beans. About all we buy is meat and potatoes, sugar and flour. There isn't anywhere near here to buy vegetables anyway. If we didn't have a good garden, we'd have to live on canned foods! I've finally taught Seth, our garden boy, how to irrigate! What a struggle that was. He was continually letting things die, because "It's time for them to die!" He just couldn't understand that some plants can grow all year around if you can give them enough water! We never have frost here, but it does snow on the mountains about thirty miles away. Gets very cold in the house, but our new fireplace will keep us warm. But of course, this is summer now. Looks like a rain blowing up. Only half hour left to sit. I'm tired of sitting.

Hope Patsy Anne isn't crying! I feel like it's time for her to eat! It would be fun to be home talking with you this afternoon! My desk in the office is stacked high with work waiting to be done, mostly new student applications. We've had to reject twice as many as we can accept. They are only letting us accept tailoring, leatherwork and motor mechanics students this year. No building or carpentry students. We get to graduate the carpentry students we now have, but new building students have to go elsewhere. I hope this kind of government never gets control in the States! It's terrible! You do what they tell you to, period! If we become a government school, I dread the red tape and government forms we'll spend our time and patience on! Please request prayer that the right decision will be made. Pray also for Phil. His legs are bad again. If our school is closed, they will probably let us continue on for two years to graduate the students we now have, and after that, who knows? However, there is enough evangelistic work to be done around here to keep us all busy.

From our 1955 Christmas letter to prayer partners and family

Rejoice with us for the Lord is working here. Already this term six students have come to the office or early morning prayer meeting to accept Jesus as their personal Savior. After a long time of seeing no results, we are made to rejoice as we feel the Spirit moving the hearts of the students. We feel Revival is on the way. The devil would love to defeat and tear down, but through your prayers, he can be made powerless. The government inspectors were here yesterday, and they told us more about the changes to be made next year in Bantu Industrial schools. A decision must be made soon whether Edwaleni will become a private school or a government school, fully controlled by the Native Affairs Department, or be closed. There are many problems connected with making this decision, and it is extremely difficult to know what the right thing to do is. We are now a government-aided school, receiving 100% government support. The students pay for their food, lodging, and school supplies. That is all they can afford to pay. The teachers' salaries are paid by the government. The only way we can retain complete control of the school is to become a private school, receiving less and less financial support from the government. We won't be permitted to continue on as we are now. Please pray that those making the decision may be given wisdom from above.

Phil has malaria

December 27, 1955, It's a beautiful summer morning, with low fog down in the river valley and bright hot sun. Just finished feeding Patsy. She's back asleep, the little angel. This is our vacation week. We may spend a few days in Durban in January, but Johnsons are here with us now and we are having a wonderful time just relaxing, not even opening the office door. They came Saturday evening after the big Christmas dinner with Rileys at Fairview Mission. Missionaries on vacation from Portuguese East Africa, and the DeMilles were also there. It seemed almost like Christmas dinner at home, so I didn't get homesick like I usually do. We had our family Christmas on Sunday here. I was Santa Claus, Paul and Nancy didn't recognize me! It was really fun to watch them. Did I tell you about Phil being sick? He had dysentery. We all get it occasionally, and then one night he called me and asked for more blankets. He was having a violent chill, it lasted about twenty minutes. I was really scared, and did some fast praying! Then his temperature shot up fast. He felt terrible and the next night the same thing happened, so Dr. Rice came over and examined him. He thinks it is probably malaria, possibly from when Phil was in the South Pacific, but he never had an attack before. He is feeling okay now. This isn't malaria area, so don't worry about us.

Last week Lily and I held a Bible school out at Esangweni School. Thanks for all the supplies you sent. We received everything we needed to have a good V.B.S. We ended up with 63 kids, good for here! About half were from heathen homes, can't read or write and don't attend

Sunday School. So it was a wonderful opportunity for getting the Gospel to them. We went out six days. The kids were so thrilled and excited. No one had ever had a V.B.S. here, at least not as far as we could find out. They responded well to the invitation we gave each day. Pray for those who gave their hearts to the Lord that they might grow into strong Christians. The last day we invited the parents. The school house was packed out with almost 100 there. Many heathen women who never go to church came. One little boy from a heathen *kraal*, David Cele, brought nine new kids during the week! He had only recently been saved in one of Lily's *kraal* meetings. We used flannelgraphs each day, The Wordless Book Visualized. You may have seen it, it's really good. It presents the Gospel story vividly. I asked Mary Current to put the Wordless Book chorus into *Zulu*. She was here recuperating. The house she lives in at Ebenezer Mission is so damp that she has a continual sinus infection. She and Lily are at Riley's, down at Fairview Mission, this week to rest.

We are having such a good time with the Johnsons here. We played tennis twice yesterday and went down to the river. They had never been down on that side of the hill before. Only two students are here now. They live too far away to go home, in Rhodesia, and if they did go home they wouldn't be allowed to enter the Union again, so they just have to stay here! Poor kids. They do the milking and separating and look after the chickens and work on the road and chop down wattle (Acacia) trees for firewood. We sell the bark. It contains tannin and brings a good price, and the wood is wonderful to cook with. Dr. Lamson is coming out here in February. The future of Edwaleni will be decided then. Four or five government officials will meet here with him and the mission executive committee to try to reach some agreement. Pray that the right decision will be made.

1956, February, Well, the 'Reaper' is at it again. The Umtamvuna River is flooding again. Only this year there are no pumpkins. Our long drought has at last been broken and some of the people's mealies (corn) will recover, but it is too late for the pumpkins. We nearly had a cloudburst Friday night and Phil had to take a sick boy to the Port

Shepstone Hospital, through the rain and mud. He got back about 3 a.m. and slept most of Saturday morning. No dull moments here! We wished we could have given the people all around us some of our generous supply of water, but it wouldn't have helped much. The sun was so hot the seeds wouldn't germinate. However, today is chilly. Phil has just returned from preaching at Emthini. He took Lily and the girls to Mbodiya on his way, and I stayed here with our kiddoes. They are all still asleep.

Praise be to God! Great things He has done! My faith is in flood like the river. The Lord really answered prayer Wednesday. The government official who met with the Executive Committee completely reversed his previous decision. He has now given us until June 31 to decide about Edwaleni instead of March 31, and he will permit Phil to remain as principal even if we do become a government school, which means a lot, because we will be able to enforce our rules of no smoking and no alcohol, and will be able to carry on our evangelistic work. We definitely feel that the Lord has marvelously answered prayer, much more than we had faith for! We were all expecting that Edwaleni would have to be closed. But through prayer, God does move even government officials! We felt surrounded by the prayers of the people at home this last week. Thank them for us. It makes such a difference. Lily already has 38 in her Bible study class, and a good attendance in early morning prayer meeting. There is a good spirit in the student body, and we are very encouraged. Patsy is nearly ready to crawl! She's such a sweet contented little doll.

March, 1956, Wish you could see Pats. She is on a blanket on the carpet, rocking like a rocky horse. Paul and Nancy are putting puzzles together and listening to their records. Phil is asleep in the bedroom. He is so tired. He worked too hard yesterday. In the morning he castrated about twelve bull calves! In the afternoon he made a concrete base for a new rain water tank. Our tanks are full and running over, but if we aren't very careful, we will still have to use river water before the rains come again. Patsy is so close to crawling you could practically say she does. She gets there anyway. It's impossible to keep her on a blanket.

Phil preached here this morning and I spoke in Sunday School. I felt led to talk on tithing, and Phil had been planning to preach on the same subject today, only I didn't know it! The Lord has been leading so wonderfully. Just little things, but so precious! One morning this week, I had planned to have the 91st Psalm in Chapel. I usually ask the Lord to guide me in choosing the right one. I had been sick and Lily had asked the Lord what Psalm she should prepare in case I wasn't able to make it to chapel, and He told her Psalm 91! Wasn't that wonderful? We feel so definitely that the Lord is speaking to students. But the devil is working overtime to do all the damage he can. Phil's legs have been bad lately, but the Lord is helping him. I believe that he will be healed completely soon. I'm sure the students and teachers felt this morning that they had been hit with a 'double barreled shotgun!' The Lord must have been getting someone's heart ready to receive light on the tithing subject. It's so thrilling to be used and led by Him! Teacher Nozisali, from Esangweni told us later that he is beginning to tithe!

Connie Nyaose and Patsy

Patsy and Mom

Rats and snakes!

May, 1956, Winter is nearly here, with its cold winds and hot sun and no rain. It's chilly today, but comfortable inside with warm clothes on. We are appreciating our fireplace these cold nights. Phil is out *kraal* visiting with a group of students. Patter is a little butterball, very independent and fast. She loves to stand holding onto things, especially the little footstools that Grandma made. She is such a little half-pint they are just her size! She has learned to patty-cake, probably would have learned sooner, but I am home to play with her so seldom. Don't know what I'll do when I have to start teaching Paul! Sure wish he could go to a real school, but will probably use Calvert Course here. We are doing intensive *Zulu* study now. Our teacher, Mrs. Nyaose, comes every weekday after school and stays until about eight at night. I am learning much faster than when I was studying on my own. Wish my brain were young again. You should have been here last Thursday,

Grace. Phil killed a big fat puff adder. He was only two feet from it when he saw it! They are nasty, deadly pests! But they do keep the rat population down. There was a huge rat in the house last week. He had chewed his way through the bathroom floor. Paul and Nancy are more afraid of cows than they are of rats and snakes! Crazy kids! John, you would probably enjoy our pigs and cows. We have nine pigs and about fifty head of cattle, and some cute little calves.

Nancy loves potatoes and Patsy 'patty cakes'

July, 1956, What a nice day this has been, and how relaxing it is to have school out! We spent several hours on the front verandah basking in the warm sun. Winter is nice here when it isn't too cold. The kids are certainly happy to have me home to play with them. Even Patsy. She is a little busy-body. She stands up in the middle of the floor, then squats down, up and down like a little jack-in-the box. She patty cakes and then laughs. She has four teeth, and she loves to grind them. I'm glad I finally got her on the cup and bottle. Well, I stopped to light the Coleman lantern and all the lamps before it got dark. Pats decided she was hungry and Paul began to yearn for popcorn. Phil is in Johannesburg remodeling DeMille's kitchen. He should be back home by the time you get this letter. It is lonesome without him. Nancy wouldn't eat her meat the other day and so I told her she needed to eat meat to get meat on her bones, that everybody had meat on their bones. She thought a minute and then replied with a saucy grin, "I got potatoes on **my** bones!"

Nancy, her doll Judy, Paul and his toy truck

July 7, 1955, From Phil to Dr. Zahniser, At the present time I am in a hospital in Joh'burg trying to find out why my legs ache so much of the time. It is school vacation time now. School starts August 3. We are trusting and praying that the next term will be a good one in which God's blessing will be poured out upon all of us. We have been trying to get Rev. Duma from Durban to hold a revival meeting at Edwaleni. He is quite busy and has not decided. The last few weeks of school were relatively quiet. I caught five boys smoking. Two of them were also suspected of having been the ones who wrote me an anonymous note, threatening to burn down the office. Therefore they were all sent home. I had heard that some students were smoking, and had warned them, but seemingly they did not believe me, I have a list of others who are reported to be smoking. I am sending a letter to their parents so they can take action before their boys return. I caught a boy on campus from the local area with dagga (marijuana?) in a bag under his coat. He pointed out two students who had ordered it. They told him to bring peanuts along to sell as a disguise. So you see, satan continues to do his best to attack the souls of the youth. Our heart's cry is still for a Bible school to train young workers. We realize there are many complications concerning such a step, but it seems that the church is dying without young men to present the Gospel. I have been digging deeper spiritually and asking God to help me to be in the place I should be. I have faith that He is going to enrich my life and use me to a greater extent. Praise His Holy Name!

Terrible accident!

July, 1956, Last night was a nightmare. We didn't get Paul to sleep until 1:30. He had slept for awhile earlier, but woke up crying and fussing. Finally we took turns sitting up and holding him until he finally went to sleep. But tonight he is better, and to make sure, I gave him a tablet that the doctor left for him Saturday. On Saturday afternoon, Paul was terribly, horribly burned. He was trying to put Patsy's bottle in the teakettle to warm, and pulled it over on top of him, hot water all over his back. His whole back is a solid mass of blisters and areas of dark red. One upper arm and one leg are also burned in spots. Thank the Lord that was all. It could have been so much worse, but if it had been, he probably wouldn't be alive. He is a very sick little boy, and it is all my fault. I should have gone into the kitchen with him. I should have known that what he was trying to do would be impossible! But it seems to be healing nicely. He is complaining now of it itching. No areas seem to be infected. I was fortunate in having a large piece of sterile gauze on hand. I first applied butesin picrate and then strips of the gauze. His tummy was all red at first. Probably only first degree, and the burn ointment cleared it right up. After I had applied the ointment and dressings and had gotten him wrapped up in clean pillow cases and blankets, I felt I should anoint him and pray for him. I did, and the Lord marvelously answered prayer. Paul immediately went to sleep! Imagine! He only roused up to drink a little water every fifteen minutes; exactly what he needed to prevent shock. Praise the Lord! When he was feeling better he told me that Jesus had made him all well and told me to take off the bandages and see, because it didn't hurt anymore! This was only about one hour after the accident! Later he told me that right after we prayed that his "burn went lower and lower until it was just about all gone. Wasn't Jesus nice?" His faith is so sweet. Every time he gets a spell of itching, he either prays or asks me to pray. I forgot to tell you that I called Dr. Rice and asked him to come over because I had no way of getting out. Phil was in Johannesburg and didn't get home until Sunday. Doctor came about 4:30. Paul was sound asleep. They dressed the burned area, practically clothed him in bandages! We call it his bathing suit! They left a supply of dressings and medication for me to use on him, but what an ordeal it is to change the dressings! Poor little boy. But he is very brave, and so far very little has stuck. Thank the Lord for that! I'm getting sleepier by the minute. Patsy is beginning to take steps alone, not quite 9 1/2 months yet! She'll be really walking by the end of this month. We'll probably go over to Youth Camp on Sunday. Can't keep my eyes open. P.S. I know Paul is going to be OK, so don't worry! Edwaleni is now a government school. The decision was approved by the Mission Board. Phil remains as principal and all departments except Motor Mechanics and possibly leathercraft will be transferred out next year, and Phil won't have to teach classes! His legs are still bad.

Monday, I just changed Paul's dressings and got him settled down for a nap. I am absolutely 'done in'. It's such a strain on me to change them alone. He hurts so much. The third degree areas still burn because of the damage to the nerve endings, I'm sure I suffer almost as much as Paul. He had a bad night last night. He wants his back rubbed almost all the time he is awake! But the Lord is helping wonderfully. Yesterday he felt so good, he said he could run now! Then he took off down the hall to show us. Even rode his trike a little. We went to Youth Camp Friday and Sunday. Today it finishes. Phil stayed last night at Ithemba Mission so he could bring the truck back full of Edwaleni's young people today. There was a record attendance this year, about 130, and the Lord really blessed. About 50 testified last night at the closing service to new victory or a first time experience. It was wonderful, and at the end of the meeting a girl was brought who was possessed with a demon. Pastor Duma has been given the gift of healing, and I'm sure the girl is all right now. As he prayed for her all the campers gathered in a circle around the family and sang, "There is wonderful power in the blood of Jesus," over and over in *Zulu*. It was a marvelous service. You could feel the power of the Lord present. Our hearts thrilled as we listened to the testimonies and confessions, and we know the Lord is going to do mighty things for South Africa. These changed young lives will mean much to their home churches. Ringing testimonies of deliverance from smoking, drinking, and immorality, and they will go home to make restitution. Our girls are different now, too. Two of them gave good testimonies last night with shining faces. It's nearly dinner time. Must feed Pats. She is walking now. Takes five or six steps without sitting down. She walked more than one step alone before she was 9 1/2 months old! She still seems so tiny. Tomorrow afternoon is the 'welcome back' for Gertie and Kathryn Hessler at Greenville Mission and Wednesday morning we have to be at Fairview Mission for Worker's Conference. I am in charge of food for the missionaries and I plan to have meetings for the children, and have to give one talk on Sunday School in the Conference. Big week ahead, please pray for us. Love you.

August 4, 1956, Paul is very much better. All the burn is healed now except the third degree area, and it is coming along nicely. He is such a brave little fellow, doesn't cry anymore when I change the dressings, and is feeling better. However, he caught a bad cold and has been running a temp with it. He is on penicillin, so should be okay soon. The doctor says that burn cases are very susceptible to pneumonia, so I **try** to keep him in bed at least half of the time. But he gets to feeling so good since I keep him on aspirin. But he runs outside at least once a day and comes back in with a runny nose. Really, I feel very much like a female edition of Job! I am not complaining, but just let me recite some of our troubles. I do hope that some good will come out of it all, and that somehow, someway we will be a blessing to someone through it. To begin with, there was Paul's burn. Then at Youth Camp we all got sore throats and coughs and temps, and the kids aren't over it yet. All three were sick at once, plus Paul's continued needs. Part of the time I felt as though I was going crazy! In addition to three kids sick, Phil had a huge carbuncle or abscess on his arm just above his elbow, and of course he has a sore throat too. For nearly a month now I've gotten only half nights of sleep. Usually I just get dropped off to sleep again when one of the three cries for Mommy. Many nights, it's been all three crying at once. I have been fighting off this cold and it almost goes, and then it's back again. However, I do feel better now, but to top it all off, Patsy developed a big abscess on her little bottom, much worse than a boil. She is fussy, runs a temp, and screams every time she has a BM because of the pressure. However, she is better this evening. It started draining today. It must have started from a bite. Phil's started from a spider bite. Oh yes, I forgot to mention the fact that we are all covered with bites from fleas, or mosquitoes, or something! I hope it's not from bed bugs. The natives all have them, and you have to be so careful or you get them in your house. I have just recently cleared up a batch of scabies(?) on Paul. A few days ago I watched a mite dig into my hand. I got it when a woman handed me a coin to pay for something. I washed and scrubbed, but it must have gotten clear in because it itched intensely for two days! They lay their eggs just under the skin and dig little tunnels. Phil said I was crazy for letting it dig in, but it was the first mite I had seen, and I was so curious! Don't you wish you lived here too? Really, I shouldn't write like this, because I haven't let it all get me down. The Lord has undertaken marvelously for us, and in the middle of it all, I've had some wonderful seasons of prayer. I'm sure I've learned patience. Oh! That reminds me, now I understand. Not too terribly long ago I prayed for more patience. Don't think I'll pray that prayer again! I do hope this is all of our trials and troubles.

It's really nice to have Gertie back. She is so full of energy and vitality, something we all don't have right now. The kids are enjoying really having Mommy home with them. I'm still working, but I can do most of it here at home. I only help out sometimes with the routine work in the office now. Paul said the other day, "Mommy, I'm so glad you don't work in the office anymore." Phil had another attack of malaria this week, but the doctor gave him some medicine that should clear it up, we hope. I am happy and full of joy in the middle of all our troubles, because I can feel the Lord so near. He has helped me to keep going when I felt absolutely at the end of myself. The devil is terribly powerful here, but we can feel the power of the Lord overcoming him. Pray that we may be able to keep the standards high at Edwaleni even though it is now a government school. Pray that many may give their lives to Him this term.

Our men trek to Central Africa

September 1956, A group of our mission men from South Africa are on their way to Central Africa to study how they were able to establish an indigenous church there. (Indigenous means self-supporting, self-propagating, and self-governing.) Besides Phil, there were Warren Johnson, Vic Macy, Ed Clemens, Wes DeMille and Tillman Houser. From a letter I wrote to Phil in Burundi: The Lord is still working here. The last two chapels have been precious. Even the 'hard ones' are drinking it all in. Praise the Lord for speaking through us and using us. Because a lot of what I say, I never thought of before I get up there to speak! I even made it out to early morning prayer meeting this morning. The five faithful ones were there. Gertie is going out mornings with a group of students to work on the road when it isn't too wet. There are some really bad places. She said the boys are doing good work. Several miles of our road are private, and it's our responsibility to maintain it. Paul wanted another pair of shorts, so he whacked the legs off of a good pair of jeans! If I'm gray when you come back, you'll know why! It looks like they want us to keep tailoring now, and said to accept ten new tailoring students next year. Finally the wind has died down some. It's been nearly unbearable, the cold wind screeching incessantly, rattling our windows! A big wattle (acacia) tree blew over down near the *naartjie* (tangerine) trees, and the garage door broke off. Teacher Shembe went out to Esangweni to take the big tent down. There were a few rips in it already. They are mending it now. We hope the weather will clear and warm up so they can put it back up again. They had the meeting in the school house last night even though it was raining. Mason says it will rain more. At least we have some water in our tanks now, which means we won't have to switch to river water this year. Thank the Lord! Patsy is much better, not wheezing anymore.

September 20, 1956, To Phil - How we miss you! Every day Paul wants to know where you are, and today I told him I thought you would be in Rhodesia. I hope you aren't getting the rains we are. They started on Saturday and the roads are terrible. We had to put on chains to get into Ithemba Mission on Sunday and back home to Edwaleni. Coming to Ithemba Mission Sunday morning, Dr. Rice slid into the bank right by Mtshali's. Even with chains we slid all over. Gertie was driving, for which I was thankful. Mason was right. It is starting to sprinkle again. Just went over to check on the kids. Pats is much better, insists on playing with Paul and Nancy. Tuesday evening she just lay on her back. I got scared. I was afraid she was getting pneumonia. The kids are over here, in the office, writing on the blackboard. Paul can write any letters now, with just a little help to begin with. They are certainly stinkers when they can't be outside to play! Got a date for you! Hope you will be back to take it. Sunday, the 28th is tithing Sunday at Ithemba Mission. J.S. will be very happy for you to come and preach on tithing at Ithemba! You'd better be back, so get your sermon prepared. All the circuit will be there, so you will get to reach all of them.

Write everything down so you can answer all my questions. If and when we ever get to make that trip, I'd like to go into Uganda. That is where the Mountains of the Moon are. Sunday morning I led the testimony meeting in *Zulu*. I had everything written out before, of course! Tell Adamsons hello for me, also Vera and Merlin. Every time Nancy prays she says, "Please help daddy to drive the car goodly." This morning at breakfast she added, "Because if I don't pray for daddy, he will have a wreck!" I really don't think I can stand another three weeks away from you, really I don't. But I hope you have a nice time. Don't get bitten by any mosquitoes, tsetse flies or crocs! Have a nice swim in Lake Kivu (key'voo) for me. Wish you could carry television with you so I could see everything you see. October 1, Tomorrow you will be at beautiful Lake Kivu. How I would love to be there with you. Weren't you surprised to get a letter there? The meetings at Esangweni have been very good. Nearly every night all the women from Manjiva's *kraal* went forward for prayer and several young people also! Their husbands have consented, so it probably won't be very long before they make the decision to '*ukupendula*', (To turn around, their term for repenting.) I gave a testimony in *Zulu* one night, and so now all the people are saying I know *Zulu*! There were 1,000 people at the opening of the new Esangweni school building. I spoke for you and received all the '*Siyabongas*' (thank you's) for you. Even the big chief was grateful, but you could smell beer on him. They killed an ox and fed everyone. What a day! Dr. Lamson wrote that they were greatly blessed while reading our report of our revival. A bat came downstairs Saturday night, and Sunday morning Nancy found him in their room. She was terrified! I finally managed to catch and kill it. Patsy wanted to grab him. You should have seen Pats and her birthday cake! She took a big handful of cake and smeared it all over her face. Paul didn't think I should let her spoil the cake! Hurry home. We need you.

October 14, 1956, Phil is finally on his way home. He has already been gone a whole month, and it will probably be another 10 days before he gets home. They have been traveling 450 miles most every day. They will put the station wagon on a lake steamer on Lake Tanganyika (tahn-gahn-yee'-kah) which will save many miles of bumpy roads. Then they will go to see Victoria Falls. In Rwanda they were privileged to see the four volcanoes at the north end of Lake Kivu, and took a welcome swim in Lake Kivu at Kumbya, the missionary retreat area.

October 18, 1956, (A letter to Mom and Betty Kline) We expect Phil to turn up within six days, I hope! And we hear that all the men on the tour agreed to grow beards. The first person who cut his beard was to get the hair clippers run up the back of his head! That's what happens to men when they get away from their wives! The last day, they drove 900 miles, after getting off the lake steamer, to Livingstone at Victoria Falls! They really had some adventures. Gertie is over at Greenville Mission today working in the hospital office, and when I called her on the phone this morning she told me some about the wild time the men had been having. One day they had absolutely no food! Didn't find any store where they could buy any, so they just went without all day. We heard later that they did have two cans of sardines and some dry bread, so they didn't starve! The crazy guys even slept right out in the open, propping up their suitcases to keep off the wind. No mosquito nets, and probably right in the middle of Tsetse fly country! It's a wonder they didn't get all sorts of diseases, or get stepped on by an elephant, to say nothing of malaria. Of course, most of them have it anyway. Phil wrote that the roads were absolutely terrible, thousands of bumps, and that they each had a sleeping bag and air mattress. I guess when they get back to South African roads they will be thankful. You can imagine what they feel like, seven men packed into one station wagon with all of their luggage, driving solid for a week! Phil wrote that they had piled everything in the back so one person could sleep on it! He also wrote that they had all taken baths in a mountain stream in Congo, which felt so refreshing. Phil wrote that he had been able to talk with Frank Adamson in Usumbura, (oo-soom-boo'rah) Urundi, and reminded him that we would like to work at Kibogora Mission sometime! They were really fortunate in catching the lake steamer at Usumbura on Lake Tanganyika, coming south. It only sails once every three weeks!

We just completed 'operation dead rat!' There was a dead rat up between the office ceiling and the upstairs floor, in the Ghormley house. By 'smelling' it out with our noses, we could just about locate it. We found two loose boards in the floor upstairs, pulled them up, and there it was, half rotten, stuck in a corner. Robert Nxumalo, a carpentry student, got some sticks and together we pulled it out. What an odor! But much better than standing the smell for a week and a half like we did the last time. Robert buried it with proper ceremony! A held nose! I have discovered on my leg what looks very much like a tick bite. It is very painful today. I certainly hope I don't get tick-bite fever. That's what started Lily's sick spells, it kept coming back.

Answered prayer at Edwaleni

October 1956, Our hearts are full of praise and thanksgiving for answered prayer. Revival has come to Edwaleni Technical College. We have seen, and we have felt the outpouring of the Holy Spirit in our midst. All but thirty of the students have taken their stand for Christ, some of them for the first time. We have marveled at the wonderful way in which God works. Rev. Duma's promised three days became six days as the Spirit worked and Revival came. From the first meeting we could sense God's presence with us, and we knew that many of you were praying for Edwaleni. Each night a few responded to the invitation, but on Sunday night the Holy Spirit came in an unusual way, and 130 young men came forward to give their lives to Christ. How our hearts leaped within us as we saw them coming, everyone an answer to prayer, how precious! Monday was to be the last day, but we all felt that it couldn't be, and Pastor Duma felt he should stay. The burden was still heavy. On Monday he decided to stay with us one more day. With thankful hearts we continued to pray for the students with rebellious attitudes. On Tuesday the Lord was very near, and as we watched, we saw the grim, set look on faces melt away; heads were buried in hands as they too finally acknowledged their need for Salvation. The power of darkness is broken, the evil spirit of rebellion is swept away, and they are still coming to the Lord. One young man was set free from a terrible fear that had driven him to witch doctors. It is wonderful to see his happy smile. Please continue to pray for Edwaleni. We believe that this is only the beginning of what God is going to do for us. Pray for the twelve students who have heard the call to full-time pastoral service. Pray for the teachers, that God may be able to use them. Several have been greatly blessed and are now radiantly witnessing for the Lord. Yes, we are seeing the long prayed-for revival, and our hearts are full of joy, but we are holding on in prayer for even greater things from God.

Edwaleni Technical College Teachers

Phil is home again

November, 1956, Even one year old Patsy is glad to have her Daddy home again. We thought she might have forgotten him, but she is Daddy's girl, and runs to him on her chubby little legs, saying "Da-da" whenever she sees him. Paul and Nancy had begun to think their Daddy would never come back. It seemed like forever to them. Nancy, three, kept wanting to save food for Daddy, "Because he might come home tonight." Paul, a big boy of five, very patiently kept asking, "Where is Daddy today?," and was interested in keeping up with his Daddy on the map. Phil is happy to be home, to put his feet under his own table, and to sleep in his own bed again.

November 30, 1956, Patsy is such a funny little thing. She insists on going outside now with the other two kids, and she invariably finds her way over here to the office all by herself. She is here now, 'helping' me type! Sometimes she starts turning around and around until she is so dizzy she can't even walk. And if we say, "Ring around the rosy," she keeps it up indefinitely! I preach here Sunday morning. Phil goes to Emthini and Gertie to Old Edwaleni, and Phil preaches in Izingolweni on Sunday night at the European service there. (In South Africa, if your skin is white, you are called a European!) Some of the third years are acting up, trying to tell us that they won't have a third year program or even graduation, if they can't have the kind of jazz and dance program some of the 'bad eggs' want! We have put our foot down and some of them are boiling. One of the Christian teachers is down in the chapel with them now, 'having it out!' Everything has been going too nicely, I guess, so the devil decided to throw this 'monkey wrench' in the works!

December 2, 1956, Yes, it's victory! I came home again to do some more sewing, but felt so terrible about the attitude of the third year students that I just stopped and got down on my knees and prayed for all of satan's plans to be defeated, utterly and completely. In just a few minutes the assurance came that all would be OK. I went over to the office to tell Gertie, and I hadn't been there long when Seth Msweli came in. Gertie asked him what the decision of the class was. Seth beamed and said, "Well, we will have to give God the glory, our prayers have been answered." In a few more minutes the program committee came and apologized to Gertie for the whole class, and said they wanted to go ahead with the program and graduation, and that they now realized their mistake. It may seem like a small thing, but little things like that can upset the whole school. Their attitude was just like it was during the strike last year, just the power of satan, the spirit of darkness. So many of the fellows are just like sheep, following blindly whichever way any leader goes. So continue to pray. You never can tell when the devil is going to brew up more trouble. Just pray that every plan he concocts will be smashed before any damage is done.

The Lord really helped me preach this morning. I preached on Sanctification, and the Holy Spirit was there, and sent the message out with power. It's wonderful to be used of the Lord and to know that He is speaking through you. No one came forward to pray, but six or seven raised their hands to indicate that they felt the need of being filled with the Holy Spirit, and were seeking. I expect some will come for talks and prayer next week. Pray that each hungry one will be filled with the Holy Spirit! We all got ready tonight and drove to Izingolweni for the service there through rain and slippery roads, only to find that the meeting had been cancelled and that our phone was out of order and that they had been trying to call us. The Lord helped us to get safely home again, and Paul prayed so cute, "Thank you very very much, dear Jesus for helping us to get home safely." He told us on the way home that the reason we didn't slide around much was that "Jesus was helping us and that he was praying." Time to go to sleep now. I'm typing in bed, so "*lala kahle*," (sleep well).

December 17, 1956, Merry Christmas! Hope you get this before then. Phil and I are in Durban at Johnsons, relaxing. School closed last Wednesday and on Friday I had dental surgery, two impacted wisdom teeth and one crooked tooth extracted. I was asleep with sodium pentothal for 1 1/2 hours while the dentist hunted for a lost root! I felt 'woozy' for a whole day afterwards! Feel much better today. Ached all over yesterday. Been getting huge doses of penicillin and get the stitches taken out tomorrow. Then home to my babies. Sure do miss them. Hot today and yesterday and last night, so humid! Glad we don't live here. Edwaleni is almost always cool at night. It is 2,000 feet higher in altitude. Would love to be with you for Christmas, but Edwaleni is really home to us now, and we are where we belong and that's what counts! School closing was very nice except that Phil caught two boys who had stolen tools from the carpentry shop. He turned them over to the police. We felt terrible about it. They were third year students who had rejected the Gospel.

January 15, 1957, We had a wonderful time with Johnsons here, at Edwaleni. Hope you had a nice Christmas. We think often of you. Patsy is the sweetest little one. She's beginning to talk, jabbers constantly in her own 'dutchy' language! Since she's so good, Phil has finally consented to having our fourth. I'm not sure yet, but it may be on its way! Johnsons expect their fourth in April. They are really thrilled! Nancy played with her doll, Judy, on my bed, dressing and undressing her until she fell asleep. She plays dolls by the hour! Patsy just climbed up on the book shelf and is now busy investigating. Paul is happily engaged in using Phil's tools, 'helping' his daddy. Phil is rewiring everything to hook up with the new electric generator. He sure needs a vacation, but isn't getting any, except relief from the responsibility of school. His legs are still bad. I will probably start to teach Paul soon. I gave up on kindergarten because there was no time. I'll just have to make time now.

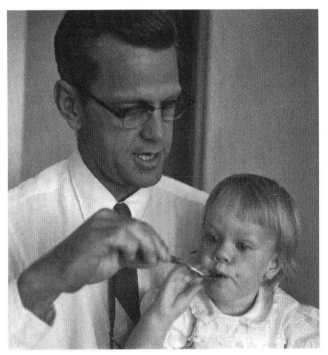

Daddy feeding his girl, Patsy

Patsy, Miss Mischief

May 5, 1957, Phil's letter to Dr. Lamson: We have been waiting for a month to hear back from Pretoria. Two officials came yesterday with instructions from Pretoria to re-open the school, selecting the students very carefully. School is to re-open June 17, and continue on from there without the usual July holiday. The enrollment was 120 but we expect it to be less than half when we start again. The officials thought some of our regulations were rather severe, especially 'no smoking'. I told them we were not prepared to let down our standards. We are thankful that we have not had to make any compromise whatsoever, but if anything, our position is stronger than before since the Advisory Committee has recommended that the Education Department approve and help enforce our Mission rules. We feel that God has overpowered satan's plans. The glory is all His. We praise Him for answered prayer. We still have unlimited opportunity for Bible instruction and evangelism in the school. About the Edendale School, I have no doubt but that Edwaleni will gradually become smaller and smaller because of Edendale taking the students for various courses which were taught here. They have already taken our building, carpentry and most of our leatherworks students.

Arlene and Elmore Clyde arrive

May 19, 1957, Phil went to Mbodiya church to preach this morning. It's drizzly today and chilly. Fire in the fireplace, nice to relax! The one day in the week I don't dig in my *Zulu* books. I've plowed through the book we have to take our first exam over, and now I'm going back over the parts I don't know. I spend most of my time these days studying *Zulu*, when I'm not chasing Patsy. She has learned how to open doors, so unless a door is locked, she is into everything. She still is an angel at night. Put her down, and that is the last you hear of her until 7:30 in the morning. Elmore and Arlene Clyde, new missionaries, arrived last week. They were here part of last weekend and we all went to Greenville Mission for a meeting with Dr. and Mrs. Watson, from Seattle Pacific College. Good to see them again.

July 15, 1957, (From the Port Shepstone Hospital) Ever since Patsy got whooping cough, after she had chicken pox, I have had only two to four hours sleep at night, and hardly any in the day. As soon as I got to sleep, she would start coughing. Then I wanted my girls to go to Youth Camp, so I let them go, figuring I could easily do the dishes, cooking, and cleaning. I wasn't even going to **try** to do a washing, too much carrying buckets of water. I got along fine the first few days. Paul brought in firewood for the stove, but it took me all day just to get my housework done, and care for the kids. I had to check the proofs for our Bantu Harvest and I decided that on Wednesday I'd get my work done sooner. I did, but I didn't rest, had some back pain. That scared me so I rested, and the next morning I took it rather easy. Phil made beds and all I did was cook breakfast. I didn't even get the dishes done because contractions started again. Doctor said to stay in bed and take pills with codeine or caffeine in them. That took care of it until evening when I had to get up and feed the kids and put them to bed. We had no more pills without caffeine. I try to avoid it because if I take it, I can't sleep. Phil went to the evening service and brought back Connie Nyaose to help me. I hate to have her miss Youth Camp, but Phil insisted. Before he came back the contractions got quite regular and after he came home, I took three pain pills to stop them. Phil called Dr. Rice, and he said to take me to the Shepstone hospital. Phil threw together some things for me and we took off to meet Dr. and Mrs. Rice at Rice's Halt, just in case the baby arrived en route. Everything stopped. Here at the hospital they are stuffing me with medicines. I will probably go home Monday. I am enjoying resting and sleeping! This is a beautiful place. A graceful date palm is outside my window, and a big old *Kaffirboom* tree with brilliant red flowers perched on brown bare branches like so many scarlet birds poised for flight. If I sit up straight enough in bed I can see the beautiful blue Indian Ocean. They just told me that I could go home today!

August 4, 1957, This next week will probably drag! The doctor said Davey Joe should arrive early, so my suitcase is in the car, all ready to go! He gave me some medicine to take that will slow things up so I'll be sure to get to the hospital in time. It takes us over an hour to get there. We just finished Sunday School. Betty Kline sends the Primary papers and handwork to our kids. They enjoy them so much. Patsy thinks the songs with motions are fun. She is forever getting us to sing "Running Over." We have LP records of the 'Old Fashioned Revival Hour' quartet and organ meditations and several with kids' music. Patsy is much better now. Hardly coughs at night, and it looks as though Paul isn't going to get the whooping cough! This is Nancy's sixth week of it. The Bantu Harvest is finally printed! We had to get more copies made this time, and still it's not enough. I am addressing envelopes. Our mailing list is about 300 now.

I just let the kids out to play since it is nice and warm, and I noticed that Phil has had the students bring their benches outside for church. Lily is preaching this morning. It's so good to have her back. She is a jewel. She reminds me a lot of you, Mother. She is your age. Gertie is in the hospital now. Phil took her in last Sunday, and the nurses assumed Gertie was Mrs. Kline, so they were taking her to **Maternity**! Ha! She was having severe pain. They operated on her Tuesday for appendicitis! She is getting along fine now. Dr. Rice says I have to go to Shepstone for delivery, just in case of complications like last time, and then if his wife, Marge is feeling well enough, they will take me to Greenville Mission for my recovery.

We've had so much company this weekend that we'll run out of bread before Tuesday, so I guess I'll make biscuits for dinner. We get to the store on Tuesdays and Fridays only, in Izingolweni, eleven miles away, but we are fortunate. We get meat sent down from Harding, thirty miles away by bus every Friday, along with the meat for the students. We have a big freezing compartment in our refrigerator, so we have all the meat we need, and nice vegetables from our garden the whole year around. We get apples shipped by train from the Cape for $1.60 a crate. African women bring bananas and oranges to sell for one cent each. We have tangerine and lemon trees, and we get eggs from our own chickens! So you see, Edwaleni is a nice place to live. Especially nice, because we know that this is where we have been brought by the Lord, and this is where He wants us for now. School is going nicely.

From our August prayer letter

We have re-opened school and feel that this is in God's plan. We only re-accepted half of our students, just those who were willing to abide by our Mission rules and who had not participated actively in the strike. We are praying that the students who are here now will give themselves wholeheartedly to the Lord. We are also praying for more young men who will feel, and answer, the call to the ministry. We praise the Lord for using our pastor, Isaac Shembe, one of our Motor Mechanics teachers here at the school. We are trying to help and encourage him with his studies so that he can soon be ordained as deacon. (2005 note: Teacher Shembe's son, Lincoln, was recently elected Bishop of the South Africa Free Methodist Church after Robert Nxumalo retired!)

Phil has been preaching tithing wherever he goes. It has been encouraging to watch the people as they find out about the blessings which God pours out when they really tithe. We are glad to tell you of an answer to your prayers. Douglas Mthembu, one of our teachers whom we asked you to pray for, received definite spiritual help at the recent Youth Camp. He has now started attending Lily Steele's Bible classes. Continue to pray for Douglas that he may be wholly surrendered to God's will and that his life will be a real blessing here at Edwaleni.

Paul, six, is in first grade this year. We fixed a nice room in the basement for his school. His teacher's name is 'Miss Jones', but sometimes he forgets and calls her Mommy! Nancy, four, won't be ready for kindergarten until next year, but she is more anxious to be in school than Paul. He would rather be out 'driving' the tractor or making roads in the sand with his toys. Patsy, two, is just like all little sisters, she 'helps' the older children play, and gets into everything. We are waiting now for the arrival of Davey Joe. The children are enjoying helping to get everything ready for our new baby. Please pray for Phil's legs. The calf muscles in both legs ache almost continually except in very cold weather. He feels tired all the time because the pain keeps him from getting sufficient rest and sleep. Pain killing drugs help, but they are habit-forming. It is a constant drag on his energy, both physically and mentally. We feel it would be to God's glory if Phil's legs were healed.

August 11, 1957, Nancy was so cute this morning. I was sitting down to fix the kids some lemonade, and she said, "Mommy, why do you feel like sitting down?" I told her that maybe we would get Davey Joe tonight! She was excited, and said, "When he gets here, please bring him in and put him in bed with me!" Phil says if this one is a girl he will trade her off somewhere! But I wouldn't mind another sweet one. Patsy is a perfect little doll, rather full of mischief, but so lovable! She is Phil's girl right now, for which I am thankful.

David Joseph is born!

August, 1957, (Port Shepstone Hospital). The nicest anniversary present anyone could ever have, arrived at 8:20 a.m., David Joseph

(Davey Joe), eight pounds, twelve ounces, 23 inches. He is a good baby; reminds me of a soft, cuddly kitten. He makes the cutest little noises. He is a very sweet one to have to remember as my last baby. Monday morning I was in the office mimeographing the preaching plan for next quarter for the circuit, and Nancy came in yelling that Patsy had gotten into my purse and overnight case I had packed ready to take to the hospital, and said that she had eaten up all my medicine. I took off, hoping she hadn't eaten my pills for carsickness and pain! When I got there and saw the mess, papers and junk all over my desk and the floor and saw she'd gotten into my medicines, I about had heart failure. Then I saw that they were still sealed shut, unopened, except for the outside wrapper, but she had eaten several sticks of gum and most of my heartburn pills!

After I cleaned up the mess and locked the door and got back to the office, I started feeling very queer and shaky! I told Lily not to be surprised if we woke her up in the middle of the night. I went to bed, but not to sleep. Got up several times, roamed all over the house, fixed the refrigerator wick, got back into bed and started timing. When I realized the contractions were getting close and harder and regular, I woke Phil up. He got the car ready and called Lily. I called the hospital, took the pills the doctor had given me for the ride in. By the time we got there they were really hard and three minutes apart. The ride was terribly bumpy, but I wasn't uncomfortable at all. We arrived about 2:00 a.m. The Sister (nurse) assured me I was well on my way, and took me to the delivery room. Sweet little old grandmother, with years of nursing and midwifery practice. She stayed right with me and rubbed my back. Phil got tired waiting and went out to the car and slept for a couple of hours. I asked the Sister if Phil could be with me for the delivery. Even the doctor gave his permission!

I realized something was wrong, because I wasn't able to move the baby. The doctor did a low forceps delivery, because this baby was also P.O.P., (face up)! Phil was so absolutely fascinated that he forgot to care whether or not it was a boy! But you should have seen and heard him when they said, "It's a boy!" You'd have thought he was at a football game and his side had won! How perfect and thrilling it was to have him there, and to be completely conscious. I'm anxious to get Davey Joe home to see what the kids say.

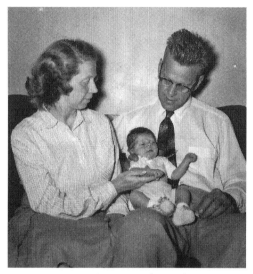

It's a BOY! David Joseph

The kids welcomed us home

September 10, 1957, Davey Joe is starting to gain weight now. He is so long and thin and has such big eyes for a baby. So sweet and cuddly. Love him! He is so good. We went to Durban to see Johnsons off, for furlough. I did quite a bit of shopping, but still felt fine when we got home Saturday evening. I hadn't hardly hoped I could go and do that much when he was only 2 1/2 weeks old. Phil agreed to take us. The kids had so much fun. Phil had caught a puff adder. We took it in a box to the snake park, so we got in free to see all the snakes. They pay over a dollar for the snake too.

September 18, 1957, Davey Joe is nearly a month old already. Hardly seems possible. He is starting to fill out. School is coming along very well. There is a wonderful spirit among the students. Most of them have 'chosen the Lord'. They are even not afraid to testify! It's really wonderful. Continue to pray, because we know that all of this is a direct answer to prayer. Pray that they will become really strong Christians and soul-winners. We can begin to see now why God permitted the strike. We have found out that some students at the beginning of the year were going around trying to get all the 'first years' to promise not to become Christians! Probably we would never have had a really Christian school like we have now if there hadn't been the 'sifting out' of the 'bad eggs' and two teachers. All things do work together for good, and we are looking forward to even better things.

November 1, 1957, The kids have been climbing trees like mad today. Paul passed his exam in Izingolweni, but he didn't do as well as I thought he might. Being with so many children was too new an experience for him to concentrate. He is doing fine in reading, but doesn't like to sit still long enough to learn how to print neatly. I suppose it is really too much to expect him to do well in both South African and State-side curricula. Calvert Course has a strong reading emphasis, while the main emphasis here is on arithmetic and writing, so I am trying to combine the two. But I feel I must prepare the kids for either transferring into a South African school or a school in the States, which is hard on all of us. Phil is getting quite grey. I have wrinkles! I looked in the mirror the other day and decided that I was middle-aged! Davey Joe laughs out loud now. He weighs fifteen pounds. Phil won't let him cry. He's going to be really spoiled, but he's adorable.

November 2, 1957, The impossible has just happened! All four kids are asleep at once! So the house is quiet. A rarity! How did you ever manage eleven, Mother? Tell Harland we got our new radio, thanks to him! We can hear stations all over the world. Did I tell you that Paul refused to listen to Superman? It scared him! He prefers to play Bev Shea records! You should hear Paul sing "The Love of God" and "What a Friend We Have in Jesus." The doctor in Durban prescribed adding a half inch into the heels of Phil's shoes. I think it is helping. We were thrilled to get the tape. Played it last night on Gerties' recorder. Good sermon, wonderful music. Closed my eyes and imagined I was home. It was so nice to hear a church service in English, from home. Thanks for sending it!

November 16, 1957, Phil is definitely much better. He has increased the lifts in his shoes to three quarter inch, and it seems to give much relief. Phil is himself again and has not had to take pain pills to sleep with for several weeks, for which we are very thankful. Davey Joe is getting so big already and is starting to lose his beautiful reddish brown hair. He even laughed out loud one day. He and Phil talk and talk.

From our December prayer letter

The Holy Spirit is working here in a way that we have not seen before. Even though the students come from many different denominations, our testimony meetings are now like Free Methodist Love Feasts! This is what we have been praying for, students unafraid to witness, so eager to testify that it is hard to get a meeting stopped! But continue to pray. The new school year begins the last week of January. There will probably be 60 new students. Pray that the revival spirit may continue. The Education Department has given permission for Edwaleni to continue as a school for one more year. We are thankful for this answer to prayer, and for this continued opportunity to reach more African young men for Christ. As we look across the deep valley to the high hills surrounding us, we see scattered here and there over the steep green slopes clusters of round, mud huts with grass thatched roofs. Most of these people walk in heathen darkness. At night we can sometimes hear drums throbbing and the chanting at their drunken dances. Pray that they too will see the Light.

December 22. 1957, Phil finally got the milking house and *isibaya,* built down by the river so the cows won't have to go up and down the hill. Should increase the milk production. Phil is milking one cow for us, and for the first time since we came, we don't have to boil our milk! We still boil our drinking water.

All the missionaries will be here for the day after Christmas, at least 38 people. Turkey and everything. We will have our family Christmas on Christmas Eve and on Christmas Day, a picnic wiener roast for the kids. Phil plans to climb the big hill to Old Edwaleni to spend Christmas Day with the Zulus in their church service, since his legs are better. The kids are happily playing 'farm' with their animals, trucks and tractors. Nancy, of course has a 'sick' baby. She just told me its temp is going down. It has the flu. Nancy plans on being a nurse, she says, and Paul wants to be a farmer. Patsy is finally starting to talk. It really slows kids down to learn two languages at once. But they won't talk *Zulu.* Patsy understands everything you say to her in either language, but won't make a sound except when she is trying to get your attention. We have electricity now in some rooms, 32 volt charger and batteries, nice! We don't run the big power plant just for us. It's really nice to have battery lights because we don't have to be in the dark after the plant goes off at 9:00 p.m. when school is in session. Elmore and Arlene Clyde plan to stay with us for several days after Christmas.

Nancy, age 4, "I want to be a nurse when I grow up!"
(After many years working as a nurse,
Nancy also taught nursing students)

1958

January 31, 1958, The kids are riding their trikes around in the basement. It is drizzly outside. Patsy is just learning to pedal. She is such a half-pint. Davey Joe will be as big as she is in another year! He turns over both ways now and pulls himself up and nearly over the side of his crib at five months. School has started. 67 boys are here and about 20 more coming. Problems already, one boy drinking beer in the dorm, but he hadn't been accepted anyway, so Phil is sending him home. Phil's legs are very bad again, so I'm sure the pressure of the responsibility makes them worse. Some people get ulcers and Phil's legs get worse! Patsy is taking a bottle to Davey Joe that has been out all morning so I'd better run. Just as I feared, the bottle was in his mouth and he was swigging away! I give him bottles to supplement because I can't begin to give him enough. He is so big!

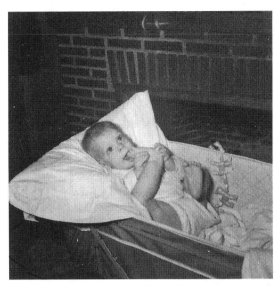

Davey Joe was always hungry!

March 23, 1958, Nancy is enjoying kindergarten. She can count to twenty and knows many of the colors already. She still says she is going to be a nurse at Greenville Hospital when she grows up. Davey Joe started crawling today. He pulls and scooches himself along until he gets where he wants to go. While we were gone to Durban an *imamba* crawled up on our roof and shed its skin, just above where the kids usually play. I'm thankful we were gone! I finally got Davey Joe to bed. This afternoon he was fussy and I was trying to interest Nancy in entertaining him. She brought him to me and I said, "I don't want him." She frowned up at me and asked, "Well, why did you have him then?"

Elmore Clyde came over today to learn how to build cabinets. Phil is going to make four sets for Greenville Mission, one for Ebenezer Mission, and one for our bathroom, all at once. He also has the Mbodiya church building started. How can he keep everything going at once? At 4:30 a.m. this morning Stanley knocked on our bedroom door and said a boy had broken his ankle, so Phil took him to the Greenville Mission Hospital, a forty mile round trip, and got back just in time for breakfast. It's 9:30, and I need to start Paul's school. Well, no Paul in sight, so I will dash off a few more lines. Workers' Conference will be held during Easter week, but school will still be on, so we will probably have to drive back and forth. I am supposed to have one class on tithing, another on church discipline and history and Phil has one on personal evangelism. I'm back working in the office again, afternoons. Gertie is in Port Shepstone studying *Zulu*, so I take Davey Joe over to the office, put him on the floor on a quilt and type away.

Chilly cold today. Winter is coming. School begins in about two and a half more weeks. Phil has gotten nearly everything done that he planned to do this vacation. He is getting quite South African; bought himself a pair of khaki shorts! After we had the blessing, Paul remarked, "I didn't pray because I had to see daddy in his new shorts!" We went down to Port Edward last Wednesday so Phil could fish and the kids could paddle in the lagoon, but it was so windy and the sea so rough that he couldn't even get rid of his bait! I didn't swim in the ocean because there have been too many deaths lately from shark attacks. The rivers are pouring muddy water into the sea, which attracts them. When we were in Port Shepstone last week we saw a shark, a grey shadow riding the waves, and then a dark triangular fin gliding slowly away. Gives me the creeps to think about them!

Davey Joe weighs 17 1/2 pounds at 4 1/2 months. He rolls over and has fallen off beds three times! Patsy has had summer diarrhea for several weeks, off and on. She has lost more weight. She has been sick so much this last year with chicken pox, measles, and whooping cough. Then four or five sand fly larvae burrowed under the skin on her little bottom, which we finally killed with dry ice! Mary Current, our mission nurse, says the diarrhea comes from eating corn, so we are not letting her have any more, but she loves it so much! We have beautiful corn in our garden.

Wonderful Workers' Conference

April 9, 1958, Please thank all who have been praying for our Worker's Conference. Many Sunday School teachers, pastors and evangelists came and the Lord met with us in a wonderful way! One day, the Holy Spirit came in convicting power and the schedule was laid aside as preachers confessed one to another and shouted with joy. One night a young man was preaching, talking rather straight about immorality, and the older men tried to stop him by singing, but he kept on preaching until conviction came and 100 young people and children knelt at the altar and cried and prayed and many found real victory! We have never seen anything so wonderful. And then the old men got blessed because the children had gotten saved! There are still many hard places and problems, but God **will** give the victory. We had left Edwaleni for the weekend rather fearfully, because there were about 60 students left on campus during the Easter holidays with not very much to keep them occupied, and there was only one teacher there. Oh, we of little faith! On Good Friday evening, the Volunteers had a meeting in the prayer hut and invited all who cared to come, and all but five came. The Holy Spirit was there in a wonderful way. Many wept their way through to victory. Isn't it wonderful how the Lord works? Praise the Lord!

Edwaleni teachers and students who attended Bible School for ministerial training, and became Free Methodist pastors

May 20, 1958, There is a very good spirit in the school now. More are joining the voluntary Bible class. Lily says there are forty-five now. Wish you could meet her. She's a wonderful person. Paul borrowed one of the boy's bikes, a big one, and taught himself to ride! So Phil is going to bring him a small one from Durban. Paul and Nancy are both doing well in school. Nancy is nearly ready to learn to read. Paul has taken a real liking for arithmetic and is doing well in reading. Davey Joe is beginning to say a few words. He is the noisiest baby we've had! The weather is perfect here now, golden, warm sunny days. I love the winters here. The coldest day still has a warm sun. We have about fifty children in our children's meetings. I go out every Monday after school to Esangweni and all of the older children and some small ones stay for our meetings. The two teachers, both fine Christians, help me.

"Build me an house ..." - 1 Chronicles 17:12

(An article written by Mary Kline for the Bantu Harvest.)

The new little church at Mbodiya stood high on a hill for everyone to see. A cluster of trees gave shade from the hot sun. With dried mud block walls freshly plastered and the roof painted, the inside gleaming with new whitewash, the little church was ready for Dedication Sunday. The rough backless benches quickly filled with worshippers until even the floor was packed full of people sitting on mats. Eyes were wet with tears as they remembered the 'building'.

The Mbodiya people had been without a church building for over a year. The old one, built many years ago, probably in the 1920's, during the ministry of Miss Margaret Nickel, had finally become unusable. The galvanized iron roof was still good. It had been carefully put away to be used again. Most of the sun dried mud blocks had been ready for months, prepared by Edwaleni student volunteers.

But what a hard job to build again! First, all must agree and be willing to work together. Then, to get a builder who could lay the blocks, when the women could help between weeding and harvesting and the rains. There was cement, sand, lots of dirt, poles for rafters, but no water. So, women carried on their heads, pail after pail of water from the river far below, toiling up the long, steep hill. Slowly the building began to rise, and with it the hearts of the people. Mbodiya would have a church again. The heathen would see that the Mbodiya church was not dead. And then it was finally ready, a place for the worship of their Heavenly Father.

Some heathen people also came on that Dedication Sunday, and listened and watched as Dr. Rice, District Superintendent, presented the church key to Pastor Shembe. Pastor Shembe was also a Motor Mechanics teacher at Edwaleni Technical College. The people came with their coins and brought their offering to the table in front. The missionary-in-charge beamed as he said, "I am glad I can say that I did **not** build this church." For the people had done the building with a minimum of missionary help.

And then one morning, after a stormy night the missionary told his wife, "The devil blew the Mbodiya church down last night." "Oh **no**! Not the new church. It **can't** be! The **poor** people." Seeing her husband's face, an indication of how the people felt, she prayed, "Oh Lord, encourage the people. Don't let them sink down into black despair. Help them to determine to build again."

That same day when the missionary arrived at Mbodiya with the pastor in his car, the people were there already, beginning the heartbreaking work of clearing away the rubble. They were not in despair, they were ready to begin again, and the missionary was encouraged to see them.

But even though they were ready, there was not enough money, and there was also a reluctance to build another dried mud block structure that would eventually fall down again. And then Miss Steele heard from a friend in England, "How much would it cost to build a church at Mbodiya?" How thrilled the people were when they learned that someone in England had cared enough to send 200 pounds, approx. $600, to help rebuild their church.

Now the making of the cement blocks is beginning, and supplies are being gathered. One day soon, the Africans will again be able to see their church on top of the high, steep hill at Mbodiya.

From our June, 1958 prayer letter

Old Mrs. Ncane (Mrs. Little) has 'chosen the Lord'. She has washed the red clay from her hair and has exchanged her leather skirt and blankets and trinkets for Christian dress. Pray for her and her husband. He is almost persuaded. He is one of the chief's head men, and his influence is great. When missionaries first began talking with him, people just laughed. Old Ncane was 'impossible' but you can see him gradually coming out of darkness. Pray that he may soon be walking in the full light of the Gospel.

The church at Mbodiya is still waiting to be built. Phil has been unable to secure a builder. We are wondering if perhaps he is supposed to build the church himself, of course with African helpers. Now he feels he hasn't an ounce of energy, nor the time, but with a month of school vacation coming up in July, he will have a little more time. Pray that God will give him the energy he needs. The Mbodiya people are bubbling over with thanksgiving. Money has come from several undreamed-of sources. The Edwaleni Student Volunteers group has spent several Saturdays building a road up the hill so the truck can carry building materials to the top. Do pray that the church will be built soon. Patricia is almost three and is in the "me do, my, and why" stage. She calls herself "Ish" and "Cookie." She is beginning to gain weight. Davey Joe, ten months, is walking, holding on to things, has six teeth and is a husky twenty-five pounds and a tall 31 inches. He is a big, noisy, happy boy.

July 2, 1958, At last, time to relax. Conference is over. We fed twenty missionaries and arranged for the feeding of four hundred Africans. Sunday noon we had twenty-eight here for dinner. I would like to hibernate for a week, but Paul's school begins tomorrow. Just had to stop and make sandwiches and juice for Nancy and Patsy for a tea party. Joe is trying to get their food. He is so big, the girls think he is a little pest. There go all their dishes on the floor, and Patsy is crying because Joe hit her finger with a bottle. Oh dear! So it goes! I'm letting Nancy's and Patsy's hair grow long. They look cute in pony tails. It was a good conference with much of the blessing of the Lord. Many women came determined to make their delegates fight for permission to continue to make beer for their husbands and still be given Christian baptism. We expected it might be an explosive issue, but the Holy Spirit 'poured oil on the troubled waters' and many of the women received spiritual help, and went home determined to refuse to make beer and to 'take up their cross' and follow Jesus. They greatly need your prayers. Please request prayer again for direction and guidance for the future of Edwaleni. We have received notice that Edwaleni will not continue as an Industrial school after 1958. Pray for God's plan to be worked out.

A Place to Worship

Written by Phil and Mary Kline and printed in the Bantu Harvest.

The truck from Edwaleni, carrying the load of workers and tools groaned up the steep hill on the new winding dirt road. The July school vacation had begun and at last there was time to start building the Mbodiya Church. First the Edwaleni tractor with the scraper blade and plow was used to level and enlarge the site. Then the cement mixer began its noisy grinding, attracting all the small boys from the scattered huts on the neighboring hillsides.

The foundation, the pillars, and then the walls, block by block, and row by row, rose higher and higher until the walls and the bell tower could be seen across the hills and valley from Edwaleni.

Elmore Clyde, Robert Nxumalo and Seth Msweli came to help plaster after their tent meetings and Vacation Bible Schools were over. The church women came each day to make tea and cook samp, (dried and pounded corn kernels, cooked together with beans), in black iron cooking pots for the workers. The crowd of small boys scraped the pots clean for the cooks while filling their tummies with samp.

Then the boys would swarm onto the truck just before it wound down, down, down to the river for sand, helping to load sand for the excitement of riding in a truck for the first time. When Paul came with his daddy the children played together, having fun, "helping to build the church," and exchanging *Zulu* and English words.

One day a heathen man came and asked if he could work and help build the church. This was the son of the man, Mbodiya Cele, who had originally given the church site to the Mission. Pray that his heart may be won for the Lord.

Lily Steele wrote another letter to England about Mbodiya; this time asking her friends to please look for a bell for the new church. Soon an answer came from her brother-in-law, an old bell had been found. One of these days we will be able to hear the bell ringing loud and clear, calling the people to worship in the new little church on top of the high, steep Mbodiya hill.

Robert Nxumalo held evangelistic meetings in the big tent

Phil falls and injures his leg

August 20, 1958, Happy birthday a week ago, Daddy! Sorry I haven't written sooner, but Phil has been in bed half of the time and on crutches the rest, so I've had quite a bit more to do than usual. About two weeks ago Phil stepped down from the top of the wall on the Mbodiya church where he was laying concrete blocks and the scaffolding plank broke and he went down with it. He scraped his shin and came home with a big 'goose egg' on his leg. We put frozen meat on it because I didn't have any ice in the freezer and the next day it looked better, so he went back to work, helping to build the Mbodiya church. Every day his ankle and foot were more swollen, but not too painful, so he kept on working. After a week he couldn't walk on it, so he went to Shepstone to see the doctor. He X-rayed and said, "No fracture," but he put pressure bandages on and got crutches for Phil to use if he had to be up. He can stand on his foot now, but still has to stay in bed as much as possible. He went to Greenville Mission this afternoon to take three sick students. Flu and possibly pneumonia. So many are dying from it all around, that you don't dare take chances.

To go to Greenville Mission from Edwaleni you go in almost a complete circle. Most of the road is along the ridges of high hills, and I can see car lights about five miles out on our road when I look out the window. One part of the road goes over past Mbodiya hill, down, down to the river and up again. It is a terrible road. Used to petrify me! Phil is home now. I always breathe a sigh of relief when he comes in from such a trip. It's so dangerous, oxen and cows all over the road, and drunk men coming back from beer drinks. But the Lord takes care of us.

Happy wedding anniversary! We grow happier every year. I suppose you do too. But we are more in love than ever before. The Lord has been really answering prayer for us. Thanks to all who are praying. Phil's legs are much better and he is no longer discouraged. The spirit in the school is wonderful. The Lord is using us. Phil preached a wonderful sermon here this morning; simple, and yet you could see that the Holy Spirit was speaking, and working. Phil is not a preacher and often gets discouraged because he can't talk as fluently and eloquently as others, but at least he keeps humble and the Lord does speak through him. We are so thankful for the blessings the Lord sends.

Sunday, August 24, 1958, We are at the Missionary Fellowship here in Pretoria with all the Rhodesia, Portuguese East, and South Africa Free Methodist missionaries. Counting all the kids, there are sixty of us. They didn't have room here for all of us, so I felt I shouldn't bring our kids. I prayed that someone would volunteer to take care of them, and Anne Brauteseth called and said that the Lord had told her to come and take care of our kids so we could come to Pretoria. Her husband came to Edwaleni also, to be in charge of the school. We were able to leave our kids and the school, because the Lord had arranged it all. The special speaker is one sent here by God. His messages have been just what everyone needed.

September 12, 1958, Davey Joe walks fast now, nearly runs. He climbs down off the front verandah feet first so there is no keeping him out of the dirt! He is big and strong, and can climb steps already. Patsy is starting to grow again. I have all the kids asleep at the same time! Rare! So it is only me in the living room and Selinah and Gladys clattering around in the kitchen, doing dishes and making a pumpkin pie for tomorrow. We grow enormous pumpkins down by the river. The chickens are "cockeling" outside. (Nancy's word) They lay eggs under our front verandah and eat my flowers. They won't stay in their pen. The warm air is heavy with the delicious perfume from the Yesterday, Today, and Tomorrow bushes in front of our house. The breeze brings the wonderful aroma right into the house. This is early spring and the three big bushes are in full bloom. I must get busy studying my sermon for tomorrow morning and my Bible story in *Zulu* for Monday afternoon. Need to wash clothes too! Not enough hours in a day.

Paul, Nancy, Patsy, and Davey Joe

Patsy, Nancy, and Paul on his trike

Picnic down by the Umtamvuna River

October 3, 1958, What a lovely day this has been! It was so hot this morning Phil said, "Let's take a picnic lunch and go down to the river." So here we've been most of the day. The kids have had so much fun wading, playing in the sand, and throwing rocks into the river with the African kids across the river to see who could throw the farthest. Davey Joe slept a long time. Nancy and Patsy took naps and Paul, Phil and I took a walk down the river. We found a beautiful spot with sand, and nice grass, just as nice as a lawn! Edwaleni is such a beautiful place. I hate to think of ever leaving. I've been working on another Bible story in *Zulu* for Monday at Esangweni and also I'll try to preach in *Zulu* at the Mbodiya church tomorrow, for about twenty minutes. I started in *Zulu* Sunday, but finished up in English. It was too hard to say everything in *Zulu* that I felt I should tell them. Joe is cutting more teeth and Nancy has tonsillitis and now laryngitis. Today I feel really tired, but it was such a thrill yesterday, to hear all those little African

ري

Kline*

kids popping up one after another to repeat the Ten Commandments, the Beatitudes, 23rd Psalm, 100th Psalm, and the Lord's Prayer; some of them with four selections, one right after another. One girl has only the Bible left to read through and the rest of the Catechism to learn. She is working very hard. I've promised them a *Zulu* New Testament with Psalms if they complete all the memory work. Fifty-seven kids had stayed for the meeting.

God uses everything we have learned to do

November 9, 1958, It seems that I've done nothing but write for the last month or so, Bible stories in *Zulu*, report for the field for Dr. Lamson's Annual Missions Report, newsletter, articles for the Missionary Tidings, Sunday School paper, newspapers here, and a history of Edwaleni. I'm about 'writ out!' Also, there are pictures I have been asked to draw, two pencil sketches to go with a story of Kathryn Hessler's, and a drawing of the Edwaleni campus for the cover of the Edwaleni history pamphlet for our final graduation ceremony. It's really amazing how on the mission field you are kept busy doing the things you really love doing. Everything I've ever learned to do is useful here. It's marvelous how the Lord prepares us for what he wants us to do.

My only regret is that I waited so long to completely surrender myself to His will. There were so many wasted years when I could have been purposefully preparing for a life of service instead of the life for self I had wanted. How foolish that selfishness seems now. When a person is in the center of the Lord's will, there is complete fulfillment. We have just gone through a very painful experience. Did we ever write about Stanley Gowe, the talented Edwaleni graduate from Southern Rhodesia who came back to work for the school? Phil taught him how to do so many things, electrical wiring, driving, plumbing, repair work, pump maintenance, plastering. He was Phil's right hand man, doing all the things Phil had neither time nor energy to do. Last Saturday he drowned in the river. We had the funeral last Sunday. So many people came. It really hit Phil hard because Stanley was like a son to Phil, and he was Paul's *isihlobo* (ee-see-hlow-bow) (friend). Paul followed him everywhere he went. We all depended so much on Stanley. But out of the loss and

120

grief the Lord led me to write a story about him. I did, and sent it to the Sunday School paper. Several Edwaleni students have been drawn closer to the Lord because of Stanley's death and a new realization has come to us how important it is to keep in the will of the Lord.

Too Late

A true story that I wrote.

Stanley was an unusual African young man. He was talented, intelligent, dependable, and always had a smile. Everyone had great hopes for his future. He had completed two years of the sheet metal course at Edwaleni Industrial School and had graduated from the course in motor mechanics. After his graduation he was employed by the Mission as maintenance man. What a load he lifted from the shoulders of the missionary! Every night Stanley was the one who started the power plant. If the water tanks were empty, he was the one who went to the river to start the pump. He did the electrical wiring, the repairing, all the odd little jobs that needed doing. He drove to Izingolweni twice a week to bring in supplies. He could drive the tractor, do plumbing, run the movie projector, do plastering, and operate the metal lathe. His hobby was photography, and he kept everyone supplied with pictures from his darkroom. He had even made his own enlarger. How many times a day the missionaries said, "Call Stanley, I need him." But more than all that, he was like a son to the missionary, a beloved son, and like a big brother to the missionary's little son, Paul, who followed Stanley everywhere. Stanley was his *isihlobo*. Stanley occasionally preached at the outstations or taught Sunday School, and the Lord blessed him. He had wonderful victory in his Christian experience. He felt called to preach the Gospel to his own people in Rhodesia. He had hoped to go to England for ministerial and agricultural training. And then he fell in love. Instead of seeking the will of God, asking God to work out His perfect plan for his life, Stanley said, "I love Tanda. I want her. I am going to have her at any cost." He sought his own way, and stepped out of the will of the Lord. He began to walk in darkness.

The missionaries counseled Stanley to seek God's will, and prayed with him. While starting the power plant one night, he was knocked unconscious, but was not seriously injured. He narrowly escaped death in an automobile accident. God was speaking to him. Stanley began to pray again, to seek God's will. He came broken, sobbing, "I have lost my soul. Pray for me." After a Wednesday night service, he finally prayed clear through to glorious victory. He completely committed his way to the Lord, and asked the Lord to work out His plan. But it was so late. Tanda was writing insistently to him. She would go to the end of the world with him. Friends were urging him to marry her soon. It was a good match for Tanda. Arrangements had already been made for the formal engagement negotiations to begin. He had already promised to marry her. The appointment with her family had been made for Saturday. An uncle was coming from Durban, one hundred miles to meet with them. Tanda came home happily in expectation. On Saturday, Stanley awoke with a heavy heart. He had begun to realize that perhaps Tanda was not the girl God wanted him to marry. He spent much time in prayer that day. He didn't know what to do. He felt obligated to marry her, and yet he didn't want to go against God's will. What could he do? If only he had never been so insistent on having his own way. His prayer that day was, "Oh, Lord, work it out for me. Your will be done. I don't know what to do."

Saturday was also the day of the annual party for the Bible study class members. This year it was to be a picnic down by the beautiful Umtamvuna River. The day was hot, a wonderful day for swimming. Stanley had pumped up an old tractor inner tube. The boys had great fun playing and splashing, swimming around it. The river was deep, and a friend had said to Stanley, "Don't swim there, it's too deep." But Stanley was having a good time; his troubles forgotten for awhile. Then suddenly he called for help. He was going under. A teacher tried to help him, but in his struggles, Stanley pulled him under. The teacher, exhausted, finally got loose, and reached the surface panting to get back his breath. Only Stanley's hand came up above the water again, mutely pleading for life. The teacher made a dive for his hand, but missed. He frantically dived again and again. Others searched and searched, but they could not find him. The missionary was called, the doctor came, but his body was not found until two hours later. The missionary found him and tenderly placed the body of his African son on the bank of the river. Stanley was gone. His troubles were over.

But oh, how he would be missed! Intense was the heartbreak and grief of those who loved him. Such a promising life cut so short. No one could take the place of Stanley. Oh, if he had never stepped out of God's will. If only he had committed his way to the Lord before he became so enmeshed in plans of his own making. If only he had asked the Lord to lead him to the girl of His choice before he let himself fall so deeply in love. God in his infinite wisdom knew the future, and could see that through death, Stanley's radiant Christian testimony would influence many. If he had lived, his testimony might have been lost. Through Stanley's death many were drawn closer to the Lord, and some sought Salvation. But this was only God's second best for his life. It was too late for God's perfect plan. Too late!

CHAPTER 3
Edwaleni School is Closed

Phil is appointed mission builder

December 1, 1958, School is nearly over. We had several days of wonderful meetings here with Pastor Duma from Durban. Fifteen students, some of them who had rejected Salvation for nearly three years went forward last night and about ten more this morning! We expect a huge crowd here for graduation. Probably seventy-five missionaries and friends and five hundred Africans. We'll have a very nice graduation. Wish we could fly you here for it. After school is out, Phil plans to finish the Mbodiya church. The Mission Board has approved that Phil be a mission builder, first in South Africa, then probably Southern Rhodesia and Congo after furlough, depending on our health. I saw the doctor yesterday. Monday I had a pain above my heart and down my arm, then tingling all over. The doctor said neuritis, inflammation of the nerves. She gave me a good check-up and Vitamin B complex and Aureomycin. I feel better, but need rest. I nearly cracked up this morning. I was hurrying to finish a model community, ten huts and the preacher's hut, ten fields and the preacher's garden, and a church for Phil to use in his newest tithing sermon. I felt the pressure building up inside. I got all jittery and started yelling at the kids. Phil came in and told me to get my blood pressure down. I felt that I had nearly lost control of myself. I've been under a terrific strain lately. The devil knows the quickest way to get me down and he has really been working overtime. Before we came to Africa I had to pray a lot to overcome my fear of snakes and lions. Now they don't bother me in the least, even though there are many snakes around, it's the 'creepy crawly' things that get me down. You plant a garden and the insects literally eat it up. However, we do manage to have a nice garden in spite of them. We've had bed bugs, fleas, lice and now worms, pinworms, whip worms and

Nancy has tapeworms! We just discovered them a few days ago. The poor child! So we are all taking worm medicine that makes you dizzy. I've got to pray through now, over all these parasites and get the victory before the devil does. We feel we should go to Southern Rhodesia so Phil can help Doc Embree with his building and maintenance program at Chikombedzi Mission. But it's hard to think of taking your kids into one of the worst malarial areas in Southern Africa. One of the Embree children nearly died from cerebral malaria. But we are going because we feel that's where the Lord wants us. I prayed through to victory over the bed bugs and my supposed 'lice' and the Lord helped us get rid of them, so now I know he'll help us get rid of the worms. I feel somewhat as though we were being visited with the 'ten plagues'! What next? But this afternoon as I was praying, I felt such a nearness of the presence of the Lord. It was wonderful! I could feel that someone was praying for us. Pray that I'll get the victory over the parasites. Mbodiya church is nearly finished. The people are happy with it.

Honor graduates at the final graduation of Edwaleni Technical College, 1958

Transformation

Patrick Cele is18 years old, and attends our day school at Esangweni. For several years he had been a problem in the school, requiring severe punishment. He hated the teacher. One day he even brought a knife to school, planning to stab a girl, but handed it over to the teacher instead. Now, during school vacation Patrick is working in my garden; a changed boy. During evangelistic meetings held by Lily Steele once a week, after school was out, Patrick gave his heart to the Lord. When I started holding children's meetings each Monday after school, Patrick's face was wonderful to see, glowing with the joy that comes with serving Jesus. It hadn't been easy for Patrick. He is an orphan, living with his brother's heathen family, who persecute him every chance they get because he had become a Christian. Then came Youth Camp time. Patrick's brother refused to let him go, and sent him to work for us instead. When I found out why Patrick wasn't going to Youth Camp, I prayed, "Oh, Lord, make a way for Patrick to go." Soon the thought came, to write a letter to his brother, offering to advance Patrick the needed money from his wages. The next morning when he came to work, Patrick told me that he would be allowed to go to Youth Camp, but there would be no money at home for his school fees and books. That was easy. Patrick could continue working for me. I needed another school boy to chop wood and help in the garden. I felt I was being part of a miracle, and what a joyous reward it was to see Patrick come forward Sunday morning to dedicate his life to the service of the Lord!

An amazing answer to prayer

Agnes Cele was an answer to prayer. We were living at Edwaleni in 1958, the last year our industrial school was in existence. It had been a hard year, a year of strain and tension, a year of sickness and discouragement. And now we learned that the two African girls who helped with our housework were both to be married soon. So, on top of everything else, I was faced with the problem of finding a suitable girl to help in our home. As I listed the qualities in my mind, I couldn't think of anyone in our area, whom I knew, that would be just right.

She had to be dependable, honest, eager to learn, quick, teachable, one who loved children, impossible, there was no one I knew.

Because of the hard things that year I had begun to learn to trust God for small things, and so when this need came, I took it to God. "Oh, Lord," I prayed, "You know how desperately I need someone to come help me with the housework and to help watch the little ones. You know I am not physically able to manage this big house alone, teach our kids, and still have time and energy left over for missionary work. You know the kind of girl we need. I am just going to trust you to supply this need. I won't ask around to try to find a girl. I'll leave this matter in your hands." As the time drew nearer and nearer to the day when our African girls would be leaving, the devil would come and sneer, "So, you think God will send you someone? Do you think He cares enough about you to bother with finding you a girl?" "Go away, satan! I have committed this problem to God. Oh, Lord, you know I'm still trusting you to send just the right person." The weeks went by. It was the closing day of school. Our girls would be leaving the next week.

Still no one had come and then after the program on Commencement day, I had walked up to our house, and was standing in our front yard. A girl approached shyly. "*Sakubona, Nkosikazi.*" (Hello, Madam.) I have come to work for you." I could hardly believe my ears. I had not expected my prayer would be answered today. I was rather startled, "*Ubani igama lakho?*" (What is your name?) "My name is Agnes Cele. I have been working for *Nkosikazi* Shembe, (the wife of one of our teachers), but I told her that you needed me, and I wanted to work for you, so she agreed."

Agnes was the answer to my prayers. She was a lovely girl, beautiful really, a quick smile, neat, clean, and I knew that anyone who had happily worked for Mrs. Shembe would be dependable, and she assured me she loved children. Yes, Agnes was an answer to prayer. The Lord had sent her. Every morning after breakfast it was our habit to have family prayers, including the girls who worked for us. So every day we would call, "Aggie, *Umthandazo.*" (Prayer time) She would come to the living room and listen intently as Phil read a Bible story from our children's Bible story book. Then one day after family prayer time, she stopped before going back to the kitchen. "*Nkosikazi*, is that story in the Bible?" "Yes, you can find it in the book of Genesis." "Oh, thank you." A little while later she came back. "*Nkosikazi*, could I borrow a Bible please. I want to read that story." "Of course, Aggie, here is my *Zulu* Bible. Let me find the story for you." This happened several mornings, and when I discovered she had no Bible, I gave her mine. Then I began to notice that Aggie was spending all of her spare time pouring over her Bible. She put me to shame. She spent more time reading God's Word than I did!

We all loved Aggie, and when the time came for us to move to Durban so Phil could help build the church there, we were happy that Aggie wanted to go with us. Aggie's happy face was glowing even more radiantly. She was not afraid to testify. She loved attending Youth Camp. From her testimony there we learned something amazing, something we had not known. She was raised in a church that did not teach the Way of Salvation. She had never been allowed to read a Bible before coming to work at Edwaleni. God spoke to her, she was convicted, and gave her life to God. When it came time for us to move to Southern Rhodesia, she shared with us her desire to go to a Bible School. Her mother refused to give her permission. We helped her make arrangements to attend Bible School. Aggie happily studied God's Word in Bible School, and she later graduated with a victorious testimony. Yes, Aggie was a wonderful answer to our prayers!

More parasites!

January 6, 1959, Now we know why we have both been feeling so lousy. The doctor in Durban says we both have amoebiasis! But it isn't really bad yet. We are thankful it was discovered early. We have been taking drugs for three months to kill the amoeba! The last pills I took made me feel like I was walking in my sleep. Thank goodness they are finished! We are both getting shots of vitamin B12 every other day. I can't stand to give an injection to Phil, so he is giving them to both of us. I'm gradually feeling better. It improves with rest. I haven't had much of that 'pins and needles' prickly feeling today.

The latest recommendation is that we move to Durban so Phil can help to build the churches and parsonages there until furlough time. So, if that happens, we can put Paul and Nancy in school there! That would be nice! We are waiting for Board approval.

February 18, 1959, I just finished hearing Paul in a reading lesson and drilling him in his two times table, and got Davey Joe interested in digging outside. You asked what I'll do now that our Edwaleni school is closed. Mornings, school work with Paul in third grade, Nancy in first grade, and Pats in nursery school! School started for us about a month ago. Paul is working hard this year; reads very nicely, is good in 'story sums', which I never was. He is practical-minded like his daddy, and he is trying to improve his writing. Nan is in pre-primer two. She wanted to start reading last year so I let her. She is beginning to learn to print, and even knows her numbers. She can write 1 to 10 by herself without copying from anything and is beginning simple sums and 'take-aways'. She is very artistic. Pats is really talking now, a mile a minute, still in her own private language, of course, but I can understand her without an interpreter. However, Phil can't. He asked Nan the other day what Pats was saying. When Nancy started to 'interpret', Pats said, "Hush! Me talking Daddy!" She and Davey Joe got on famously with Arlene and Elmore while we were on holiday, mandated by the mission group for our health! Clydes have a dachshund puppy named Bouncer. So now at night Pats prays, "Bless E'more and Auntie E'en and Bouncer Boy." She prays for about two minutes, names everybody she knows and ends up with "Jesus Love Me. Anem." She is so cute that everyone spoils her rotten. She asks every day, "Me make cookies?" So we did yesterday. She did the sifting and beating and Nan did the measuring, except Pats 'measured' the salt! They aren't too salty if you drink lots of milk along with them! Pats is real proud! Cookies!

About 10:30 I start racing back and forth from the school room in the basement to the kitchen, fixing dinner and teaching all at the same time. I have two new girls I am training now. The one I had trained to cook, left to get married, so now I do most of the cooking myself. I like it much better that way. Monday mornings we sandwich in the washing.

I run the machine to preserve both the machine and our clothes! I always regretted teaching our former girls to run it. My new girls didn't know how to iron or wash dishes or hang up clothes. At home they throw their washed clothes on the grass, a fence, a bush, or drape them on tree branches! Afternoons, after I put the younger kids down for naps, are *Zulu* study time. I write a Bible story each week in *Zulu* and go to Esangweni School on Monday afternoon for the children's meeting, tell my story and listen to memory work. Also, I am beginning to get ready for furlough, going through everything. Gave a big box of very worn-out clothes to Mrs. Shembe for the church ladies to mend and patch and then sell for a few pennies. They were glad to get them.

Please continue to request prayer for future plans for Edwaleni Mission. A tuberculosis center, or a Conference Church Center for annual Conference, Conventions, Camps? Pray that God will lead us to His solution. Well, it's almost supper time. What shall I fix? The wood stove smokes terribly. The chimney needs a good cleaning, but the girls are ironing today, so we have to keep feeding the wood to the fire to keep the flat irons hot. Guess I'll fix tomato soup and corn pancakes. Don't have enough fat left to fry fritters, and our bread is gone. When Phil goes to Durban to consult with the architect, he brings home groceries. Our nearest store is eleven miles away, so we don't go unless it is absolutely necessary, and if I forget to put something on the list, that's just too bad, because I get to the store about once a month! Phil buys most of our things in connection with other trips. Anyway, you hardly have any choice of brands unless you shop in Durban. Phil went to Izingolweni today to bring petrol (gasoline) in drums, cow feed, chicken feed and groceries, and maybe a water tank to catch drinking water from the aluminum roof on the Mbodiya church. I dread the thoughts of moving. I love Edwaleni and don't have enough energy to pack! Phil killed a six foot green *imamba* snake yesterday. We had all been within ten feet of it! And the day before that, Paul, Nancy and Patsy were three feet from a black *imamba*! But I know no one will get bitten. Praise the Lord!

Paul, Nancy, Patsy, and Davey Joe, have lots of room to play at Edwaleni

March 4, 1959, A letter to Orlean and Bill Keller (Mary's sister and brother-in-law) Today has been blistering hot, but it is raining now. These hot, humid days leave you feeling flatter than a left over pancake and twice as soggy! Yes, we are still missionaries. To be a missionary means that you are more concerned with winning people to the Lord than anything else. Some missionaries are doctors, nurses, or teachers, but their constant prayer is to be able to lead those around them into a personal saving knowledge of Jesus. That's why we are here. Much of missionary life is just living, except it is harder, and very necessary that we live close to the Lord. If we neglect to pray and don't consciously strive to do God's will, then everything goes wrong, because the devil doesn't want us here. I dread the thoughts of packing and traveling with our four! Some day this week we plan to take the kids to the beach. We go so seldom, and it is only thirty-five miles from here.

March 13, 1959, Seven, five, three and one year old, they were all sick with a throat infection. I had just issued the evening ration of pills and water and had tucked them all in bed when I heard the eternal call, "Mommy, more water, please" I took three-year old Patricia to the table where four small green glasses stood side by side. I picked up the one that I thought had been hers. She loudly protested; pointed an accusing finger inside the glass, and wrinkling up her tiny nose, stated authoritatively, "**Germs**!" Patricia was given a clean glass.

We move to Escombe, near Durban

April 30, 1959, At last I can sit down and write. I've really been going around in circles for weeks. Packing, cleaning, unpacking and cleaning, making Nancy's school uniform, and sewing on school badges! Most everything is finally well enough organized so I can sit down and rest a little. Warren Johnson found us the nicest little house, just made for us, even to the color scheme. Three big bedrooms with lots of storage space, even built-ins in the kitchen! Something unusual in South Africa! What a change for us! Electricity all the time! We don't have to boil drinking water any more. No wood to chop and carry, no ashes to empty. We can use our toaster, vacuum, electric mixer and iron! No kids for mommy to teach. That's the best part, and they love going to school. It's really a treat for Paul and Nancy to be with English speaking kids. They are both like their father, they make friends easily. So we are all very happy. We brought Agnes Cele with us. The kids love her, and she is so good with them. She is also a good worker. Phil has gone with Warren back to Edwaleni to bring in the rest of our furniture and to check on things there.

Warren has put me to work already. They want to print a brochure to help raise money for the new church. He found it would cost $150.00 to have a perspective drawing made by the architect of the proposed new church, so he asked me to try. I studied Phil's architectural drawing book, and managed to sketch something that doesn't look too bad. Now I have to put the finishing touches on it, and ink it, and help write the copy. Next week is our annual mission meeting with the missionaries from Southern Rhodesia, Portuguese East Africa (Mozambique), and Transvaal. This year we are meeting at Hibberdene, right on the coast, at a big beach resort, so it will be relaxing and fun as well as inspirational. Pray that the Holy Spirit will fill each heart with love for one another. The devil tries so hard to cause disunity and division, so pray for harmony and unity of spirit. You can tell the Ashcrafts that the book they gave us, "Calvary Road" has been such a help and blessing, and the Lord has given me several opportunities to help others, using it. The Ashcrafts were retired missionaries to China, wonderful people. They lived near my parents.

The perspective drawing of the proposed Glebelands Church and
Youth Hall, drawn by Mary, for the brochure to be distributed
in Durban to help raise money for the building fund.

June 16, 1959, Please begin now to pray for the annual Youth Camp to be held July 6-13 at Ithemba Mission. Pray especially that the Lord will call more young men to the ministry, and that they will dedicate themselves to this work. Please also pray for Phil as he has begun to supervise the building of the new church at Umlazi Glebelands, near Durban. Pray that the construction may progress smoothly.

June 27, 1959, Another glorious sunny day. I love it here. I'm sitting in our bedroom, near the bay windows, overlooking the hills and the distant sea. This is a wonderful place to sit and read or write. Nancy and Patsy just helped me mix up some donut dough. It is chilling in the fridge now. Did I tell you Phil found an ancient fridge, 1928, in perfect running order and in good condition! Davey Joe just woke up, so he is cuddled on my lap, looking over my shoulder out of the window. He is such a big boy, but so good. Soon we should see the end of the diapers! We have all had colds. I am just getting over a touch of sinusitis. Patsy and Joe are taking medicine to take care of another intestinal parasite!

My last lab test said I'm OK and so is Nan. Hope this is the end of pill taking for this family, but the kids are really good about it. Phil took Paul to the church site today. He loves to be with his daddy. School winter vacation began today. They have nearly a month off now. Nancy is rather sad that school isn't still on. She loves school and seems to be at the top of her class in everything.

Back in my sunny corner again. Phil came home early. He fixed the stopped-up sink drain and the kids and I polished the car. On Sunday Phil took the kids to the closest evangelical Sunday School at the English speaking Full Gospel church. We picked them up later and drove downtown to the Baptist church. A Salvation Army Colonel preached. Then after church, to Johnsons for lunch and then out to the native town, Lamontville, for the African service. Because we have no church building yet, we have to meet in the community hall. The kids stay at Johnsons and play, then we go back to Johnsons for Sunday evening dinner. I usually furnish the meat and dessert and Jean does the vegetables. Then back home at night. Poor Phil doesn't get a real day of rest at all. He gets so tired on the job and his legs are still aching. Please pray for physical strength for him. Physically, he was ready for furlough before he started this church. I must go now to the butcher's for meat. It's only a five minute walk down this little hill, and up and over the next. Good exercise.

I get more done when the kids are in school. I worked late last night on the banner for the front of the church for Youth Camp. I'm ready now to start painting it. It says *"Nifunani na? uJohane* 1:38" (What do you seek?) Articles are beginning to come in for the South Africa Missionary Tidings issue for October or November. I have been given the job of compiling the material and sending it on to the editor. We have our prayer letter ready to mimeograph, but no paper, so that will have to wait a few more days. Wish you could see Davey Joe now. He is such an adorable child, talks quite a bit, jabbers a lot, and does the cutest things. Put him in his bed and he says, "Bye bye." and off he goes to sleep!

July 21, 1959, School began again today for Nancy and Paul. It is still winter, but very nice and warm in the middle of the day. We didn't even get to the beach once during the kids' school vacation. We planned to, but never got there. Phil is trying to get the building finished, and just won't take time off. He has about fifteen African men working and has to spend a lot of time supervising everything carefully, and showing the men how to do things properly! They have put some windows in the youth hall already, and have the foundations poured for the Sunday School wing and for the church. The building site is on quite a slope, which makes it all more difficult.

Paul and Nancy in their school uniforms

Youth Camp has been over for a week. It was a wonderful success this year. One hundred-eighty attended. William, who is the night watchman for the new church building here in Durban, decided at youth camp that he would try to win some of the workmen for the Lord. So, two days after youth camp, it rained so hard they had to stop working in the afternoon. He got two fellows together and began talking to them about becoming a Christian. After they had talked quite a while, he brought them into the shop office at the building site, and told Phil and Warren that these two men were ready to become Christians. So right then they all knelt down and prayed with the men. Please request prayer for them that they may stand true and grow spiritually. Also pray for William. The Lord has called him to the ministry, but the devil is trying to persuade him not to. We think that he should be in Bible School now.

We have a huge old wild fig tree up in our back yard near the road. Paul and the boys next door love to climb up and sit on the very top of the tree like the egrets that perch there every morning just after sunrise, a whole flock of them, beautiful white birds. They sit and fix their feathers and then fly away. During the day each bird finds a cow and sits on its back, picking off the ticks. We call them tick birds.

Beginning this Friday, the first Free Methodist South African Women's Convention will be held at Fairview Mission. Jean and I may go on Sunday. If the women can only be challenged to live Spirit filled lives and to teach their children about the Lord, it would make such a difference in our church. Beauty is ironing for me, so I can spend the rest of the day typing. She is such a lovely girl. Have I ever told you about her? Her father was one of our best preachers, but he was poisoned, and died. The cup of tea he drank was meant for someone else! Several years ago she first came to me for work during school vacation. I really didn't need her, but let her work for me just to help her out. She came back every school vacation. Last year Seth Msweli, who had been one of our students, and a future preacher, proposed to her. He had been one of my garden boys at Edwaleni. She prayed about it for a while and then accepted. She was debating at the time whether to enter nurse's training or to go to a girl's Bible school. I had the privilege of counseling her to commit everything to the Lord. She finally decided to go to Bible school. We are helping her through school, and to say thank you to us she has come to work for us. We all just love her. It was definitely an answer to prayer because I had been praying that she would, so I could let Aggie go home for a visit. Then Beauty and Seth will get married. We won't be here to see the wedding, but that is a small matter, I guess. It was through Phil's influence that Seth joined our church, and enrolled in Bible school, so we really feel that they are our children. Pray for them. We think that they are the most promising young couple in our church.

New Churches in South Africa

By Phil and Mary Kline, printed in the Missionary Tidings

The new Mbodiya church has been completed. This is a lovely little church. The sanctuary measures twenty four by thirty four feet, with a bell tower at the entrance. We had hoped that we would have a large bell to install in this tower to call the people to worship. Watches are rare instruments in this area, which makes the need more imperative. We have borrowed a small bell from Edwaleni to use temporarily. (An old bell was later donated by Lily Steel's brother, from England, and was installed.)

The Mbodiya church grew out of the labours of Miss Margaret Nickle many years ago. The mud and pole structure eventually fell down, battered by the rains and the many goats, cattle, and donkeys that chose the church as their favorite shelter. Another dried mud block church was built by the people, using the same good old iron roof, but shortly after its dedication, it was demolished in a terrific wind storm. (Tornado, maybe?) The people then began to pray for a new church, and the beautiful cement building standing now is the evidence of answered prayer. A fence around the church yard will keep out the animals. How the people rejoiced on dedication Sunday and continue to rejoice as new converts join them in worship there. Please continue to pray that this little church on a high hill will be as a lighthouse probing the darkness all around it with the light of the Gospel.

After many years of missionary endeavor near the fast growing industrial city of Durban in the Glebelands native area, an African church site has been granted and construction of a church and educational unit has begun. For many years there has been a struggle to maintain a flock without a church building. Many efforts had been made to obtain a church site from those in charge of the African Locations. Money was raised for the building, but now it actually has been started! Praise the Lord for all His goodness.

The church is located near the south edge of the city, overlooking the Durban airport with the blue Indian Ocean on the horizon. It is surrounded by the homes of thousands of Africans who have no church to attend. North of Durban, is another huge African housing area, Kwa Mashu. We have been granted an additional church site there. This is a new residential development. People are moving by the thousands into the houses built by the government. A small church should be built soon in Kwa Mashu.

The opportunity is great. "The fields are white ... Pray the Lord of the harvest that He will send forth labourers ..." John 4:35, Matthew 9:38. Dedicated African young men are needed to pastor these churches. Also pray that we will not only build a building, but that we will build the true church, the church of Christ.

The new church building at Mbodiya

One of the churches Phil helped to build in Durban

August, 1959, Please continue to pray for the problem we have been so concerned about. The Lord is working even now and it is really thrilling to be able to see the workings of the Lord. He has led us to do nothing about the situation but pray. All the missionaries have been drawn closer to the Lord and closer to each other. We have seen marvelous answers to prayer. But, of course, the most precious to us is Phil's healing. It has been the means of increasing the faith of all of us. Phil had been so depressed and discouraged over the constant pain in his legs that he was almost ready to give up and go home. I felt so burdened in prayer for him that the Lord would give him real victory over his legs, and would heal him in His time. It happened in a prayer meeting. All the missionaries had gathered together at Fairview for a fasting prayer meeting on Saturday. After all had prayed, Phil was groaning in prayer, asking the Lord to either give him victory or healing. How wonderful it was to hear that! All joined in prayer for him. We anointed him, and the Holy Spirit met with us in a marvelous way, and several said they knew the work had been done, but Phil just couldn't believe it because the pain was still there. Then on Sunday we were praying together at the Johnsons instead of eating. Phil again felt the terrible burden of pleading for victory, and then suddenly he said, "You know, the pain is gone!" What rejoicing! Praise the Lord, and then he continued to seek the re-filling of the Holy Spirit. He prayed through about that early this morning. The Lord told Phil to preach on 2 Chronicles 7:14. We are expecting great conviction to fall on the people and especially on this certain person. We are praying that the Lord will work in such a way in solving this problem, that all the people will know that this has been done by the hand of God. We believe revival is coming soon. We are looking forward expectantly to seeing it. You know, it's quite an experience to fast. We have discovered that we have much more power in prayer, and one's spiritual senses are sharpened. The Lord led us into this experience separately, but in all four of us about the same time. It is nice to be able to encourage one another. This is our fourth day and we aren't sure how long the Lord will have us continue. We are rejoicing in His leading and guidance. Praise the Lord!

Paul just blew in. He took his socks off so he could walk in puddles on the way home from school! His shoes are plastic. One room in the Youth Hall is now ready for use, so we can have our services there instead of in the big old hall at Lamontville that is full of echoes. There have been some marvelous conversions in the last two months, and it all started the Sunday after the Lord healed Phil. There is a spirit of revival on nearly every circuit now. Just the beginnings of what the Lord is going to send.

October 19, 1959, This has been a drippy, rainy day. Looks as if tomorrow will be too, so no wash, even tomorrow. Thank goodness we don't use many diapers these days. Phil is late again. He must be talking with Warren. When those two get together, the hours fly! Nearly time to put the kids down. Patsy and Joe have been very sick, a strep throat very much like diphtheria. I'm certainly glad we live in the day of miracle drugs. Nancy's tonsils are bad, but we don't want them out unless absolutely necessary. She is getting medicine to help clear them up. We'll see what they say in the New York Medical office.

Davey Joe talks a mile a minute these days. His favorite expressions are, "I'm going store." Then off he starts up the driveway with a penny in his pocket! "Fix it!," "My money!," "Where pocket?," "Where daddy going?," "Where Mommy, Aggie?" Phil finally made it home, so I need to stop now and feed him. Tuesday - My prediction was right, more rain today. Joe is asleep and Nancy and Patsy are playing their own version of Old Maid on the living room carpet. I've recently discovered something encouraging about Patsy. She is a clever little cookie! Really bright! Hardly anyone outside of our family can understand her, she talks so 'dutchy', and I always assumed that she might have a hard time in school. But the other day when I went hunting her to see what kept her so quiet for so long, I found her with a game of Traveling, neatly sorting out all the different kinds, matching them perfectly by the numbers, and by big words like collision! The next day I tried her out on a first grade matching word game. She breezed right through it, very carefully checking the words letter by letter! Was I surprised! When she starts kindergarten, her speech difficulty will probably clear up. It is mostly habit now, I think.

I'm not too sure of our furlough plans, except that we plan to leave here March 23 on the Italian ship, S.S. Europa. I am really looking forward to seeing the Suez, and possibly a little bit of Egypt, Italy, Switzerland and France by train and a week or so in England. We hope to be in Winona Lake for General Conference in June and will probably have to do some deputation work in July and August. The Kline family has planned a family reunion in Colorado in July, so maybe we can make it to Los Angeles in August. I'm hoping to settle down in Los Angeles, in Hermon, to put the kids in school. However, I'd love to go on deputation with Phil. But with four kids? I shudder at the thought of all the travel that is ahead of us! By the time we get to L.A., I'll be ready and glad to stay forever! But seriously, we are praying that in all of our furlough plans that God will lead and direct. We want to always be where He wants us to be.

How God answered prayer

I copied the following from the December, 1959 Missionary Tidings (used with permission). At the top of the page I had written, **"The Lord spoke to us through this letter."**

"A Doctor's Day" by Paul Embree

(From Chikombedzi Hospital, Southern Rhodesia, now Zimbabwe)

You awake to a thousand jobs, some of them are not your own, and you turn first to the Lord, praying that today His work might go forward. And so you wait on Him and read His Word.

After that, maybe you find a bit of time for a medical journal to renew contact with your past training. Then the day is upon you with a rush of static, "ZEE 33 calling ZEE 34." Radio contact is made with Lundi (Loon'-dee) and Dumisa (Due-mee-sah) Missions. Usually there is some business, sometimes medical advice is needed or transportation for a patient. Family worship around the breakfast table follows and then you have prayer with the African workers.

First you attend to the builders; corrections and alterations are made. More work is laid out and often demonstrated. Next you do the same for the carpenter, and then you find some job to do yourself which nobody else knows how to do - and usually you don't either. Here's a sampling of the present list: fix an oil leak in the generator engine, reattach the fuel return line from the injector on the same engine, re-align the generator belts on the standby generator, repair the parking light on the truck, the emergency brake on the jeep, the kick starter on the washing machine, the handle on the pressure cooker syringe sterilizer. They all need to be done now.

You work like fury on some job and then with a sigh of frustration you leave it half finished because it's past time to see the out-patients. Miss Strait brings them in. There are many. They come from far and near. They have strange diseases. Some are coming for the first time. Some are leaving, and want to say goodbye, truly grateful for the help they have received. Many need spiritual help, just like the people on the streets downtown in any American city. And when you sense the need, you try to help. Prayer is not infrequent in the examining room. Some have found God there.

Patients are still unfinished, but you stop at one o'clock for lunch. Afterwards the morning's schedule is repeated. Occasionally minor surgery or emergencies replace the mechanics, but more frequently, emergency mechanics replace the medical routine. About 4:30 or 5:00 o'clock you see the hospital patients and Miss Morris points out the ones who need special orders. One very frequent question is, "Where do we put them?" There are sixty patients, nine of them babies, and only twenty-six beds. After that you finish the morning's out-patients. Supper is late and then Mrs. Embree helps with the correspondence, the bills and the reports. Then you are alone with the building plans and estimates. Finally you quit, and as you recline in your thirty-inch galvanized tub for a hot soak, you think things over. It doesn't bother much anymore that the record player you bought four years ago is still not built into a cabinet, or that the full-sized bath tub, which was donated to the Mission eighteen months ago is still sitting outside. It does bother some that the pump and engine sit in the sun and rain without a building, that the orderly has no kitchen, nor the cook for the TB patients, and that the clinic, X-ray dark room, and lab have been waiting three years for cupboards. It bothers even more that the surgical instruments are stored in three different places because of lack of proper cabinets, that there are sixty patients for twenty six beds, that there were eleven new TB admissions last month, no discharges and no room for next month's admissions.

You realize that there are still 999 1/2 jobs left and that before morning a couple of those will produce twins. The work will never be done, so why beat yourself out? Be content with a day's work of ten or twelve hours and committing the rest all into the hands of the One who cares the most, pray for strength for tomorrow's work, funds for tomorrow's expansion and if He wills, personnel for tomorrow's needs. P.S. After writing this, my job has been made easier. I no longer have to spend time laying out the carpenter's work. He quit today!

If My People

Written by Phil and Mary Kline for the December, 1959 issue of the Bantu Harvest

"If My people, which are called by My name, shall humble themselves, and pray, and seek My face, and turn from their wicked ways, then will I hear from heaven, and will forgive their sin, and will heal their land." 2 Chronicles 7:14. This is the verse God has been using in South Africa. Revival is coming. Continue to pray. God has laid this verse on the hearts of one after another, for prayer meetings, for sermons, and even missionary prayer meeting. "If My people," My Christians, church leaders, My missionaries, "shall humble themselves," will admit that there is sin in our hearts, will confess, will pray the prayer, "Lord, search my heart, show me the things in my life that aren't pleasing to You." Then when God does point out something in our lives that He calls sin, let us be quick to pray, "Lord, be merciful to me a sinner." The precious blood of Jesus is ever available to cleanse anything we are willing to admit is sin. He cannot cleanse us if we merely make excuses, rationalize and refuse to humble ourselves.

"And pray" ... How little time we have spent in real prayer, in intercessory prayer, in prayer that cries out in anguish for the souls of the *Zulu* people, and we have confessed this lack of prayer as sin. "Lord, teach us to pray." Since we have begun to pray more earnestly, giving prayer a more important place in our lives, God is answering our prayers. He has given us a greater measure of His Spirit, His power, His love. He is teaching us to make allowances for each other because we love one another, and seek His face, seek to be conformed to His image. Oh, that others can see Jesus only in us! That when we speak, our every word will convey to others the Love of Jesus. "We would see Jesus." Let weariness never be an excuse for impatience or cross words. Let our every action be Christ-like. Let our whole beings be so filled with the love of Jesus that every thought, every attitude that we permit to remain in our minds will be like Jesus. Let us walk in the continual consciousness of His presence. Let us live in the spirit of prayer, in unceasing communion with Him. Let the best hour of our days, that time which we would spend on ourselves, be spent in prayer.

"And turn from their wicked ways." What? Can a Christian have sin in his heart? Can a church leader have sin in his heart? Can a missionary have sin in his heart? **Yes**! And God has been convicting our hearts of sin. We have had to confess to God and to one another our critical attitudes, our lack of love, our resentment, our talking behind each other's backs, the kind of things we tend to excuse ourselves for and are reluctant to call 'sin'. But God has shown us that He cannot send the revival we have prayed for so long, until there is revival in the heart of each missionary and each church leader. Unite with us in prayer that this may soon become a reality. We are continuing to pray, "Lord, search my heart, keep my 'cup' clean and overflowing."

"Then will I hear from Heaven and will forgive their sin and will heal their land." We are beginning to see the answer. We are beginning to see the Spirit come in convicting power. Souls are being saved; there is real hunger for Salvation. There is new awareness of the fact that spiritual growth comes through fasting and prayer. He is teaching us to pray, and there is a new consciousness of the things that are sin in God's sight. Revival is coming.

In Durban, we are seeing the beginnings of revival. Several Sundays the people have come, seven at a time, seeking Salvation, some with heart hunger for a closer walk with God, others burdened for the souls of the unsaved. The church people are gradually beginning to pray the prayer, "Lord, search my heart." Other circuits in the conference are also experiencing the beginnings of revival. This has come in answer to your prayers. Every victory that is won, every soul that is saved is a direct answer to prayer. United prayer brings the answer. We have been so conscious in recent months of a continuous volume of prayer being offered on our behalf. Your prayers are being answered beyond anything we could ask or think. Keep on praying until these flickering flames are fanned into mighty revival fires. Praise the Lord! He answers prayer!

We will postpone our furlough

November 13, 1959, My desk, a card table, is stacked high with many things I need to get done. I need to stencil our prayer letter, the envelopes are half typed. I need to send out twenty air mails to those who received the SOS for prayer in June, and there is the usual stack of correspondence from Women's Missionary Society ladies, but I feel I must get a letter off to you. The kids have had bad cases of tonsillitis again, first Joe, and then Patsy, and now Nancy. But finally they are all playing happily again. Nancy's temp is below normal today, so she and Patsy are playing dolls. Please request prayer for the health of the children. It takes so much of our time and energy when they are sick. Just yesterday we received a letter from the Board requesting us and Embrees to postpone our furloughs because they just didn't have enough money to cover everything, and there are so many of us whose furloughs have come due at the same time. This is the first time in fifteen years they have had to ask anyone to wait. Please don't be too disappointed. We'll probably see you in 1961! But this isn't the whole story. The Mission Board may not realize it, but their decision has been directed and ordered by the Lord! Just wait until I tell you and you will be rejoicing with me. I have been walking on air, nearly unable to contain myself, just marveling at the way God works. Please don't take me wrong. I'd love to see you, and there is a part of me that aches inside because of the human longing. Oh, how I'd love for you to see our precious little Davey Joe. His talk is such an amusing mixture of English and *Zulu*. But before I have us all bawling, let's get on with the story.

When I read the Board's letter, I nearly shouted for joy because I **knew** that this was God's plan. Do you remember reading Dr. Paul Embree's article in the November Tidings? Before I finished reading it, the Lord started telling me that He wanted us to go to Chikombedzi Mission! I felt really sad because we would have to leave South Africa before Annual Conference in April. But we couldn't stay for that and still arrive home in time for General Conference. So our plans were made, but I prayed that if these plans didn't meet God's approval that He would block them! And now, we have the answer! Isn't He good to us! When we make mistakes and still are yielded and longing for His guidance in our lives, He so gently and lovingly rearranges things so we are kept in His path! Are you beginning to rejoice with me? Let me tell you more. Before we left Edwaleni, I tried to sell all of the first and second grade books and equipment I had accumulated, except Calvert course things. We had invested quite a bit of money in South Africa school things, but at the last minute the person who had planned to buy them didn't, and I felt that I might need them even yet some day, and so I will! Because there will be the Embree children as well as ours and every bit of our books and equipment will probably be used. And because of the kids' sickness I had been unable to stencil our prayer letter, even though it had been written for a week. And now it needs re-writing. It won't arrive for Christmas. Honestly, everything is falling into place. We can see the pieces of the puzzle fitting together. This is in the Lord's will, and a year goes fast. We will see you before too long.

The Board had sent a letter to us suggesting that Embrees take a long vacation away from the malarial area, and they are asking us to go to Rhodesia to give Dr. Paul an assist with his building program, and lift his morale. So, Southern Rhodesia, here we come in about May, 1960. Do you remember that we had planned on going to Rhodesia after we left Edwaleni, but the mission group here felt that we should stay and help build the church in Durban. It has been such a change for me that I feel rested and ready to go back to the pressure and responsibility of living on an isolated mission station. Even the malaria doesn't worry me, though we will probably all get it. In 1957 after Patsy had recovered from whooping cough, and Davey Joe was still tiny, we began to be visited by the 'ten plagues!' Somehow, we had been invaded by bed bugs, and I didn't realize it until they were all over the house! I nearly went insane. Every night I would walk through the house, carrying a kerosene lamp, hunting bedbugs, killing them with my thumbnail before they ate my babies! What a nightmare! We took all the furniture outside, doused everything with boiling water and DDT, and finally found an effective tablet to burn that would fumigate the house. Well, the bedbugs were finished, but so also was I, and then I discovered what I thought were **lice** crawling all over my **baby**, on Davey Joe's head and basket and in his ears! Again I nearly went frantic. Of course, I thought I had lice in my hair too. You should have seen us. It's funny now, but I was desperate then. I got down my good old parasitology book and applied every remedy I could think of to the heads of my poor family! DDT powder, kerosene and olive oil again and again, and I still felt them running around in my hair. But that was just nerves! We learned later that it wasn't really head lice, but a bird parasite from the bats that live in the attic. When finally that nightmare was over, we discovered we all had worms and Nancy had tapeworm, so we began taking worm medicine. By that time, it was 1958 and I realized I had to pray through about parasites and get the victory over them once for all.

The Lord gives Mary victory over all the parasites!

When I had nearly prayed through about the bed bugs, the lice, the worms, the scabies, and the fleas and the ticks, the Lord started putting thoughts in my head: "Mary, does this consecration apply to amoebiasis too?" "Oh no! Lord, not that. Please don't let us get **amoeba**. That is too awful." But finally, "Yes, Lord, even amoeba." "What about malaria? I might ask you to take your family into malaria country some day." "Yes, Lord, even malaria." "What about the bad kind of malaria, the kind that kills people from cerebral malaria?" "Yes, Lord, even that and any other of the millions of parasites in Africa. I am yours, my husband is yours, and my children are yours. Take us where you will, regardless of what it means." And so, I had the victory and then shortly after that we discovered we **did** have **amoebiasis** and **giardia lamblia**, and I was stricken with neuritis and a possible slight heart attack, but we got rid of them, and the Edwaleni School was closed and we moved to Escombe (near Durban), and the Lord has been doing wonderful things for us ever since. But He had to allow me to go through the 'valley of the parasites' to get me to realize my consecration wasn't complete, and to bring me to the place of complete surrender and yieldedness to His will. So, please don't feel badly about the malaria. Embrees say they get on pretty well if they take a double dose of preventive drugs. Our kids are good pill swallowers by now, so it is with joy and eagerness that we look forward to what the Lord has in store for us next. Certainly seems strange to think of going to Rhodesia now instead of home. It feels like walking in a dream, rather difficult to readjust my thinking. But the Lord will work everything out.

Measles!

December 14, 1959, Happy birthday, Mother, but it will be late in getting to you. We are finally over the measles! The last I wrote to you we thought Paul had the flu and when he seemed well enough, I sent him back to school and you should have seen him when he came home! Such eyes! Even then, I never dreamed it was **measles**. But after I had called the doctor and he had prescribed penicillin, then Nancy tells me, "Oh, yes, Mommy, there are eleven kids in my room, sick with the measles!" So, of course she got it next, but very lightly. Paul ended up with bad styes and eyes a little weak even yet. Then Davey Joe, so broken out there was hardly a pink patch left on him, but the Lord greatly helped him and he recovered very suddenly even though he had started a bad cough, and then Pats. Her glands and ears got involved, but even she is running around now!

Both Paul and Nancy passed to the next grade. Nancy's report was excellent and Paul got the Progress Award for the school year, a nice book for the student who had improved the most during the school year. In some subjects his grades increased thirty points from the beginning of the year! Every report was better than the last had been, and he had learned how to behave like a 'town kid' in school! So we are all proud of him. He was so thrilled, because he had been afraid he wasn't going to pass. Thank you very much for the exhortation to pray more for the kids when they are sick. It came at just the right time! We haven't been able to get their polio shots yet, and I have been almost worried about that, but I have claimed by faith now that they won't get polio, so that worry is gone. It has been marvelous how the Lord has been sustaining me through all the weary nights and exhausting days. Just when I would almost reach the end of my strength, the Lord would give me a verse, "Delight thyself in the Lord." Psalm 37:4, or "They that wait upon the Lord shall renew their strength." Isaiah 40:31. And then would come flooding in the joy and strength of the Lord. What a wonderful experience! That infilling would give me enough strength to go on for days. Never have I felt the nearness of the Lord like that. I am almost glad for the measles because those times of the Lord's presence were so precious!

Christmas is Different in our Land
Merv Russell requested that I write this article
for the December Youth in Action

It's Christmas time again in the Union of South Africa, that country stretched across the bottom of the map of Africa beside the warm Indian Ocean. But no! Who feels like Christmas now? It's as hot as the 4th of July! Well, it should be, this is the middle of summer! But according to the calendar, it's really Christmas. How confused can one get! Christmas in South Africa leaves Americans feeling rather frustrated and homesick, dreaming of a white Christmas and friends and relatives back home. Christmas cards, unless imported, are decorated with summer gardens and flowers instead of the traditional winter scenes. One can find very little Christmas music on the radio, and oh, for a Christmas tree that smells like a Christmas tree! However, the children like Father Christmas every bit as much as the American Santa Claus. After all, it's what he brings that counts! The day after Christmas usually finds all the missionaries together for a big happy family turkey dinner with all the trimmings, even a can of cranberry sauce, especially hoarded for the occasion, and a warm at-home feeling begins to replace the homesickness of the day before.

Many South Africans celebrate the day with a picnic at the beach, or have a *brai-vleis* (like a weiner roast). For many non Christians in South Africa, brown, black, and white alike, the Christmas holidays, like Sundays are just another opportunity for drinking parties. Many people take their three week summer vacations at this time, and the African men who work in the cities board buses and trains and return to their families in the 'Native Locations', way out in the country. Many African men are with their wives and children only once or twice a year. The main preparation for their homecoming and for the holidays is usually a big pot of home-made *utshwala* (beer).

They celebrate for days with drinking and dancing, and beating of drums, ending with the inevitable fights, injuries, and deaths. African religious publications appeal to their readers to keep Christmas a Christian observance. There are Christmas morning services in most churches, English, Afrikaans, Coloured, and African - each singing in his own language the great traditional Christmas hymns. *Zulus* love to sing - they have an amazing ability to harmonize, so much of their time together on Christmas Day is spent in singing. After the church service is over they hurry home over the green hills to their round, thatch roofed, whitewashed mud and wattle huts for a feast, and what a feast! They love to eat almost as much as they do to sing. Many days there is not enough food to fill one's stomach, but on Christmas there is plenty. An ox has been killed or a goat and chickens. Just smell that delicious curry gravy cooked with dumplings and chicken in a black iron pot over an open fire! Pour it over your plate of mealies, rice, cabbage, pumpkin, and samp and see who can eat the most. Samp, their staple food, is dried corn kernels, cracked and cooked with beans until soft. Eat meat until you feel you will burst! You may not taste meat again for weeks. Rural Africans do not own refrigerators, or even have electricity, so eat it while you have it. Even the dogs get a bone today. This is Christmas! Gifts of clothing, dishes, soap and other necessities are often exchanged on Christmas Eve, on the 24th, Boxing Day, the day after Christmas, or on New Year's Day. A gift of peaches, a peanut vine, or a sweet potato plant, complete with roots, expresses true friendship. Yes, the celebration of Christmas is different in our land - South Africa, but what is Christmas, really? Christmas is the adoration, the worship of Jesus our Savior, and the thankfulness for His coming to earth - in the heart of every believer - and that is the same the world over.

The Setting, the Life, the Prayer of the Missionary
This article, written by Mary, was printed in
the October, 1959, Missionary Tidings

South Africa - land of beautiful scenery, green hills, swiftly flowing rivers, and sunny winter days - has been for centuries a settler's paradise. Europeans came by ship, then by plane, while the *Zulus* drifted down by foot from Central Africa, bringing their cattle with them. Later came the cane field workers from Asia, whose sons became shop keepers and peddlers.

This multiracial country, now endeavoring to maintain separate development of the races, (*Apartheid*) educates its children well, but separately. There are African schools, Indian schools, Coloured schools, English schools, and Afrikaans schools. Each child learns the three R's in his 'mother tongue'.

The ancient, poverty-stricken mud and wattle (acacia pole) hut continues to be built by Africans in the rural areas. Their city 'cousins' live in small government constructed houses or in tin shack hovels. The

European population builds modern, ranch-style homes with 'American kitchens'.

The cities boast of expensive beach front hotels, huge industrial plants, and tall office buildings. In luxurious department stores, complete with escalators, the white society matron garbed in the latest Paris creation, shops beside a brown-skinned mother from Zululand, clad only in beads and leather skirt, her hair packed with red clay, her baby slung in a blanket on her back. Beside them waits an Indian woman, gracefully draped with the traditional silken sari, the red mark of Hindu worship on her forehead - all three without Christ.

Jet planes roar overhead - electric trains zoom by - thousands of people flock to Durban for the annual horse races. Carefree vacationers crowd the beaches. On a thousand dry brown hills in the country, far from the frequent coastal rains and the noise and smog of the city, the cattle munch what food they can find. African girls walk gracefully along the dusty roads, balancing on their heads long, heavy loads of firewood. A car speeds past and clouds of dust settle thickly on grass and bushes. Around the mud huts, on the grass, and over the bushes are spread the freshly-washed clothing and blankets. Africans file past on the path, dressed in their brilliant heathen finery - the men carrying their shields and *knobkerries*, the women with big pots of beer on their heads - all going to a big wedding feast and dance, all without Christ.

But whether in the city or isolated rural areas, the missionary labours on, planning and preparing for youth camps, daily vacation Bible Schools, women's meetings, teaching African church workers, quietly 'making disciples', counseling, preaching, the ordinary routines of living, managing one's own children, supervising building, repairing the pump, the engine, the lawn mower, caring for the sick, training nurses, securing supplies, keeping the endless books and records, preparing and promoting Christian literature, speaking a word about Salvation to this one, an invitation to surrender his life to Christ to that one, carefully taking advantage of all opportunities to witness to the wonders of God's love.

But most important of all, spending time in the systematic study of God's Word; alone with God in the closet of prayer, pleading for the

Salvation, the strengthening, the spiritual growth, the sanctification, of these our African brothers and sisters. Oh, for a church on fire for God, a ministry earnestly proclaiming the Gospel. Continually breathing a prayer for guidance - to be kept in God's will, to be filled and motivated by the spirit of love, to be more Christ-like. This is the setting, the life, the prayer of the missionary - South Africa, 1959.

December 26, 1959, Letter from Mary to Dr. Byron S. Lamson, Missionary Secretary

Dear Dr. Lamson, Re: Personal Testimony - I thought perhaps you would be interested to hear of God's recent dealings with me. Immediately after I finished reading Dr. Embree's article in the November Tidings, which we receive airmail, the Lord began showing me that He wanted us to go to Southern Rhodesia next. Of course I did not know that the Commission had already made that decision! For a long time we had been praying for God's guidance concerning our future, and I had prayed that God would block our travel and furlough plans if they weren't in His will. I didn't tell anyone of the Lord's leadings, but only prayed that He would lead us to Southern Rhodesia in His time, and that He would also make His will clear to Phil. Of course, I figured that this would be after our furlough, since our deposit had been paid to the travel agency and reservations had already been made. The Lord had already led me in 1958 to the place where I was ready to make a complete dedication regarding taking our children into malarial country. He had allowed us to go through the 'valley of the parasites', a time in 1958 when we were absolutely besieged by several different kinds of disgusting parasites. When I had practically lost control of my senses fighting these bugs, the Lord showed me that my consecration was not complete. So as He led, I prayed through to real victory over all the 'million and one' parasites in Africa, even the kind that cause cerebral malaria, the kind that live around the Nuanetsi (Noo-anet-see), Mission! And so when the Lord began speaking to me about going to Chikombedzi Mission, I was immediately willing and ready to go.

You can imagine my joy when your letter came informing us of the Commission's request that we go to Southern Rhodesia before returning to the States! I practically shouted. The presence of the Lord was so real. Tears of gratitude filled my eyes. To think that the Lord had answered our prayers for guidance in such a definite way, and so quickly! Our children kept wanting to know, "But Mommy, what has happened to make you so happy?" We called the travel agency and asked them to cancel our travel reservations and to try to recover at least part of our twenty pound deposit. The next week a letter came from the agency with a check for the entire amount, twenty pounds! We thanked the Lord for this additional indication that our going to Rhodesia was His will for us, not just merely a decision of the Commission. I am continuing to rejoice in the knowledge that when we are completely yielded to His Will, the Lord leads us in ways more marvelous than we could ever imagine. Praise His Name!

(And within a few days we received a copy of Dr. Embree's article in the mail from Phil's sister, Betty, who was working in the General Missionary Board office. Someone in the Winona Lake General Mission Board office evidently thought it might help convince us that we were really needed at Chikombedzi Mission. What they didn't know was that we had already received the Tidings airmail, and that the Lord had already let us **know** that we should go to Chikombedzi Mission! Triple sources of assurance!)

January 8, 1960, What a lovely summer day this is! Nice breeze straight from the ocean so it isn't hot. We'll really miss our ocean view and cool air in Rhodesia! And our Saturday afternoons at the beach. We do go occasionally. We went to the beach New Year's Day and took the Johnson kids so Jean and Warren could spend their whole day getting their account books up to date. That was fun, but rather tiring, watching all eight at once. The surf is so treacherous here. But I did get a nice swim in the tidal pool, a concrete and rock pool that the waves fill at high tide, but is safe. A huge wave came crashing over the walk and steps leading to the pool. Phil grabbed the shirts I had laid there in a corner with my shoes, and down fell Johnny Johnson's glasses. The water was still rushing by and so they disappeared. I quickly breathed a prayer and began frantically searching in the sand under the water. Just then a woman came up with the glasses. The water had washed them way over beyond us and she had grabbed them!

The kids are all in bed, supposedly asleep. Our 'lawn mower' is out mowing the lawn. An old African man comes around every two weeks or so to cut grass. He works all day for $1.00, and that is three times what you pay a man in the country for a day's work. He uses a long sharp piece of steel, a bush knife, and that is the accepted way to get your lawn cut in Durban! At Edwaleni we had a power mower.

Did I tell you about our Christmas? We had corn on the cob, pork roast, ice cream, and the next day we had watermelon, and right now I am eating some luscious grapes. Johnsons came to eat Christmas dinner with us. We are sending our African girl, Aggie, to Bible School in February. That will make two of our 'daughters' in Bible School. Which will also leave us here without any help, but I am trusting the Lord to send someone reliable. The kids go back to school February 3. They will still be wearing last year's uniforms, so I don't have any sewing to do for getting ready for school. But I should sew a few things for furlough as I probably have more time here than I will in Rhodesia. It still seems strange to think of our moving up there, not quite real. The Embrees want us to come right away, but as far as I know now, we will stay here for Conference in April, and then move after that. Beauty Hlophe is here with us now so I have a little more time. Aggie left on vacation on Wednesday, so I did all my own work for a few days, good for me, I guess. Good for the kids too, to do dishes once in a while! But it leaves little time for my work, which is mostly writing now. The biggest thrill in my life, I think, was receiving the letter from Merv Russell asking me to write that Christmas article for Youth in Action. The Lord gave me the ability, and I have given it back to Him, so anything I write you can give Him the credit. My purpose is to live so close to Him that He can write through me. So if anyone comments to you about anything I write, you can tell them I belong to the Lord, and what I write is to bring honor and glory to His Name.

I received the sweetest letter from Ethel Ward, the other day. We have corresponded quite regularly ever since we arrived here. I will always treasure her letters. She has always meant a lot to me. (When the Ward family was home on furlough from India, she was one of my Sunday School teachers when I was a young child.) She says she has tons of junk to dispose of before she sails in February for Los Angeles. She is retiring, and returning to the States with all her belongings in one trunk, the same one she took to India in 1911! Well, I must get more envelopes typed for our prayer letter when I can get it mimeo'ed. Please request special prayer for meetings at the new Glebelands church. Phil is putting the glass in the Youth Hall windows today so it will be ready for services. Our Bible school boys are holding Vacation Bible School for the African children next week and are calling in the homes intensively. These city people are so hard to reach. Pray for a great spirit of conviction, for the church people to have a greater concern for souls, and more to keep filled with the Holy Spirit.

CHAPTER 4
Our Furlough is Postponed

January 31, 1960, Last night all our Bible School students were here for a farewell service. There are eight of them now, five boys and three girls. We had a wonderful time of fellowship together. I've been sewing this week, getting my African 'daughters' ready for Bible School. We'll probably never see them again in this world! The church building is going very slowly now. It is almost unbearably hot, 104 temperature, and 80% humidity! One day it was 99 degrees and 99% humidity! Yesterday the wind was just like a blast furnace. Paul had trench mouth, but is almost well now. He gets another penicillin injection this morning. He has been really sick. It went into his glands. He picked it up at the dentist's office! Davey Joe got Trench mouth from drinking out of Paul's glass! When I took him to the doctor's office to get his injection, he told me, "Mommy, you go in. I'll wait here for you. You'll be right back!" Poor little guy! But his finally cleared up also.

April 24, 1960, Davey Joe had a severe attack of croup at Fairview Mission when we were there for Conference. We steamed him, and he seemed much better, but that night he fussed and complained of his chest hurting. We took him to McCord's hospital. They gave him penicillin and powerful cough stuff, and said he should have three more injections. He has been closer to pneumonia than any of our other kids. Today he is chipper, slept all night, which was an answer to prayer. Patsy has the sniffles again and I am fighting a sore throat. I'll be glad when we get away from this damp climate. Everything is working out all at once. It is beginning to look as though this is God's time for us to go. We finally got our new passports. The Rhodesia Missions group doesn't want us to spend time at Baker in the Transvaal, building the classroom unit for their Bible School. But, thanks be to God, He is bringing new life to our church. It is so wonderful to hear the African people themselves say, "We need to be filled with the Holy Spirit. We need a clean church."

May 29, 1960, Dear Family, We are still here, but practically ready to go. Last minute packing to do, but nearly everything is sorted. We will go back to Edwaleni for a week so Phil can build the built-ins for the Clyde's house. They are living at Edwaleni now. June 15, Phil has the kitchen nearly finished, finally. It really looks nice. By the time you get this we will probably be in the Transvaal at Baker Memorial Farm. Phil is supposed to get a Bible School classroom building started for them, and show Don Crider how to finish it. Our Rhodesia papers have been cleared, and we have been notified that our entrance is approved, so it will only be a short time until we get our visas. Elmore Clyde is turning the big Motor Mechanics shop building at Edwaleni into a chapel. Youth camp will be held there in July.

I would love to stay here, but we know that God is really leading us, and we will follow Him. His plan is unfolding step by step. God has been teaching me how to keep filled with the Holy Spirit. I need to daily surrender to God's Will, and continually be obedient to His Word. Now my heart is so much more in God's work here. It is really hard to leave, but it is really marvelous to see how every door has opened from the beginning. When we first knew we were to go to Chikombedzi Mission, there was much criticism from some of the South Africa missionaries of our going, taking our kids, especially Patsy, who has been so sick, into that bad malarial area? But I began to claim by faith the promise that God would supply all our needs, material, physical and spiritual. The children's health has improved. Three doctors have given them medical clearance to go to Rhodesia, and God has been supplying the things we needed to take with us.

June 20, 1960, A note from Lily Steele as we were preparing to transfer to Southern Rhodesia:

My dear Mary, Accept this with my love today, Psalm 37:3,
"Trust in the Lord..."
May you be kept by Love divine
Such is the prayer of this heart of mine.
We know not what the path may be
As yet by us untrod;
But we can trust our all on Thee,
Our Father and our God.

Mary, may the radiant presence of Jesus continue to flow through you where ever you go. My love, until we meet, Lily Steele.

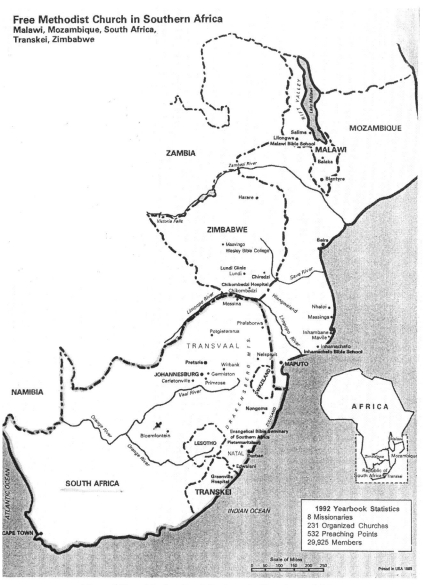

Free Methodist Church in Southern Africa
Malawi, Mozambique, South Africa,
Transkei, Zimbabwe

MOZAMBIQUE

ZAMBIA

Salima
Lilongwe
Malawi Bible School
MALAWI
Balaka
Blantyre

Zambezi River

Harare

Victoria Falls

ZIMBABWE

Beira

Masvingo
Wesley Bible College

Lundi Clinic
Lundi Chiredzi
Chikombedzi Hospital
Chikombedzi

Save River

Messina
Phalaborwa
Potgietersrus

Limpopo River

Hlengweland

Nhaloi
Massinga

Limpopo River

Inhambane
Mavile
Inhamachafo
Inhamachafo Bible School

TRANSVAAL

Nelspruit
MAPUTO

Pretoria Witbank
JOHANNESBURG Germiston
Carletonville Primrose

Nongoma

AFRICA

NAMIBIA

Vaal River

Orange River
Bloemfontein

Orange River

LESOTHO

Evangelical Bible Seminary
of Southern Africa
Pietermaritzburg

NATAL Durban
Edwaleni

Greenville
Hospital

Malawi
Zimbabwe Mozambique
Republic of
South Africa Transkei

SOUTH AFRICA

TRANSKEI

INDIAN OCEAN

ATLANTIC OCEAN

CAPE TOWN

1992 Yearbook Statistics
8 Missionaries
231 Organized Churches
532 Preaching Points
29,925 Members

Scale of Miles
0 50 100 150 200 250

Printed in USA 1993

Map of Free Methodist Missions in Southern Africa
This map was produced in the Free Methodist World Missions Office
Used with permission

--

We move again

July 1, 1960, (In the Transvaal, still in South Africa) I guess it's about time I let you know we are still alive and very happy. We are finally settled in our own little house after a month of living with Clydes, Johnsons and Criders. We had a pleasant trip up here and I do mean up! The altitude here is 3200 feet, and it is lovely. We are living in a rest camp on a fabulous citrus farm, beside the Crocodile River. Paul keeps telling the other kids that there aren't any crocs for about three or four miles down the river! Harvest is in full swing and we can have all the fruit we can pick up. Enormous oranges and avocadoes! The kids are enjoying having school at home, and are really working surprisingly hard. They love to get stars for neat and correct work, a system they used in the school at Escombe, and it works! We are praising the Lord for his goodness to us. We gave most of our furniture to the young African preachers in Natal and brought only our bedding, linens, dishes, etc. On our small trailer we had one drum, one crate, several small boxes and our good bedroom suite, all covered with a big tarp, but silly Phil tied our dust mop and dish drainer on behind so we looked like real 'Okies' moving! The Lord knew we weren't bringing furniture with us, so he provided this nicely furnished place for us. Our hearts are full and running over with thankfulness for such a lovely place to stay, and it isn't cold! Phil and his crew ran the footing for the Bible School building today. He is really happy working here, but of course, he gets very exhausted. Keep praying for him. The Lord is helping him and is answering prayer for him. I'm sleepy now. 5:30 comes too early and there's breakfast to get ready before 6:15 on our little kerosene stove. Pray that they will be able to get the Bible School registered with the government soon.

On our way to Chikombedzi

August 7, 1960, Criders went to an outstation, so I had Sunday School here, about thirty kids, eager and bright. I taught them the chorus "The Wise Man Built His House" in *Zulu* and we had the Bible story in flannel graph to go with it. The Bible school building is nearly completed. The roof is ready for the iron to go on and walls are being plastered. The floor also is almost ready to be poured. Paul and Nancy love making no bake cookies. They can both fry eggs now. I am re-learning how to cook on a wood stove. Paul keeps me supplied with chopped wood. We get waste wood free from a nearby mill. It is beautiful here. The hills are covered with pines. There are springs and waterfalls all around, with a blue mountain in the background.

August, 1960, Happy anniversary, Mother and Daddy! We celebrated our anniversary by driving up to Pilgrim's Rest. Pilgrim's Rest, in a gold mining area, was the location of one of the first Free Methodist Mission Stations in South Africa in 1919! Don Crider was there holding a District Quarterly Meeting at a gold mine church. These people understand Zulu, but they speak *Swazi*, *Sheetswa*, or *Shangaan*. Anyway, it's nice to be able to pray and testify in a language they understand.

We met under the trees because the old church had fallen down. We get to come back tomorrow. Phil and Don will stay here to work on the Bible School, but Caroline will take up a load of cement, tools, windows and doors because the people have decided to rebuild their church. We will take a picnic lunch and stop by a stream. There are beautiful waterfalls, ferns and mosses, clear crisp air and lots of trees. We are still all well, thanks for your prayers.

We are beginning to take our anti-malarial pills. We plan to leave here September 5, hoping to arrive at Chikombedzi Mission in Rhodesia by September 8. We will get to go through the Game Reserve, Kruger Park, on our way. I made Davey Joe a 'choo choo' train cake for his birthday. Did his little eyes ever pop! We'll eat the engine on our picnic tomorrow. Joe is such a little character. He ate tangerines all the way home this evening! Patsy can sing most of the books of the New Testament. She learned by just listening to Nancy and Paul. You should see the Bible School building. It looks beautiful with a long, low roof line, and overhanging roof. Native flagstone walls up to window height and plastered above. It will be painted pale green with a green roof, and will have a big flagstone fireplace inside. Phil is getting a lot of satisfaction out of building it. The weeping willows are getting their leaves now and everything is turning green. The view from our backyard is breath-taking. How lovely to be here. But anywhere is wonderful so long as you are in God's will.

Bible School building in the Transvaal, built while we
stopped on our way to Chikombedzi Mission

From our Prayer letter of September, 1960.

Dear Friends and Prayer Partners, So much has happened to us since
we last wrote to you, that it is difficult to know where to begin. It has been
six months since we packed our belongings, disposed of our furniture
and began our trip to Southern Rhodesia (now Zimbabwe). It was hard
for the children to leave their friends and school in Durban. For us, it
seemed as though we were like Abraham, following God, not knowing
where he was going. (However we had a map!) But we knew we were
following God's leadings as we headed toward Southern Rhodesia, in
the South Africa Mission's Chevrolet Suburban. We drove away from the
warm Indian Ocean, northward up over the Drakensburg Mountains.
We climbed steadily upward to the flat plains and rich farm and mining
country of the high veld. Such excitement when we awoke in a fairyland
world, glistening with heavy frost. Shivering with the unaccustomed cold.
The children scraped handfuls of the fragile crystals from the car, tasted
it, watched it melt, and wished for snow too. Our two months at Baker
Memorial Farm with Caroline and Don Crider sped by too quickly as the
attractive, new building for the Bible school took shape. What a change
from the dark, bat-infested, former chicken coop/school room they had
been using. We prayed that many young men, studying God's Word in

this building would become rooted, grounded and established in Holiness. The time was long past for us to be in Southern Rhodesia. Overloaded to the point of exhaustion, the Embrees have nearly given up hope that we would ever arrive. Leaving the finishing of the Bible school building, and the evangelist's cottage to Don Crider and an African crew, we loaded our trailer and the Chevrolet and once more took to the road. Leaving the splendor of the mountains behind, we were soon in the low country near the eastern border of South Africa and the Kruger National Park, a sanctuary for the fast disappearing game of Africa. We were fortunate. In the two days it took us to drive from the lower end of the park to the north gate, we saw everything we had hoped to see, elephants on the road just in front of us, lions, Cape buffaloes, impala, a wide variety of gazelles, hyenas, ostriches, giraffe, zebra, baboons and monkeys, the favorite of the kids. This was Africa, the way it used to be.

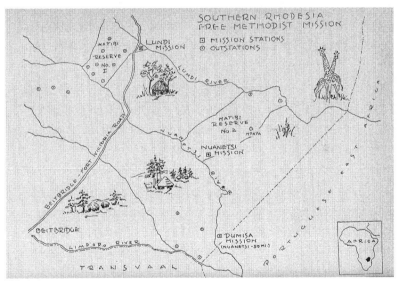

This map was drawn by Olive Teal for the book "Lights in the World,"
written by Byron S. Lamson, 1951
The Chikombedzi Hospital was located at the Nuanetsi Mission.
Southern Rhodesia is now called Zimbabwe.
Portuguese East Africa is now called Mozambique.
Used with permission

Endless mile after endless mile of Mopani bush, always the same, sparse clumps of grass, dry sandy soil, scrawny trees, but always the low, thick bush. Then over the high pass through the boulder strewn mountains of the northern Transvaal, back down to the heat and the bush, and finally, the Limpopo River, a dry expanse of sand, the Rhodesia border. As we crossed the border we heaved a sigh of relief to finally be away from the oppressive rules of the South Africa *Apartheid* government! More miles of dry bush. Darkness was falling. We weren't sure which way to go. A sign indicated that the Nuanetsi Police Camp was down that dirt road. "How far to Chikombedzi Mission?" "But you aren't planning on making that trip for the first time tonight?" The young policeman shook his head, "It's only 45 miles, but this road, you say they are expecting you? Well, I hope you make it all right." Not a very encouraging entry into unknown territory. It was getting darker and darker every minute, and an African night without a moon is **dark**! Giraffe stood in the road and gravely observed us before rocking off into the bush. Zebra trotted by on their way to the river. What other wild animals would we see before we reached the Mission? Lions? Leopards? What if we had to sleep in the car? We recalled the elephant stories we had heard. Cold shivers ran up and down our backs. We mustn't let the kids get scared, and so we sang. We had never seen such a road. Could you really call it a road? Bump, creak, jolt, scrape, shift into low, creep down a steep bank and abruptly grind up again, hoping the trailer hitch didn't catch on the bottom. No wonder they had advised against bringing a passenger car. We were glad we hadn't. More ruts, dips, holes, many sharp drops into the inky blackness, then groan up the other side. How much longer? Must be nearly midnight. No, it's only 8 p.m., only five more miles to go, but at the end of five, no Mission lights in sight. On another five and another. Finally a village near the road, "Please, where is the Chikombedzi Mission Hospital?" "Just down the road, I'll show you." With sighs of relief we rolled to a stop behind Embree's house. They hadn't heard us. Good. We stole up to a window and shouted, "Surprise!" "No! Not the Klines! We don't believe it! Not really! We had given you up." Gratefully we sat down to a picnic supper - complete with potato chips! Potato chips in the middle of the African bush! Who would believe it? Crisp and fresh, too! How good to be here. It felt just like home. Amazing! But we belong here. Our long journey was ended. This was where God wanted us.

Our days at Chikombedzi Mission have been happy ones. Full of work for Phil. Long hard days of laying blocks, keeping the African workers at their jobs, pouring cement, fighting the frustration of hard to get supplies because of the isolation, trying to keep the vehicles, light plant, and pump in working order. They are all old and need to be replaced. It is fun living in the middle of a zoo, with elephants only five miles from the Mission and lions ten miles. One usually sees impala and sometimes zebra and giraffe on trips out. Quite exciting, especially when elephants come crashing at you through the bush. Life anywhere else will seem dull by comparison! How can we even begin to describe life at Chikombedzi Mission? And Embrees told us many years later, that the *Zimbabwe* government had turned much of the area around Chikombedzi Mission into a Game Reserve, and had improved the roads!

Everything was brown and dry when we first arrived. But finally the rains came, and with them came an overnight transformation. New leaves on the bush, first gold, then red, then green. The bare ground was suddenly covered with green grass. Yes, the rains have come, but not enough. Already the grass is dry. Hot day follows hot day, with only the occasional cooling of a sudden rain. Many fields are brown and dry. There will be no harvest this year. Again there will be hunger. With the rains also came big, green caterpillars, an African delicacy when roasted! Swarms of huge flying ants, really termites, which taste just like popcorn, when fried and salted! Enormous beetles, even dung beetles, scorpions and snakes, but very few mosquitoes! Amazing! Malaria is gradually being stamped out even here in the low bush country. Fruit is hard to get, eggs are scarce, but there is a lovely vegetable garden, what is left of it when the insects get through! If we were to write a book, we would call it, 'Africa, Land of the Creepy Crawlies'. A lizard just caught a moth on the window screen. That was a crunchy mouthful! The light plant rumbles on. How nice to have electric lights at night, even though they don't stay on all night! Our children are healthier here than anywhere else we have been in Africa. They are even getting a little fat! We know that the Lord is answering your prayers for us. We are finding unequaled joy in knowing we are in the Lord's will. We do not know what the future holds for us. We expect to return to the States this spring, possibly in May. However, we are determined to follow God's plan for us, whatever, wherever, and whenever. We have learned that the only place of real happiness is in the center of God's will. We wouldn't want to live any other way.

Please remember to pray: (We are sure these requests are up-to-date, even today.)

1. For the African preachers, that they may be able to consistently live, and teach the Spirit filled life.
2. For more young African men to answer God's call to the ministry.
3. For the ones in training in our Bible schools, that each will realize the importance of living lives completely surrendered to God's will.
4. For the African church, that it may grow in grace, and be able to resist the temptations coming with the turmoil which is engulfing Africa.
5. For each of the missionaries by name, and for us.
   Yours Victoriously, Phil and Mary Kline

September 10, 1960, Chikombedzi Mission, Southern Rhodesia, Dear Family, Yes, we are here at last, and we really feel 'at home!' But if you are in God's will, you feel that way wherever He leads you! We do like it here very much. On our way in here, fifty miles of narrow, rutty, dusty, dippy, terrible roads in the dark! You should have been with us. Spooky! We sang nearly all the way in to keep our courage up. We nearly had to creep with our heavy load. Anyway, we saw a herd of zebra, several impala, and a giraffe right in the road! And farther down this road, if you can call it a road, toward where Housers are at Dumisa Mission, there are elephants that chase cars, and lions! I don't know if I'm brave enough to go down that way or not! Phil and Dr. Embree and their sons went on a fishing trip down that way this afternoon. They will undoubtedly be full of exciting stories when they get back. They should be back any time now. Yes, here they come. Hope they caught some fish! Both men needed to relax and have some man fellowship and also to spend some time with their sons. These men push themselves so hard that they wear themselves out before they get old! We are sleeping in the empty half of the single ladies house until our little cottage gets ready. The house is getting painted for us. We are waiting until the hole gets dug for our out-house before we move in. We'll continue to use one of these rooms for a school room. The first project Phil has started on is fixing up Embree's bathroom, so Dr. Paul Embree won't have to squeeze anymore into their little wash-tub to take his bath! They have a real bathtub and stool and are getting a wash basin, so they really feel luxurious after all these years of wash tubs, wash pans, bucket showers and chemical toilets!

Well, the fishermen have returned with no fish. But full of stories! They saw tiger fish, but couldn't catch them, a crocodile, a big herd of elephants that ran away, kudu, impala and nyala - different kinds of gazelles, and zebra. They spent one hour fishing, the rest of the time getting there and coming home. They took the Land Rover and the gears stuck. The trip would have been impossible without the four wheel drive. But they enjoyed themselves!

We had sauerkraut and weiners for dinner and impala steak last night. Yum! Two geology students from Leeds University, England ate dinner with us today. They come and make geological surveys and maps of this 'unexplored' country while working on their doctorate degrees. They will be around for several days. Last night Esther and I went chasing down another bumpy road to bring in a patient who was having a miscarriage. Esther is the 'ambulance' driver. The 'ambulance' is a pick-up. We saw a steinbuck (small gazelle) and rabbits. *Shangaan* is one of the languages here, and, in some ways is quite similar to *Zulu*. They whistle instead of 'clicking', some of which sounds like pulling a cork out of a bottle. Esther and Paul are so nice. Dr. Paul and I were at Seattle Pacific at the same time, and Esther's mother was in daddy's class at Los Angeles Seminary! Esther was at S.P.C. the same time as

Sue. We have a lot in common. We both like to write, so we have lots to talk about. The kids seem happy. Honestly, I can't get over how much this seems like home. Isn't the Lord good?

Just returned from Sunday evening missionary fellowship at Embree's. We sang ourselves hoarse. Embrees have a piano! Our packages were here waiting for us. Were we ever surprised when we opened them! Just like Christmas! Everything fits perfectly. I had wished for enough money to buy more pants for the kids and T-shirts for Joe and stockings for me! But the Lord knew we needed them and He supplied our needs again. The girls' dresses are so cute and fit nicely. That was something they desperately needed. They are growing like weeds! My dress is an exact fit! Words can't express our appreciation and love for you. Davey Joe is so cute. Every time he puts on a pair of his new shorts, he says, "Grandma Nana gave me these." And is he ever proud of his little angel shirt! Just what he is, too! All the kids are continuing to adjust remarkably well. Only Davey Joe shows signs of feeling a little insecure. Even Phil is relaxed and happy in his work. There is nothing more wonderful than to know you are in God's will. Perfect weather so far, coolish and a few drizzles. Embrees have a wonderful garden. Esther says that Dr. Paul is beginning to feel release from the terrific strain he was under, trying to keep up with everything. Thanks again for the packages.

September 20, 1960, We are finally nearly settled in our new cozy little house. Our bedroom looks like a cabin on a ship. Just room to walk between our beds. Phil made us a nice headboard and shelves for our clothes, so we are getting along nicely without all the furniture we left in South Africa. The Lord is still marvelously supplying all our needs. There was an old kerosene three burner stove here that had been left by Dr. Naomi Pettingill. I had been planning on using it, but Gwen Houser, bless her, brought me her nice new propane gas stove! Gwen says she is gone most of the time and likes to use her wood stove anyway. But I know she is making a real sacrifice to make life easier for us here. Her new stove, a small two burner with a nice oven was her pride and joy, especially during the hot season. But I am so thankful to have it.

This kitchen gets roasting anyway and kerosene fumes might be the straw that broke the camel's back. Anyway the Lord knows. His Grace has been sufficient for us for everything so far and we are all very happy.

The kids are continuing to adjust well, much to our surprise, with only a few complaints. Our Paul doesn't like powdered milk. All the cows are dry this time of year here, and Paul wishes he could go to public school, but those are only minor problems. We have lots of vegetables from the garden and an abundant supply of beef at twenty cents per pound. People bring us eggs for two cents each. Bananas are two cents each instead of one cent like they were in South Africa, and not so plentiful, but the bus brings our mail to our doorstep twice a week! Our outside toilet will soon be ready and they are beginning work on an additional room for this house. That will mean a lot. All four kids are squeezed into a tiny room now, but it is wonderful to be finally in a house we can call ours. We do feel more at home and relaxed than we have anywhere else in Africa. This is a cute little place, and it is fun to fix it up. I only have three drums left to unpack and curtains to hang and covers to make for shelves. The kids think our tin wash tub makes a nice bath tub. The Embree kids are crazy about their flush toilet. They fight over who gets to flush it! The kids are really enjoying popsicles. Thanks again.

October 4, 1960, The bus will take the post out again day after tomorrow. I can't tell you how good it seems to know we won't be moving again very soon. There is nothing I dislike more than moving, and that is about all we have done lately, but we are here and we feel just as though we have always been here. We just belong! I thought you might be interested in hearing about last Sunday. Phil was very tired so we had decided we hadn't better go to the District Quarterly Meeting at *Chompani*. Gwen and Tillman Houser had been there for the weekend, camping out as usual. He is in charge of the District work, and holds church business meetings, inspects schools, does the work of a conference superintendent and is superintendent of the Mission besides. They are great people. They were also at Seattle Pacific the same time I was. Embrees were going and planned to eat Sunday dinner with Housers after District Quarterly Meeting, (D.Q.M.). Early Sunday morning Esther came over and said that Dr. Paul had to go to bring in a critically injured man. He had been a Christian, but had gone back into sin. He was drunk Saturday night and was on the back of a truck. He went near the edge to urinate over the back, a very common practice among the Africans, and fell off. He had internal injuries, a broken leg and ribs. Then another patient was brought in with a broken shoulder, and a woman had a premature baby. So Dr. Paul was swamped with work and couldn't go to D.Q.M., but there were two carloads of church members wanting to go, so we decided at the last minute to go and take a load. They crowded in like sardines in the back of the Chevrolet Suburban. We quickly grabbed some cans off the shelf and a couple sacks of potato chips and off we went in a cloud of dust.

Of course we were late, but the preaching service hadn't begun. The church was crowded. We sat in the back row with Gwen Houser. She had brought along a couple of folding chairs, for which we were thankful. The benches were backless, as usual, but these were of very rough slabs, twisted and rickety and too narrow for comfort. After about an hour your tailbone felt as if it were going to break. The floors were freshly smeared with cow dung. It makes a nice clean, rather fragrant floor finish! And most of the pews were built up of dried mud, very narrow, and also plastered with cow dung! The church had fallen down, and they hadn't gotten around to building a new one yet, so the service was being held in one of the school buildings with a blackboard across the front, with Monday's lessons all written on it. No desks, the students hold their slates on their laps.

The service was good. We could understand a little of the *Shangaan*, but none of the *Chikaranga*. There are three language groups in this area and only the *Cindebele* people can understand our *Zulu*. The African preacher preaches in one language, and after he is finished, another one gets up and summarizes the sermon in the other language. When they sing, they alternate between the two languages. Gets rather confusing. The work in this area was begun by Rev. Ralph and Mrs. Jacobs among *Shangaan* people, who had not heard the Gospel before 1938. The other two groups of Africans have since been moved in. Prior to that time the government would not permit Europeans to live in this southeast corner of the country. There was so much malaria, it was considered a death trap for the white man, but the Jacobses came, survived on quinine and then came the Housers and Dr. Pettingill, then the Embrees and several nurses, and now all of us. The Mission work here is still in the early stages, compared with South Africa. The people are very responsive, but very few of them can read and write. Before the missionaries came, there were no schools for Africans.

We had a lovely day. It was fun for a change, almost like a picnic, but it would take a lot of consecration to 'camp out' like the Housers have done for years, the majority of the time. They get home to Dumisa Mission about every other weekend just long enough to unpack, wash their clothes and pack up again for another week or two of 'trek'. They sleep on the floor of their Volkswagen on squishy air mattresses. Till's feet stick out the door. No protection from the mosquitoes or the cold night air, and the nights get terribly cold. They cook on an open camp fire and set up their camping equipment in a school building. A big box serves the purpose of kitchen built-ins. They have a clever little folding camp table with four seats and two nice folding chairs. Gwen says the hardest part is doing without their nice beds. They are back here at Chikombedzi Mission tonight.

We are chased by elephants!

October 9, 1960, Sunday night. It's late and everyone is asleep but it's too hot for me to go to sleep, so I'll write to you by kerosene lamp light. It was 104 in the shade at noon today, and there has been a hot north wind blowing steadily all day. They say it doesn't get much worse than today, and usually the nights are cool. The wind is from the south now and feels cooler. We went on a picnic Friday afternoon. Phil and Dr. Paul wanted to go fishing way down the Nuanetsi River where the Tiger fish are, so we all decided to take a picnic supper and go along. We had turned off the main road, which is just a narrow dirt strip, and were whizzing along through the bush, with hardly a trail to follow. An African boy, Scotch, had come along to point the way. Suddenly Dr. Paul stopped the Land Rover. "What is it?" "**Shhh! Elephants**! A whole family! Aren't the babies cute?" They were eating and going off through the trees. Maybe it was safe for us to start, and so we started slowly down the track. Suddenly the enormous leader wheeled around, huge ears flapping, trunk raised and charged straight at us. We were petrified! "Hurry, faster, faster! Oh Lord, make him stop. Protect us! Faster! Oh Lord, keep the Land Rover going. He's getting nearer!" Scotch was wildly pointing the way through the solid wall of bush. We careened, twisted around this bush, over that one, around those trees, down a gully, and slowed down going up the other side. "Oh, hurry, hurry, they are still crashing after us!" And on through the bush we plunged at break neck speed. We were white with fear, shaking violently. The kids buried their faces and sobbed. Would this nightmare never end? Would they chase us clear to the river, would we meet more? Finally we couldn't see them anymore and we slowed down to a safer speed. We hoped they weren't coming.

We arrived at the river and watched a huge troop of baboons on the rocks. Paul Embree caught a Tiger fish! It was fantastic. Every time you threw in your line a small fish grabbed it. I was still too scared to relax. Everywhere there were elephant tracks and elephant droppings. What if they came now to drink? Where would we go? What would happen to us? Night came. We reluctantly stopped fishing, built a fire and got out our food. We roasted weiners and even had potato chips, but I could hardly force myself to eat. I dreaded the trip home. All the way up the trail, we smelled fresh elephant dung, but saw no elephants and finally reached home safely. Thank the Lord! I don't want to go there again! Embrees have been there many times. But we still love it here, and are happy.

October 10, 1960, The climate will be mostly hot from now until we leave. Cotton is the most comfortable. There is hardly a breeze tonight. Today was just as hot as yesterday. Poor little Patsy went into the kitchen to get a drink and almost stepped on a huge rain spider. They aren't poisonous, but she was frantic. Then when she was almost asleep, one got on her bed, and she says she dreams about elephants! She is in bed with Phil now. The kids have so much fun with the Embree kids. Patsy and Ruthie are just six months apart. Nancy and Martha are practically twins, and Paul is about nine months older than David. We are all very happy here. (And who would have imagined then, that in 1979 our Patricia would become the wife of David Embree! They accused Dr. Lamson of being a match-maker, since he is the one who sent us there. No, it was the Lord!)

The Chikombedzi Kids
Paul Kline, David Embree, Nancy Kline, Martha
and Ruth Embree, Patsy and David Kline

At last, a good wind has come, really feels good. Well, I have to type an article for the Missionary Tidings tonight before the mail leaves on the bus. Lots of love to everyone. Keep praying for us. We are still in good health. The mosquitoes haven't come yet. I hope the kids don't get malaria, but I've committed that to the Lord, so I don't worry about it. Esther has a lovely piano and I am trying to teach Paul and Nancy a little. David Embree can play quite nicely.

October 26, 1960, Dear Family, The men have gone on another fishing trip. They drive themselves so unmercifully that if they don't take off an afternoon once a week they would be more exhausted. Hope they didn't see any elephants! Last week they took their sons along and saw elephants while they were walking. Our Paul was so scared he felt sick all the next day! Normally, though, elephants are afraid of people, and run away if they catch your scent. They don't like cars because too many people have shot them from cars, over the border in Portuguese East Africa, (now it is called Mozambique), so sometimes they attack cars. The kids are all in bed, supposedly trying to go to sleep. Today has been very hot. Dr. Embree thinks a real rain is coming. The rains don't really begin until December. Everything will be green then. So dead and dry now, except a few trees are getting green leaves. Phil has been busy this week. He overhauled the truck and got it running, and took the cement mixer apart and got it fixed up. He has one crew making cement blocks down by the day school. The government will pay for a big new school building if it is done this year, so they are crowding it into the building schedule. Tillman Houser is in charge of all the African schools around. There aren't any other missions for a hundred miles! The enormous spaces here! It's just unbelievable how far we are from anywhere and how long it takes to go even a few miles, the roads are so terrible.

I went with Esther to get a woman who had been gored by a bull, only about twenty five miles away, but it took us two hours to get there! Huge stones in the road. I learned how to drive a Land Rover on that trip. The steering wheel nearly jerks your arms off. They need a new one badly. Any other vehicle just wouldn't go where they have to go. I took the church people out calling last Sunday afternoon. It was blazingly hot, but they didn't let that stop their zeal. We visited about six villages. One was very large, all one family. The man probably has several wives! So the big crowd of children we gathered together for a children's meeting while they had the other meeting, were all brothers and sisters! Each wife has a separate hut and woven storage bins built up off the ground. This enterprising family even had a truck, but it looked as though it hadn't been running for quite a while! The Africans in this area seem very friendly and not a bit anti-white.

The kids are having a wonderful time playing with the Capp kids. Kenny Capp, David Embree, Paul and Nancy each have a bike, so they go racing around. The little girls all mother Joe and pretend he is their baby! It is so nice to have kids close for them to play with. The men should be getting back soon, that is, if they ever do! Phil was rather apprehensive about going back where the elephants come to drink.

I just got through cleaning seven small fish. Not even one strike from a Tiger fish. But they came home with a story as usual! They had fished until nearly dark. They had seen elephants up the river a ways and had gotten near a high rock in case the elephants came their way. Dr. Paul and Phil Capp went closer to the elephants, lying on their stomachs on the rocks to watch them. There were about thirty or forty, quite a few young ones. When the elephants started coming their way, they ran and just managed to get to the big rock. The men were only about ten feet above the elephants. The elephants just stood and stared at them, but couldn't figure out what those small creatures were up there! They couldn't get their scent. I don't know who was the most curious, the men or the elephants. Finally the elephants went away, so the men could get down and come home. While they were eating their supper near the car, they could hear the elephants' stomachs rumbling down by the river! Shiver!

November 2, 1960, It is nice and cool this morning, but will probably get hot later. Still no rain. The country around Chikombedzi Mission is simply parched. I am so sleepy I can hardly keep awake today. We didn't get home until two this morning. Yesterday morning very early, a woman had a premature baby, just three pounds, twelve ounces. So they decided they would have to take it to the Morgenster Hospital where there would be sufficient staff to care for such babies. That is about 150 miles from here, on the way to Fort Victoria. Dr. Paul was at Lundi Mission for clinic. Gwen and Tillman were there also, en route to Fort Victoria, so they decided Esther should take the baby and its mother to Lundi Mission so Housers could take them on to Morgenster the next day. Esther didn't want to go all that way alone, about 90 miles, so she asked me to go with her. That sounded great to me, because I hadn't gotten to see Lundi Mission yet. We took Patsy, Joe and Ruth along and left the rest of the kids with Carmena Capp and my Phil.

Lundi Mission is a beautiful place. It is near the Lundi River, and hippos come up onto the Mission grounds at night, to eat the green grass. Lundi Mission looks like a park with big trees. The buildings are nice, especially the new school building and Capp's new house. The views all around Lundi Mission are majestic, *kopjies* (strange rock formation, small hills), made up entirely of huge boulders jutting up sharply, and dotted with flat topped acacia trees. Fits exactly my mental image of Africa. What a contrast to the area near Chikombedzi Mission! When we arrived at Lundi Mission, Ruth Morris took charge of the preemie. She had just gotten back from a vacation, which was spent studying *Chikaranga*, another language used around here. Nina is the nurse at Lundi Mission, but she is sick.

Car trouble in the middle of the night

Dr. Paul had Nina come back to Chikombedzi Mission to see if he could help her. Ruth Morris didn't feel she should leave the baby with Nina, so she decided to stay overnight and come back the next day, bringing Nina. We had had a little trouble with the Chevrolet pick-up so we left the Land Rover for her to drive. We left Lundi Mission about 9:00, pulling a heavily loaded trailer with three fuel drums. I bedded my kids down in the back and sat with them. Ruthie slept between Esther and Paul in the cab. After we had turned off the main highway which is only tarred in parallel strips, and on to the bumpy dirt road, we began to have trouble with the engine. It coughed and had no power, and then 45 miles from home it stopped running. Dr. Paul climbed out and wearily investigated the engine. He cleaned the spark plugs, checked the fuel pump. It wasn't acting right. Well, it was **empty**! Could we be out of gas? But there had been more than enough to get us back to Chikombedzi Mission. It must be using extra gas because it wasn't running right. We had a drum full of gas on the trailer, but no can and no hose. We emptied a water jar, and Paul cut a hose from somewhere. He opened the air hole on the drum and began to siphon out gas. Esther held the torch, (flashlight), I held the jar, and Dr. Paul operated the siphon. The kids didn't wake up. We could hear all sorts of animal noises in the night. Zebras were braying over by the Nuanetzi River, and about a mile away baboons were calling. We shivered because we knew that there were many lions and leopards all over that area, but we didn't hear any. Esther told us a grisly story about some policeman who just recently fought barehanded with a big leopard close to where we were! Finally Paul succeeded in starting the engine. We piled in, and jolted on. We went about a mile, and then we heard something dragging under the trailer. Dr. Paul stopped the pick-up. The tie rod was broken. He fastened it with wire and on we went. Five more miles, the wire broke and we stopped again. Again we could hear zebra and baboons. This time he tried twisting the four wires a different way. Thinking that should hold, we went on more slowly. We crept on over the ruts and rocks and dips. It got later and later. The road was monotonous and unending. Dr. Paul couldn't hold his eyes open, neither could Esther. I was wide awake, so I drove the remaining fifteen miles to Chikombedzi Mission. We arrived at 2:00 a.m. What a night that was! So I'm sleepy today. How good to be home again. Transportation is always a problem here. The Land Rover also broke down on the way home. The gears came loose, or something. Phil got them both running again. We are still marveling at the sweet peace and inner joy that wells up when we think about how God led us here. What a privilege to be here.

An adventure in the night

November 8, 1960, We don't know for sure when we will be coming home. However, we are hoping we can leave sometime in April. According to our tentative plans, we will probably fly, arriving in New York, go through the medical office, then on to Chicago and Winona Lake to see Phil's mother and his sister, Betty. We plan to visit with family in Kansas and then on to California in August. When we get to California, I want to stay there. Phil has said we could probably put the kids in school in Hermon, at my old school. That is what I have always dreamed of. We don't know if we will be returning to Africa. It all depends on Phil's legs. The need is so desperate here that many people would be disappointed if we didn't return.

We spent a night out on a cliff above the river. It was exciting! We took sleeping bags and a picnic supper. Just after we finished eating, a hippo came out of the pool below us, about 300 yards below and up-river from us. The cliff was about 100 feet above the river. There were several pools within sight. Hippos make the most awful noise. They come out of the water in the evening to eat grass and leaves. Then some Cape buffalo came. The moon wasn't up very high, so they were difficult to distinguish, but we could hear them drinking and hear their hooves on the rocks. After the buffalo left, we heard a leopard chanting his hunting grunt, but he wasn't close. Then we heard elephants trumpeting up river about two miles. We kept hoping they would come near enough so we could see them. We slept awhile, and then woke up with a start when the African guide said, "Elephants are coming." There they came, single file down across the sand, thirteen of them, some huge ones, and one baby. The moon was high and everything was nearly as light as day. Dr. Paul had his binoculars along, which brought them up close. They splashed into a pool, and churned up the water with their trunks. They were side by side, with their trunks all the same way. They drank for about half an hour, and started to leave. Three big elephants, that were probably the guards for the herd, crossed over to the opposite side of the river, almost directly across from us. They ate a few leaves, stood around a bit, and then all of a sudden took off back toward the rest of the herd. Immediately they all quickly took their positions in single file and padded off silently into the night, and they were gone. Probably they had gotten our scent.

We didn't see more animals that night. The hippos kept bellowing often, and then we could hear many birds. Tiger fish made splashing sounds in the pools beneath us, and we could hear way off in the distance a lion grunting as he hunted. We hoped he didn't come any closer, but we weren't afraid and slept until morning. The morning was beautiful, clear, cool, full of bird calls and baboons noisily roaring in the rocks and trees. Coming home in the morning, we saw kudu, impala, water buck and some small gazelles. The magic spell of that night in wildest Africa lingered a long while. I would love to sleep out there again. Phil stayed home to take care of the kids. I had gone with Nina, Ginny, Dr. Paul and a couple Africans.

The verandah of our little house is finally screened in. That is a big improvement and it gives us so much more privacy as well as protection from the flies and mosquitoes. We are using our new privy. Phil even rigged up a flush system for it, with holes drilled in the bottom of a hose. You turn on the water, and it flushes, using only what water you need. Phil built us a box seat. It means so much not to have to walk half a block to use the toilet! We have a big wash tub for a bath tub. Phil put a drain in one end near the bottom, so you don't have to tip it up to empty it. Don't I have a clever husband? They are pouring the foundation for the school building today. It will be very nice. Nina just came and asked me to go out with her to bring in a woman who is having twins, but the second one won't come. It is only three miles, so maybe I can get back in time to have dinner on the table for my hubby. Well, I didn't go because the trip turned out to be **thirty** miles instead of three! Mo went instead, but when they got there the woman had just died. They suspected that the old woman in the village had done something, because they wouldn't let Mo and Nina see the bodies. One twin survived. Poor people.

Fishing on the Lundi River

Tillman, Phil Capp, Nina, Dr. Paul, Esther, and my Phil have all gone on a long-dreamed of fishing expedition. This will probably be the last fishing trip this season, because the rains are coming. The sky is heavy this morning and it feels like rain. I hope they get back home before things get too wet. They took the Land Rover just in case they get caught by the rain. They went to some pools on the Lundi River where the fishing is fabulous, and there are many wild animals. The last time some people camped there, Cape buffalo came during the night, went on both sides of their tents, many of them, and the people didn't hear a sound! They just found their footprints the next morning. So they will undoubtedly have some exciting stories to tell when they get back. Embrees have wanted to go there for years. Esther needed to get away. She does so much entertaining and is forever answering the door.

I really almost feel guilty, but after six years of never-ending, day-in and day-out pressure, I am really enjoying not being the wife of the missionary-in-charge! The only people who come to my door are kids with eggs to sell. They got the foundation laid on the school building. The workers are filling it in while Phil is gone. They will pour the floor on Monday and start up with the walls. Gwen is kid-sitting with the Embree kids. She brought me a sack full of succulents for my new rock garden. Grass is too difficult to grow here, so we plant cactus to have something green around the houses. I have over a hundred little papaya trees starting to grow. I plan to plant them all over the mission station, everywhere people throw their waste water, so all the people who live on the mission will have papaya to eat. Fruit is so scarce that most of the Africans never get any to eat. Water is a problem. They carry buckets of water for at least a mile unless they live near a bore-hole well. The government has put down bore-holes every six miles, or people wouldn't be able to live here at all. They are experimenting now with an irrigation project that should help to raise the standard of living for the people. Part of the year there is a lot of water in the rivers, but the rest of the year they look just like Southern California rivers, nearly dry, except where big rocks keep the water in pools.

November 14, 1960, The electric plant just went off so I can't sew anymore, so I will try typing for a while. Phil has gone to Lundi Mission with Dr. Paul. Phil will go on to Fort Victoria tomorrow to do shopping. Wish I could go, but Esther is too tired for me to even think of asking her to take care of my kids while I go. The rains have come, and what a change!

Overnight, there is green grass and lots of beautiful red amaryllis flowers. Before the rain came there was just the bare ground. Now there are lots of green leaves on the trees and bushes. The sudden transformation is unbelievable. We have had several good rains, stormy again tonight, but not much rain. The Africans in this area with cars have discovered that Phil is a good mechanic. They are all bringing their vehicles for him to fix. Takes time, but creates good will, and may win some to the Lord. There isn't a garage or service station within one hundred miles of here! The isolation of this place is absolutely unbelievable until you are here and see it for yourself. I hope we come back after our furlough. This Thursday we are all going to meet out at the police camp, forty miles from here. It is halfway to Lundi Mission. This will be the first time all the Rhodesia missionaries have been together since we have been here. There is a swimming pool at the camp, so we will all go swimming on Thanksgiving Day! Hope it is a good hot day and not rainy. We were all set to go to Beira with the Embrees for a month at the beach, but then we discovered that the only rooms available would cost us $12 per day. So, unless Phil Capp finds something a lot cheaper than that for us, we will stay home. He is going to telephone from Lundi Mission for us. We don't have a regular phone here, only a radio/phone for communication between the Mission stations. They talk every morning at 6:00 a.m. I have to have breakfast on the table by 5:30 every morning except Saturday and Sunday because Phil starts work at 6:00 and he has prayers with the workers before that. We still can't make up our minds whether to fly home or go by boat.

We go on vacation with the Embrees to Beira

December 2, 1960, We are on holiday at Beira Beach, Portuguese East Africa, beside the Indian Ocean. Wish you could be here with us. We came with Embrees in Capp's Volkswagen Kombi, all eleven of us! On the way here we stopped on the road in the middle of dense bush country for a 'pot stop'. I went behind a bush to do my business, got back in the Kombi, and yelled, "Let me out! I've got pincher **ants**!" I had gotten too close to a trail of termites, without having seen them, and they were vicious! I finally got rid of all of them, and we were on our way. We have an eight-bunk 'chalet', actually a small cabin, with a partition down the middle. Our Paul and David Embree sleep in the Kombi. Our family sleeps on bunk beds on one side, and the Embree family sleeps on the other side. It is too expensive to rent a whole cabin for each family. We are having a marvelous time. Early this morning at 2:45, Dr. Paul and Phil took off for a fishing trip up the coast about twenty miles. It is supposed to be a fisherman's paradise! Talk about wild country! They'll have to get an African to row them across an estuary in a dugout canoe to get to the beach. The bush and banyan tree growth is matted into an impenetrable barrier. We went with them yesterday, hoping to see the beach there, but we couldn't even get close enough to see the surf. The tide was coming in, blocking the only trail cut through to the beach. The men will sleep in the Kombi tonight and walk up the beach an hour in the morning to the mouth of another river, where they catch the big fish. You should see this beach. It is unbelievably perfect with mile after mile of wide, clean, flat white sand, just gradually sloping, so that at low tide you can walk out in the small surf for a long way. The waves are small and gentle. No undertow or riptide, just idyllic. The kids are all brown. I'm the only burned one. We rigged up a tarp for shade and only let the kids in the sun in the early morning and late afternoon. They are having a wonderful time digging in the sand. You never saw such white sand, maybe of coral origin? Needless to say, we are relaxing completely. We may stay here two more weeks. We have been here one week already. Just depends on how our money holds out! Food is quite expensive except for fruit, which is cheap and yummy! Pineapple, papayas, bananas, oranges, mangoes, and cashew fruit.

We came through Fort Victoria and Umtali to get here. Beautiful country with mountains. Lots of big mahogany trees, jungle, blue butterflies, water lilies, and lots of mosquitoes! The kids are all asleep. Esther is reading. The moon is full, the tide is low. The beach is gorgeous. Long, low, white breakers, shallow water running slowly back to the ocean, crabs, clams, snails, small fish. A strong wind tonight with blobs of clouds. Hope it doesn't rain before the men get back. You never saw such a terrible road. Makes the roads near Chikombedzi Mission seem like highways! You creep over the bumps one wheel at a time, creaky bridges made of poles, sand, and swamps! But Phil would go anywhere to fish. Took us more than two hours to go twenty-four miles. They should get back sometime tomorrow night if it doesn't rain. Lots of ships in the harbour, bright colored houses and buildings, modern architecture, hot, hot sun. Chinese shops and restaurants. Open air fish market, fruit market in a square with small shops all around the edges.

Plazas everywhere, sidewalk cafes and very few people know English. But we manage to make ourselves understood.

December 8, The men are doing the dishes. Terrific tropical storm last night. Roof leaked! We are still having a wonderful time. We plan to go back to Chikombedzi Mission next week on the 19th. School is out so more people are coming now. There are 200 units here, so probably the place will be crowded. But we have found a secluded beach, protected by sand bars so it is just like a huge swimming pool. We are teaching our kids how to swim. The water is so warm, almost like a bathtub, but you don't dare go barefoot on the dry sand, because the sand is scorching hot! We have to walk thirty minutes to get there after the road ends, but it is worth it.

December 11, We are still in Beira, being lazy on the beach under our big tarp. We have another week before we start back. How lovely to really relax! We've been feasting on fish and fruit, both hard to get or unobtainable at Chikombedzi Mission. We had our own church this morning, nothing but Catholic churches here. We will go out to dinner, maybe to a Chinese restaurant downtown, and then out about ten miles to a small rain forest where the vines and bush and trees are impenetrable. Several roads have been cut through so we'll go exploring. Cool there. Hot today. We went out again yesterday to our lagoon. We took inner tubes and the kids had a marvelous time. We played 'train'. I was the engine, floating on my inner tube. The first kid held onto my toes and I pulled all seven of them, each on his own inner tube! They are all making good progress learning to swim and float. We saw a ship that was probably on its way to Bombay from Durban with many Indians on board. Port cities are fascinating with so many different kinds of people. (Monday) Rained last night, cool this morning. The rain forest was wonderful. There were vividly colored butterflies, cool, dark, damp, mossy, ferns, tall, tall trees hung with vines and creepers. When we get back to Chikombedzi, I'm going to start mailing stuff home. It is so hard to pack, not knowing if we'll ever return. But whatever the Lord's will is, that's what we want. Merry Christmas to all!

December 22, 1960, (Back at Chikombedzi Mission) Well, we are home safely once more. Good to be here, but the heat is rather hard to take after basking in the sea breezes for three weeks. However, it rained a few minutes tonight, so the air is cooler and a small breeze is stirring. We had a wonderful vacation. We left Beira at 5:00 Monday morning, reached Fort Victoria at 6:00 that evening, stayed in a hotel there that night, shopped all day on Tuesday, slept last night at Lundi Mission, and came on home this morning. We stopped at the Nuanetsi Police Camp for a swim in their pool, very refreshing! But that is two hours from here, so even with the swim, we arrived here hot and grimy. Nancy is very sick, temp, sore mouth, looks like trench mouth. Just about all of us have had tummy aches and diarrhea. Must have been something we ate or drank in Beira! I feel better this evening. I'll start school with the kids tomorrow, finish unpacking, set up the Christmas tree, and try to get settled in again. Sure helps to have a girl who does the dishes! We all have a little more energy than we did before our vacation. Even Phil feels a lot better. (Thursday morning) What a lovely rain we had in the night, so that means that at least three days will be cool before the heat builds up again, thank the Lord. The ground is covered with green now, except around the houses which we keep bare to discourage snakes. While we were gone, my celery seed sprouted, and the little papaya trees are growing. Really is nice to be back home, sleeping in our own beds. They got one unit of the new school building all finished except for the roof while we were gone. The sheets of galvanized iron roofing were so hot during the day that they couldn't put them on the roof. Asbestos is better to use, but it is so hard to get here without breakage. Government plans specify iron. Today won't be so hot, so the roof should go on today. The kids will be wanting breakfast soon. The oatmeal is on the stove, hot. I have a huge wash to do. Nancy doesn't have a temp this morning, so maybe she is on the mend. So much to do today, I hardly know where to start, so I guess I had better get started!

Christmas in the middle of the summer

December 29, 1960, We had a wonderful Christmas. Hope you did too. We had turkey, done just right, dressing, mashed potatoes, red applesauce, pumpkin mashed with butter and sugar, peas, celery, olives, pickles, and we were too full to eat the fruit cake, so we had it for snacks after our carol sing that night. Ginny and Mo ate with all of us at Embrees. Thank you so much for all you sent us for Christmas. We appreciate it all more than we can tell you. The DeMilles were here on Tuesday. Good to see them again.

An African chief was brought into the clinic some time ago with a terribly broken arm. He had been cutting down a tree way off in the forest, and it fell down on him. He walked home a long distance. Someone came to ask for a car to bring him to the clinic, too far for him to walk. So he was here for several weeks. *Mamani* Tema, the African missionary from P.E.A. (now Mozambique), who does evangelistic work in the hospital, spoke with him every day, showing him the way of Salvation. Then just before we left on holiday, he accepted Jesus as his Savior! He is still radiant and is a changed person. It means so much when the chiefs become Christians. Pray for him that his witness will be bright. The General Missions office has asked Esther and me to write a children's skit to be used on Compassion Sunday. We think we may use the story of the African chief. Anyway, neither of us have ever done anything like it, so we hardly know where to start. Hope what we turn out will be worthwhile, and will accomplish its purpose. Must stop and get to work teaching Paul and Nancy. Groan! The best part about coming home will be to get the kids into a real school. Lots of love. Thanks again for all the packages.

January 9, 1961, Another **hot**, sticky evening, not hardly a breath of cool air. Phil is going over some building plans, and our Paul is lying on the cool floor beside him, reading. Some nights we take our bedding outside onto the slab beside our house and just lie there, looking at the stars, and one night, we even saw a satellite slowly moving across the dark expanse and it looked like it was right up there with the stars! It looks now as though there may be more projects to be completed before we leave for home, so we may not get gone from here until June. They are begging Phil to come to Lundi Mission to put up a classroom building before we go home, and Dr. Embree is trying to get a few more plans approved for here.

Please continue to pray that we will do what the Lord wants us to do. Phil's legs still ache a lot. It is exceedingly hard for him to keep going. Phil is hauling cement again today from the railroad at Makambe, fourteen miles from here over dusty, rutty, bumpy roads in a rickety truck. The cement comes from Salisbury. It is an exhausting job to haul it in. We are thankful that now we can get real milk because of the rains and new grass. Of course it is always dirty and must be strained and boiled. We pay five cents a quart. We are so thankful to have milk. A boy brings a big can of it every morning. The hardest part about living here is that so much food is unavailable. We rarely get eggs, and we can only get fruit in town. However, meat is very cheap and is delivered to our door once a week. When Embrees first came to Chikombedzi, the only meat they ate was what Doc Embree brought in when he went hunting. There is a nice garden with plenty of vegetables, and we can buy canned goods in Fort Victoria. Phil went to Lundi Mission last week for a few days to help Phil Capp put in their new water system. They have to filter the water through the sand near the river to remove the Bilharzia parasites. Phil found a huge scorpion with about fifty little babies on its back! How hideous! It was six inches long and six inches from claw tip to claw tip. Body is 1 inch wide. It will go in my collection of creepy crawly things! Paul Embree killed a big Egyptian Cobra in their wood pile yesterday. It had killed five chickens! The other night Dr. Paul was working very late trying to get a fractured leg set, but it just wouldn't go right. While they were still working on him, in came another man, hardly able to breathe with an advanced case of T.B. These poor people wait until they are about dead before they come to the hospital. We got to bed by midnight.

January 16, 1961, Still no rain. The people are getting desperate for rain for their gardens. They have been praying to the spirits for rain, drinking too much beer and making sacrifices to appease the spirits. We went to Malapati Saturday to get corn ground into meal. All of us went along to get a swim in the pool, only 7 miles from here. We had only been in about fifteen minutes when a huge black cloud came swirling over with sheets of rain and blasts of wind, thunder, lightning and hail! When the storm slacked, we jumped in the Land Rover and headed for home, only to find that not a drop had reached Chikombedzi Mission! Our Paul left for Lundi Mission, with Phil this morning, a very happy boy. Phil went to work there to get the school building started. He will be pouring a floor today, and finishing it down too, so that means he will be really tired tonight. This heat is so hard on him. Esther told me a story yesterday about a woman named Setsetyane, who had been given to another man when her husband went to South Africa to work in the mines and didn't return for a long time. When he finally came back and found out about his wife, he was so angry he went to the witch doctor and had a curse put on her. She came back to him. The curse was that when she had a baby, it would die at birth, her second baby would die within a few days of birth, and if she had another, she and that baby would both die. The first two parts of the curse had taken place, and she vowed she would never get pregnant again. When Dr. Naomi Pettingill went home on furlough she asked people to pray for the poor woman. One woman in the States who had prayed much for her was certain that the curse was broken. Shortly after that news reached Chikombedzi Mission, the woman came to the clinic pregnant, and the missionaries assured her that people had prayed for her and that this baby would live and so would she, and that is exactly what happened. But she is still not a Christian.

Esther gets an elephant foot for a wastebasket!

January 28, 1961, We had quite an adventure this morning, with an elephant, but this one was dead! One of the workers came with the news this morning that an elephant had been killed near the road, and would the Embrees please take them so they could get some meat? Embrees like elephant meat too, and they had been wanting to get another elephant foot to make into a waste basket to use when they were on deputation. Esther asked me if I would like to go with her. We took all of the kids in the Land Rover. We took off down the road toward Dumisa Mission. After about five miles we were told to go off the road.

We looked and could see nothing but tire tracks, no more road. So for two miles we zig-zagged through and over the bush, knocking down small trees until we came to some big rocks and the Game Warden's jeep. We parked beside the jeep, and started walking. The people had complained that this elephant had been raiding their gardens, so the Game Ranger had tracked down the elephant and killed him with one shot to his head, a very proud hunter. He was standing there, and had already confiscated the ivory tusks. It had taken us about twenty minutes to walk, scrambling over rocks and bush until we reached the big grey hulk. Men were chopping on the skull with axes. Soon they penetrated the abdominal cavity, it sounded like a jet, and what a stench! Joe cried and said he didn't like it. Every time they punctured the cavity there was another blast of foul air, and a screech just like a tire puncture! The meat was still fresh. Some men were filling large baskets with hunks to take home. There were so many flies, you could hardly see the meat. A small fire was sizzling a few pieces of meat. Someone was too hungry for the meat to wait until they got home! These people get very little meat, and are not allowed to shoot any animals except small game, so this was a big treat for all the people who lived nearby. Esther got her huge foot and a nice slice of back strap to make steaks from. We will let you know later what it tasted like! This elephant had an old injury in his trunk and had survived a previous bullet, so that is why it had become so troublesome, and it was only five miles from Chikombedzi Mission! Please pray that we will all get over this attack of amoebiasis. My tick bite fever is gone. The place where he bit me is almost well.

February 1, 1961, It's the middle of the night, 12:50 to be exact, but I can't sleep, so I might as well be doing something constructive! This drug I'm taking for amoebic dysentery gives you insomnia and you can't sleep except fitfully unless you take sleeping pills! But you can't keep that up every night. So this is my night for staying awake. I'll take some sleeping pills tomorrow night and get a good night's sleep. I'm feeling much better. The dosage is less now, and I have more energy than I've had for months, so it must be killing the amoeba. I'm writing by the light of a flashlight. The wind blew out my kerosene lamp and I'm too lazy to get up and get a match! I'm lying in front of the window on the foot of the bed to get the benefit of every breath of air. Stifling tonight. Phil is still at Lundi Mission. He'll probably come back tomorrow. The rest of us just came back from Lundi Mission today, but Phil stayed over to go to Fort Victoria to do purchasing of building supplies. He will also bring us some fruit.

We had a Missions meeting with Vic Macy yesterday afternoon to make preliminary plans for the African Fellowship Conference which they hope to have in September. We've invited the Conference to be at Lundi Mission, since it is centrally located.

On our way home from Lundi Mission, this morning, Dr. Paul stopped to load the trailer with building supplies. The big delivery lorries won't go on our terrible roads. We got to go swimming in their nice pool while Dr. Paul was loading, and enjoyed the water for two hours! How refreshing after a long hot drive! The sun was so hot I really got sunburned. We started off again for home at three, feeling fresh. We had gone only fifteen miles when **whoosh**, a tire blew out on the trailer, so we all piled out while Dr. Paul searched, but couldn't find anything that would fit the trailer wheel nuts, so he just changed tubes! He didn't have the right size tools. The kids were getting restless, so I took them exploring. We followed a dry stream bed until we found a shady place big enough for them all to sit down and play in the sand without getting covered with ants.

Africa swarms with ants of all sizes and descriptions. They are about to take over our house. (Too bad I didn't know then what I know now. Ants will not cross over a chalk line!) It's an endless struggle to keep them out of food. They even get in the fridge! I'll have to get some more DDT powder from Esther tomorrow. Just before I started writing, I had gone to the kitchen and discovered ants walking away with the milk I had put out to sour to make cottage cheese! So, I sat the pans in the sink in water. Then I found that they had gotten into the new packets of crackers! So I had to open them, brush the ants off each one, and put them in Tupperware. You don't throw food away here. It's too hard to get as well as being expensive. You sift the bugs out of your flour and oats and go ahead and use it. They come from the store with them in. When you open a new sack of flour, you get out an old pair of panty hose, and sift away. You don't throw away buggy flour! It took me a long time to get used to that, but this is Africa!

We finally got the trailer tire fixed and crawled on home. The 120 mile trip took us seven hours counting the stop at Nuanetsi! Were we ever glad to get home. We saw a huge roan antelope today, quite rare, a beautiful animal, and lots of impala with young ones.

Joe is very restless, cries and chokes every night. I'm sure he has roundworms again. They are going to do lab tests on him tomorrow. He had a bad spell tonight. But he finally settled down. Our Paul is just recovering from a very rare and serious eye disease, Iritis. Fortunately Dr. Paul had a new drug that cures it quickly, so there was no damage to his eye and the other one wasn't affected at all. He can get up and play tomorrow. He didn't go to Lundi Mission with us. Ruth Morris had to stay here to run the hospital, so she took care of him too, so I could go to the meeting. She is so sweet. Paul played records and sang most of the time we were gone. I was very proud of him because he was willing to sleep all alone in our house last night. We are so thankful he won't have his sight impaired. It often causes blindness if untreated or undiagnosed. We think Dr. Paul is a wonderful doctor! Now maybe I can sleep a while. Wonderful victory in spite of all of our troubles. Praise the Lord! He is able to keep us rejoicing in the middle of it all!

February 18, 1961, The young people's meeting had just started at Embrees. Esther was playing the piano and we were all singing, when a jeep drove up. A government man had come to ask Dr. Paul to go with him to the scene of a stabbing. One was dead, and one was injured. But Paul and Phil had left that afternoon for Dumisa on mission business, so Ginny said she would go and give first aid before they brought the woman back to the clinic, but she didn't want to go alone with the men. She asked me to go with her. I took Joe with me and left the other kids with Esther. If I had known how long we would be, I wouldn't have taken Joe. We started out about 8:30.

The roads were very rutty with some mud holes, but passable. Finally we left the road and started following a path through the grass. The path got smaller and smaller, and the bush got thicker and thicker. We bounced and bumped, and it seemed endless. It was a dark night with brilliant stars. Joe slept in my arms. Finally after we had driven about 40 miles we came to a clearing and saw a lantern. Several men were carrying a double bed spring frame with a woman on it bundled up in blankets. They had left her in the field where she had been hoeing when she was stabbed, and when they returned after taking the dead woman away, they found this one was still alive. Ginny had to go certify that the other one was really dead, so she did. We proceeded to load the injured woman onto the floor of the jeep. Ginny gave her drugs to help her stand the trip, and we took off again.

The Africans had neglected to tell us a road was close. They had directed us there the way they had walked! The trip home was much shorter and easier, only about 35 miles. We had to go very slowly so that the bumps wouldn't be too much for the injured woman. Finally, about 2 a.m. we arrived back at Chikombedzi Mission. Ginny and Mo fixed her up for the night and gave her tetanus and antibiotics shots. Her injuries didn't look very deep, but when Dr. Paul came back the next day and started to sew her up, he discovered that she had many punctures! He worked on her for about eight hours. He couldn't give her general anesthesia, because there must be two doctors to do that, so he filled her full of pain killing drugs, and hoped she couldn't feel it too much. She finally went to sleep. Paul was drenched with sweat, and so was she. We all felt so sorry for Paul having to work under conditions like that. He is really a good surgeon, and you can imagine the frustrations of having to put up with such inadequate facilities. He finally got her all stitched up, and everyone marveled that she was still alive. The police came today and told us that the man who stabbed her was her husband. Several years ago he had killed his father and a son, but they had never locked him up! He must be a mental case.

Travel plans

March 8, 1961, At long last I can write you something definite about our coming home! It still doesn't seem real, but I guess it must be. We went to Fort Victoria yesterday to get our yellow fever shots which are required before we fly to the States, since Central Africa is yellow fever country. While we were there we went in to see the travel agent. We decided to go to the missionary fellowship in Pretoria, South Africa. All the Free Methodist missionaries from South Africa, Mozambique, and Southern Rhodesia meet together every other year. We had forgotten that this is the year, and so hadn't planned on going, but when we started thinking about it, it seemed too good to pass up, so that is what we want to do.

After the meeting is over we will leave Johannesburg by plane. It is only thirty miles from Pretoria. The conference ends on Sunday and we will fly on Wednesday, May 5. The price is the same as if we were leaving from Salisbury, but this way no one will have to make an extra trip to take us to the plane, and best of all, we will get to see the Clydes and the Johnsons once more before we leave! It seems too good to be true. I am just singing inside. Those missionary fellowships are really wonderful. Times of such rare Christian fellowship and spiritual growth. Isn't it all just great? As you can see I have finally let myself get excited. But before, it all seemed so far away and remote. The only thing I feel badly about is that Paul and Esther still don't know for sure when they can leave. We are praying for the Lord's will to be done for them, but it is hard for them, especially since we finally know what we are going to do. We made our reservations, planned our itinerary, and the travel agent is making hotel reservations for us in Europe. We will fly through Salisbury to Nairobi, Kenya, stop one night in Athens, three nights in Rome, two nights in Switzerland, see the Alps, go through Paris, stay three days in London, and arrive in New York on Monday morning, May 15. We will have to stay there several days in order to go through the medical office that clears missionaries, and then on to Winona Lake by train.

After that, we aren't sure, since Phil wants to go to Mayo Clinic to see if they can do anything about his legs. So we still aren't sure when we will get to Los Angeles, but we will get there as soon as possible. Do you think you can find us a house to rent near you for a year anyway? We aren't sure what we will do after that year, but I know the Lord will reveal His plan to us in His time. I am looking forward to putting the kids in school at Hermon, and getting to live near you. That has always been my dream, but I am willing to follow the Lord's plan if He has something different planned for us. Patsy's and Joe's smallpox vaccinations didn't take, so I will have to take them back next week to get it done again, but I don't mind, because then I get to see Phil again. He has about two more weeks yet before he will get the school unit done at Lundi Mission. It was terribly hard to leave him there. We stayed Monday and Tuesday nights at Lundi Mission, and came home this morning, long old trip, but we brought the Capp's Kombi back with us again so the trip wasn't too bad.

We were so happy to receive this letter from Aggie Cele in Bible School in Swaziland. It was sent to us at Chikombedzi Mission. I have copied her letter exactly as she wrote it.

12th March, 1961, Dear *Nkosikazi*, I greet you in the precious name of our Lord. Before I say anything, I say sorry to be so late to reply this letter. Since I came here this year I didn't have time to reply you, for I have been going out to Sunday Schools. I am thankful for I am continuing the work of the Lord. This is the time I have got to reply.

In this week we are praising the Lord of having the great revival meeting by Rev. Mpaphu of Pretoria. We thank the Lord for this opportunity to listen to His Word. I again thank very much with the money you sent to Mrs. Johnson. From that money I bought the rain coat, and I paid for the bus, then the other for pocket money. The greatest thing I thank is Him who saved me being nothing on earth. I ask to pray for me. I like the Lord to do everything with me. I am ready to go anywhere he likes me to go. In my heart I am asking the Lord to really show me where to go at the end of this year. In all I like the Lord to do his will. A long time I have been begging the Lord to show me what to do at the end of the year. I haven't seen it even now. I thank very much to hear about Nancy, Patsy, Joe and Paul that they are growing. I am much happy to hear that you know how to speak the *Shangaan*. Does Mfundisi know how to speak it?

And I too will write to him with *Swazi*. I like to have picture of all children but I would like Nancy to laugh and see her teeth. *Nkosikazi*, you tell *Mfundisi* to write to me when he had learned *Shangaan* very well, I am not troubling *Nkosikazi*, but I remember them too much. I think God is with you there keeping close by him. Like His with me. Pass my regards everyone whom I know not. May God bless you all. Yours in Christ, Aggie (How precious to hear from Aggie.)

March 21, 1961, The kids are all asleep and I am lonesome again. Phil had to go back to Lundi Mission. The trailer is broken and he had to go there to repair it so they could bring back the mixer part of the cement mixer. If they have gotten the well parts, he will finish putting in their sand well. They found out that if you filter the water through sand it takes out the nasty parasites. But you still have to boil it to make it safe to drink. Chikombedzi Mission has a good well, but the water is extremely hard. Never again will we take good water for granted. I have been sewing like mad, letting down hems and taking up hems, and making pajama tops for the girls. We are giving all our old clothes to the families of the evangelists. The churches are unable to support them. Only a month now and we will be on our way. Doesn't seem possible, and I am a long way from being ready to go. Two drums with all our electrical appliances, are being sent from Durban to Los Angeles, but it will probably take them at least two months to arrive. It will be nice to have them to use at home since we can't use them here, not enough power. The kids are getting so excited about going to America. Pray that Mayos will be able to help Phil's legs. He is even taking Codeine during the day now. It is hard to understand why the Lord doesn't heal him permanently.

April 12, 1961, The kids are asleep and so is Phil, so all is quiet. I just about have all my sewing done, except for mending some khaki shorts of Paul's before I give them to *Mamani* Tema for her grandsons. She is doing such a wonderful work among the patients in the hospital. She is always coming with a glowing report of another one who has repented. Since I can't talk directly with any of the people here because I don't know *Shangaan* and they don't know *Zulu* or English, I am trying to help *Mamani* Tema as much as I can with food and clothing. Pray that the Lord will raise up more like her with a real zeal for personal evangelism. We've reached the stage in packing where if we pack anything else, we'll be digging in the drum again for it, so until we quit using our stuff, there is not much more I can do. When I realize there are only two more weeks, I get panicky inside. Wish we could just push a magic button and be home. The thoughts of traveling with all the kids, stopping in so many places in Europe, scares me, but we want to **see**! I think we are crazy! Embrees finally heard that Dr. Kuhn is coming from Ruanda-Urundi to replace them, so they will get to leave in June as they had hoped. They will arrive in California before we do.

We just got word today that Phil has an appointment at Mayo's on May 23. That is just a very few days after we arrive in Winona Lake. The plan is for us to stay with Mom and Betty Kline while Phil is at Mayo's. The Lord is answering prayer in a marvelous way for Phil. In spite of the fact that he is in pain all the time, he has victory now all the time! Praise the Lord! The next two weeks will be hard on him. He is working hard now to get the storage shelves built for Dr. Paul's surgical instruments and medical journals. That will be a big boost to the efficiency of the hospital. He also has a building under construction to house the out-patients and their families who stay with them to cook their food while they are here for treatment. There are only hospital beds for the maternity and TB cases. All the rest sleep in huts, in little branch and grass shelters, or lined up one after the other, rolled up with a blanket over their heads, of course, to keep out insects and animals, on the cement floor of the hospital verandah, and it gets cold some nights. There is a lot of sickness around now, smallpox, diphtheria, measles with complications, malaria. We are so thankful for the extremely good health we have all been enjoying. We know it is in answer to prayer.

You should see Davey Joe eat. I just can't get him filled up, and only a few weeks ago I had to force every mouthful down him. Guess he must have gotten rid of his nasty parasites! Going back to public school in the States will be a big adjustment for Paul. Patsy is starting to learn to read. She knows her alphabet and can count to 100, so she will be more than ready for first grade, even though she hasn't had kindergarten. She is really eager to begin school. I had nightmares last night about losing things on our trip through Europe, but in my dream I decided to make a check list, so at least something good came of it!

April 16, 1961, Everyone is asleep and the light plant is off. I'm writing by the light of a kerosene lamp and it feels as though a million insects are buzzing around. Only one week before we leave here, and I'm neck deep in drums and stacks of things. We are allowed forty-four pounds each on the plane. We will jet most of the way. Phil has quite a bit more to do on the storage cupboards for the hospital. He is working on the doors, and has to fix the pump again. While he was gone to town the petrol tank caught on fire and did some damage to the pump. We were without water half a day. Patsy, Esther, Ruthie Embree and my Phil all have mild cases of tick-bite fever. I'm immune now.

Years later one of the missionaries who had worked at Lundi Mission told us what had happened there during a time when angry men were attacking mission stations! The Christian Africans told the missionaries what they had seen. When it looked like the mob was going to break into the mission, all of a sudden, the mission was surrounded by angels! The mob became quiet, and left, and did not return! What a tremendous answer to prayer! Thank You, Lord for your protection!

Furlough time

May 3, 1961, At last we are on our way home. What a delightful way to travel! Johannesburg to Salisbury, about 1000 miles in one and a half hours! We just had time to eat a delicious chicken dinner, 6 1/2 miles high at 580 miles an hour. We had a wonderful Missionary Fellowship time with much of the presence of the Holy Spirit. Our prayers for Phil have been marvelously answered. He is completely surrendered to the

Lord's will! As he led a testimony meeting the Holy Spirit broke us all up. Confessions were made and some found real victory over problems that had hindered them for years. We had considered going down to Durban when we learned that the Natal, South Africa missionaries wouldn't be coming, but we felt we should stay for the conference, so we prayed that the Natal missionaries would change their minds and come, and they did! Arlene and Elmore said they came just to see us, but I know they came in answer to prayer. They needed the inspiration and encouragement of the fellowship. Jean Johnson, Gertie, Laverna and Kathryn came with them. How wonderful to see them all again!

On the plane, writing a letter to Esther Embree

May 3, 1961, Johannesburg, Dear Esther, We just got on the plane, two hours late because of engine trouble. Now we are starting to taxi. How exciting! This is huge. Bigger than a train coach, three seats on each side. We are all in a row so we have two window seats. Beautiful interior. Hardly any sound, but the runway is bumpy. No butterflies in my stomach now, but there were when we pulled up in front of the terminal. We are climbing steeply. We are directly over the wings. There is a little turbulence occasionally. We are already quite high. We arrived at Guyers about 11:30 and had *boerwors* (sausage) in buns for dinner. We took the kids to the barber and hairdresser shop for haircuts. They all look nice. Then back to Guyers for baths. Gwen and Myrt also did some last minute mending and pressing, for us. They were so nice to us. Bless them! Myrtle found one of Dean's old sport coats and we shortened the sleeves for Paul, a pretty good fit. It's brown and goes perfectly with his brown trousers. Much nicer looking than his old blazer! Another case of "All things working together for good!" Rather cool, but a coat is too warm. (8:15 p.m.) We are now over the Limpopo River! And we just finished a most delicious chicken dinner! We will soon be in Salisbury. You are probably about home now. There are the cutest little tables that pull down in front of you. What a lovely way to travel. Feels as though we are starting to go down already. Joh'burg to Salisbury, just long enough to eat your supper. (9:45) We are on our way down. One and a half hours to make a two day trip! Down already and hardly a bump. Wow! That was a fast slow down. We are back on the plane already, 10:00. That was a short stop. Just had time for a drink of orange juice and wrote one letter. Very warm inside now, but it will cool off as soon as we get going.

Salisbury is quite a bit warmer than Joh'burg. Queer, but I feel none of the strangeness and lostness I felt in 1954. I feel like a seasoned traveler. The kids have been good. 28,000 feet high now, going up to 31,000. 11:30 now, Nairobi time. Due to arrive there at 1:40. Joe and Paul are asleep. They are passing out blankets and soft drinks now. Over Kenya now, going down into the clouds. Wish I could see. This is the part of Africa I've always wanted to see. Another smooth landing. Well, that was Kenya. Saw just enough to want to see more. We bought an ebony elephant and an African man's painting of Mt. Kilimanjaro! We are two hours late. I should go to sleep, but who can sleep? Up again over the Mediterranean. Crete looks beautiful. The kids slept like logs, one kid on the floor, rolled up in a blanket, one kid stretched out on the seat. The arms are removable and I am stretched out with my legs up on a little table, swathed in a blanket. Economy class overnight is not luxurious. Phil and I didn't get much sleep. I'm glad we'll spend the rest of our nights in hotels. The Mediterranean is much larger than it looks on the map. Islands look like big rocks poking up out of the blue. 8 a.m., going down sharply now. Greece! Athens is an interesting city, old, old buildings, and new modern ones with marble everywhere, one million people, a big beautiful city. We can see the Acropolis from our hotel balcony. We are going on a tour of the city this afternoon. Poor Phil caught a cold on the plane last night. His nose just drips and his head aches. Hope he gets over it soon. We really feel queer around so many people who don't know English. The hotel people and air terminal people do, however, which really helps. We saw all around Athens. The Acropolis is all everyone ever said. Breathtaking! We could see the Parthenon from our hotel window all lit up at night. Athens is balmy and coats are excess baggage today. However, it did rain yesterday.

Off for Rome. This is a small jet, about 80 passengers. Seems as though we spend a lot of time waiting in lines and going through customs. But I'm glad we came. The kids are still being good. It's really a thrill to take off in a jet. The Mediterranean is so blue that with clouds underneath you, it seems as though you are looking down into the sky! Many brown islands surrounded with greenish blue water. Airplanes are chilly compared with the ground temperature.

You should see all the fancy new airplanes! We have been living in another world! But a very nice one. Rome. We've fallen in love with Italy. Everyone is so friendly. Greeks seem more solemn. The kids had a wonderful time looking out our windows in the YMCA, down at the street cars. It's fun to see the kids' reactions to things that are commonplace to us, but that they have never seen before. Phil and I went window shopping. Americans everywhere! You can tell them by looking at them! Guess we don't look very American except for Phil's hair! We plan to go see the Coliseum tomorrow via streetcar. We took a bus to Vatican City this morning. Saw St. Peter's Cathedral and the Sistine Chapel with Michelangelo's awesome paintings. This afternoon we went on a bus tour to some other beautiful churches and the catacombs. Miles of tunnels underground. We saw more gold today than we've ever seen before! Saw the stairs Martin Luther went up on his knees. People were there going up the stairs like he did. Poor people. They didn't understand that Jesus paid the price for the Salvation of all who believe in Him, love, and obey Him. We are so glad we came. It's so much fun to see the things you've always read about.

Monday, Joe has 3-day measles, I think! He has a rash all over now, but it is nearly gone from his face. Wonder where he picked that up! We've kept him in bed since yesterday. He seems quite frisky today, so we hope he will be OK to go on the plane this afternoon. We saw the Coliseum yesterday morning. What an enormous place! You can imagine how we felt, standing where hundreds of Christians were martyred. Yesterday afternoon I took Paul, Nan and Pats to the zoo. Seemed real sad to see the poor animals in cages after having seen them in the bush! The kids had a wonderful time! Tuesday evening. If we thought Rome was nice, then Switzerland is out of this world! So much beauty! On Monday morning Joe got sicker and sicker and his temp went higher and higher even with aspirin. I gave him a Nivaquin, for malaria, and when the kids and Phil went down to eat I stayed with Joe to pray. It just seemed as though the devil was trying to mess everything up. Only a few hours until plane time and who could take such a sick baby out? But when I was through praying, I knew Joe would be OK and that we should stick to our planned schedule. While I was praying he fell asleep. It was time to go down with our luggage to call a taxi. I woke Joe and gave him half an aspirin. Of course he cried and then began to vomit. Our suitcases were all in the hall by the elevator. Phil had gone out too, and there I was still in the bathroom with Joe. When I thought he was finally through, I carried him to the elevator and just before I stepped on with him, he started vomiting again! I ran back to our room and finally reached the toilet. The maid was already in, cleaning the room. I felt awful, leaving so much for the poor lady to clean up! Eventually we reached the taxi and by the time we arrived at the airport, Joe's temp was normal and his spots were hardly visible on his face! The rest of him was absolutely covered with the worst rash I've ever seen! But he feels OK and we had a lovely trip to Zurich, over the Alps. We were in a propeller plane, so we were close enough to see everything. The grandeur of the snow-covered, jagged peaks, immense valleys and lovely lakes! The kids got scared when it got rough just before we landed. Felt just like a roller-coaster! This morning we took a train to Goldau and a *bahn,* an electric cogwheel car, up and over Rigi Mountain. Gorgeous views, but cold up on top! Then we took a steamer down Lake Lucerne to Lucerne and back to Zurich by train. What a day! Switzerland is beautiful. Green, with flowers, waterfalls, and classical music. How lovely to have nothing to do but relax, and do what you want to do and not feel guilty about it! What luxury to sink into the feather beds in our hotel! We are so glad we are making our trip home like this. So far it's all been even nicer than we had hoped for and not too expensive. We also stayed three days in London, visited Madame Toussaud's Wax Works. What a strange feeling to walk through, looking at all those real looking, life-sized figures, so real looking you would expect them to be able to talk. We loved the subway system in London. So nice, so clean, such a great way to get around in the city. Westminster Abbey and St. Paul's Cathedral were awe inspiring with all their grandeur and history. We went through the Tower Bridge, saw the fabulous royal jewels, gawked at Big Ben, and looked down at the famous Thames River.

Back in the States!

No more letters in 1961 to Mary's parents. We followed our plan of stopping in New York for our physicals and clearance by the Medical Office. They check out all the in-coming and out-going missionaries. While we were in New York, we thought it would be a great adventure to take the kids on a New York subway since London's had been so nice. So, we decided to take one to go see the Statue of Liberty in the New York Harbor. When we were lined up, ready to get on the subway car, Paul jumped on ahead of the rest of us and the door started to close before we could get on. I was frantic, but Phil calmly stuck his arm in the door before it could completely close. Of course, that stopped everything. An alarm went off. A conductor rushed to the door, scolded us for putting the system off schedule, but kindly let us on with our bewildered 'bush babies'! Did we ever feel like 'hicks from the sticks'! How thankful we were that Paul hadn't gotten lost in New York all by himself! I still get goose bumps just thinking about it all these years afterward! Then we went to the magnificent Statue of Liberty, and we climbed clear to the top, huffing and puffing. As I recall, Phil stayed at the bottom with at least the youngest and waited for us.

Then on to Winona Lake by train, to visit with Mom Kline and Betty. Betty introduced us to s'mores! We thought they were really yummy! We visited with the Johnsons in Michigan, and went through our church headquarters in Indiana. Then on to McPherson, Kansas for a good visit with a lot of good old friends there. Also in McPherson we purchased a used 1955 VW Kombi to drive to Los Angeles. We visited with relatives in Colorado. In Los Angeles we ended up living in the Ugly Igloo, the family nickname for the little old house where I was born, originally built by my great grandparents before 1924.

Living in Los Angeles, California - 1961

The rent was extremely cheap, and right on the same lot as my parents, in the same little house of my birth! Our children attended the same school as I had as a child, and we all went to church in the same church I had attended as a child, and the same one in which we were married! Phil did missions deputation speaking all over the Mid-West and Northwest, and I spoke in quite a few of the Southern California churches. I was asked to be the speaker for our Ladies' Retreat at Camp Glen Oak Pines. I didn't feel adequate to be the only speaker, so they invited another missionary to speak also. I had never met her before, but she had also lived in South Africa. Even though I didn't know her, the Lord convicted me of what my attitude had been of her when we were at Edwaleni. Instead of going to lunch, I spent time in prayer, confessing and seeking the Lord's guidance. He moved me to go to her, ask her forgiveness, and the Lord melted us together in love and harmony. The Lord brought real blessing to that Retreat. Many were burdened for the Salvation of loved ones, and renewed praying for them with a greater measure of hope and assurance that God does answer prayer, and the burden is lifted when we praise the Lord and thank Him for what He is going to do!

Nancy and Paul enjoyed getting to attend an American school. Patty was so shy the teacher didn't know until the end of the school year that she hadn't made much progress in learning to read! I was so relieved to have the kids in school, I didn't keep in touch. I should have been helping Patty with her reading. Maybe the drastic move had been too traumatic for her. Years later she was reading as voraciously as her mom!

We received our furlough salary check from the General Missionary Board quarterly, $1,000. One day when I had planned to take it to the bank, I couldn't find it! I searched high and low, everywhere I could think of. Finally, in desperation I prayed, "Oh, Lord, you know where that check is. Please help me find it." The thought came immediately, "Look in the waste basket!" I looked there even though I **knew** it couldn't be there. I **wouldn't** have thrown it away! But, I looked in the wastebasket, and there it was, still in its envelope! It's amazing how wonderful it is that God cares so much for us! After Phil was through with traveling around on deputation, he secured employment at Los Angeles Pacific College, up on the hill above our house. We were happy to visit with relatives, and to have our children get acquainted with their cousins and grandparents. When their cousins first saw our kids, they very disgustedly said, "They were born in Africa, but how come they aren't black?"

September, 1963. A poem I wrote a few months before we started our second trip to Africa. It was printed in The Missionary Tidings.

A Missionary's Consecration

Take all of me, Lord, My time, my talents
My loved ones, my will, my money, my all.
Here am I, Lord; I answer Thy call.
I am willing to go, I am willing to stay;
I am willing to pray, to give of my time,
To intercede, that they might hear.

All Thou hast given me, this Lord, is Thine.
My money is Thine; Use it, Lord, as Thou wilt
I would not withhold of silver or gold
It all belongs to Thee,
Nor selfishly grasp or hoard for myself
When there are millions who perish

They have not heard of the Living Word.
They perish
And the guilt is mine if I do not love
If I will not give as He gave, His all
My all, oh Lord, is Thine.

I wrote another poem while we were on furlough in Southern California. One day we had taken the family to a beach. As I sat on the sand, watching the little waves as they washed the sand again and again, these words came to my mind, and I wrote them down.

Reflections

The sand builds no barriers,
The sand near the water;
Unresisting, surrendered,
It yields
Unceasing, forever.
The waves cleanse the sand.
The clutter
Is gone.
The wet sand,
The sand being washed,
Reflects like a mirror
The sun.
Radiant reflection,
A brilliance not its own,
But that of
The sun.
Uncluttered and calm,
Continually cleansed,
The soul that abides
In Christ.
Radiant the life
Surrendered to Christ.
The image reflected
is His!
Mary Kline, 1963, (printed in the Missionary Tidings)

Years later, after we had returned to California, after we had spent five years in Central Africa, and we were living in Modesto, I received a letter from a lady who had been one of our prayer partners all the time we were in Africa. We had met at church in Stillwater, Oklahoma, probably in 1952, before we knew we were going to Africa! Her letter was dated July 31, 1977.

Dear Brother and Sister Kline, Greetings in Jesus Christ, our Savior. You have meant so much to me since I met you in our newly organized church in Stillwater, Oklahoma. While you may not remember me, you have been one of the uppermost in mind, heart, and prayers. If I remember right, your youngest was a baby in arms, or I think a year or two old, a toddler, I think. You called him Paul. Nancy had not yet arrived, but was on the way. After you left Oklahoma, I have tried to follow you through the Tidings and church. I think one of yours is called Patsy. One of the things, Sister Mary, that keeps me uplifted here at the Health Care Center where I now reside, is the poem you wrote. I read it in the Missionary Tidings. "Radiant Reflection." The sand builds no barriers, the sand being washed, the sand near the water, reflects like a mirror the image not its own, but that of the sun. I carry a copy of it in my Bible. A blessed encouragement.

Sincerely yours in Jesus, Nettie V. Rogers

What an unexpected blessing, to realize that something the Lord had inspired me to write had been an encouragement and help to someone else! I am filled to overflowing with the Joy of the Lord! Thank You, Lord!

CHAPTER 5

Congo

Preparing to go to Congo, 1962 to 1963

We had just about decided that we might not get to return to Africa, but we both knew that we wanted only what God's will was for us, and that we would not try to push open any closed doors, so Phil was looking around to find a job teaching, when we received a phone call and a visit from Vic Macy. He brought with him a request from the Free Methodist General Missionary Board, that instead of returning to Southern Rhodesia, would we consider going to Congo? A builder was needed to supervise the building of the much needed hospital at Nundu (noon'doo) Mission in Congo, on the shores of Lake Tanganyika. Would we be willing to go? Oh, yes! We had wanted to work in Central Africa for a long time. We would have to be ready to go by the end of the year. Also, since French is one of the official languages of Central Africa, we would need to spend at least six months in Belgium studying French before we could work in Congo. So, Phil was appointed missionary builder for Congo. Our hearts would go back to Chikombedzi Mission with the Embrees when they returned, but we had to follow where the Lord was leading us. Phil would have to study linguistics for a few weeks in New York because he had never studied French in school.

Friends and family went with us to Pasadena to see us off. We boarded the train, bound for Kansas, leaving our VW Kombi with Mary's parents for someone to purchase. What would we ever have done without all the help Mother, Daddy, Harland and Orlean and many friends gave us? Phil would go on to New York for a few weeks, and the rest of us would stay in McPherson, Kansas, with Joyce and Mitch Allmon, and I would put the kids in school there for a few weeks.

In McPherson, Kansas

January 11, 1963, It's a white world here again. Blizzard nearly this morning. But it is only snowing lightly now. Still quite a bit of wind, so drifts are forming. Seems strange to have time to sit quietly. McPherson seems like home still. (We had lived there for six years after we were married.) The kids are all happily in school. All of them think these schools are better, except Joe, and he says the California schools have better blocks! Patsy is rather unhappy because the second grade here is so much ahead of the Los Angeles school! They really stress phonics here, and poor Pats hardly knows the sounds of any of the letters, but she is learning. However, she can't read the second grade book. I know Pats is a slow reader, but she could do much better if she knew how to sound out words. (So, I ask myself these many years later. "Why didn't I try to teach her myself, like my great grandmother taught me?")

January 18, 1963, Still in McPherson. What a mad rush today, and I have two suitcases yet to go and a couple items to squeeze into the crate. Got a special delivery letter from Phil this morning with some more items to pick up. So, I've been running around nearly all day and picked up a pair of shoes for Phil that had just come in. Got school books for the kids to continue on in. We washed nearly all day yesterday. I thought I had kept things pretty well washed up, but when I began going through suitcases, I found a whole stack of dirty clothes! The girls had worn their red jumpers so much I finally had to wash them. I had some of my things on the line for three days. The sweaters I had hung out were dripping, and the blouses froze stiff before I went back in the house. Then the sweaters all grew icicles and didn't lose them until after we finally brought them into the house. It is supposed to get down to zero tonight, but not much snow. The wind cuts right through you.

Joyce brought me over to her hairdresser to get my hair done to relax me. I got a perm two weeks ago. I am sitting under the drier and am just now beginning to relax. Nancy has been sick for two days, flu, I guess. She felt better today. I hope none of the kids get train-sick. Patty wants to stay here with Joyce. We found out years later that every day at school in McPherson, Patty purchased the half pint of milk I had given her money for, and then because she didn't like milk, she buried them, one by one in a bank of snow, all along the sidewalk! Then in the spring, when the snow melted, the teachers found all those little half pints of milk, all in a row. The principal of the school, told us about it when we came back from Africa in 1968! Paul also would like to stay in Kansas. He likes the school, and seems to be doing really well. He took their semester science test and only missed two! He had learned it all from their review and pre-test.

January 21, 1963, New York. Well, we made it this far. We're all packed and all our luggage is downstairs waiting for the man to take it. Because of the dock strike the regular systems aren't operating, so there is a forwarding agent who takes missionaries and their things to the ships. He will have to make two trips. He has a station wagon and a trailer and it takes about forty-five minutes to drive from here to there. The train trip to Chicago wasn't bad at all, but from Chicago on, cold, dirty snow, ice, and slush all over when we had to change stations, and me with four kids and about eighteen pieces to keep track of! And to top it all, our train was 2 1/2 hours late, which only gave us a half hour to change stations and trains in Chicago. One of the kids dropped their carry-on case. Things scattered all over, but we managed to get it all put back together. Our car was way up by the engine, and we felt we had walked a mile! But we slept on the train and felt some rested. We arrived in New York about 10:30 yesterday morning. Phil was at the train to meet us. Today was hectic. Had to type ten copies of all drum and crate contents because they are planning on sending the things as soon as they find out where to send them! We met the other family who is going with us, Margaret and Russell Peters and their two kids. Between the two families, we have two trunks, five foot lockers, nine suitcases, about twelve little pieces, six kids and us! Phil took the kids out for a hamburger. When we arrived, it was warm here. It's really chilly now, but no snow.

So Send I You . . .

To Congo

Phil, Mary, Paul, Patricia, David and Nancy Kline

Pray ye therefore

We had prayer cards made to send to our prayer partners

January 23, 1963, on the S.S. Rundam, Holland America Line. (Postcard mailed in Halifax, Nova Scotia)

Hi! This is a lovely ship. The food is excellent, beds are good. We are taking Dramamine and are feeling OK. Just a bit rough this morning. We are nearing Halifax. We'll get 'shore leave' for a few hours. Patty is the only one who doesn't feel well. Joe has been coughing some, but isn't sick. Warm in the cabins, chilly on deck. We are nearly in port now, so no more rock'n roll.

February 2, 1963, Brussels, Belgium. We are here, but not settled. I've spent the whole time here so far being nursemaid. Nancy got the flu on the ship. Pats was sick the day before we landed, and is just now feeling OK. Joe got sick on the way from Rotterdam to Brussels and Paul is sick too! Joe is feeling the worst. Bad headaches and temp, and of course, they don't like the food here. Too different from American. I like it, except for the too rare meat! Also, I guess I have the flu too, or something, but I keep taking aspirin and keep going. We located a building with two apartments so we can all be together, but since our kids are ill, and there is only one apartment open until February 6, we'll stay here in this little hotel. It's really quaint, used to be an old family mansion. Tall ceilings, enormous windows, queer plumbing. There is a lavatory in each room for washing hands and face.

There is a scarcity of coal and natural gas here and so hot water is limited. It's only warm. But there is no scarcity of cold air. We are lying in bed with three heavy blankets. My nose and hands are a bit chilly. And this hotel is 'well heated'. Guess since it didn't snow today, they must have let the furnace die down. Each room has two steam radiators, but with these fourteen feet ceilings, not much heat stays down where we are. They say this is the worst winter in Europe in twenty years. Coldest since 1927! We can believe them! If the kids are well enough tomorrow, we plan on moving into the apartment with Peters. It will be crowded, but cheaper and maybe we'll be able to fix food the kids will like. It will only be for two days until our apartment is vacated. Most of our stuff is already over there. Quite a few Americans live in that neighborhood. One of them came with a VW to help Peters move over there. We'll just go over in a small taxi. All the kids are feeling much better today. 7 p.m. It is warmer now. They must have started the furnace again. Anyway, it is comfortable in the room now with only one sweater on. The kids are busy coloring and Paul is reading a second grade reader for lack of anything else to read! I brought along some of the school books from Kansas, but I should have brought more, I guess. They will have plenty to do when they start school. There is an eleven year old boy who has been here four months and already sounds French, but his parents don't! Our ship trip was rough. One day was extremely rough, and most of the passengers were sea-sick. All of us were sick except Margaret Peters, and we were all taking Dramamine. We just couldn't keep it down that day. We just lay all over the lower bunks and floor of our coolest cabin, each with his little white paper sack made for the purpose! Phil and Paul never did get hungry after that until the last couple days, in the English Channel, where it was finally calm. The sun shone beautifully one day out of the ten. There was quite a bit of drizzle, chilly out on deck, but not icy. Don't imagine I'll ever get Phil on a ship again. When I asked the kids, "Who would like to take another trip on a ship?" there was dead silence and blank stares! So Joe wanted to know if I was going on a ship! Too much continual motion! But I miss not being rocked to sleep at night. It was such a strong storm that they took the precaution of boarding up all the porthole windows! Our ship was late because of the rough sea and when we did arrive in Rotterdam on the mouth of the Rhine River, there was so much ice, the ship couldn't dock properly. We waited three hours before we could get off. Cook's travel agent was waiting for us with a Ford limo and a trailer and a chauffeur to transport us here to Brussels. It was 10 p.m. when we finally located this little hotel. It is right downtown. Phil's brother, Burton may send some welding materials. Please try to get them in number seven drum. Please send me a list of the things you've added.

February 4, 1963, We arrived January 31 late at night with one sick kid, so of course all of them have come down with it. The doctor is coming this evening. The Peters, are young and enthusiastic. We are enjoying their fellowship. You should see our window. Like a fairyland, it is snowing heavily. Large white flakes that quickly cover the dirty, churned-up slush in the little cobblestone street. A horse and buggy just clopped down the street, looked like a delivery man of some sort. The people walking by look cold, wrapped up in fur coats and fur hats. Even Phil is wearing a cap these days. It has warm flaps to cover his ears. The doctor just came and went, and because he does not speak English and we don't know much French, the hotel manager's wife came along to interpret. Patty's flu has turned into bronchitis, but the other kids are on the mend. *Parlez-voux Francais? Oui? Non.*

We study French and our kids attend a French speaking school!

February 17, 1963, More snow, but with warm clothes on we are cozy even though our apartment is a bit chilly. However, our kitchen gets very warm and we shed our sweaters in there. Davey Joe is still sick, but his temp is down a lot from yesterday. The kids have either intestinal flu or bacillary dysentery. We were having bottled milk delivered, cheaper than the milk at the store. We were enjoying it and drinking lots of it, but when the little kids got diarrhea, we began to wonder.

We found out that everybody **boils** their milk! So we are switching to sterilized milk. Keeps for a month, but it doesn't taste as good. You can buy pasteurized milk, but the doctor says it isn't safe either! We have a rather heavy schedule of studying French. I am attending the Alliance Language School. They were on lesson fifteen, but I can understand most of it. We are studying with tutors, me too, in addition to the school. Everything in the class is in French.

It's fun for me to be studying again. It is coming easily and I am really enjoying it. Phil is rather discouraged, but he is understanding more, and is beginning to make sentences. Thanks so much for taking care of things for us. Sorry we left so much undone. Nancy and Paul made a snow man yesterday in the back yard. It's below freezing today and keeps snowing. I wish it would stop and warm up again. Patty is complaining of ear ache again. Tomorrow we have to take all the kids with us to the police station to get our identity cards. Then Margaret and I have to take our clothes to the laundromat. Much cheaper than sending them to the laundry. That will take the morning, then more study.

March 14, 1963, Hi! Can't cram another French word into my tired brain tonight, so I'll quit for today. Everyone else is asleep. I'm on lesson thirty-one. I'm going faster and beyond the language school now, but I still go there for review. They only do three lessons a week. I try to do six. A lot of it I remember from French in high school, which helps muchly. Phil is making real progress and thanks to everyone who is praying, he is keeping encouraged! We've seen several men wearing wooden shoes. They must be warm and waterproof. We get fruit from Spain and Italy; cheese and peanut butter from Holland. Phil bought some really good tools, inexpensive, from France. Mr. and Mrs. Hugh White were here. They invited us all to dinner at their very nice hotel. There is fresh fish every Thursday, stacked up in the fish shops. There are so many tiny shops side by side, with apartments two and three floors above.

March 24, 1963, The kids are all sick again, covered with a red rash. We don't have any idea what they have. We found out later it was what they call the fifth disease! Phil rented a TV to help keep the kids quiet. Last night was "My Three Sons," with French words. There is a typhoid epidemic in France. Glad we have had shots for it. **Clang**, goes another streetcar. About every twenty minutes one goes by each way. We have the windows open and the street noises are noisy! We never saw such speeding on side streets. We buy our bread in little bread shops. They slice the bread with an electric slicer if you want it sliced, and put it in a paper sack. Your package with Nancy's jacket and magazines arrived. The kids were thrilled to get them with all the things to do and read. Thanks too for the Sunday School papers. Doesn't seem like Sunday without one. Thanks so much for all you do.

April, 1963, A nice sunny day, but still chilly. The kids are out in the back yard playing with parachutes we made out of plastic bags. Nice to have them out of the apartment. Yesterday was the first day of their Easter vacation. They have two weeks. At church this morning, I could understand almost everything the pastor said. Phil said he could understand much more than he could last week. So, we are making real progress. I am enjoying learning French more than anything I've done for years. I have started the second book now because there was a class beginning it last Friday at the French school where I go. So they let me drop the other class in the middle of the first book and join the more advanced class. I'll finish the first book with our tutors. This means a change in schedule, which makes Joe happy because I can pick him up every noon at his school. He is much happier now and even says he likes school. They all have a two hour lunch time. Joe can count to twenty in French better than he can in English! Nan can count to one hundred in French, and they all are beginning to understand their teachers. Before we came, we had been assured that there would be an English speaking school our kids could attend, but we found it was full. The Bates and the Johnsons will all be stopping on their way back to Burundi. Dr. Lamson might come by on his way home from South Africa.

We have lots of guests

April 27, 1963, Phil is shaving in our kitchen/bathroom and I'm relaxing. We had some very interesting guests today and last night, the Ogdens. They live near Paris and stopped to see us on their way to Holland. He will be teaching at Seattle Pacific College next year. Davey Joe was so cute yesterday. When I took him to school his class was in the auditorium playing and singing "The Farmer in the Dell." When I went back to get him at noon I asked him if the kids had sung it in French. He said, "Yes, but the piano sang it in English!" He has a hard time deciding which language is which. He always counts in French!

Monday a.m. Back from the *Wasserette*. I had five loads of clothes. I'm really tired! I'll let the kids put them away this noon. I usually go on Tuesdays, but with all our company coming tomorrow, I had to get it done today. I managed to get three driers going at once, so it only took me two hours. It's nearly time to go get Joe for lunch. As long as I'm there early for him he keeps happy, but if he has to wait on me, then his feelings of insecurity get the better of him and he cries.

Tuesday. Phil and Russell have just left to meet Dr. Lamson at the Sabena Air Terminal downtown. We have kept the Bates busy ever since they arrived, answering our questions. They must be exhausted. I'd better study some more.

May 5, 1963, Happy Mother's Day, Mother! Wish we could see you. Well, our company has all come and gone, and we went too. Yesterday was the missionary bus tour of Holland. It was fabulous. It is tulip time, with many gorgeous flowers of lots of different kinds. I wish you could have seen it.

July 7, 1963, I hate the thoughts of moving again. The kids are getting more unhappy all the time in the French school. Glad there are only two more weeks of school. By the time you receive this we will be packing! We are scheduled to fly to Usumbura, Urundi, July 30. Paul's ticket doubles on July 31, his 12th birthday, so to save the money, we will rush and leave. The Clydes will be with us for five days ending the

29th. Prof. Helsel comes tonight for two nights. Our neighbors just left today, so we are renting their apartment in addition to ours for the rest of the month, so we'll have a guest room and in between guests, Paul will have a room, and Joe won't have to sleep in the baby bed next to the fireplace which he is afraid of. Imagine, snakes here, on the third floor! Kid's imaginations! We went down Friday and got our medicals and vaccinations and Phil has many downtown trips yet to make before we get our visas. The Board has stipulated we spend three months in Usumbura in intensive *Swahili* (swah-hee'lee) study. The Congolese won't be happy about that. They say **they** can teach us *Swahili*! As of now, there is no way to get there until the Mission buys a boat. The lake has risen five feet and all the bridges are out and the road is inundated. It's good that we are going sooner than planned, because Nancy and Paul will be able to start school at Mweya (mway'yah) Mission in September. Did I tell you I passed my exam in French, fifth place, '*tres* (very) honorable!' I was really surprised because it was a very hard exam, mostly based on a difficult dictation we had never seen before. I expected to come in last since all the others speak French more fluently than I. While we were talking about going to Congo the other day, Joe piped up, "Let's go right now. I can talk French," and he rattled off the French numbers! "*un, deux, trois, quatre, cinc*" - (1,2,3,4,5)!

July 18, 1963, What a hectic day. Phil is packing our trunk to go surface from here. I am exhausted already, and the day is only half gone. I'm at a self-service laundry. Olive Bodtcher came yesterday. It is helpful to have her here while I am packing. She knows the climate there. After we get to Urundi, please sew a cloth wrapper around anything you send to us. You can write the address right on the cloth with ballpoint or magic marker. This is evidently the safest way to send anything overseas. Sunday, relaxing, surrounded with packed suitcases and trunk. Beautiful day today.

July 30, 1963, On the airport train. We are on our way after a hectic day yesterday, but God's Grace was and is sufficient for all! Our plane leaves at 10:45 and will arrive seventeen hours later in Usumbura! We are really loaded with things to carry and they let us through without weighing what we carry. That is an answer to prayer. All our company left yesterday morning early. I did a big wash and ironed and finished packing! Nearly there.

On the plane to Usumbura, Urundi

August 1, 1963, We thought you'd like a letter from us while on the plane. This will be sort of a flight diary. We are airborne over Germany in a DC 70. What a hectic day yesterday. We had to have everything ready by five to take down to the air terminal to get weighed in so we could know if we were going to be overweight. We were, but when we did the final weighing in today, they didn't weigh hardly any of our twelve pieces of hand luggage. That was an answer to prayer, because overweight charges are sky-high! And even in the middle of the mad rush, the presence of the Lord was precious. His grace **is** sufficient.

Over the Alps now. Breathtaking sights. Fields of snow, roads like trails zigzagging up the steep slopes; emerald lakes nestling way up mile high, tiny toy villages dotting the bottom of every deep canyon, cottony clouds rubbing shoulders with the peaks, and of course, bumpy air and butterflies in your stomach. Above the blue, azure, and sea green Mediterranean now. The brown shore line below, of Italy, near Brindisi, is scalloped, startlingly embroidered in sand-beige, with a white lace edging of breakers.

It doesn't seem real, that this is really us on our way to Congo. We are at peace about going now, but still very disappointed that we were unable to stay in Belgium until December when Phil's tutor said he would have been able to converse in French. However, he has most of the basic grammar and vocabulary.

Nearing Greece now. It looks like a relief map, overhung with billowy mounds of summer clouds, giant scoops of vanilla ice cream, floating on hazy blue shadows. Phil has a new toy; our camera dream come true. A Leica M3 with a 90 mm lens, at such an enormously reduced price we couldn't pass it up. Later we hope to add a good telescopic lens so we can show you Africa as we see it. We are about to collide with the billowing white cotton towers of clouds. No, we are climbing above them, and our ears are popping again. Skimming through a cloud canyon now, and then engulfed in the fuzzy mist and made dizzy with the tossing around given us by the air pockets. A soft woolly blanket below us. We are glad to be above its turbulence. Phil and Nan are sleeping through it all, happy in their Dramamine dreams. The plane is full with Belgian families moving to Burundi, Africans returning home after a year or two of study in Brussels, several Catholic Fathers, the Peters and us. A constant stream of Europeans is pouring into Central Africa now. We've left the bank of clouds behind and all is hazy below. It looks warm down there. We'll know soon. We are beginning the glide down to Athens.

Back on the plane in Athens, it is **hot** here! We had a wonderful five days just before we left Brussels. Elmore and Arlene Clyde from Edwaleni Mission in South Africa, and Prof. Helsel from Seattle Pacific College were with us. We rented a VW Kombi and took a two day tour through Holland. In Holland we had toured through the windmill area south of Rotterdam. We saw the Hague, the Capitol, and the Maduradam toy town again. We stayed all night in Lisse in the heart of the tulip fields. They are harvesting the bulbs now. We had planned to sleep in the car, but we would have shivered all night. Prof. Helsel insisted on treating us all to bed and breakfast in a clean little Dutch Hotel. What a breakfast! Not the skimpy coffee-roll kind that you find in most of Europe! All for $2 a person. Living in Holland is much cheaper than Belgium. Then we drove up through reclaimed land near the former Zuider Zee, which is now a fresh water inland lake. We drove through several towns where many people still wear the quaint native dress and still more wear wooden shoes. We bought a pair at a tourist shop and Nan and Pats dressed up in lace Dutch caps, aprons and wooden shoes and Phil took their picture. A bus load of American tourists came along just then and also took pictures of the two little 'Dutch' girls. Guess they got fooled! We went through a cheese farm in Edam. Good cheese!

We're up again and two hours and twenty-five minutes from Cairo. Hope it's still light enough to see the Nile and the pyramids. The Mediterranean Sea is no mere puddle as it appears on the map!

219

Holland was so green and very cool. Quite a contrast to the heat and brown dry land here in Greece! We drove north up over the dike that separates the North Sea from the lake that was once the Zuider Zee. The dike is twenty miles long and one hundred feet wide! What a structure! The northeastern part of Holland is hilly and very much like northern Germany, with lots of big trees, and ferns. It was a lovely trip. Most of all we enjoyed the Christian fellowship with our good friends.

It's dark out already, so we'll see nothing but lights down in Cairo. We can't help thinking how different this trip is from our first one in 1954. Everything seemed so strange and foreign to us then. This trip we are at ease. We feel just as much 'at home' in a European or African environment as we do an American one! Wednesday. We were awakened too early this morning after a night of 'off and on' dozing by the announcement in French, Flemish, English, and another language or two over the plane's loud speaker that in one hour we would land in Usumbura, Urundi. Still dark below; we were over Entebbe, Uganda, and then Lake Victoria.

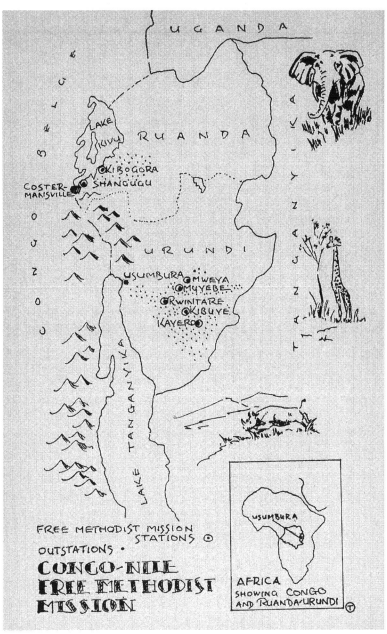

This map was drawn by Olive Teal for the book "Lights in the World,"
written by Byron S. Lamson, 1951
Used with permission
The name of the Mission is now Central Africa Mission,
which includes Congo, Burundi and Rwanda

We arrive in Urundi

At the Usumbura, Urundi airport to meet us were our good friends, Hazel and Frank Adamson, Shirley and Jim Johnson and several Congolese. We were the last off with our four kids and heavy loads to carry, typewriter, projector, and tape recorder. We couldn't let them out of our sight! Customs took a lot of time with its endless forms to fill out in French, its long lines to wait in, and the fast talking, that is, as fast as we can talk in French, necessary to convince the African customs agent that all our things were very used since they looked new and we had no sales slips to prove they were purchased six months ago! But we finally got everything through OK. Customs over, we loaded up in three cars and drove to the Mission station in Ngagara, the African residential area of Usumbura. Unpacked now and ready to sleep off our buzzing 'airplane heads'. See you tomorrow! Sleeping here is slightly different from sleeping in Brussels. Noisy old streetcars in Brussels, right below our bedroom windows. Here, it's crickets, frogs, dogs, and the constant hum of African voices and drums, and the forever odor of wood cooking fires. This is the closest we have ever lived to such a dense African population area. It will take some adjusting to. When we left Brussels, the air was crisp with a nip in it that made coats or sweaters comfortable. It was the end of July! Here it is middle of winter dry season, hazy, windy, pleasantly warm. But you know it is Africa. There is nothing bright, shiny and modern here, drab, dusty shops downtown, reminiscent of the general 'country store era', with a pitifully small jumbled assortment of things to buy. You buy what you know you will need, when you happen to find it! Importing is expensive and carefully controlled and many things are often scarce. Of all things scarce now, no deodorant! No shop in town has any! Ordered, but not here yet. And everything we saw yesterday was expensive! About twice the price of things in Belgium, and we thought things were terribly expensive there! But food is fairly cheap here and lots of tropical fruits and good meat. Better wind this up so we can mail it when we go shopping in the morning. We start studying with our new tutor in *Swahili* Monday. So, "*kwa heri.*" That's "goodbye" in our new language.

CHAPTER 6

A Brief History of Free Methodist Missions in Central Africa

In 1885, ten years after the death of David Livingston, the Free Methodist Church of North America contributed $3,000, hoping to establish a Mission in Central Africa, near Lake Tanganyika. Instead, the members of the little missionary team, the 'Africa Band', followed the advice of Bishop B. T. Roberts. He had advised them to seek a healthful elevation near the coast. They began a Mission in Portuguese East Africa, and later another in South Africa, both near the coast. In those days, it was extremely difficult to get to Central Africa, and more expensive than traveling to Eastern and Southern Africa.

In 1923 at Fairview Mission, South Africa, the Lord spoke to missionary John Wesley Haley in the words of Deuteronomy 2:3, "You have compassed this mountain long enough. Turn you northward." Rev. Haley felt that God was calling him to take the Good News of the Gospel to the 'unreached' in Central Africa. No new Free Methodist Mission field had been opened for many years because of World War I, and lack of finances. Rev. Haley felt he should investigate the possibility of missionary work in Central Africa, the land north of the area explored by David Livingstone, and in the area where Stanley had done some exploration. Rev. Haley had learned of Ruanda-Urundi, two small mountainous countries, about a hundred miles south of the equator. In Urundi were more than two and a half million people, a dense rural population of two hundred per square mile. In these countries, there were people belonging to three tribes. The tall, slim *Batutsi*, of Hamitic origin, who probably had migrated down from Ethiopia, with herds of long horned cattle, and had become rulers of these countries. The *Bahutu*, of *Bantu* origin, who were farmers of very small plots of land, and had submitted to the harsh rule of the *Batutsi* because they wanted to own some of the long horned cattle; and the *Batwa* pygmies, originally from the rain forest. All the natives of Urundi spoke a *Bantu* language, *Kirundi*. A similar language, *Kinyarwanda*, was spoken in Ruanda. *Swahili*, an East African trade language, which was much simpler, was understood by many.

Because of the Great Depression in the 1930's, there was no money available to fund mission expansion, so J.W. Haley convinced the Free Methodist Mission Board that it would be wise for his family to skip their furlough in the States, and instead, for him to travel up north to Central Africa, trusting the Lord to supply their needs. Rev. Haley had contacted a Danish missionary from that area in 1932, but it wasn't until 1935 that he was able to establish the Muyebe (Moo-yeh-beh) Mission in Urundi, on a site where German missionaries had briefly worked prior to World War I. Before the war, Congo and Ruanda-Urundi were part of German East Africa. After the war, these countries had become protectorates of Belgium. There were five Mission station sites that had been granted to German missionaries in Urundi.

Rev. Frank Adamson, missionary at the Edwaleni School in South Africa had also felt led to spread the Gospel to those in Central Africa who had not heard. Frank Adamson had accompanied Rev. Haley and his son, Blake, on their exploratory trip up the 'Great North Road' by car. Before they had reached their destination, Frank had to return to South Africa by the time school started at Edwaleni. Rev. Haley continued his trip by boat up Lake Tanganyika, to Usumbura in Urundi. Mrs. Haley and their daughters were finally able to join him in 1935, sailing up the coast, from Durban, South Africa to Dar es Salaam (Port of Peace) in East Africa, and then by train to Lake Tanganyika. Their first dwelling at Muyebe Mission had a grass thatched roof, dried mud floors and sun dried mud brick walls which became damp during rainy season. Later they were able to build a house with kiln burnt clay bricks, with a tile roof, and a fireplace. This house could not be destroyed by termites, nor would rain dampen it inside.

To begin with, Rev. Haley concentrated on learning the difficult *Kirundi* language. After he had gained the confidence of the people, he was able to win a few men to Christ, and taught them to read from some New Testament books that had been translated into the *Kirundi* language by the Danish Baptist missionaries. These few became pastor/ teachers, teaching people who were eager to learn how to read, and spreading the Gospel.

Peace Haley, their daughter, was able to start a small dispensary at Muyebe Mission, where she treated people with many tropical diseases. Since most of the people had very little money, the payment for medicine or a treatment, was a piece of firewood. His other daughter, Dorothy, became a teacher. Even the adults wanted to learn to read and write. The Central School at Muyebe Mission eventually became a training school for teachers, which is still in existence.

Rev. Haley strongly believed that the African church should from the beginning, be **indigenous**; which meant that the churches should be self-supporting, self-governing, and self-propagating. The *Barundi* built their own church/school buildings, similar to their own dwellings, built with acacia wood poles, plastered with mud, with reed thatched roofs. The Lord blessed their work, and the church grew rapidly as the Holy Spirit convicted many to confess their sins and to accept Jesus as their Lord and Savior.

During 1936 to 1938, missionaries Rev. Ronald and Margaret Collett, from Canada, and Ila Gunsolus, teacher, from the South Africa Mission, Margaret Holton and Marjorie Peach, nurses, and Rev. Frank and Hazel Adamson, from South Africa, came to Urundi to work with the Haleys. The Free Methodist Mission in Central Africa was originally called the Congo Nile Mission.

Beginning in 1938, Hazel Adamson treated hundreds daily in a small dispensary at Kibuye (key-boo'-yeh) Mission. The Kibuye Hospital was built in 1946, and Dr. Esther Kuhn was the first doctor there. God sent a spirit of revival in answer to fervent prayer by the missionaries and their first converts. In Urundi, by 1947, there were 123 pastor/teachers, a church membership of 3,000, and 11,369 attending schools. More Free Methodist missionaries were eventually sent out from the States, and other Mission sites were developed, including Mweya, where they were able to build a Bible School and later a seminary for the training of African preachers, and a school for the children of missionary families.

Missionaries also came from other Mission groups - National Holiness Association, which became World Gospel Mission, Evangelical Friends, and the Church Missionary Society from Britain, in addition to the Danish Baptist, who had been there first.

Each Mission group was given a certain area in which to work, and they all worked together so well that they formed a cooperative, supportive group, The Alliance of Protestant Missions. Both schools at Mweya Mission were operated by the cooperation of all the Mission groups. World Gospel Mission built a building at Mweya Mission to house their printing press.

In 1964, when we were refugees from Congo, Dr. Len and Marti Ensign and nurse, Doris Moore took us in at Kibuye Mission. They gave us housing and work, and together with other missionaries, provided for our needs. God's extra-special gift to us, our 'bonus baby' daughter, Janet, was born there in May of 1964.

In the 1970's, Dr. Frank Ogden, at the Kibuye Mission, began the manufacture of his mixture of nutritious grains to feed hundreds of small children who were suffering from a fatal protein deficient disease, *Kwashiorkor*. He called the food *Busoma*, and it is still helping many children in the tropics to survive and grow.

Frank and Hazel Adamson, in 1942, were the first missionaries to live and establish work at Kibogora Mission in Ruanda. Kibogora is in the area that is called the 'Switzerland of Africa'. It is on a high hill overlooking the beautiful, mile high Lake Kivu. It is about one hundred miles south of the Equator, and is near the equatorial rain belt. Rev. Haley wrote that the *Barundi* and the *Banyarwanda* were a pagan people, who lived in fear and darkness, in primitive conditions and superstition, a people skilled in cunning and deceit. The *Batutsi* men carried six foot spears with a very sharp point. They believed in one god, the creator, *Imana*, (ee-mah'-nah) but their religion was the appeasing of evil spirits.

Thousands responded to the Gospel, as lived and demonstrated by these pioneer missionaries. Ila Gunsolus also worked at Kibogora Mission for many years, until she retired and married former missionary to Southern Rhodesia, Ralph Jacobs.

When we were at Kibogora Mission in the late 1960's, Rev. Paul and Estelle Orcutt, Dr. Esther Kuhn, Dorothy Orcutt, RN, Myra Adamson, RN, and Rev. Merlin and Vera Adamson were also working there. Later, Dale and Janet Nitzsche, nurses, Dr. Floyd and Alice Hicks, and the Dale Brock family joined the Mission group at Kibogora. After these two small countries, Ruanda and Urundi, obtained their independence from Belgium, their names were changed to Rwanda and Burundi, and Usumbura became Bujumbura, (boo-joom-boo'rah).

In the early 1960's, the Free Methodist Mission in Burundi was invited by the *Babembe* people of Congo who lived along the northwestern shores of Lake Tanganyika, to send missionaries to work with them at Baraka (bah-rah'-kah) Mission, Congo, and to build a hospital at Nundu Mission. This was an area formerly evangelized by a British Mission, but because of problems and disagreements, all of those missionaries felt that they had to leave their work there, and returned to Britain, in 1961.

The first Free Methodist missionaries sent to Congo, the Phil Kline and Russell Peters families, had to evacuate to Burundi in 1964 because of the *Simba* (seem'bah) Rebellion war against the Congo Central government. Many teachers and preachers had also fled, because the *Simba* Rebel Army was killing many leaders who had been taught by missionaries. Many Christians were martyred.

In the late 1960's and early 1970's, Free Methodist mission work was revived in Congo, under the leadership of Gerald and Marlene Bates. Schools and churches were revitalized and the hospital at Nundu Mission was finally built. In 1968 there were 21 Free Methodist churches in Congo with a membership of 10,694. In 2005 many Congolese were still refugees in Tanzania and Kenya. In 1978 a mighty revival came to the secondary school at Kibogora Mission in Rwanda, and spread to many of the churches. A total church membership of 10,990 was reported that year by the Free Methodist churches in Rwanda.

When independence was granted to these countries in the early 1960's, Burundi and Rwanda were kingdoms, but both became republics, with the *Batutsis* in control in Burundi, and the Bahutus in control in Rwanda. There was intertribal conflict and genocide in the

1960's and 70's in Burundi, and 1990's in Rwanda, between the *Batutsis* and the *Bahutus*. Thousands were massacred, and many *Tutsi* fled, leaving the *Hutus* in control of the government in Rwanda. In Burundi in 1978 there were 167 churches with 11,636 members, and political instability there finally settled down. The church work was mostly turned over to the African pastors.

More educational institutions have since been established in Central Africa, the Myron F. Boyd Seminary at Baraka Mission, the Nundu Mission Deaconess Hospital, with a school to train African nurses in Congo, and the Hope Africa University in Bujumbura, Burundi. It had an enrollment of more than 5,000 in 2013, after only 13 years! It offers over 30 bachelor's, master's, and doctorate degrees in education, medical studies, theology, and several other fields of study. Medical students take their practical training at the Kibuye Mission Hospital which is, since 2010, a branch campus of Hope Africa University. In 2013 former missionary to Burundi, and former Bishop in the United States, Rev. Gerald Bates, and his wife, Marlene, were again working in Burundi! Gerald was asked to fill the position of Rector of the University, since the African Rector had unexpectedly died! In January 2015, an African man, one of the first graduates of the university was selected to be the new Rector for Hope Africa University. There is also a secondary school and a program for training nurses and medical assistants at the Kibogora Mission and hospital in Rwanda.

If you are interested in more history of Free Methodist Missions in Central Africa, read "But Thy Right Hand," by John W. Haley, "Lights in the World," by Dr. Byron S. Lamson, "Soul Afire," the story of the life of J. W. Haley by Rev. Gerald Bates, "Frank and Hazel, The Adamsons of Kibogora" by Glen Williamson, and "New Ventures," by Leona Fear. These books were published by Light and Life Press, Winona Lake, Indiana. Some of the material that I have written in this brief history came from reading these very interesting books, and from information sent out by the Free Methodist World Missions Headquarters in Indianapolis. (All used by permission.)

CHAPTER 7

Waiting to Go to Baraka Mission, Congo

Studying *Swahili* in Usumbura, Urundi

Jambo, Bwana. Habari gani? (Hello, Mister. How are you? In *Swahili*.)

August 4, 1963, Sunday afternoon, and I've been snoozing. Still feel drowsy. We've been going to sleep with the birds since we arrived. It is dark at 6:30 and there is no TV. Even the kids are willingly asleep by 8:30! Must be the change in climate. In Brussels, it was light still at 8:30! Some change! Snappy air there and warm comfortable air here, but chilly at night with almost always a stiff breeze. Nan has caught a cold already. Her bed was in a draft. The kids are wearing their heavy p.j.'s to sleep in, but they will need cotton pajamas when it gets warmer. The kids are happy. Nine American kids are here, Peters, two, Johnsons, three, and our four. Paul is rather at loose ends, but is finding books to read. Next week the Child Evangelism lady here is having an English Vacation Bible School, and has offered to drive all our kids to town every day. So that will be nice. We are settled in. There are four Mission residential units here, like a double duplex, all with running water and electricity, but you have to boil your drinking water. So many similarities between *Swahili* and *Zulu*. Numbers almost the same, many words identical, and pronunciation the same. Will be glad to get to Congo with all our things.

Our Los Angeles shipment is waiting in Dar-es-Salaam. We can't get to Uvira (oo-vee'rah), Congo from here, a bridge is out. The kids don't like the fleas, mosquitoes, huge roaches, and chiggers that lay eggs in your toes! We got mosquito nets for the children. The kids like them. They give a feeling of security! We begin language study tomorrow with a Brethren missionary. Phil has already repaired one car, a hot water heater and our fridge! We are thoroughly enjoying the delicious papaya. We eat it three times a day! Fairly cheap and plentiful. Meat is good and less expensive than at home. The reason they had us learn *Swahili* is because it is a 'trade' language, used all over East and Central Africa, and is a rather simple language compared with the more difficult tribal languages of *Kirundi*, *Kinyarwanda*, and *Ebembe*.

August 18, 1963, Just finished the nightly ritual of tucking in the kids' mosquito nets. Malaria is rampant here, and the mosquitoes are thick. So are the fleas! The houses are screened, but the mosquitoes manage to get in anyway. Rarely a night goes by that the light doesn't go on two or three times to hunt for a pesky mosquito that buzzes our ears or fleas that tickle as they crawl to find a new spot to attack. But, even so, this is better than Belgium and we are happy to be back 'home'. Africa gets in your 'blood'! Warm tonight, after a shower, and a strong wind. Dead still now, and muggy. At least the air is cleared of the dust and smoke. This is the season when they burn off the dry grass to make the grass grow green sooner for the cattle, but it is hard on my nose. Phil, Russell and Jim Johnson are on safari to Congo. They'll be gone seven to ten days. Land Rover to Uvira, Congo, then in African dug-out canoes on the lake down to Nundu and Baraka Missions. What tales they'll have to tell when they get back. Safari sounds glamorous and exciting, doesn't it? But it is just the *Swahili* word for trip. While they are gone, we are trying to cram in *Swahili* vocabulary. I average ten new words a day. Some words lend themselves to my crazy memory schemes, such as chair, 'a kitty likes to sleep in a chair', '*kiti*' (keetee) is chair. I can remember better all the words that I can think up systems for. It's really something to lie here, listening to the African night. There are crickets, frogs, voices, drums, sometimes loud jazz from the open air beer joints, and then what a thrill to hear a strong whistle, an African man whistling one of the great hymns of the church. He is not walking in darkness, because Christ walks with him. Nancy and Paul are nearly as tall as I. She is 5 feet tall and he is 5 feet, 1 1/2 inches tall. We are getting them ready for boarding school at Mweya Mission, sewing name tags on clothes. I'll try to measure the girls tomorrow. If you send packages, less than two pounds, (*petit paquet*), with a value less than $10.00, there is no duty to pay and no trouble with customs.

I would appreciate some fine point ballpoint pens. My precious ones are going dry! Thanks.

August 21, 1963, Happy Anniversary yesterday! The men really had a trip! They slept in boats, on the beach, and in deserted Mission houses. When they slept on the beach the last night, they woke up to find hundreds of people all around them, right in the middle of the 'fish market'! They felt like 'monkeys in the zoo'! White people are rare over there now. After Phil's suitcase was unpacked and everything put away, I found a **bedbug** in the suit he had taken! We investigated their sleeping bags and they were full of bugs! So you can imagine the tizzy I went into! I've gone over all our beds and floors and sprayed two bottles of bug spray. Hope I found them all! Phil thinks they got them on the boat coming home, an African-owned thirty foot putt-putt. It took them twelve hours to make the sixty mile trip! The first morning one of them gave the can of oatmeal to the African helper to cook for them and he cooked their whole ten days' supply all at once! It is Quaker Oats, compressed into a small can a little larger than a coffee can. One can lasts our whole family a week! So their breakfasts were rather skimpy the rest of the time! Such items are unobtainable over there.

Nancy and Paul start school at the Mweya Mission boarding school

September 7, 1963, Just a quick note before we dash off to language class. Vera and Merlin Adamson, who live at Mweya Mission came down today for a dental appointment, and I do mean down! It's 6,000 feet up there and about 2,000 here. We really like the climate up there - so nice and cool. Even greenish in spite of it being end of dry season. We took the kids up to Mweya Mission, after visiting all the Mission stations with Frank Adamson. We came back down the next day. Seems empty here without Paul and Nan. We hear they seem to be adjusting OK. Nan was in tears when we left and Pats was also. She wanted to stay there with Nancy. So did Joe. So, I guess we'll send all four next year. They don't take first graders - too young to live in a dorm. It's such a nice place, a bigger hilltop than Edwaleni, with several missionary residences, a Bible School for future African preachers, and the school building and dorm for the missionary kids. Kathryn Hendrix is their teacher. She is so nice. Another couple are the dorm parents. So hard to leave our kids there, but it is for their good. This Land Rover is so bouncy on these bumpy roads, but at least it is dust-proof! All the dirt roads are coated with a thick layer of dust!

September 23, 1963, I assume you have returned from your travels and are home again. Do you know what to do with yourself, Daddy, after all those years of the going-to-work habit? How did the VW do on your trip? Did the bouncing wear you out? If you think it is rough, you should come try our Land Rover on these roads! You feel as though you have a churned gizzard and a smashed liver by the time you get there! I've been here at Mweya Mission, visiting Paul and Nancy since Wednesday. I brought Pat and Joe along. We are staying with Vera and Merlin Adamson. He is in charge of the Bible School. We knew Merlin in McPherson when his parents were on furlough from Rwanda. Merlin and Myra Adamson had attended Central College, in McPherson, Kansas, in the 1940's, when we were there, and then Merlin married Vera Bean. Phil was acquainted with her in Wichita before he went to the South Pacific! He had even given her a ride on his motorcycle! I was friends with her brother, Roy Bean, at SPC. He helped me limp through Analytical Geometry!

At Mweya Mission there is also a World Gospel Mission printing press. They print hymnals, tracts, and Sunday School supplies, in several different African languages. I've been watching our kids from a distance, and they look happy and busy. There are many shelves of books to read, so that should keep Paul happy. We ate dinner today with the kids in their dining room. Phil is working over at Kibuye Mission, doing some cabinets for the hospital. I'll go this evening and spend next week there while Phil finishes up the urgent projects. A Congolese fellow is trying to teach Phil *Swahili* as they work! I am wading through an endless list of *Swahili* verbs!

October 6, 1963, My clothes on the line got rained on this morning. I hope rainy season has started. Yesterday was almost unbearably hot. There are fewer fleas and chiggers now, but I dug a chigger egg sac out of Patty's toe the other day with a big safety pin! That is the standard way to dig them out! Doesn't hurt. She didn't even know it was there! It was about half the size of a pea! We received notice that our washing machine is missing. Hope they find it. I don't want to be without one for long.

October 21, 1963, We are at Kibogora Mission in Rwanda, above Lake Kivu. No wonder they call this the "Switzerland of Africa." It is twenty degrees cooler here, too, and that is welcome! So much nicer to sleep here than in Bujumbura. Quiet here, few mosquitoes. Lake Kivu looks calm. Lake Tanganyika, a much larger lake, is like the ocean, afternoons anyway, when the wind is up. Paul and Estelle Orcutt are here and Ila Gunsolus, Myra Adamson, RN, and Dr. Kuhn. They have a booming clinic here, and are planning on building new ward buildings. We are going over to Kumvya today, the Missionary Alliance rest camp, after Phil gets through fixing Myra's car. You may wonder why we are here. Our visas expired yesterday, so we probably shouldn't even be here. Hope we don't have trouble at the border. We'll go on over to Bukavu (boo-kah'-voo), Congo tomorrow. It's on the west side of Lake Kivu, and it used to be a Belgian resort town, but it's something like a ghost town now! We will try to get a three week visitor's visa for Burundi there and finish getting registered in Congo and try to do some shopping if there is anything left there to buy! Food that we are used to is almost non-existent in many parts of Congo.

Phil and Russell went last week over to Baraka Mission, Congo. The road, which has been impassable since May, has become fairly good. It is still under water for several miles, but only knee-deep. In our Land Rover it took them only three hours to go from Uvira down to Baraka Mission, which is so much better than three days to go up and around the other side of the Congo mountains. Our Los Angeles and New York shipments still have not arrived in Uvira, but should within two or three weeks. We are all packed up ready to move over to Congo as soon as they arrive. Our four drums from Rhodesia are waiting in Uvira and our stove and trunk from Brussels are in Bujumbura finally. The light plant and Phil's saw and jointer from Durban are in Dar-es-Salaam, Tanzania, so they should arrive within six weeks or so. Maybe we'll be settled by Thanksgiving. We hope to get up to Mweya Mission to see Paul and Nan before we move. We talked to them on the Mission radio last night. They sounded happy. Pat is sitting here trying to read over my shoulder. She is doing much better with her reading. The missionaries call Phil the 'man with the golden hands'! The Africans call him *'Bwana Fundi'*, (the man who knows how to fix things). I call him Mr. Fixit! He has fixed nearly every one of the Mission cars. What a pile of junk most of them are! But these roads! They are worse than some roads in Rhodesia because they are so mountainous. They all need Land Rovers. (And in 2013, I heard that some of these roads have been paved!)

We can just barely see the outline of one volcano at the north end of Lake Kivu. Still hazy because the rains haven't really started yet. I've been sitting in the sun because the air was chilly, but now it's too hot! Must go now to see about our lunch. (Same night, back in the Kibogora Mission guest house.) It's a *rondavel,* which is a round hut, brick, and with a tile roof instead of grass thatch! Kids are in bed. On the Mission radio/phone, we heard from Bujumbura that the Orcutts hadn't arrived yet. They left from here early this morning. She drove the car and has a sick pastor with her, and Paul Orcutt was driving the Kibuye Mission truck back down. The last time the fan came loose and he spent a night out on the road. Seems like these people are forever having car trouble! We had a wonderful time swimming and got quite sunburned. The water was chilly. Estelle Orcutt's car had problems - the drive shaft fell off!

Bukavu, Congo, Tuesday. It looks as if everything is OK. We have Burundi visas for another month, as well as permits to go in and out of Congo. Tomorrow, right after breakfast, we plan on driving down to Uvira, Congo, on the northwest corner of Lake Tanganyika. We'll check to see if our shipment is in, and store the things we bought here, which are mostly tools! Some were cheaper than in the U.S.! We did find a carton of salmon, a 100 pound sack of flour, some cans of yeast, shortening, and Quaker Oats cheaper than in Bujumbura and a few other items. So nice and cool here. It will be hard to go back down to the valley's hot climate! At the southwest end of Lake Kivu, water rushes down into the Ruzizi River (roo-zee'-zee), and here they make electricity out of it for the city of Bukavu, and for Bujumbura down at the north end of Lake Tanganyika, which is a good 150 miles south of Bukavu. We've been staying in a lovely rest home for missionaries, overlooking Lake Kivu that used to be the grand estate of important Belgian officials. There are beautiful grounds with gardenias, azaleas, bougainvillea, cedars, palms, and flowers everywhere and a vast expanse of lawn and swings for the kids. So we've all been happy here.

November 14, 1963, The kids are asleep. Phil is over in Congo again. We haven't moved over yet, but Phil and Russell are spending about half of their time over there. We are in Bujumbura again, half unpacked and ready to pack up again. We got to be with Paul and Nancy again. We drove up to Mweya Mission, got them on Friday afternoon, then we took them to the Ensigns at Kibuye Mission. Marti and Len Ensign and Doris Moore have been so good to us. Of course, they always find something for Phil to fix! We had a wonderful weekend. The day before we left, Thursday, our trunk finally arrived from Brussels! So I hurriedly unpacked it and took out the things for Paul and Nan, and repacked it to go to Congo. The same day, your package for Nan and Pats arrived. They love the nighties. They are so dainty and sweet. Thanks for the deodorant. Still can't get any here! Also, the same day, the Calvert Course books arrived. The kids are so thrilled with their new books and supplies! Also, two packages of magazines have recently arrived.

Our Los Angeles and New York shipments have finally arrived at the port in Uvira. Phil has arranged for a barge from Bujumbura to take them on down to Baraka Mission. We are almost ready to move over to Baraka Mission, Congo. The men will set up the beds before Margaret and I and the kids go over. I do hope they get all the **bedbugs** killed first! No missionaries have lived there for three years. The last trip they made it from here to Baraka Mission in 3 ½ hours. That is, even with several miles still under water and five bridges still out. The water is higher than in the pictures in the Tidings, but is down to floor board level in our Land Rover. The trip over jolts all your insides loose! I just hope it won't be too scary! We plan to really move over next week. Most of our things are already over there. Only our good equipment and our suitcases are still here. I hope we'll be able to grow a garden in Baraka Mission, even though there are probably lots of insects and goats! Patty and Joe are such good kids. While I was taking my siesta this afternoon they swept the whole house! Nancy is almost as tall as Paul, which makes her about 5'2"! Paul weighs 102 pounds! Pats is putting on weight and is shooting up too. Joe is still small and rather thin. They are anxious to get moved over to Congo so they can unpack all their things they haven't seen for so long. I don't share their enthusiasm. I dislike moving, change, new surroundings! Maybe after we retire I can find a nice comfortable rut to vegetate in! (Grumbling! Evidently I hadn't yet learned to praise the Lord **anyway**! And now that I am 89, and I **do** have time to 'vegetate' if I feel like it, I've discovered that it is rather a very boring thing to do!)

Our family and the Peters family moving to Baraka Mission, Congo

In Congo!

November 24, 1963, At Baraka Mission, Congo. We have finally arrived and are somewhat recovered from the moving process, but far from being settled. We have opened a few drums, and have partially unpacked and stuff is all over our living room. We don't have any furniture anyway, except beds, a table and three folding chairs! We have some ordered, but it may take the African man all year to make them. We found out that the man with the boat was ready to take our things from Uvira down to Baraka Mission on Wednesday morning early. We decided it would be best to be here when the boat arrives, so we started out in the Land Rover, after dinner on Tuesday. We had no difficulty at the border. We were very heavily loaded and they could have searched everything, but they only looked in one suitcase! Were we ever thankful! We had to check on gasoline, kerosene and oil drums in Uvira. That took an hour and a half. Then we drove on down to the port to check on the boat and our stuff, and there they discovered something wasn't quite cleared yet, so Margaret and I and the kids waited in the car until 5:30! Fortunately we had bread and meat and plenty of water. I found three candies left from our airplane trip in my purse and three fizzies. Margaret had a few cookies, so we managed to keep the kids occupied! After the men finally got through we started out down the lakeside.

It was nearly dark when we went through the first place where the road was under water. The waves were big and one splashed up over the hood, in through the ventilators, and got us wet! We were so thankful to have a Land Rover! When we reached the deepest water it was totally dark, but the waves were smaller by then. Even so, it was scary, but exciting. The waves broke on my window, splashed over onto the overhanging cliff and back again onto Phil's window! We had the vents closed so we didn't get wet except it leaked in a little around the doors. If the lake gets much higher, this 'road' **will** be impassable. The boat the Mission is hoping to purchase still isn't ready. We don't plan to go back over to Bujumbura until December 20 when Paul and Nan will have a two week vacation. They have to be back January 3. The rest of the road was wet, rainy and in some places muddy. There are about twelve gullies that need bridges that don't exist, and some have huge cave-ins.

We were thankful for camp cots when we finally got here, even though there were no pillows, no blankets, but plenty of sheets. Fortunately it wasn't cold! It was 9:00 p.m. by the time we arrived. We were thankful to sleep. Our drums and crates arrived the next morning on a boat that anchored near the swampy shore. Everything then had to be unloaded onto a smaller boat that could be poled up our little canal to dry land.

School boys rolled all the drums up, Peters' and ours from the States and Rhodesia, and also drums of gasoline and kerosene, up, up the little slope to our house. The Land Rover made many trips to bring up the crates, some inside, some on top, and the heaviest ones dragging behind on a cable. We wish we had taken more pictures. It was really something to see, and there was a crowd here to observe. Again, we felt like 'monkeys in a zoo'! The process took two days and the unpacking two weeks. We felt better when we finally had curtains up, and began to feel that this is 'our house'. We 'camped out' here for four days until we finally discovered our stoves had come after all. They were in such big crates we never imagined they were the stoves. You can imagine cooking for 8 people on a couple of pump-up temperamental burners! Our Coleman camp stove even acted up. What a joy our little apartment size bottled gas stoves are. They even have thermostats in the ovens! I am learning to be thankful for some things I have always taken for granted. Don't think I've ever appreciated anything so much in all my life. Peters have moved into their house and we are all relaxing today. Unpacking is fun, but tiring. I'm sorting tomorrow!

December 12, 1963, Merrry Christmas and Happy New Year! Phil is getting the Land Rover ready to make another emergency trip out to Bujumbura. On the last trip, they took a man to the hospital at Uvira in the middle of the night. He had been gored by a Cape buffalo three days before! Hope he is still alive. He has eleven kids! Anyway, that was one nightmare trip. Guess the best thing to do would be to go ahead and write whenever anything happens to write about even though there is no

mail service! We have all been sick this last week with dysentery. I am
still rather weak in the middle. We are finally almost all unpacked and
settled. One footlocker yet with clothes in it, but no chests of drawers
to put anything in, and the two small closets are full. Phil built some
rough shelves out of crating, which are a big help. The 'desk' on which
I am typing is one of the crates from Los Angeles, not the huge one. It
went to partition off part of the living room area in the Peters' house
for their kids to sleep in. Everything came through in fair shape. The
huge crate proved to be too big, just as we had feared, and was broken
on one corner, but evidently nothing was lost. Then in order to unload it
here from one boat to the smaller one which came up the little swampy
canal to dry land, they had to take off the top, and take out most of the
heavy stuff! You can imagine me, when I saw only half a crate coming
up on top of the Land Rover! Phil managed to assure me that everything
was OK and that he had done it, and that everything was on its way
up. There were a few dents in things, but nothing broken except two
mirrors from the Kansas crate and one little glass dish. All of the big
glass bowls and pyrex weren't broken. It was a good feeling to finally
be surrounded by our possessions. We hadn't seen the Rhodesia things
for almost three years!

Phil made some kitchen shelves and counter tops and a buffet, all
very rough, from crates. Temporary, of course, until lumber is available
to build some nice ones, but it was wonderful to have somewhere to put
things. Our bottled gas stoves are lovely. They are tiny, but work like a
dream. We bought them in Brussels and had them sent here, and our
wringer washing machines putt-putt nicely. No electricity here! We heat
water outside in a drum over a wood fire, but the former missionaries
also had the hot water piped into the bathroom in this house, such
luxury - we take hot baths in a big dishpan! There was a big old cement
bath tub in our bathroom, but it looked so skudzy that I couldn't stand
to make myself use it! Water has been a problem with no rain for a week,
and all the water drums went dry. We had to use lake water one day, but
the risk of Bilharzia was so great, we rigged up more rain barrels, with
screens too, to keep out the mosquitoes. They were thick when we first
arrived, but we have managed to get rid of some. We don't even have to

spray the bedrooms at night now. We trimmed the tangle of beautiful bougainvillea that had practically covered the front of this house. It had grown up onto the roof, through the gutters, and into the ceiling of the office! The mosquitoes swarmed on the porch and when it rained, water poured all over the porch. I even found a mosquito **larva** swimming in a puddle on the steps! All the water drums are full now. It has been raining nearly every night, but we are not wasting the water.

Sugar is unavailable here now and our supply from Bujumbura is nearly gone. We hope Phil will be able to find some when he goes over tomorrow. He is taking a man and his wife who had a baby three months ago, and she is sick now from complications. They are paying for a one-way trip to the hospital, so we will get some more supplies and our mail, but poor Phil, such a hectic trip to make. When we came over the lake was high, but it is even higher now. We are hoping the boat will be ready one of these days, because it probably won't be long before the road will be impassable again. Then Phil has to make the same trip next Friday to get Paul and Nancy. Someone is bringing them down to Bujumbura from Mweya Mission, so we should have our family all together next weekend for the Christmas vacation until January 6. That is, if the car gets through and they don't tip off into a gully! What a wild ride! Rhodesia had some dillies, but nothing to compare with this road. It is a mess, and every rain makes it worse. About a dozen bridges or culverts are out between here and Nundu Mission, plus the four really deep water places on the road, up near Uvira. Phil can't find lumber to make screen doors for Peters' house, nor any to make beds for our kids' foam rubber mattresses. They are still on sleeping bags and cots.

This is a pretty place. The lake is beautiful, and just across the bay is a wild peninsula where very few people live. No roads, but it is full of elephants, lions, leopards and Cape buffalo. The African men around here fish at night in their dug-out canoes with kerosene pressure lanterns to attract the fish, and nets. The lights from their boats out on the lake at night look like a big city most of the night. There are many hippos and crocs in Lake Tanganyika, but only a few near here. It's about ten miles across the bay, but it only looks like two. They say you can hear the lions roar from there when the wind is right. Exciting! I would like to go over there to see. I have really missed the animals of Rhodesia. There are so many people in Burundi that there are only a few animals left. We love the new records the people in Circle 6 gave us. They make it seem a little more like Christmas. Sure hope we can get some sugar before Christmas. Can you imagine Christmas without sweet things? Would love to be with you.

Army ants?

December, 1963, If you could come in out of the hot summer sun to sit on our cool verandah in one of our new, comfortable African-made lounge chairs, and look out over Lake Tanganyika with us on this quiet Sunday afternoon, you would be as relaxed and happy as we are. Yes, even Mary, after all her fears and forebodings, thinks Baraka Mission, Congo is a nice place to live, even though it is rather isolated. But in the few weeks we have lived here, we have made some decidedly great improvements. The mosquitoes no longer drive us crazy. Small interruption, Davey Joe just came in screaming with two bites. He foolishly got too close to an army of huge black pincher ants. Ice cubes on the painful spots and in his mouth brought prompt relief! Could they have been **army ants**? Our two youngest are happily discovering that African kids are just as much fun to play with and to share popsicles with as were any of their friends in America. However, they still longingly talk of California, where cousin Terry lives, and where there are apples and grapes and Santa Claus.

I was standing near our front verandah steps, talking with some people, when here came a huge column of big black ants, some enormous ones with big long pinchers! They poured up our steps, determined to get into our house! I screamed, ran inside, grabbed a spray can of DDT and sprayed and sprayed until they gave up, and marched out in the dirt again. I hope they didn't get into some else's house! (I wonder what the Africans thought about me. "Silly woman! Afraid of **ants**?")

Sugar shortage!

We are counting the days until Nancy and Paul come home from boarding school at Mweya Mission. It has been a month since we last saw them, a long month, knowing we were too far away for them to come home for Thanksgiving. They had a happy time at Kibogora Mission, up in Rwanda though, with Jon Orcutt, Paul's pal and roommate. But in six more days, they will be here with us for a joyful two weeks of Christmas vacation. It will be their first time to be in Congo. Their first time to ride in the Land Rover 'in' the lake, just like a boat! On Phil's last trip out to Usumbura to take a sick person to the hospital, the lake level in several stretches of the inundated road was six inches above the floor board, but hardly any leaked in and the trusty vehicle kept purring right along, even though Phil could hear the fan throwing water all over the engine. The sugar refinery has run out of some necessary chemical, so there is a sugar shortage. We have been low on sugar for a week, and without any for a whole day. And I was having grim thoughts about Christmas with no sugar! But Phil came home with a whole 120 pound sack he had talked somebody out of! It's not the cleanest sugar I ever saw, but it is sweet. Rejoicing in the Kline house! Davey Joe can have cinnamon toast again, and we can make bread pudding and ice cream and even kool-aid from our precious little hoard! And when the kids come home, we can have fun making Christmas cookies and candy. Wonderful to have sugar! Thank You, Lord!

December 19, 1963, Phil leaves early in the morning for Bujumbura to get Paul and Nancy. He'll bring them on Saturday. Pats and Joe are so excited! I won't let them decorate the tree until the other kids arrive. It's so pretty and sparkly, looks just like a tree covered with snow! This is the artificial tree we packed and brought from California. We probably won't be able to have Christmas on the 25th. The Africans have a big meeting every Christmas, at their church. This year it is a three day affair way up at Nundu Mission. Phil and Russell will probably have to be there from the 24th to the 26th, so we'll either have an early or a late family Christmas. Today has been a scorcher! Humid and sticky and lots of flies! I wish it would rain. Our water supply is getting low and my garden is very thirsty. Sometimes it rains every day and then no rain for days. I have curtains up now in our bedrooms and bathroom.

Slow going when you have to do it all by hand! We'll be so glad when our power plant arrives.

Would you please make me a couple of muumuus, modest ones, you know, not too scoopy. (I should have been ashamed of myself. I didn't tell my mother I was pregnant! But we had thought a pregnancy would be impossible!) Use some of the material I left, if you think it's suitable or buy more, and I'll send you a check. Make sure it's drip-dry, please. I weigh 130 now, probably size 15-16. (And when the muumuus did arrive, an older missionary told me I shouldn't wear such short dresses. I'm sure she didn't know I was pregnant, either. The problem was, that before we had left the States, Phil had had a vasectomy, because when Davey Joe had been born, the doctor told me **never** to get pregnant again, especially way out in the '**boonies**' because of the prolonged and difficult delivery of both Patty and David.)

It will be nice to get our mail again. Phil has been going over to Bujumbura nearly every week for the last three weeks, which makes it nice. We are afraid to use the mail service here. It's too unreliable, and Bujumbura postal service is about the best in Central Africa. One Sunday evening we were lying in bed, reading Sunday School papers mother had sent from the States, when suddenly here came a huge, enormous hairy spider running across my pillow. I screamed and jumped out of bed, and the thing headed for Phil. He jumped too and so did the spider. It was probably more scared than we were. He hid under the bed. Phil swooshed him out, and clobbered him with a shoe. Well, he was probably harmless, but too big to stay alive in our house! Our family is all together in our own home for two weeks! How wonderful it feels! Paul and Nancy are having such fun discovering all their old treasures. Paul is overjoyed to be finally reunited with his football, train, bike and our good assortment of children's books. Davey Joe wishes audibly, every now and then for "our electricity to hurry up and get here so I can run my train!" We are wishing too. Don't know what is holding it up in Dar-es-Salaam.

1964 – In Bujumbura, Burundi

January 12, 1964, We have returned to Bujumbura after taking the kids back to school at Mweya Mission. The Missionary Retreat at Kibuye Mission was good. Seems nice to be in civilization again! There is even a shop where you can buy hamburgers and something like Dairy Queen cones! Nice to be where you can buy things again. Only thing, we are only allowed to take $10.00 worth per family across the border! Phil made a three day trip up to Bukavu, Congo, and hardly found anything there. He did bring back six large cans of dehydrated onions, for which we are thankful. We are stranded here in Bujumbura until the Mission can buy a boat. However, we got here OK. The water was about one and one half inches below the door handles. We stalled only once and that was after we pulled up out of the deepest hole. Phil dried off the distributor cap and we went merrily on our way, 'putting' just like a boat! Now the lake is six inches higher. Phil says that makes the deep holes in the Congo road too deep for safe family travel. Phil will attempt it alone, and expects to stall several times, which means the car will get rather full of water unless he climbs out the windows! But I don't think he can do that. Don't know for sure what we'll do. Either we'll wait here until Phil returns in a little African boat, or if the Mission is able to purchase a boat here, Phil will go in the car and the rest of us by boat. Rev. Ron and Margaret Collett plan to go to Congo with us. Ron is supposed to hold pastors' institutes. They will live with us and the men will make safari trips from there. They will probably only stay with us a month or so, then they will go to Kibuye Mission.

Now, a piece of **shocking** news! We wish desperately it weren't true, but if all goes well, you will have another grandchild, maybe by May 22! So, the impossible has happened, but I am well and feel fine and plan to make the long trip to Kibuye Mission a month early. The mission hospital is well equipped and I will be under expert care, so I'm not worried, so don't worry! Just still wishing it weren't true! Phil has accepted it with more grace than I. I am less unhappy about it than I was, and I am just trying not to feel sorry for myself. When she is sixteen, I will be almost sixty! Old enough to be her grandmother! (How did I know she would be a **she**?) The last part of Isaiah 46:4 is the Lord's promise to me, so I can't grumble! After all, this may be a **special** gift to us from the Lord. (Little did we know how special Janet would be, a miracle, really. The verse the Lord gave me, "I have made, and I will bear; even I will carry, and will deliver you.") Wow! Thank You, Lord! (2013 Editing note: I know, I took it out of context, but it just jumped out at me, so I assumed the Lord had called it to my attention! And I **really** felt He had sent it to me! I had written in my old King James Bible, that my worries had disappeared! That was the only Bible I had in Africa, and I still have it, very worn and well-used.)

The Frederika. Our big 30' diesel powered boat!

January 22, 1964, (In Bujumbura, Burundi.) Just a brief note to let you know we are ready to go over to Congo in the Mission's new (very old) big boat. Phil is waiting. He returned from Baraka Mission in an African boat and hitch-hiked in a truck from Uvira. Phil, Russell and Ron Collett had taken the Land Rover through the water-covered road. The water was up to the door handles, but didn't even stall once! Phil said it was just like going through the Red Sea! Miraculous!

January 26, 1964, (In Congo.) Phil is leaving again in the morning, so here is another unexpected chance for mail. This time he will take our boat to Bujumbura, and then go by airplane way up north to Bukavu, Congo. The diesel engine on the boat isn't acting quite right. I hope he gets there OK. We had a lovely trip over here. It was calm almost all the way until just at dusk we hit a squall and really got tossed around. But it's a good boat, thirty feet with a cabin below deck with six bunks and even a chemical toilet! Really makes it nice for traveling with kids. The fuel line clogged up and we stalled several times. What a weird feeling to be in the middle of that huge expanse of water and no other boats in sight, and no power! The fuel was coming directly off the bottom of the tank, but Phil fixed that. What is wrong now, he can't find. It sounds as though it is missing. He has had it all apart and can't find anything. Phil will leave it with someone to check it over in Bujumbura. We are all well, but tired.

Phil, Russell, and the Colletts went up to Nundu Mission yesterday and got back today, middle of the afternoon. The Colletts are very nice people and we are enjoying having them with us. Ron and Margaret Collett had been pioneer missionaries in Burundi, beginning in 1936, with the Adamsons. Next weekend they are planning on visiting the church people up in Epupu (eh poo'poo), way up in the Congo mountains. We can see the mountains from here. They are 8,000 feet in elevation. It really gets cold up there. We could use a bit of cold here. It's really been uncomfortably warm. It rarely rains daytimes now, but will later. When we do get a rain at night it is usually a tremendous cloud-burst. Our garden is growing, but what a battle with the insects!

The trouble spots in Congo are a good long way from here. We are in such an isolated area that even if Kivu province got in an uproar, it probably wouldn't reach us. Ask the people to pray for government subsidies for our schools. The teachers are unable to live on the small amount they get now. A man is bringing some lumber in the morning. Can you imagine Phil with no wood, no bricks and no cement?

February 26, 1964, (Still in Congo.) When Phil came back from his trip to Bujumbura to take the Colletts over there, we were overjoyed to see all the packages he brought back with him. There were two Christmas packages from you, the muumuu you shouldn't have sent airmail, but it's nice to have, thank you! Two of the packages contained Tupperware, and two were from the Women's Missionary Society in Long Beach. So we had Christmas in February! You should have seen us. Don't know who was the most excited. Thanks for it all. It is a good thing you sewed all the packages up. One would have been lost long before it reached Bujumbura, but with the sheeting sewn so securely, nothing was lost! I was so glad to see the jar lids. I have a few jars, so as soon as the guavas start getting ripe, I will can some. Then I gave her a list of baby clothes and things that I would need! I don't know if I have covered all the necessaries or not. It has been so long since I've had any anything to do with a baby I'm sure I'll be all thumbs.

Hey! Guess what! We have **electricity** for the first time! What a difference. The lights are so much brighter than the Coleman lanterns that it almost hurts my eyes! And guess who is the most thrilled? Davey Joe got his train rigged up first thing, so he is satisfied now. He was even willing to stop it long enough to eat supper! They are wishing Paul were here so he could get his train going too. And I'm sure if Paul knew, he would be quite unhappy they won't be coming home for Easter vacation. We have been invited to spend that week at Kibuye Mission. I guess the doctor thought I'd better go up there for a checkup. I've been only once, but with the good pills and capsules he gave me, I keep feeling OK. The girls were thrilled with their slips. They are growing like weeds! Thanks for all you've sent.

Prayer letter to our friends and prayer partners, written in Congo

What's it like living in Congo, 1964? Baraka, is a place of beauty. The vivid hues of bougainvillea combine with palm and eucalyptus trees to frame our front verandah view of Lake Tanganyika, that fearful and enormous 'Sea of Storms'. It provides us with an endless change of scene, now calm, quiet, picture-like loveliness in deep blues and greens, then early morning splendor. The lake is pale blue with streams of gold pouring from the rising sun into the swampy channels near the shore and then fully living up to its name when all the fury of a tropical storm lashes the water into six foot waves that beat upon the shores with the roar of an ocean. All night in calm weather, the lights from the dugout canoes of the fishermen far across the bay and a few near our shore, glisten like strings of diamonds against the black of the African night. Hundreds of lights, so many, you'd think for sure there was a big city across the bay, but it's only the fishing canoes. In the middle of the night we can hear them banging their oars on the sides of their boats to scare the fish into their nets, and oh, the fish they bring for us to buy! Flopping fresh, some three feet long, Nile Perch, but our favorite is a smaller trout-like variety. This is the first place we've lived in Africa where fish are abundant and cheap. It's a nice change, but there's hardly any beef available here. What else do we have to eat? The Africans keep selling us eggs, vegetables, tropical fruits in season, chickens, and an occasional goat, which we have discovered to be good eating. We have a garden with green beans, cucumbers, corn, peppers, some scrawny lettuce, vines of pumpkin, watermelon, cantaloupe, and sweet potatoes. From the local shops in the tiny village of Baraka, three miles from our mission, we can purchase cans of powdered milk and sacks of buggy flour, sugar, cooking oil, and a few other items. Nearly everything else we must purchase from Bujumbura, Burundi.

How we look forward to those times when someone has to go to Bujumbura! It's a tiring seven-hour trip in our thirty foot diesel powered boat up north and across the lake. We don't go very often, but Phil does make the trip over every three to four weeks. Then he brings back our mail! What excitement at our once-a-month mail time! Also he brings back fresh vegetables from the market in Bujumbura, scrumptious papayas from the mission there, canned goods, butter, beef, and bacon! Twice a week we bake bread and sweet rolls with that tempting bakery aroma, and how fast those hot rolls disappear! Our family is glad we 'live in the sticks' and have to bake our own bread! (I didn't bake the bread, our African helper did! He must have been trained by the former British missionaries who had lived here! I was so thankful he was already trained.) Our water supply? This is rainy season, and as long as it rains twice a week, we catch plenty of good, clean water in drums from our galvanized iron roof. Of course, we have to boil our drinking water. Just this week, however, we got down to our last couple gallons. Tomorrow we would have to have a drum of water hauled up from the contaminated lake. We had prayed for days as our water supply got lower and lower, "Oh, Lord, send us rain." But there was no rain in sight, and our African helpers said, "This is a dry month, no rain is coming." But that night the Lord sent us a cloudburst and filled all our drums full to overflowing, a week's supply of safe water! When our kitchen helper arrived in the morning, he said with a beaming face, "*Mungu* (God) sent you that rain, *Madamo*. Outside the mission, it rained only a little!" I knew it was from the Lord. As the first noise of the storm had awakened me in the night, I had lain there listening to the crashing of the thunder and the heavy rain beating down, thanking God for His tender mercies and loving watchful care.

He sends eggs too. When our eggs are nearly gone, I pray in my early morning 'alone time', "Oh Lord, you know we need eggs today." And without fail, someone always comes along that morning with eggs to sell. "Thank you, Lord!" Knowing that He who loves us with a never-ending love is here with us, enabling us to pray with the Psalmist David, as we lie down to a peaceful, fear-free night's sleep, even when we hear gun-shots in the night. "I will both lay me down in peace, and sleep: for thou Lord, only, makest me dwell in safety." Psalm. 4:8. Thank you for continuing to pray for us.

A fisherman sold us a Nile Perch he had caught
from Lake Tanganyika
Patty, our African helper, Davey Joe, Mary

Danger is near!

We were shocked to learn recently when our African helper burst in unexpectedly one evening begging for shelter for the night, that there are drunken and undisciplined *Simba* rebel soldiers in **our** area, breaking into houses, beating up people, intimidating the young men into joining them, throwing the resisters in jail, pillaging, stealing, and some nights we have heard gun shots! And people tell us the good officials of this province have been jailed and 'bad' ones have taken their places. All this, to make sure the coming election goes 'their way!' Oh pray that the Congo Central government will remain a 'good' one. General elections will be in June, and it is predicted this will be a time of much trouble and unrest. Pray for strength for the good government officials, and for the success of their attempts to stamp out the terrorist activities of those who are making desperate attempts to gain control of not only Congo, but all Africa as well. (We learned later that the *Simba*, rebel revolutionary soldiers, had lists of people that had been educated by Christian missionaries, including teachers and Christian leaders. They were all slated for execution.)

How do we feel when suddenly confronted with the knowledge that danger is nearly on our doorstep? Shook-up, to say the least. Here we had been feeling so secure in thinking that our peaceful little corner of Congo was too isolated, that it wouldn't happen here as it had in Kwilu Province where 300 missionaries had recently been evacuated, leaving everything behind. We prayed for them as we heard the terrible news, "Oh Lord, give them peace of mind." But when the very real possibility comes so close to our home, there is such temptation to become fearful and anxious. "Should we begin packing the things we treasure most? How best to plan a quick escape? Will they leave us unmolested? Oh Lord, help us to be willing to lose all our possessions, help us to be able to radiate your joy even if called upon to suffer imprisonment or possible martyrdom for your Name's sake." Yes, it's different when the threat of danger comes close to home. We are sure you will be praying with us and for the Congolese Christians, for His protection, for strength, courage, and hearts so full of love, peace, and joy that there is no room for fear.

CHAPTER 8

We are Refugees, but God Supplies All Our Needs

While we were still in Congo, some of our *Babembe* church leaders had come to us and begged us to leave quickly for our sakes as well as for theirs. They had told us that it was no longer safe for them to have us living there! So, we hurriedly had packed, taking what we could, as well as the kids' bikes, our typewriter, recorder, some of our clothing, my little portable sewing machine, our Bibles, some food for the journey, our slide projector, our passports, our baby books, and a few important papers. We thoroughly expected to be able to return to resume our work at Baraka Mission within a few months, after the election. Phil did return several times for short visits to give direction and assurance to the people that they had not been abandoned. But at the time we left, evidently there was close and imminent danger of the *Simba* Army (*Swahili* word for lion) coming nearer, because our church people kept urging us to hurry.

After we were all on the boat, Phil, Mary, Patty, Joe, and the Peters family, Phil tried to start the engine on our thirty foot diesel powered boat. It would not start. Finally, he stripped off his trousers, climbed off the boat, went down into the swampy channel, swam down under the boat, and was able to remove the vines that had wrapped themselves around the propeller! He climbed back on board and when the engine finally turned over we all cheered, and prayed together for the Lord's protection for all of us. I was nearly eight months pregnant, and as the children and I huddled down in the cabin of the boat, I began to feel nauseated by the fumes from the engine. I remember feeling very sick as we chugged across the lake into the dark of the night. I don't remember if the water was choppy or calm. I only remember my feelings of relief when we **finally** docked in the harbor at Bujumbura. We were refugees.

We had left most of our belongings behind. Many missionaries in other parts of the Congo escaped with only the clothing they were wearing, and some others, like the Catholic Fathers, whose mission was only one mile from ours, were martyred. (Little did we know that we would never be able to return to Congo to live and work there. We only knew that God had delivered us from the hand of the Evil one who had taken possession of many of the young African men.)

In the big city of Bujumbura, Burundi

March 18, 1964, We are once more in civilization. How nice for a change. We had also liked the peace and quiet of our 'quiet' little corner of Congo, but elections are coming up, and it is anything but quiet there now. So, we are here in Burundi until Congo election time is over, and things settle back down to normal. It's a good feeling to be here. Thought I might have the baby on the boat! What a wild ride that was! We ran into a squall and Patty and I took turns 'urping' into a bucket. Phil and the Peters stayed up on deck in the fresh air, so they weren't feeling so bad. Phil was so thankful for the compass because he couldn't see a thing in the fog. I'm feeling better now, but still not up to facing the rough ride up to Kibuye Mission. We'll go on up next week. It was so nice of the Ensigns to invite us to spend Easter vacation with our kids at Kibuye. Guess maybe they figured it would be a good way to get me up there when they had told me to come **two** months ahead of baby time! I figured I could wait until May first to go. Anyway, I'm glad this much of the trip is behind us! Glad to hear Daddy is really enjoying being retired! Give our love to the rest of the family. Please request prayer for the elections in Congo. You know who is desperate to gain control of the whole country, and the people are so dissatisfied, that the bad guys might win!

March, 1964, (in Bujumbura, Burundi a few days later) Just a brief note before we begin to load up. Phil is putting a new brake line in the Kibuye Mission car. It broke yesterday when Doris was on her way down here to get us. Phil and Doris went in to town this morning, and maybe miraculously, Patty's Calvert Course third grade stuff came in the mail!

She is just finishing second grade this week! And my elastic stockings! Thank you so much. It is chilly up there at Kibuye. I was hoping they would arrive before I left to go up-country. I firmly believe in a loving Heavenly Father's care for us. I am recovered from the boat trip over here. Patty has been very ill since we arrived here, strep throat. All the Johnson family have had it too, but Dr. Alexander came along with some pills to prevent getting it for Phil and me, so it looks as though we will escape. Pats is OK now. We are all excited about getting to see Paul and Nan soon. They get out of school on Thursday afternoon, and we will have a whole week with them at Kibuye Mission. Patty is so thrilled about her new school books that she is working hard at it already. Glad for something to keep them happy - all their toys are packed and ready to load in the car. Must stop now and rest a bit if there is time.

I am now staying on at Kibuye with Doris Moore and the Ensigns, awaiting the arrival of our 'unexpected/expected child of our old age!' Maybe the Lord is sending us this one because He knows how hard it will be next year to send Paul, Nancy, Patty, and Joe, all of them, away to boarding school. But we are thankful to have such a wonderful place for our children to live and attend school. It is so much better for them there at Mweya Mission with other missionary family children of their own ages, than to be on an isolated mission station. With every hardship come even more blessings! Thank you for continuing to pray for us. As you pray daily, please remember to pray for the *Babembe* Christians, and other Christians in Congo. Some have already fled, some have already been persecuted and martyred because they were Christians. Pray also for Phil, who is back in Baraka Mission, Congo, trying to 'carry on' without Mary and the kids and the Peters' family.

We purchase a little '55 V W!

April, 1964, (A letter from Phil in Bujumbura to Mary's parents), Surprised to see a note from me, I suppose! Mary is up at the Kibuye Mission where our hospital is, waiting, and I am in Bujumbura preparing to go farther up north to Bukavu, Congo and back here and then south to Baraka Mission, Congo in the middle of the week. All of us are OK. The kids are back in school. Another missionary is selling a 1955 VW passenger car. She is going on furlough. We are buying it for $500, and so, of course, we need some money from our account at the Credit Union. Will you please take this note to the Credit Union and ask them to make the transfer? Will you also find out when they make the transfer, and let us know so we can draw from our bank account? This gal needs the money to pay for her ticket, so I would like to help her out. I think Mary just wrote to you, so no need of my taking your time to read a long letter, so will close and get ready for breakfast. Thanks a lot. Love, Phil

Up in the mountains in Burundi

April, 1964, Conference is in full swing here at Kibuye Mission, and I am also still here. Eileen Lehman was unable to come, and her husband, Stan, stayed with her, which left an extra room for the kids and me. I had planned to go to Mweya Mission to teach for Kathryn Hendrix, but one night I had contractions half the night, so I was given orders to stay here. Mornings I have 'fun school' with the little Johnsons, Nicki Ensign, Virginia Orcutt, my kids and the little Adamsons. Afternoons, I rest and usually sleep. Pat and Joe are really enjoying being with other American kids. I am feeling fine, have six weeks to go, and I'm not so uncomfortable now. I have to take it easy, but I don't mind being lazy! A package arrived from you containing Tupperware, the pretty dress you made for me, and this pen. Thanks, really appreciate it. Also a package from L. Fisher, containing seven pair of knit slippers! They were so welcome. It's chilly here and I forgot to bring any slippers along! I'll write to her to let her know how much we appreciate them. She probably sent them from her Women's Missionary Society Circle. Immediately following Conference, we will have our Congo Mission meeting here with Vic Macy. Phil is back home at Baraka Mission now, but will cross the lake again and drive up here on Friday. Then the men will safari back again to Congo on the boat. Vic wants to make a film and there are many church council meetings, to be held there. Phil is arranging for them now. We contacted him by radio yesterday, and he said everything over there seems to be OK for now, so we assume the soldiers are gone, the local election is over and everything is peaceful once more. However, since the general Congo elections are in June, and there could be a lot of unrest in May and June, please continue to pray. Marti Ensign flew home, hoping to arrive before her father dies. I am helping to take care of Nicki. I've been letting down hems again! That Nancy is just growing too fast! Then when I can't let them down any more, I put them up again for Patty! Did you receive my letter with the kids' measurements? Have you found out where to order name tapes?

April 27, 1964, Doris and Len are going to Kitega tomorrow to take the car in to get the hole in the oil pan fixed. With these roads they all need new Land Rovers or VW Kombis! Dr. Len told me tonight that the baby's head is engaged already! He doesn't think I'll wait to have it until May 22. Goody! I'm getting so tired carrying all this excess weight around! The men will be coming back to Bujumbura from Baraka Mission this weekend. Sure hope Phil can come on up here. Paul and Nancy have a free weekend and will be here. Mweya Mission is only a forty-five minute drive from the Kibuye Mission. It's nice to be so close. Paul is doing very well in piano. One of the Friends' missionary men gives all the Mweya kids lessons each week. They have the same Sunday School quarterlies and memory work system as at the Hermon church, and both Paul and Nan are working hard to get trophies. Bed time again. Seems like I sleep a lot here. It's certainly a good feeling to be here. I've finally got a prayer letter ready to send.

May 4, 1964, At Kibuye Mission, Burundi. Still waiting, very impatiently. The head is engaged and doctor says it can't be much longer. Hope not! Paul and Nancy were here for the weekend. We had a nice time together, except Phil was over in Baraka Mission. He reports that everything seems OK there now, but the American Embassy in Bukavu must know something because they are insisting that he maintain daily radio contact at a set time to report on conditions there! It isn't a very good feeling to know your husband is constantly under the threat of danger! We do appreciate the prayers going up for him. I'm not worried or anxious. He is in God's hands. Thanks for letting us know the money has been transferred. Yes, we will keep the VW here in Bujumbura to have for transportation after we get off the boat. The lake is getting higher and higher, so it will be a long time before we can drive over in the Land Rover again. Phil said tonight on the radio/phone that the road is now impassable even between Baraka and Nundu Missions! The lake is deep over the road in several places! So that makes him dependent even more on the boat. The kids have two names finally picked out, Janet Kae or Daniel James (Danny Jim). I don't care what it is, I just want to get it out! I am very tired of being PG! Doris just told me the baby could arrive any day now. It probably will be at night, and we've no electricity now. The water tank collapsed that cooled the generator engine, and let it overheat! Such is life here.

May 10, 1964, Happy Mother's Day! We have just returned from Mweya Mission with Nancy and Paul. Phil arrived at Kibuye Mission yesterday afternoon from Baraka Mission, Congo. This morning we decided it would be nice to go over to Mweya and bring back the kids for the rest of the day. We did and took along a picnic lunch. The first time we had done anything like that since we left the States! We found a nice secluded, grassy clearing in a grove of Eucalyptus and Acacia on the edge of Mweya Mission, and ate there. It was a lovely spot. It's so difficult to find a private spot anywhere here. Certainly different from sparsely populated Rhodesia and South Africa! Phil wanted to come back so he could really sleep. Poor fella, I kept him awake half the night. I have a hard time really sleeping nights any more. He will stay for a week. We are hoping the baby will arrive while he is here. The head is so low it can't be much longer. A surgeon was here yesterday doing surgery with Dr. Ensign, so in the afternoon he re-did Phil's vasectomy, and found an **extra** tube! Tuesday. The baby's head is back up again, so I may have another one to two weeks yet! Jim Johnson just arrived with the mail and will be going back to Bujumbura tonight so I'll send this with him. Your letter of May 4 to Kitega just arrived. Glad you got the name tapes. Hope you sent them in a package instead of a manilla envelope, they get torn in transit. Half gallon milk cartons come through in fine shape, especially if covered with cloth and sewn securely. We will need some sponge hair rollers for the girls next year. The girls have to wash and do their hair on Saturdays, so that's why we'll need more than we have now. I'm feeling disgustingly good and am resigned to more waiting. Not even any more night contractions!

Our precious baby arrives!

May, 1964, It's all over. We have an adorable little girl, Janet Kae, 21 inches long, 8 1/2 pounds, lots of light brown hair, fat little face. She's a sweet little doll and we all love her, especially the girls! The boys are a bit disappointed because she wasn't a boy, but I'm glad she wasn't twins! She arrived yesterday evening after a whole day of mild contractions and 1 1/2 hours of good hard ones, but only ten minutes of pushing her out! That's the shortest second stage I've ever had, and thank the Lord it was a perfectly normal delivery. I was so afraid it would be a long difficult delivery like Pat and Joe's. This one seems just like a miracle! Phil, of course, got to watch. He has become quite interested in things medical around here. He is up watching them do a C-section now. He watched a difficult forceps delivery this morning. This is the 6th baby this weekend, but all day yesterday, I was the only one going and had constant and loving attention. Both Len and Doris were angels. They took turns sitting with me all day! They started me on an I.V. Pitocin drip at 7 in the morning, but I didn't begin to dilate much until 4 in the afternoon. I'm so glad the 'pit drip' worked, because Phil has to go back to Congo tomorrow and Len needs to go to Bujumbura this week to purchase supplies for the hospital, but wouldn't leave Kibuye Mission until I delivered. Phil brought Paul and Nan over so they could see Janet. Their school is out June 5. By that time she will be two weeks old, and I will be 'myself' again! I feel fine today. They let me up for a little while this afternoon and I'll get up for prayer meeting tonight. You have probably been hearing the news about Kivu Province. The area that has been taken over by the *Simba*s is about fifty miles north of our station. Too close for comfort. Don't know what Phil and Ron Collett will find when they go over this week. So far all has been quiet down in our area. If things get 'hot' they will come on back. No sense staying and taking chances! Phil has so much building to do it is rather frustrating to have things so uncertain. Do pray for their safety and for the other missionaries in the area. Some have evacuated and one large station farther north is encircled, and so far no one has been able to rescue them.

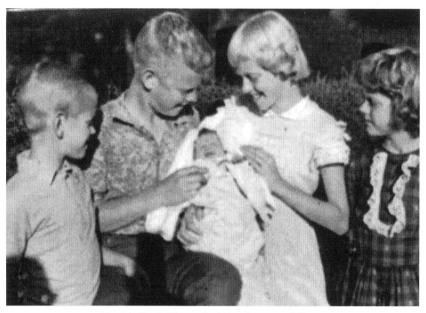

David, Paul, Nancy holding Janet and Patty

Last day of school

June 5, 1964, Just a quick note. We came into Kitega to register Janet's birth, an hour's drive from Kibuye Mission, only to find out that the office is open only on Mondays. So that means another trip. We are on our way to Mweya Mission for the last day of school program and to bring the kids back to Kibuye Mission. Phil drove down to Bujumbura, but returned here within a few days. They can't go over to Baraka Mission until they receive assurance that the boat won't be confiscated. You've probably heard more in the news about Kivu Province than we have. Albertville is 200 miles south, and Bukavu where most of the action is now is about 150 miles to the north, but the *Simbas* have taken over all of the territory in between. So, I guess we'll be setting up housekeeping in the old 'white house' at Kibuye Mission, where Colletts were living. It is all newly cleaned and whitewashed and aired out, so it won't be quite so cold. Everybody says they have things we can use. We just hope all our nice things at Baraka Mission won't be bothered, and that it won't be too long before we can go back to live there. However, the way things look now, it may be a long, hard struggle because the *Simba* soldiers aren't going to give up easily! At least, maybe our family can be together for awhile, and there is lots of work on all the mission stations here for Phil to do. Stanley Lehman wants Phil to come to Muyebe Mission to help him re-roof his house. Phil has already gotten many things in running order at Kibuye already. Kibuye Mission is our favorite station here in Burundi. Of course, the hospital is here! It's a pretty place with lots of trees and grass. We are at the post office. Phil is loading up packages for the hospital, twenty-one today! All the Women's Missionary Societies' are sending baby gowns, but they need them, because they give out so many! Phil may go on over to Congo if he can, and bring back a load of our things. Pray!

June 24, 1964, (from Kibuye Mission) Hope I get this written before Colletts take off. They are taking a load of things to Mweya Mission, where they will live next year. He will have charge of the Bible School. Merlin and Vera Adamson, who have been there, leave for furlough the first of next week. The Colletts are leaving a lovely garden here for us with beans, peas, lettuce, tomatoes, and strawberries. They have rejuvenated all the fruit trees they had planted near this house years ago. There are orange trees, tangerine, grapefruit, mulberry, avocado, and blackberry vines, plus a whole orchard full of guava trees. Guavas make wonderful jelly. Phil is in Bujumbura again. He came up just for the weekend. He took Paul down with him last time, so Paul could get his dental work done. Phil is working Doris' car over now. She plans to go to Nairobi, East Africa, for vacation with several other single ladies, and Phil won't let her go with her car as it is, so that is his work for this week!

Did I tell you that the Alexander family is moving to Kivimba, a Friends' Mission station to fill in there while their doctor is on furlough? The Alexanders were planning on storing their furniture in a house here at Kibuye Mission because the doctor at Kivimba left a houseful for them to use while there, so, the Alexanders, when they heard that we had practically nothing, said, "Why don't you use our things?" Just another of the wonderful provisions of the Lord for us! It's just marvelous the way everything is working out for us. Phil is rather discouraged. I think he blames himself because he wouldn't believe that the rebels were really going to take over in our area, and he left so many of our things over there that he could just have easily brought to safety in Bujumbura. All his tools, and equipment, to say nothing of our linens and all my nice little kitchen gadgets, but as I keep telling him, the Lord has graciously supplied all our needs so far, so I am not going to cry over the things we left behind over there. Of course, they would be nice to have. Maybe he will feel better after we get really settled here. We are still living with Doris Moore. Bless her!

The 'white house' is nearly ready for us. They are re-mudding the ceilings in a couple of rooms, and can't get whitewash to finish it up, but may be able to find some in Bujumbura. The cement floors are freshly waxed and cleaned, and it all looks so nice. Phil plans to put shelves in the kitchen, and will even put a toilet and wash basin in the bathroom, if he can find some that aren't too expensive! So, we will have it nicer than what we had in Congo. The climate is so much more pleasant here, and so much more quiet, except when they beat the drum. It rumbles! They use the drum instead of a bell for the school and church. It is so close to our house, and it is so loud it frightens Janet and she screams, and we can feel the vibrations from the deep bass sound waves all through our bodies!

Living over in Congo was the most difficult place we ever had to live and work. However, I'm perfectly willing to go back, if and when the Lord opens it up again. But it's so much nicer here that I am thoroughly enjoying being a 'refugee' here in Burundi, even though we have practically nothing of all the things we have been accumulating all these years. I do have my sewing machine, typewriter, and all the clothes we need, and a few other things even, so we have much more than many missionaries who have just recently had to evacuate! Some of them have absolutely nothing but the clothes on their backs. So, we are fortunate. You can see why I am so thrilled over the dishes that you are now sending! The missionaries here will lend us some until they arrive, but it will be nice to have some of our own! Please send jeans for the boys and pedal pushers for the girls.

A place of our own

June 29, 1964, We'll be in Burundi indefinitely. It looks as though it will be a long time, if ever, before we can go back to Congo. Alexander's furniture will be here next week. The kids are getting anxious to get moved to some place they can call their own! One set-back, the mud they were plastering the kitchen ceiling with has fallen off in spots! The floors look nice. Ron makes his own floor wax with melted paraffin, kerosene and coloring. Some rooms have green floors and the others red; much nicer than drab cement color. Guess we will buy some African sleeping mats made of reeds to use for rugs. Colletts are going down to Bujumbura today to see Merlin and Vera Adamson off for furlough. Then they will move to Mweya Mission later in the week. Janet is growing. Don't know how much she weighs. She smiles quite a bit now and Nancy is a very good baby sitter. She loves changing her and dressing her. Janet is sleeping better. She goes five hours in the night between feeds. I'm glad we have Janet. She is a doll. Never thought I would feel like this about a baby again. But she's an angel.

Down in the big city of Bujumbura

July 11, 1964, Patty had her dental work done Thursday, but has to go back in two weeks for permanent fillings. I was surprised that I had no cavities! Phil brought us down in our little VW, all seven of us. Then he took Jim Johnson back up-country because Jim doesn't have reliable transportation. Jim, Len and Phil have all gone hunting today. There are cape buffalo, elephants, and many others, down closer to the eastern border. Phil is supposed to bring Jim back down today and take us back up to Kibuye Mission. There were seven packages for us in the mail, full of lots of things we needed. We were so thankful to receive them. The little pajamas are so cute. All the baby things are sweet, just love the little clown suit. Thanks, Orlean, if it all came from you! You should see Janet now! She is growing and is so sweet. She sleeps eight hours at night now, which is wonderful. Really helps to get that much good unbroken sleep. She is such a good baby and happy. She smiles a lot and nearly laughs. Don't know what we ever did without her! The name tapes arrived! The first unbroken manila envelope! So good to have them. We are sewing them on already.

The latest news from across the lake - our house is untouched. The *Simba* soldiers couldn't get the Land Rover started. Phil had removed and had hidden the distributor. So they pushed the vehicle out of the garage and several soldiers are living in the garage! They are killing the resisting Christians, but many are fearful and are submitting. Request prayer for them, please, and for the church leaders who have fled to other countries, or are in hiding. Thanks for sending all the nice things.

July 22, 1964, We just returned from Mweya Mission. They had the annual Missionary Convention there this year instead of up in Rwanda because of the political situation there. It was really good. Doris is in Nairobi, Kenya on her vacation. She'll be gone another two weeks. We are still in her house. Phil is getting ready to put a toilet and wash basin in our bathroom and cupboards and a good sink in the kitchen. He's here and ready. They are begging for us to come up to Kibogora Mission near Lake Kivu in Rwanda to help them. They are about ready to build a hospital ward building. The people have already burned clay bricks in a kiln.

August 9, 1964, Glad you are making good use of the VW Kombi we left with you. That beach trip sounded like fun! I'm sending pictures of Janet in this letter and three in another. Phil is fixing his car, getting ready to go down to Bujumbura for a Congo Mission meeting with Gerald and some of the church leaders who are also refugees. We are in our house at Kibuye Mission with Alexander's furniture, dishes, kitchen utensils and linens! We are so glad they had extra things, and so many are identical with the things we brought out and left in Congo! Phil has our sink installed in the kitchen with hot and cold water. Our hot water heater is a 44 gallon gas drum, bricked in, heated by a wood fire underneath, and piped into both bathroom and kitchen. Our kitchen will be so nice. Phil hasn't done a kitchen for me since he built our house in McPherson! Guess we'll begin eating here tonight for the first time. The kids are anxious to be in our own house. We've been sleeping here for a couple weeks and with a fire in the fireplace, we don't have to wear sweaters in the house. Phil resurrected an ancient refrigerator, so we even have that luxury. I'm cooking on a two-burner bottled gas plate, so we are all set. We feel that we are the most fortunate refugees in all of Africa! Bujumbura is full of others. Doris returned from Nairobi, loaded with things you can't buy here. She and two other single gals drove Phil's car since hers wasn't reliable. They had a nice three weeks. They even stopped to see Ngorongoro Crater where there are thousands of wild animals. I'd like to see it someday.

We lived in the 'white house' at Kibuye Mission

August, 1964, School begins at Mweya Mission September 1, and we are still sewing on name tapes, patching jean knees, and lengthening dresses! I've had a touch of the flu and so, of course, Janet has been fussy, and the kids are all a bit upset with school time so near and the tension they sense of the uncertainty of everything here. Do pray. We know not what tomorrow will bring, In fact, we wouldn't be at all surprised to see you much sooner than what we had anticipated. The kids do need a sense of security. Only the Lord can give it to them. It won't be easy to leave them at school even though we live only forty-five minutes away! We had a wiener roast in our fireplace this evening! We can get wieners in cans and with some of Hazel Adamson's good pickles that she left for us, it was delish! The only thing lacking was good mustard! We can get catsup, but the Belgian mustard is hot! I also french-fried some peanuts, much faster and better than roasting in an oven. Paul will grind some up and make peanut butter tomorrow. The packages for the boys arrived. Their jeans fit just fine. Joe will soon be size 10. Thank you! We have a strawberry patch and a few bushes of blackberries. I made five pints of jam from mixed berries the other day. I've got some guava jelly underway now. The trees are loaded. One good sized guava has 400 units of Vitamin C! We eat them raw, cooked, made into sauce, almost like apple sauce, or in jelly. So thankful for all the good things here. Our tomato plants are bearing heavily. Margaret Collett had planted them before they moved to Mweya Mission. The radishes we planted are big enough to eat already, and the beans are nearly six inches high, the peas are up and the carrots and lettuce. We'll have a nice garden, much nicer than what we had over in Congo. I'm lengthening Nancy's red corduroy jumper by putting a piece in at the waist. I've used all of Joe's name tapes and he still has clothes unlabeled.

Phil saw the school director from Baraka Mission, Congo. He got permission to come over to Burundi. He said that when the *Simba* soldiers came to his house to kill him, he said, "All right, kill me, I am ready to die!" When they asked him if he wasn't going to flee, and he answered, "No, I'm staying right here." So they went away and left him alone! I don't think I'd have that much courage!

Paul, Nancy, Patsy, and David at the boarding school at Mweya Mission

September 5, 1964, It's just like 13 years ago, just Phil and me and the baby. Too quiet around here! I keep wondering how Joe is getting on. He was so big-eyed and white that first day, but he took our leaving them at Mweya better than the girls. Nancy came the closest to crying of any of them. She and Patty are in a room with Virginia Orcutt. Virginia is Joe's age. Joe is in a room with two other second grade boys. I forgot laundry bags for Pat and Joe, so I drew Yogi Bear and Boo-Boo from the kids' color book on Joe's with crayon, and ironed it and put fish and a frog on Patty's. I used 100 pound flour sacks inside out. It's unbleached heavy muslin. I would love to see their faces when they see them! Finally got all their clothes ready with name tapes on. The clothing inspection committee didn't like my temporary home made tapes, so if you haven't already mailed the new tapes, maybe you'd better cut off two dozen for each and send them air mail. I'm sure the ones I made will last through quite a few washings, but they want me to get the permanent ones on as soon as possible! Did you get my second letter with Janet's pictures in? Mother, you sound very busy! Would you have time to make a pair of flannel pajamas for each of the kids before Christmas? Make Paul's to fit John, Nancy's to fit Orlean, Patty's to fit Dottie, and Joe's to fit Terry! How many jeans have you sent the boys altogether? Right now Joe only has two pair without patches and they are supposed to have six each! I must have left a lot of larger sizes of clothing for the kids back at Baraka Mission!

September 27, 1964, All our kids are here, home for the weekend, plus little Virginia Orcutt. She lives too far away to go home for a weekend. They have really been having great fun, but Nan, Joe and Paul all have bad colds! Janet just got over the three day measles! A boy came to school with them and Janet was there that first day! She has been quite fussy, but is OK now. Hope she doesn't get the kids' colds. It's been so nice to have all of our children home. Patty doesn't want to go back. It's hard on all of them to have to live away from home, but it seems especially difficult for her. However, I think she is making real progress in learning to read. How is the washing machine doing? How I wish for mine with all these diapers! I just hope we find it all in one piece, if and when.

Ants!

October 15, 1964, Hi! I'm almost too shaky to write! I just went out to our garden to see if the aphids were fewer on the peas and to tell the gardener it was 4 o'clock. I was standing near the last row of peas looking in beside the blossoms when I heard this rustling sound, almost like big drops of rain falling, and then I looked closer. The sticks on which the plants had climbed were covered with big ants. Then I looked down, and so were my feet! I ran, but everywhere I ran, hundreds of ants were swarming all over the ground! Finally, I ripped off my shoes and socks, left them on the ground, and took off! I finally got the last ant off me, and the gardener bravely rescued my shoes and socks! He then proceeded to show me where to walk to get out of the mess, and he got right in the middle of another swarm! He ran like a scared jack rabbit and so did I, right after him! Glad no one saw us! We've just had our first heavy rain of the season and the ants are everywhere! I DDT'd them out of our kitchen. I hope they don't get into our bedroom! Many are small, but mixed in with them are these huge giants. They are long and have pinchers. Ouch! The kids practically go hysterical when they are near them. I've always laughed at them, but now I understand! You can't just brush them off, either. They attack and won't let go! The kids are coming home tomorrow evening. I'll go with Marti to get them. She is going to record some songs at Mweya Mission for the Christian radio station, CORDAC, in Bujumbura. I'd better get busy and make up beds for the kids. Must bake bread tomorrow morning.

October 20, 1964, The kids were home for a really nice weekend and it didn't rain. Our garden is beautiful. Finally got the aphids killed off. Sorry this is so messy. I'm holding Janet. She is fussy. Had her second DPT shot last night. Phil says to please put a bar of sal ammoniac in a package to be sent regular mail. It is the stuff you put on a soldering iron to keep the solder from sticking to it. He has a new electric soldering iron. Then I gave her a Christmas wish list that she had asked me to send. Don't know how we could have managed without our faithful parents.

October 29, 1964, Hi! Happy Halloween! The kids are having a party tomorrow night. Paul will be a miner, Nancy a Dutch girl. She wishes she had her wooden shoes! Patty a witch, and Joe, a girl! I'd love to see them, but I'm sure they don't need a lot of parents around. The kids will be home next weekend. Sure do miss them. I'd like a couple bottles of Mennen's Baby Magic and two boxes of a good kind of baby cereal. Janet is a fussy eater! She has diarrhea now from something I've given her to eat. I hope it wasn't carrots, because that's one thing she does like! I use Marti's food processor to make baby food. Phil has a lot of 'irons in the fire' right now. Plans for remodeling present Kibuye Mission hospital buildings to more adequately use the space they do have, and change the electric system to 220 V since 110 V light bulbs are scarce. He is also supervising the building of a house for the school director. Janet is a beautiful baby and so alert! She can crawl now, at 5 months! All the Baraka and Nundu Mission schools are closed in Congo. Much fighting there now and the town of Uvira is just about leveled. The British missionaries who were 100 miles inland from us finally got out. They had been under house arrest and without adequate food since June 1. I'm so thankful we were here, thanks to God's gift of Janet, and the Lord's provisions for us. Phil is up helping Doris make a cast for a broken upper arm. Doris really enjoys having Phil to help.

November 6, 1964, The kids come home this afternoon for another weekend. They will really be surprised to see Janet. She already crawls and gets wherever she wants to go! We have lowered her low-sided play pen from the open divan to the floor. Phil will have to build up the sides soon or she will be out and into everything, including the fireplace! A fire screen will be next on the list to make. Phil still is working on the electricity changeover. Then the hospital pharmacy gets remodeled, with new shelves. Guess Marti and Len will be leaving for furlough in a couple months. No replacement is available! We have women's and girls' sewing classes going. If one of the Women's Missionary Society groups wants to do something for the work here, we could use lots of embroidery thread, all basic colors, the brighter the better, also white '50' thread and needles. The Orcutt kids are coming this weekend. We'll have a houseful! We'll have hamburgers and baked beans for supper. Guess I'd better finish getting beds ready. Phil will be ready to leave soon. We continue to need much prayer, for Burundi as well as Congo. I see your missionary conference is on now. Wish I could be there! Paul's bike part arrived already! He will be thrilled! Thanks so much!

November 20, 1964, I'm just waiting for Phil to come to breakfast. He is working on a Kombi from the Kayero World Gospel Mission. They brought in a girl with a possible fracture. Phil is showing William how to diagnose VW 'illnesses!' You should see Janet! She stands up nearly all the time she is awake. She even lets go with both hands, braces her tummy against the side of the play pen, and walks along! She doesn't know she is too young for such stuff, and crawls everywhere! None of the other kids stood this young! But she has been practicing ever since she was 3 weeks. She never would cuddle, just stiffened out, exactly like Mother told me I did! She is so strong. Phil is making a real playpen and none too soon. She is about ready to climb out of the low-sided one he fixed. We have chairs all around the outside to keep her in! The kids will come home next Wednesday afternoon for Thanksgiving weekend. We are having tacos for supper tonight. Doris knows how to make really good tortillas! Phil and I are evidently both allergic to cedar trees. I've been gathering seed to grow more cedars and he has been trimming branches away from the electric lines. We both have an itchy rash from it, feels like sunburn! Our corn is about 7-8' high. Maybe we'll have corn to eat by Christmas.

Janet walking, holding on at 6 months!

Mom's precious treasure. Janet Kae.

December 4. 1964, Today is like a typical California December day. So gray and drippy with a few real downpours. We have had so few days of steady rain. This will probably mean the end of my peas and maybe the tomatoes, but so good for the rest of the garden. The corn is 11 feet high now. It is nearly ready to eat. I'm going to try to grow some popcorn. Hazel Adamson left us some she had grown. We popped most of it, but I saved some for seed. You should see Janet and the kitten, especially when they both want the same toy! I gave her a rubber canning jar ring to chew on and the kitten tried her best to take it away! Phil made Janet a very nice play pen. She stands up most of the time. When the kids came home for Thanksgiving and saw it, they wanted to know where it came from. When I told them their daddy had made it, they said, "Well, he couldn't have, it looks too professional!" They can't remember the nice stuff Phil used to make when he had good material and time and his equipment. There is a little power saw here and he has Merlin Adamson's little jointer. Phil's good tools and power equipment in the Congo are probably going to rust and ruin. But he has been able to get some fairly good lumber here, so he has something to work with.

Patty and Joe are both making real progress in reading. Kathryn Hendrix is an excellent reading teacher. When Patty started at Mweya Mission she was only reading beginning second grade level. Now she easily reads third grade material and likes it! Joe reads really fast now, and Patty has learned how to figure out new words! Jean Johnson and Gwen Houser sent Janet a baby book from South Africa. The kids all love their baby books and browse through them every now and then. So glad I managed to bring them along when we left Congo! Did I tell you I am growing African violets now? Nancy brought some home from Mweya Mission for Mommy to take care of! The package containing two pair of jeans for Paul arrived this week, mailed July 20! Thanks. The string and tags were lost, but the package was OK and unopened! Hope the ones you sent for Joe arrive sooner than that. Most of his are patched already! From now on, better send size 10 things for Joe and size 18 for Paul! Nancy is taller than me and Paul weighs 120 pounds! They will come home for Christmas vacation December 18, for two weeks. Janet has a tooth! A lower one. I thought kids always got their uppers first!

Earthquakes!

December 27, 1964, Happy New Year! Phil is about ready to take off for Conference in Bujumbura. The kids and I are staying here. We are all well, had a lovely Christmas and are enjoying having our kids at home. Phil will be back Thursday or Friday. There were two violent earthquakes the other day with lots of small ones. The first bad one cracked a lot of the dried mud plaster in our house and the second knocked down a big batch of plaster in the kitchen. Thought for awhile we were in California! We didn't know it, but many of our roof tiles were shaken down, out of place and so when a big rain came along, it soaked up the dried mud ceiling and another spot came caving in! Phil and Paul spent most of two days on our roof shoving the tiles back in place, trying to cover all the holes! What a mess! But it could have been so much worse. One bad earthquake they had here several years ago shook most of the tiles off into the patio! I saved out the crayons to give to the kids for Christmas. They were all happy. We are having corn and squash from our garden and peaches and still strawberries and avocadoes.

CHAPTER 9

Phil is Appointed Central Africa Builder

January 4, 1965, I thought I was going to tell you in this letter to address us for the next three months at Kibogora Mission, but now I don't know! Estelle Orcutt said they had been 'alerted'. Conference decided Phil was to go build a hospital building for Dr. Kuhn at Kibogora Mission, in Rwanda, as soon as possible. We thought we could make the move within the next two weeks, providing we could secure the proper papers, but the way things look, we had better sit tight for awhile anyway. The kids were extremely unhappy at the thoughts of not seeing us for three whole months, and we certainly don't relish the thoughts of starting to move around yet. Please follow the news regarding the Lake Kivu area. You will undoubtedly hear more than we do. The only reliable news we get is from BBC and Voice of America, also from Time Magazine, that Ensigns get. We have a radio now, an old one that belonged to Clara Sparks. Phil took it down to Bujumbura and had it repaired. Do pray. This threat places the Orcutts, Myra Adamson, Dr. Kuhn and Ila Gonsolus in the same position we were in last April! Pray that we won't make a foolish move.

We have had some really nice air mail, but no surface mail at all. Must be a holdup somewhere. How we would love to come home! But the Lord is good and helps us over the times of feeling that what we do is futile, and lifts us up out of our feelings of apprehension and tension. I am at Mweya Mission right now. Doris and I brought the kids back to school. We took Patty and Joe into Gitega to the dentist. Janet has four teeth now! We are waiting now until the African Conference secretary gets through helping Evelyn Rupert with the conference minutes. They are mimeographed and we all helped put them together.

To Kibogora Mission in Rwanda

January 19, 1965, We arrived at Kibogora, the mission station founded by Frank and Hazel Adamson in 1942! I was really surprised. I had apprehensions about the trip. Paul Orcutt's and Jim Johnson's new Land Rovers arrived in Bujumbura. So Phil, Janet and I drove down there on Wednesday, stopping at Mweya Mission to see the kids before school. All the papers, permits, and visas, didn't get cleared until Thursday afternoon, so we didn't leave until Friday morning at 6:30. We were close to the Congo border most of the way, all the way up the Ruzizi valley. We didn't know it, but a battle was raging at Uvira. We were not far from there, and when we arrived at the Rwanda border, we heard about it and also of a battle in the hills just above us there. We had an hour and a half wait for an official to come to sign our visas and count Paul Orcutt's duty money. Soldiers were milling all around with their loaded guns and camouflaged uniforms. A truckload of Congolese soldiers roared past coming back to Bukavu from the Uvira fight. In it all, we were peacefully aware of the Lord's presence with us. At another road barrier, we had to unload everything. A drunk soldier snooped through all our suitcases and finally let us go on. We rejoiced that we hadn't been turned back. The trip was a pleasant one, and none of my pessimistic apprehensions came true! They are still on alert here at Kibogora. No one knows what tomorrow will hold, but the Orcutts, Ila, Myra and Dr. Kuhn are all firmly convinced that this is no time to sit back and wait. All the building they have planned, will be useful even if the missionaries have to leave! We were only able to secure permits to be gone two weeks, so we'll have to be back in Burundi by January 29. We'll fly down. The kids will be glad. They thought even three weeks would be too long. Marti told us on the mission radio that four packages had arrived for us, so we'll have Christmas when we get home, back at Kibuye Mission. Maybe now, the surface post is starting to come through again. There has been nothing but air mail for more than a month. Another miraculous detail about this trip. Because of the murder of Burundi's Prime Minister on Friday night, all roads had been closed. No one could travel anywhere until today! Phil and Paul Orcutt are in Kigali today to check on building supplies, and get permanent visas for us. They will probably return Thursday. Wish you could see this beautiful lake and lovely flowers.

The building starts

January 26, 1965, We are still at Kibogora Mission. Tomorrow morning at six we leave for the airport. Don't know when the plane takes off for Bujumbura. Phil and Paul Orcutt are laying out the building today, using a water-filled plastic hose for a level. Africans are bringing stones for the foundation for the hospital, and while we are gone they will do the digging and final leveling and bring sand. Myra and Dr. Kuhn are quite thrilled at the prospects of their dream building really coming true. Another project will be to enlarge an office building into a missionary residence. Phil has the plans drawn up, nothing fancy, but adequate. At this stage, we all feel that it is senseless to invest much money in providing comforts for missionaries! I'm all packed. With no electricity, you learn to get such things taken care of in the daylight! Janet is squealing in the play pen, an old one Drusilla Orcutt had outgrown. There is also a nice baby bed some Congo missionary refugees left at Kumbya, and Drusilla's old stroller, so Janet is well taken care of here too. I imagine we'll set up housekeeping on a limited scale the next time we come. Orcutts have fed us these two weeks. Janet stands alone quite often now. She is a rare one! Never quiet unless she is asleep. We have enjoyed our stay here. What a treat to be this close to this fantastically beautiful lake! But it will be nice to be back at Kibuye Mission again and have our kids home for a weekend. If anyone wants to send Phil something, he desperately needs six pair of good quality work socks, size 12. If no one offers, you'd better buy them, let us pay for them and get them mailed! Small packet, please. Please request prayer for our Burundi permanent residence visa to be granted quickly.

Back to Burundi

February 1, 1965, In Bujumbura again, and it's hot and muggy. We had quite an adventure on Wednesday when we came here from Kibogora Mission. We were supposed to be at the airport at Cyangugu at 8 a.m. We were, but no plane is expected until 1:30, they said, and maybe not even then because when the pilots get in 140 hours, they quit! We waited and waited and were almost ready to board a small charter plane when ours arrived. Only four passengers in a sixty seater! It only took us twenty minutes to fly down the Ruzizi valley to Bujumbura. Rather rough ride, but pleasant. A good way to really see the country! We plan to go up home to Kibuye Mission tomorrow. We have new visas for here good until March 1. They say we should be getting our permanent ones soon. Pray! The last report from where we used to live was that our things are still in good shape. Even some stolen things had been recovered and were being taken care of by some of the church members! Very few mission stations in Congo are still in as good shape as ours. Many are completely demolished.

Janet loves to hold on to the top rail of a baby bed or play pen and jump up and down. She is forever letting go so she can play with toys with both hands, and down she goes, plop, on her fat little 'sitter!' She is the strongest, most agile and active baby I've ever seen. Everyone marvels at all she does! She also climbs up the dowel rods with her bare toes while holding onto the top rail with her hands, just like a little monkey!

Our car is still in the garage, so we can't go up to Kibuye Mission until tomorrow. The kids get a long weekend. They don't have to go back to school until Wednesday, so that will be nice. Things here are looking more hopeful. Guess the ones in authority finally got their eyes open. We heard that the 'reds' were expelled yesterday. Maybe things won't be so 'anti Uncle Sam' with them gone.

Thursday night. Finally our car is ready to go. We'll leave in the morning for Kibuye Mission. It's a four hour drive up into the mountains. As much as we both dislike traveling around on these roads, we need our heads examined for offering to do this kind of thing! We're really nomads! I'm thankful we have to wait until March before we can make the trip up to Kibogora Mission again. That will be one month at home, at Kibuye Mission. The last couple days have been cool here! Lots of heavy rain, cloudburst type of thing with too close lightning! Good for the gardens, though.

February 7, 1965, (Letter from Nancy to her grandparents.) Dear Grandma Nana and Grandpa, Thank you very much for the pajamas you sent to me. We were very glad to get the other things too. We opened the packages when we got home from school at Mweya Mission. I am doing fine in school, although it gets pretty hard sometimes. There are three other kids in my grade. I take piano lessons with most of the other kids in the dormitory. Paul Thornburg teaches the older ones, and we teach the little kids. I teach Patsy. We are home at Kibuye Mission now, but we will go back to school on Wednesday. Then on Friday we will have a Valentine Party. Good-bye for now. Sincerely yours, Nancy. A note from Patsy: Thank you for the red dresses you sent to Nancy and me, and the p.j.'s too, Love, Patsy

February 13, 1965, We had stacks of packages waiting for us and how thrilled the kids were to get their pajamas and name tapes! Of course, they didn't enjoy sewing them on, but I made them! Nancy got my new tennis shoes, and I got my old ones back that she has been wearing. The new ones were too wide for me, but OK for her! The slippers are perfect for these cold, hard, cement floors! Certainly nice to have aprons that match my dresses! Thanks for all and a double thanks for the popcorn and Phil's socks! He was really desperately in need of them. He likes his shirt too. Both Doris and I jumped for joy when we saw the oregano. Stews, soups and spaghetti are flat without it! We've already used the good chili mix. We love it! Everything came through in really good shape. Glad to get the dishes and bike parts. Only 10 cents duty on each package! We were surprised because quite often they charge $1 or $2 on packages over two pounds. Janet is recovering from bronchitis. She picks up everything. She has really been sick, but her cough isn't quite so bad now. Sure hope Doris can find some baby vitamins in Bujumbura. We should have had some sent from home a long time ago. Maybe you'd better send some airmail anyway. We'll get it before we leave again for Kibogora Mission if you send it right away. Your packages come through in better shape than anyone's. I think sewing the cloth wrapper really helps. Please put in a couple tubes of Blistex too. Phil is putting in bigger windows and built-ins in Doris's house. Then they will white-wash all of her rooms with colored tints. We heard Phil's tools had all been stolen and I really miss my stove and washing machine. We need some more sheets and pillow cases of our own, but there is the possibility that someday we'll get our things back. We hear so many conflicting reports. We'll be coming home in three years for a long furlough, maybe a permanent one! You should see Janet in her new crawlers, nice fit, so cute. Thanks for what you sent.

February 20, 1965, Janet is asleep and Phil has gone to Muyebe Mission and Bireha, our houseboy, has gone to the market to buy meat, at 15 cents a pound, so I'm alone. Doris should be back this evening. She's been in Bujumbura seeing Lehmans off. Phil was in bed all day yesterday with an attack of malaria. The medicine made him feel worse than the disease did, but this morning he felt better than he has for a long time, even his legs didn't ache so much, from staying in bed. I hear Janet saying "da-da." She says "ma-ma" when she gets really mad! Guess I'd better bring her out and put her in her play pen. What a sweet little cherub. She has on the pink trousers you sent her. She looks so cute in them. Phil went to Muyebe Mission to help Jim Johnson set up a water system. They have an electric generator now, so they can pump up water from a spring. All these years they have had water carried up the hill in buckets! You should see Doris's house! They scraped off the old smoke-stained white-wash in the living room yesterday, but we got her bedroom done, pale pink. It looks nice. The kids will come home next weekend. I get so lonesome for them. Phil was going to stop to see them at Mweya Mission this morning. Wish I could have gone.

Janet is getting mad. Guess she wants some attention. She is just like a little monkey in a cage! But I can't resist her begging to be picked up and held. She's spoiled rotten! She likes to sit on my lap and chew on my plastic belt. She is determined she is going to grab this letter. Everything still goes in her mouth. She is so strong and active she has broken all of her rattles! But she has several soft plastic squeaky toys that so far have resisted her strength! She is on 3 meals a day now, and drinks milk really well from a cup. I still nurse her when she insists. Have you sent any more baby cereal? If you haven't, here's a suggestion.

Put a plastic bag inside of a milk carton, fasten the top with a rubber band, fill it with baby cereal, packed solidly. Sew up a cloth around it as usual. Send regular mail. Try a couple that way, and I'll let you know how they come through.

February 22, 1965, (In Bujumbura) We finally have our permanent visa for this country! We got a letter saying to be here in Bujumbura at 8 this morning at the immigration office. All was ready; they stamped our visas in our passports, and gave us identity cards, so now we can go back and forth with less expense and bother. We are going back home now, to Kibuye Mission. We came in last night. Phil was at Muyebe Mission helping Jim Johnson, so when Doris brought the letter, we went to let Phil know yesterday. It is hot here. We'll be glad to get back up to chilly Kibuye Mission.

February 26, 1965, (A letter from Betty Kline, Phil's youngest sister, age 38, who had been working in Winona Lake, Indiana, as Financial Secretary for the General Missionary Board. Dr. Byron S. Lamson had previously been her boss for many years.) Dear Phil and Mary. There is some exciting news that we want to share with you. For some strange reason, your friend, Byron Lamson, has fallen in love with me. It has taken me a little while to realize this, but I have learned to love him too. We plan to be married the end of July. Mother is happy for us and is quite willing to make her home with Jeanne and Glen in Kansas. I wrote to Jeanne last Monday and she called back Wednesday night to extend her congratulations, and to invite Mother to live with them. We think it will be possible to build a living room with a small kitchenette in their garage for her. I am sure she will be content if she has something like this of her own. She has been wanting to move back to Kansas anyway, since she feels her sinus trouble is better there. You have received the last Kline Klatch, so you know as much about the family, I guess, as we do. Mother is keeping well and is still reading about a dozen books a week. We had a blizzard yesterday and there is about ten inches of snow on the ground, but there was a strong wind and some of the drifts are several feet deep. It probably will melt fast this time of year. Give our love to the kids. Betty

(At the bottom of her air form letter was this note from Byron,) My Dear Phil and Mary, Some day I hope it will be possible to have a good leisurely visit with you and tell you how very recently, our eyes have been opened and our hearts warmed. Betty was quite surprised when I spoke to her of my feelings. I didn't know for a few days just what she would decide. In a beautiful, beautiful way, her regard and appreciation of me has gradually been turning to love. Both of us are so happy, and our friends too, seem excited about it and happy for both of us. So, I hope you will approve. You know of my long time regard for you and my respect for the quality of your work out there. God bless you, and share the news with the missionaries as you see fit. As ever, Byron.

March 1, 1965, At Kibuye Mission, Burundi. It's late, Phil and Janet are asleep, and I'm in bed writing by Aladdin lamp light. The kids were home last weekend for Phil's birthday. The nice work socks arrived just in time, so the kids wrapped them up to give to him, also two pair of shorts that we had bought at Sears in Sierra Madre! We used the cake decorator you had sent. Patty decorated the cake since Nancy was sick. So were Paul and Joe, with some kind of violent intestinal bug. We had a lovely time, in spite of the tummy aches. The Orcutt kids were here with us. Paul spent most of his time setting up his train and working it over! Phil let him drive our car a little, so he was thrilled! Doris's house is still in a mess. Phil is starting to fit the built-ins in the kitchen. What a difference it all will make! He got the toilet hooked up in the hospital. That should make Doris and Len happy! Imagine, all these years without one for them up there! Were the sewing class ladies ever thrilled to get the bright green embroidery thread! We were completely out! Thank you!

Wednesday, Last week Janet fell out of her stroller and just missed cracking her head on the concrete floor. Oh, oh, she just woke up crying. Sure hope she isn't getting sick. Well, she went back to sleep. The package arrived from Grace in Oroville with some really nice things in it. Sure glad to get the jeans for the boys. Joe is really going through his fast. They sent the cutest pink tights for Janet. She likes them! She just gets cuter all the time, the little angel! She plays peek-a-boo now and cuddles up to Phil when he tells her to love him, and she understands what 'no' means. Smart kid! They are really charging duty now. We paid $10 duty on a package the other day that was valued at $20! Let's try for a pair of jeans for Paul, size 18, and please send a couple more pair of plastic pants for Janet. Please request prayer for the countries of Tanzania and Uganda. They are our neighbors, and they are in danger. What a difference here, now that Burundi has expelled the trouble makers. We can breathe easier again! Direct answer to prayer! Pray that our neighboring countries will wake up before it is too late. The *Simba* supply rail line is from Dar-es-Salaam, Tanzania, across that country, and then by ships across Lake Tanganyika to Baraka, Congo! I'm so glad the Lord got us out of there at just the right time!

March 6, 1965, (Phil wrote): Dear Betty and Byron, we received your welcome and surprising letter the other day. I must say that it is rather shocking, and pleasantly so, to realize that the man who has been my friend and boss for so many years is to be part of our pleasant little family! However, I imagine Betty's surprise far surpasses ours! Congratulations and best wishes to both of you. Byron, of course, I expect you to use your influence to get me back to the wedding, because I must give Betty away! (Their father died when Phil was 7.) Another thing, remember that before final wedding arrangements are made, there is the little matter of *labola,* (dowry), to be discussed, agreed to, and paid. Among other items, there will be at least fifteen head of cattle, due to her education and long experience in the General Mission Board office! Ha! But seriously, we are anxious to hear more of your plans. Betty, are you going to keep your house for an investment? Are you going to keep on working for the General Mission Board? What are your wedding plans! I expect to see some love stories in the 'Free Methodist' any time now!

Betty, I wrote to Rev. Kirkpatrick about the cars. There is a misunderstanding about those for Bujumbura. There is only one Kombi on the field. It is now in Bujumbura. The mission voted to send the '59

VW little passenger car to Bujumbura mainly for the medical people who will be taking some required tropical medical training there in the next few months. This car is nothing super, but will be OK for that purpose. We propose that the mission purchase the used Kombi from Bukavu for the building work. Two should be ordered by the office from Europe soon, or there is going to be a real shortage of transportation. This currency change is sure going to hit hard. Tell Mom I was a naughty boy, I did not even wish her a happy birthday. We really did, but she just could not hear us on the 5th! Cannot think of more to write, so had better get my Sunday afternoon nap. Write soon. Love, Phil

(On the back of Phil's air form): Dear Betty, wasn't Phil nice to write such a short letter so I can have some space for a change? You asked what we plan to do about Paul for next year. We are hoping they will be able to go ahead with plans for ninth grade at Mweya Mission. There is an excellent school at Kijabe, Rift Valley Academy, not far from Nairobi, Kenya. But it is terribly expensive, and so far away, especially with such tense political situations all around. We'll just have to wait and see. All the kids are doing really well at Mweya Mission, and are we ever enjoying living so close! So far they have been able to come home for a weekend every three weeks. The Orcutt kids only get home to Kibogora Mission in Rwanda for Christmas and Easter. Guess our latest plans are to go down to Bujumbura next Monday to try to get military permits to travel by car to Kibogora Mission. We heard on the radio telephone that our passports had arrived back in Bujumbura with visas for Rwanda for three months. So, we'll try it anyway. Building materials are so hard to get. So many of the borders across which materials must travel are closed, or demand export/import licenses and tremendous duty! What days to be building in! Things are looking worse and worse over where we used to live in Congo. That official report about the condition of the mission over there is right as far as the buildings go. We were told that two of our personal radios were stolen, plus some of Phil's clothing, plus all of his tools, plus various and sundry other things. But even at that, we are fortunate. At the British station everything was completely demolished! But we aren't complaining. The Lord is teaching us a few things about being content to live without our own personal possessions.

The other missionaries, especially the Alexanders, have been so generous about sharing their things with us, so we are comfortably set up. I do miss my stove and washing machine, though. You asked if the games and books had arrived. Yes, and thanks so much. The kids really enjoy them and were just as thrilled as I to see the hymnals. They are all getting piano lessons at Mweya Mission with quite a bit of emphasis on learning to play hymns.

March 1965, (In Bujumbura) Last night I finished up a letter which I put in an envelope with some pictures of our family. It is so bulky it may not reach you, so I'll write this to tell you some of the news it contained. We were successful in securing all the necessary permits to travel by car and to temporarily export Phil's tools. We'll leave this morning. It's 5 a.m! The first barrier doesn't open until 7, so there's no reason to leave early, early! We came down here Tuesday. The kids were home last weekend. I drove over to Mweya Mission to get them. Janet just woke up. The little early bird! Hope she goes back to sleep! She didn't.

The most wonderful thing happened yesterday! Phil's camera came from Congo where we used to live! His **Leica**! It's been months on the way. We'd certainly like to know where it has been all this time. We still haven't met the person who brought it. It was carefully wrapped in a plastic bag and paper, and it was concealed in a woman's sewing bag, a small unbleached muslin bag with 'learning-how' embroidery on it. I was so thrilled I was nearly speechless. Bates' houseboy brought it to us yesterday evening. The person who arrived with it had sent it on with him. The really amazing part about the whole thing is that it arrived while we are here! Certainly restores our faith and brings encouragement! I sort of feel that the Lord sent it to us now to send us off on this dreaded trip with new faith and courage! We are so thankful to have it back! Time to get up and pack.

March 1965, (From Kibogora Mission, Rwanda.) What a really nice trip we had up here. We left Bujumbura about 7:30 a.m. and after about 45 minutes we came to a barrier and a little bridge about to go out, but since we had such a little car, they let us through. Lots of trucks were waiting on both sides. We may have to fly back because there is a big bridge about to go out now! One military barrier is no longer on the road. We had no trouble at any point. All the soldiers and customs officials were most helpful and congenial, and miracle of miracles, not even one was drunk! We were so thankful! We had a car full of tools and equipment, but had government papers to export them temporarily, so all was in order. No delays, and no searching our car! When we arrived here I didn't even have a small headache. No aspirins needed this trip. Thank all who have been praying for us. But please request they keep on praying. We have two more trips coming up in April! Prayer really does make a difference. When a trip goes as nicely as this one did, you know He has gone before and has smoothed out all the rough places. I'm not speaking of the road. It is horrible with mud, ruts, holes, slosh, and stones! But this is Africa, and good smooth highways are exceedingly rare! What a beauty spot Kibogora is! It has been quite clear in between rains. The volcanoes at the north end of the lake are a magnificent sight. I still haven't seen the active one glow at night! Ferns everywhere, all shapes, sizes, varieties, all wild. Embankments are covered with them along the roads. Phil has the house for Merlin and Vera Adamson underway, and also the hospital ward unit.

Janet is asleep. She goes so hard now. On her ten month old birthday, she took off and walked halfway across the room! So now she goes everywhere. She gets insulted if you put her in a playpen!

Phil builds a saw!

April 6, 1965, Still at Kibogora Mission. Phil has the foundation for the little house capped and is making door frames now. The hospital foundations are nearing completion. Did I tell you about the power saw Phil made? He bought a saw blade, a big round, flat one and a mandrel and a long V-belt, built a wood frame and hitched it all together to a little gasoline engine. He even rigged up a system so by turning a handle down below he can raise and lower the blade! Rather rough, but it works! He does miss his good equipment, though!

How we enjoy our little doll! So nice to have a baby angel around when you are forty! But what a bundle of energy! She climbs everything in sight. I should lose a few pounds chasing her. I put a box in front of the fireplace (no fire) so she couldn't climb inside. She tries to eat ashes and charcoal! I was sewing with my back to her, turned around, and there the little 'monkey' was sitting on her haunches on top of the box all ready to crawl into the fireplace! We hear the kids get out of school the 15th, a day early, so we'll have to leave here the 13th. Guess Paul Orcutt left our passports in Kigali when he went to try to get longer visas for us. Sure hope we get them back in time to go! Kigali is a six-hour drive in the opposite direction from Bujumbura!

April 12, 1965, Today is the last day here at Kibogora Mission until after Easter. We leave early tomorrow morning to travel down to Bujumbura. We will do some shopping, and then back up into the high hills, home to Kibuye Mission, altitude about a mile high. On Thursday afternoon we get our kids! It's been a month this time since we last saw them, but we'll have them home from the 16th until the 26th. That's a lot better than just a weekend. We debated about having our kids fly up here with the Orcutt kids for their vacation, but it would cost $60 or more, so we decided it would be cheaper for us to drive down. Phil has several projects he needs to do at Kibuye Mission anyway, and this is rainy season in earnest here now, so it isn't a good time to be putting up walls of buildings. They have really had a struggle to get the footings filled in before they filled back up with mud and water! It rains part of every day, so it is really a lot of lost labor. Phil's jobs at Kibuye Mission will be mostly indoor work to finish up the built-ins for Doris Moore. Then he is going to build an addition onto the guest house where another nurse will live, giving her an indoor bathroom and a closet and more storage space.

We saw something really exciting this morning. There were two waterspouts out on the lake. Must have been about twenty miles up the lake. We watched them about thirty minutes. Glad we weren't near them in a boat! Lake Kivu is one of the most beautiful places in the world, we think. This part of Africa is called the 'Switzerland of

Africa'. The storm that was out on the lake has moved this way, but its violence has dissipated, thank goodness! Seems like it rains an awful lot here, but that's what makes it so beautiful. Green, when a lot of Africa is bone dry! This area is in a corner of the equatorial rain belt. There is a rain forest not too far from here. Sure hope we get to see it. There are monkeys, and maybe even baboons. I know gorillas live at the north end of the lake up on the volcanoes. We can see the volcanoes when it is clear. One smokes all the time, and one erupted in 1948. Earthquakes are quite common in all this area, but not really bad ones.

I hear Phil out in the back yard with his improvised power equipment! You should see the saw he rigged up, but it cuts! He got tired of working in the sun and rain, so he built a roof for a shelter. Leave it to Phil. Never saw such a man for fixing things up! All the missionaries really appreciate all the little things he does for them. Wish you could see our youngest daughter! She just will not stay penned up. This afternoon she managed to crawl over a chair I had blocked off the door with. She went over on her little head onto a sharp concrete edge. She walks everywhere, but I can't let her outside alone because she tries to eat dirt and rocks! Sure wish she would acquire some wisdom soon! Wish you could look out this window with me. The lake is a breathtakingly beautiful sight, especially the volcanoes, fifty miles up at the north end of the lake. One is pouring out clouds of white smoke and spilling some down one side. It's too beautiful to be real.

Back to Burundi

April 22, 1965, At Kibuye Mission. The kids' vacation is more than half over, and what a nice time we are having just being all together. We have to take them back to school Tuesday morning. Sure nice having so many good baby-sitters! Only thing, they all want Janet at once! We went to Muyebe Mission on Monday. Jim Johnson wanted Phil to come over. Guess he wanted some advice about the building projects he has underway there. Phil has the addition on the nurse's house about ready for windows. He has been working today on the power plant. The starter won't work. Also he put Doris' VW back together again with a new rear oil seal. It was leaking oil badly. Guess we won't get back to Kibogora Mission before the first of May. Phil wants to get the plumbing done before he leaves.

Guess what? We have a nice new stove in our kitchen, apartment size with an oven big enough to hold a cookie sheet! It's not ours. Martha Pedigo loaned it to us because she is living with Olive Bodtcher, who also has a stove. It's really nice to cook on a stove again after using gas plates and a tiny portable oven for a year! Everyone has been so good to share their things with us. The Lord really does supply all our needs. We can only trust Him to continue doing so because everything in Congo is gone, everything except the power plant, power saw and jointer. A letter came telling about how a mob came to the mission and took everything away from all the residences, the church and school about March 10. It said that there isn't even a scrap of paper left! They even took doors and windows! It isn't clear if the buildings are still standing or not! We feel the worst about all our pictures! But nothing will bring them back. At least our family is intact! So many Congo missionaries didn't get out and some were killed, so we do feel fortunate. The kids took the bad news very well. We have been expecting it would happen, and yet we hoped and prayed that somehow our Mission would be spared. But things are getting really 'hot' around there. It is the rebels' only supply line left, and the government forces are closing in. Glad we aren't there, and glad we don't have to go back.

April 26, 1965, In Burundi. What a lovely time we have had with our kids! They are so nice. Of course the girls fight some, but not a lot. When they are gone tomorrow, Janet is going to be one lost cookie! So am I! What a process to get kids ready to go back to school. Make sure all school clothes are washed, and of course it rains, so I have jeans, undershirts and socks drying on the fireplace screen. Cut the boys' hair, sew on more name tapes, press dresses for tomorrow, and help Patty curl her hair. Seems like all vacation I've been taking down hems and re-hemming! They grow so fast! Paul is very proud of the fact that he now weighs as much as I do! He is about 5'7". Nancy isn't far behind at 5'5"! Paul was so pleased when I pulled out the last T-shirts I had bought for him at Sears before we came, size 18 and perfect fit. We probably won't leave to go back to Kibogora Mission until the end of the week. Phil needs to get the roof on the addition to the guest house, and the floor in. He has spent so much time re-working the shut-off and starting systems for the power plant. Each house now has buttons to push that control it remotely, Phil's invention! The main difficulty is that he needs to put up one more wire all the way around, but that is expensive. Guess he has the problem solved, because he isn't sitting up drawing diagrams tonight! He used the magic markers you sent, Mother, to draw the different colored wires! He wants to take a course in electronics on our next furlough. We think Phil has stomach ulcers and the doctor says he has bursitis in his shoulder joint. It is a lot like arthritis, very difficult to get rid of. He gets so discouraged trying to work with makeshift, inadequate equipment, makes a person really sick to think of all the good tools he lost in Congo. Please request prayer for Burundi. Elections are May 10 - 12. Tension and unrest is expected and will probably restrict travel. Pray that God-honoring men will be elected to every government office. I'm sure the bad guys haven't given this country up. Pray!

Up to Kibogora Mission again

May 3, 1965, In Rwanda. We made the trip in one day, and arrived here about 7:30 Friday evening. But what a trip! There had been a lot of rain and the trucks had made deep holes in the road! Bump, creak, grind, and jerk! We had to crawl a lot of the way. The ruts were dry and so were bumpier! Phil got a bad headache and we had to wait from 12:00 to 2:00 at the Burundi check-out point. We got there ten minutes too late! Finally got going again and Phil got to feeling worse and worse, and decided it was either flu or malaria. Ran into slick roads up here, so had to creep again. Phil could hardly drive, he was so sick, but he wouldn't let me drive. By the time we got here he nearly collapsed. Dr. Kuhn doped him up and sent him to bed. They had brought a nice double bed from the mission rest camp at Kumbya for Phil. Was he ever glad to see it! He is still in bed, but is feeling much better and wants to get up tomorrow. Guess he had the flu, but doctor treated him for malaria too. So many Anopheles mosquitoes around here now, just swarms. You hardly ever see them at Kibuye Mission, just the harmless buzzy kind. Janet is a little rascal. Opens cupboards, goes exploring through every open door, tears up magazines, pulls things off tables, and is hardly still a minute. She knows what she isn't supposed to do, but she is so determined and persistent! We love her dearly! Guess we'll bring the kids here to Kibogora Mission in June.

May 15, 1965, Janet and I are well again. We've had the flu, really knocks you out! Makes you feel like a piece of over-cooked macaroni! Janet is still fussy. Her head is stopped up and tummy aches. She didn't sleep well last night, but seems OK now. Vic Macy is here. He went to Kigali with Orcutts and is leaving again. They were having elections in Burundi, so no one could drive anywhere, so he flew up here on a commercial flight. His plane is being worked on. He nearly ran out of gas flying his plane up from Salisbury, Rhodesia, so he is having an extra fuel tank put on. He leaves in just 30 minutes and the mail will go with him. He will be back June 10 to make a film. We plan to drive down to Burundi June 2 with Orcutts. Mweya school is out June 4. We'll come back up here June 10. Estelle and I will take the kids over to the missionary rest camp at Kumbya to supervise cleaning up for the missionary retreat. The kids will get to go swimming every day! I'm making myself a swim suit. Mine was left in Congo. I'll have to buy Paul one in Bujumbura, I guess. He is growing so fast.

May, 1965, Today is Janet's birthday. She is one year old, weighs twenty pounds and is our precious little doll. She is forever on the go. She calls us "Mommy" and "Daddy" and says "no, me, there, bye," and hugs our necks, kisses and holds out both hands when she wants us to pick her up. She comes to us when we say "come," and never walks when she can run. A Belgian fellow who was here has an eight month old who is just now pulling herself up to stand. He thought Janet was "*fantastique!*" when he saw her running all over. Everyone says they've never seen a baby like her. Aren't we the proud parents! We had a birthday supper for Janet and Myra Adamson last night. The volcanoes are just barely visible. It's nearing dry season, which brings increasingly limited visibility. But today has been gray and drizzly. I just finished preparing a whopping big Ward's order. Orcutts have a catalog. I'm having it sent here since duty charges are less and there is less mail theft. We'll try it and see how it works. If you have things you are planning to sew for us, please send them to this address too. I'll be here all June and July, and will return in September probably after school starts. At least Phil will still be here building. I plan to go back to Burundi in August with the kids, but we'll bring them up here the second week in June so we can all be together. The kids will love swimming in the lake.

Myra Adamson, RN, and Janet celebrate their birthdays

May 31, 1965, Mail goes out with the porter who walks to Cyangugu and back! Takes him two days. We'll get the mail he brings back on Wednesdays. Janet is entertaining us. She is such a clown. On Thursday we leave with Orcutts to go down to Burundi to bring the kids back! And we really get to go through Astrida, and miles of rain forest! How exciting! Did I tell you Estelle and I will live at Kumbya with all our kids. Their family will have one cottage and we'll live in another. The men will come over when they can. It's about three miles from the Mission to Kumbya, and as expensive as gas is, they can't come every day. I'll do the cooking, Estelle will do the sewing and we'll all go swimming every day and supervise the cleaning up of the grounds for the missionary retreat in July. There's lots of grass as tall as I am!

June 15, 1965, I'm sitting in Orcutt's Land Rover at the immigration hut near Bukavu, Congo, We are on our way to the United Nations dentist in Bukavu. Patty lost a couple fillings and now has a gum boil and a swollen face. Dr. Kuhn gave her penicillin this morning. We had gotten temporary fillings for her in Bujumbura. The Dentist told us the tooth was infected, and that this might happen. Poor little girl, she has had a lot of tooth trouble, more than all the other kids. We arrived at Kibogora with all our kids Friday evening. Phil is starting building again today on Merlin and Vera Adamson's new house here, at Kibogora Mission. Estelle and I are to pick up Vic Macy at the Cyangugu airport. He is flying up from Bujumbura this morning in his little plane. Waiting now in the dentist's office. He took an X-Ray and said he had to pull both teeth, couldn't save them. So we are waiting for the medicine to take effect. He is starting to pull now. Patty is an excellent patient, really brave, but she couldn't help crying. I guess she was frightened mostly. Estelle and Jon Orcutt are in now and Patty and I are in the waiting room. This is the first time I've been back in Congo since we left Baraka Mission. We saw downtown, with shot-out windows and bullet holes in the shop buildings. This used to be an absolutely gorgeous town, but it is getting raggedy, with weeds and long grass, but the flowers are still beautiful. The missionaries from this area are trying to get U.S. permission to return to visit their ruined mission stations and start helping in the church work again, but it remains to be seen how soon permission will be given. All is quiet in the northern Kivu Province section right now, but down where we were, it is getting hotter and hotter! The Bates said they often hear the guns from over by Uvira! We are back in Rwanda now. On the way we picked up Vic Macy at the airport. His plane had a flat tire, but he landed safely!

At Kumbya in Rwanda

June 27, 1965, Just a short note to let you know we are having a grand time here at Kumbya. We just told Vic Macy goodbye. We all had supper here. He and Paul Orcutt and the 'girls', Myra Adamson, Adeline Fast, and Dr. Kuhn, just left to go back to Kibogora Mission tonight. Paul Orcutt will take Vic to the airport early in the morning.

Phil is going back to Kibogora also and Joe is going to go with him so he can go into Bukavu with his daddy to get a filling. We didn't know his only filling had fallen out, until he sprouted a gum boil! Phil has the walls on the hospital ward building up to window level. They haven't been able to get the windows yet. They were ordered long, long ago from East Africa, but that's the way things are here now. So many shortages. However, we can buy flour and sugar, finally! Anyway, life doesn't get dull around here! We are all well but Janet. She has a croupy cough, but the doctor gave her some medicine. The kids are really enjoying swimming twice a day.

July 4, 1965, We spent a very quiet 4th here at Kumbya, enjoying all being together. Did you stay home too? I keep forgetting to ask you to please send two 17" or 18" khaki colored zippers with ends that open. They are for Paul's uniform jackets for Rift Valley Academy. So they should be good and sturdy, not the nylon kind. Please send them airmail, sewn up in cloth like you usually do, directly to Mrs. Marlene Bates, in Bujumbura, Burundi. Please put a note inside: "For Paul Kline's uniform jackets." I have already told Marlene I would ask you to send them directly to her. Paul's uniforms are being made by an African tailor in Bujumbura. We just heard on the news tonight of another uprising in Kivu Province, Congo. And here we were feeling it would be getting more calm! Pray! Only two more weeks until Kumbya Convention time. We hope the new crisis in Congo won't keep people away from the meetings. However, all the borders will undoubtedly tighten up again!

Tell Lois her packages arrived while we were at Kibuye Mission! We were so happy to get them. The socks and pants fit the kids perfectly. Jon Orcutt has a sore throat and Estelle has some mission business to take care of, so the Orcutts have gone back to Kibogora Mission for a couple days. Phil will leave early in the morning to go work on the hospital some more.

Kumbya Convention

I can't find a letter in which I probably told my folks about the Kumbya Convention of 1965, and I don't remember much about it. That may have been the time we stayed in a hut instead of in one of the cottages. That year we were all sick with some virus that caused diarrhea and vomiting, all at the same time! That was miserable! However, a Kumbya Convention is always a wonderful occasion, full of fellowship, spiritual growth, and lots of good food, fun and laughter. Each year we were stationed at Kibogora Mission, we helped Orcutts get ready for Kumbya, and I helped Estelle with the food planning and supervision of the kitchen. Don't remember how many came in 1965. That may have been the year there were several families who had evacuated from Congo, who joined the camp. The only paper I have from that year contains the notes I had written to share what the Lord had taught me when we had to evacuate from Baraka Mission, Congo.

I was able to tell the group, "I am rejoicing because I know God's grace is all sufficient. However, I will not pretend that this has been a year of constant victory. This has been an extremely difficult and painful year. For months I struggled not to indulge in self-pity, feel resentful, or ask 'why?' about Congo. We were there such a short time and were able to accomplish so little, it all seemed pointless, a mistake. And we had nothing left, but some of our clothing, our Bibles, my typewriter, portable sewing machine, Phil's cameras, and some of the kids' toys. But the Lord has marvelously supplied our needs! Other missionaries generously loaned us the necessities and made it possible for us to stay and work in Burundi and Rwanda. And then the Lord began to show me that I had been too attached to our possessions. He helped me to see that 'all those things' I thought we had to take to Congo with us, weren't really necessary. We could have lived OK without them. And after all, we are much more fortunate than were many other Congo missionaries. We are still alive! Our children were spared emotional shock. The Catholic Fathers who lived near us in Baraka didn't leave. They were killed. Phil left Congo the last time just three weeks before the rebels took our mission! In July, the Lord helped me to see that I had been struggling to maintain the right attitudes and to keep victorious in my own strength. How much better to rejoice in **His** strength, **His** victory, **His** power. **His** Grace **is** sufficient! I need to be thankful and content in all circumstances. I feel we are in the center of the Lord's will. This is His place for us now."

July 17, 1965, (letter from Byron Lamson and Betty, Phil's sister, Cattaraugus Camp) Dear Phil, Mary and family, As you can see, I am here for the camp meeting. It seems so strange to be away from Betty these last days before our wedding. I will be home four days to help with last minute arrangements. Betty is a good organizer and has listed every conceivable item. These she is caring for. It is simply amazing to me how well organized she is, and how calm. Perhaps it is good that I am out of her way. We are both so very happy anticipating our life together. Your kind and thoughtful suggestions to Betty were so good, but Betty is the most thoughtful person I have ever known. She thinks of my wants and needs before I think of them myself. We are having a great time. We have completed plans for our trip. We will be gone about two weeks. Hope we can write you from our 'hideout' and tell you all about it. These last few years have brought me sorrow and pain. Sometimes, I was tempted to think that the Lord had forgotten me, or that I had disobeyed the Lord and was being chastened. The events of the recent months fill my heart with praise and thanksgiving. God's goodness to me is so undeserved. We think of you, love you, and pray for you. I wish the church would send me to Africa, perhaps on World Fellowship business. I wouldn't come without Betty. I suppose our next letter will be after our marriage. Blessings on your family and your work, Yours, Byron

August 5, 1965, Saddle Lake, near Bangor, Michigan. (From Betty) Dear Phil and family, We are in a comfortable cabin here near Bangor. We decided it was too far to drive to Ottawa. We are so glad that we decided to come here. It has been quite chilly since we came, but we have a nice fireplace and we keep comfortable. It is warmer now. We are having a nice time, just being with each other. We are able to do our own cooking, so we do not have to go out very often. Monday, we went to South Haven, and I think we will go into Grand Junction a couple miles from here to mail some letters. The wedding went off real well. I found planning a wedding and reception wasn't bad, but getting the house cleared out so the Haslams could move right in was a job. We got most of the things down to the Park Avenue house and we will take the rest when we get back. Glen and Jeanne packed the trailer with Mom's things on Friday morning. They wanted to leave early Saturday morning. I hope Mom made the trip OK. I am eager to hear from them. Love, Betty

Still at Kumbya

August 2, 1965, Janet is playing with oranges in a half bucket of water. She is pretty good now about not putting everything in her mouth, except guavas. She loves them, green, ripe, or rotten! She has learned to climb out of the big pen we had built for her outside, up the rocks and over the brick wall! So now, there is no keeping her put and she runs away like mad! We have little jingle bells on her shoes so we can keep track of her! I finally put her in the little playpen in the house. The kids are all out exploring and the boys are out with the boat. This is the last day the Orcutt kids will be here. They are moving back to Kibogora Mission today. We will stay on here and Phil will drive back evenings. There is more room here for the kids. They are all begging to go back 'home' to Kibuye Mission, in Burundi. Only 3 1/2 more weeks until school begins at Mweya Mission. Patty is already feeling sorry for herself because she can't stay home to have school. This 'nomad' life is really hard on the kids, but they are having a wonderful time here. Swimming twice a day, jungles to explore, boats to row. They have all learned to swim really well. All jump off the diving board and Paul dives beautifully. He swam to Kirehe, an island about 1/4 mile from here twice. On his birthday he swam to Three Hump Island, a very small unpopulated island, about 1 1/2 - 2 miles from here. He made it in 1 1/2 hours. Phil rowed the boat alongside him and took Patty and Joe along. They got to see the huge bird that lives out there. We haven't been able to identify it. Paul's latest achievement is driving our car out to the main road, about a mile. Of course the mission road is narrow and curvy, but that makes it more exciting, I guess! He has known how to drive before, but his achievement is that he has convinced us we should let him practice! Janet jabbers and jabbers! She will soon be talking!

Back to Kibuye Mission in Burundi

August 16, 1965, Happy Anniversary! Mother and Daddy, How nice to be 'home' again at Kibuye Mission! We arrived Thursday night, tired and dusty after a thirteen hour trip! The miles aren't so many, but the roads are rough and we were quite a load for our little VW! Too much, in fact, because even though we went very slowly, the frame broke. Phil is going to try to weld it up at Mweya Mission tomorrow on his way to Bujumbura with Paul. Last trip down to town before school starts. The kids need shoes. I'm not going down, just sending a huge list along with Phil! We were finally able to go through the rain forest coming home from Kibogora Mission. We saw two families of big monkeys, beautiful scenery, all the mountains covered with tall trees, but not really as dense as I had expected. We had to wait two hours at the border again. Drunk official asleep, plus the fact that we arrived at the lunch hour! The trip took much longer than we had anticipated, so we were really exhausted when we arrived. Doris Moore had supper waiting for us. She is living in our house now. She still sleeps in hers, but she is in the process of moving out so Jim and Martha Kirkpatrick can move in, so the Hicks family, the new Canadian doctor and family, who arrived Saturday, can move in to the big house where the Ensigns used to live! Clear as mud, huh? Doris will live in our house, using the things she and Alexanders have loaned us while we are at Kibogora Mission. She goes home on furlough in December. There are four missionary residences here at Kibuye Mission. School starts at Mweya Mission, September 1, and Paul's at Rift Valley Academy starts September 8. Guess we'll try to drive Paul over to Kenya after we take the other kids to Mweya Mission.

August 22, 1965, Phil is about ready to take off for Bujumbura to take Dr. and Mrs. Hicks back down there. They will go by way of

Muyebe Mission so they can meet everybody there. Phil got down to Bujumbura a day later than he thought he would because the whole frame, on our little V.W. was broken! He got it all welded up, and I guess we'll go on over to Kenya to take Paul to school and will also take a Friends missionary's son too. Anyway, Phil came home the same day he got down to town to bring the Hicks family. They have to go back Monday morning to begin their period of training there, about six weeks. I've been sewing like mad. Made the girls' robes, finally got all the name tapes sewed on, and now I'm going to sew up a couple of dresses for the girls.

We take Paul and Phil Thornberg to R.V.A. at Kijabe, Kenya

September 11, 1965, We are at the Mennonite Guest House in Nairobi, Kenya. Really seems strange to be back in civilization again and still be in Africa. You can buy absolutely everything here! Certainly different than in Burundi and Rwanda! We have gone through twice the amount of money we intended to! Nairobi is a **big** city. We drove through three game parks on our way here and another one yesterday, near Nairobi. We had parked in an area in the park where you were allowed to get out of your car and walk a ways to see the hippo pool. Janet was asleep in the back seat, so we left my window open. Suddenly we heard her **screaming**! We dashed back to the car and were horrified to see a **baboon** inside our car! As we approached, he grabbed our lunch bag, jumped out the window, and ran away. We were so afraid for Janet, and thanked the Lord for protecting her. Baboons are so unpredictable and strong! Hope I never get close to one again! We've seen everything but rhino. Serengeti is the best, absolutely thousands of animals all the way through, but a lot of tsetse flies. We all got bitten. Hope the flies weren't carriers of sleeping sickness! We brought Paul and his friend, Phillip Thornburg to Kijabe Wednesday, and after doing some shopping, we are actually just loafing. Hard to relax after you have worked so hard and fast for so long. Rift Valley Academy is big, more than 340 students, about half high school. Paul's dorm is 8th and 9th grade boys, only! He is taking Algebra, biology, English, French, Bible, P.E. and piano.

September 16, 1965, We are between Kampala and Entebbe, Uganda, at Lweza, Corrie Ten Boom's favorite missionary rest home. She is still here resting on doctor's orders before she begins another strenuous year of travel and speaking. Have you read her books? "A Prisoner and Yet" is her story of her imprisonment during World War II in Nazi concentration camps. She is about 73 and still going strong. Next year she will be going to the States. When I read her books I never thought I would have the privilege of becoming acquainted with her. We were sitting in the living room visiting, and I was holding Janet firmly on my lap. I was afraid she would break some of the lovely things in the room. Corrie told me not to hold her so tightly, to let her go! But I knew what a mess she could make. I was so embarrassed! We are having heavy rain today, but there has been a bad drought in East Africa. This is normally in the equatorial rain belt, a beautiful forest area, but this is the first heavy rain they've had in nine months! It usually rains all year round here!

Back at Kibogora Mission, Rwanda

October 5, 1965, Mail day again. Don't know why I don't write except just before the mail goes out! I am spending most of my time studying *Kinyarwanda*. This is the fifth language I have studied. However, English is the only one I am really fluent in! Anyway, I love studying, so I'm having fun! And it would be nice to be able to understand the people who live here. Phil just had another bout with malaria. He just gets more and more tired, and then we realize another attack is coming on. After a course of medicine to knock it, he feels better than he has for days! The kids seem to be happy in school. They have two new teachers this year and both are very nice. Haven't heard from Paul yet, but I imagine he is having a good time. Have you heard on the news about the government forces taking the Baraka area in Congo? That cuts off the rebel's supply line! Government troops already have the rebels almost surrounded except along the lake. They are bombing the area near Baraka Mission. I imagine there won't be much left when they get through! It would be nice if the rebels would get discouraged and quit.

Phil built a nice kitchen for me. Now I can cook and play house! We live in a *rondavel*, that is Kibogora Mission's guest room. It is round like a hut, only it has a concrete floor and a tile roof and is nicely plastered inside and white-washed, with brick outside, with a chimney and fireplace in the middle. It has a partial partition halfway through the middle, dividing the sleeping and living/dining areas. Phil added a work surface along in front of the partition and set my plastic dishpans through holes in the boards to make a sink! I have two, two-burner gas plates to cook on. Myra brought down dishes, kettles, and silverware that had belonged to Ila Gunsolus, and so we are all set up to do housekeeping here! Up until now we've been boarding with Orcutts! Janet is still a pill! She can make three messes while I'm cleaning up one! She tips over the wash basin, drags out her wet diapers, mops the floor with them and while I'm cleaning that up, she dashes over to my desk, grabs my pen and scribbles on everything! When I really want to get some work done, I send her out for a walk with an African boy who works for us! She is as fast as lightning. People say she must be a lot like I was at her age, but I'm sure I wasn't that lively, nor as noisy! However, she is learning to whisper and sing in a tiny sweet voice. We love her and wish you could see her, even though she'd make a shambles of your house in nothing flat if not restrained!

The cute little *rondavel* guest room we lived in for a while at Kibogora Mission

October 15, 1965, The Dodgers won the World Series! Phil stayed awake until midnight last night listening to the last game on the Armed Forces Radio Service! I went to sleep! We hear there is terrible warfare going on around Baraka Mission, however the government has re-taken all that area. They are 'mopping-up' now. We wonder how many *Babembe* people will be left when they get through! We got three letters from Paul. He is doing well and is having piano lessons. Patty and Joe's teacher is Mrs. Braddock from the San Fernando Free Methodist Church. They like her very much. Phil was able to buy a used saw from a Congo missionary who has gone to another area, and with Merlin Adamson's blades and other equipment, he is pretty well set-up now to do the woodwork on the new house and hospital. Merlin and Vera are living with Myra until their house is ready. It is being painted now. Phil has inside doors to make yet, closets to fix, the kitchen to do, and the plumbing, quite a bit remaining. We have decided to spend December and the last week of November in Burundi with our kids. Please continue to send all mail and packages here. They take five to six months to get here anyway. It's fun having Christmas at Easter time! Things people send for the kids' birthdays usually arrive just before Christmas!

Trouble in Burundi

October 19, 1965, I suppose you have heard the news about the outbreak of violence in Burundi. Right now it seems to be a racial thing between the two African tribes, the *Batutsi* and the *Bahutu*. However, it could erupt into something very ugly. Please request prayer for the safety of the missionaries and the Christians and our kids in school at Mweya Mission. We have no further word from Congo. Did I tell you Janet smashed her baby finger and lost a fingernail? We hope she gets another one! Then on Sunday she fell, whacked her head, and got a gash, which is nearly healed, but she still has a 'goose egg'. Phil is working on doors for Adamson's house. None available, of course, so he has to make them all from lumber that has been hand sawn. He has a surfacer, a power saw, and jointer rigged up. Merlin had some parts that fit the used saw Phil was able to buy in Bukavu, so he is quite well set up. Did I tell you the Board has approved the plans to enlarge our 'house'? It will have two bedrooms, a kitchen, storeroom and a really-truly bathroom! Our 'privy' is covered with a beautiful passion flower vine, granadilla. The present round house will be the living/dining room with a nice big picture window looking out over the lake and the volcanoes. Also they have sent $700 to purchase tools for building! Only problem is, there are none to buy here and must be ordered from the States! Another prayer request, that building supplies will become easier to obtain. It takes so long to get anything. We have been waiting since March for the steel windows for the hospital! Still aren't here! When I sweep, Janet brings me the cardboard I use for a dust pan. She brings Phil his shoes!

Janet is a doll!

October 28, 1965, Our kids in Burundi are coming home to Kibogora Mission, Saturday, we hope. This is a month sooner than we had anticipated, but things are going from bad to worse down there, and an extended vacation has been recommended. They may be here with us for a good long time. They will be bringing their books and lessons. Many of the church leaders have already been 'done in' and more are expected to get it any time. Evidently only the big city down there is under control. We'll feel so much better when our kids arrive safely. Olive Bodtcher has volunteered to go to Mweya Mission to get the children and take them down to Bujumbura. Then Gerald Bates will put them on the plane. If all goes well, Phil and Merlin Adamson will meet them at the Kamembe Airport about an hour from here. Unless things settle down, we won't be going down Thanksgiving time as planned. You have to have special permits to travel anywhere in Burundi now. The missionaries at Mweya are trying to get travel papers for all the kids. We had a special prayer meeting here tonight. It could easily be 'Congo' all over again, down there. Do request prayer for the safety of all the missionaries in Burundi and their families, and the church leaders who remain. Glad you received the pictures. Janet says, "Hi, I don't know, milk, more, again, no," and is very independent. Of course she spills food and milk, but usually insists on no help! You should see her dance the 'twist'! It's really funny. She has more energy! Don't know what we ever did without her! Phil has the nice built-ins nearly done except doors for Adamsons' house.

Our children escape from Burundi!

November 5, 1965, Have we told you yet our kids are with us? So Olive Bodtcher, brave soul, loaded all our kids, the Orcutts, Adamsons, and Klines into Jim Johnson's Land Rover. But they forgot to take Nancy's passport and the other kids' I.D. cards! So another couple sped down to Bujumbura the next morning with all of those papers just before the kids had to go to the airport. Tense drama! We were chewing our fingernails and spending most of our time listening to the radio transmitter. The Burundi missionaries were having radio contact every hour, expecting anytime to have to evacuate! However things aren't quite so tense, and only two missionaries were threatened. However, several pastors and teachers were brutally slaughtered. Johnsons are in Bujumbura and are waiting to see how things turn out. At all the road blocks, Olive let the guards think all seven kids were hers! She had a great time! Do continue to pray for the situation in Burundi. It is hanging in the balance. Still under martial law, with the Red-trained ones just waiting to take control. We will not be going down for Thanksgiving and Christmas as we had planned, since our kids are here. Paul will also come here December 7, we hope. Pray that nothing will go wrong in his getting here. His passport has been sent to get a visa for here. Pray that it will get returned to him in time, and also that his plane schedule will be worked out so there will be no difficulty in his reaching here. Also, please request prayer that the missionaries will not have to leave Burundi! We are having school here for our kids. Rather hectic, to say the least, but we are so thankful to have them safely with us! Our kids may be here with us for the rest of the year.

We risk a trip to Burundi

November 14, 1965, (This letter was begun at Kibuye Mission, Burundi.) We are rather surprised to find ourselves here at Kibuye Mission! We felt we should come down and get the rest of the things we had left here and the kids' clothing and more books from the school at Mweya Mission. We have decided to keep the kids with us at Kibogora Mission at least until after Christmas, or until things settle down here. I woke up in the night on Thursday and felt strongly that we should make this trip this weekend. Phil was very much opposed to the idea, so I dropped it, and prayed that if this trip was of the Lord, that Phil would agree. I did feel rather relieved that he had said "No," because some missionaries had been under house arrest at Muyebe Mission, and several pastors and teachers had been killed, and there was violence in many areas. But, the next morning, Phil woke up and said we should make the trip, so we started Saturday morning at 6:30 a.m., and had the best trip we have ever made! We even arrived here at Kibuye Mission in good time for supper, having stopped for an hour to visit with the Bates and Johnsons in Bujumbura. The trip was such a pleasant one that we did not feel overly tired, and I did not have a headache, which I had fully anticipated I would have! Someone was really praying for us! Even thinking about the trip had made us almost shake in our boots. Paul Orcutt said the kids' things weren't worth the risks involved, and Patty said she would rather do without her things than to be an orphan! But we both felt we should make the trip, so we came. Of course we haven't gotten back yet, and we could run into a batch of trouble yet, but I still feel that the Lord has paved the way before us. Nan, Pat and Joe are with the Orcutts at Kibogora Mission. We brought Janet down with us. Phil thought he should come alone, but I insisted on coming along. I thought our presence in the car with Phil might be helpful. And it was. Janet smiled and jabbered at all the soldiers along the way.

At Kibogora Mission, Monday evening, November 22. I was dreading the trip up more than I had dreaded the trip down, because we very foolishly put Paul's B.B. gun in the car, under everything else, of course. It isn't illegal to possess and carry it, but it looks like the real thing, and the country being under martial law, it was an extremely foolish thing to do. You never can tell what the drunk soldiers will do! We packed the car full to over-flowing at Kibuye Mission, went to Mweya Mission, loaded on the kids things, ours, Adamsons, and Orcutts. We had two footlockers on top, plus the back seat loaded to the ceiling! Phil was sure the torsion bars would break, but he couldn't buy any in Bujumbura. We stayed in Bujumbura two nights, did some shopping, and planned to leave at 6:30 Thursday morning, which we did. The earlier the better. You get through the barriers and past the border before the soldiers have time to get drunk, and you arrive home before dark.

Before we reached the first barrier, I remembered I had forgotten to thank and praise the Lord for what he was doing for us, how he was paving the way before us, so when I began to thank and praise Him, my fears left, and that horrible dread that had tied my stomach in knots for days, just disappeared, and of course we didn't have one speck of trouble or unpleasantness on the whole trip. The headache pills I had brought along, we gave to the customs and immigration men at the border who were sick! They didn't even ask to look at one suitcase, and they could have demanded that we unload everything! An absolute relief when we crossed the border and were back in Rwanda again!

While we were in Burundi several World Gospel Mission stations had their radio-transmitters taken away from them, and several more missionary families are under station arrest. Pray for them. Our stations still have their radio/phones. The single ladies have also returned to Muyebe Mission and have opened the school and dispensary. Two Friends families have already had to return to the States. Only prayer can save the country. Just two more weeks until Paul will be with us. We really miss him more with all the other kids home. We had a lovely swim Saturday at Kumbya. We fried chicken and potato chips and took a picnic lunch along. Please continue to pray.

Our VW Bug loaded with the rest of our stuff

Paul finally arrives!

December 6, 1965, We have come to Cyangugu to pick up Paul at the airport. There will be nearly a whole planeload of kids coming from Kenya. We came in the Land Rover and brought the Orcutt kids and Dr. Kuhn along. There are still two mission stations in Burundi, both World Gospel Mission, where they are under station arrest, and their mail is being confiscated. Poor people! We are at the airport now, and the plane is late. It only takes twenty minutes to fly from Bujumbura to here, but it takes us two hours to drive here from Kibogora Mission! Phil discovered a broken bolt in the steering, so he has gone back to Cyangugu to get it fixed. Well, Paul finally arrived, an hour and a half late! We are on the way home now.

Strong storm

December 19, 1965, Sunday afternoon again with thunder rolling in the distance. We had a whopper of a storm Friday that ripped off the shop roof. Phil threw planks up on top to keep part of it on to keep some of the lumber dry. He has such a time getting seasoned lumber anyway! I was having art class with my students, and sent Nancy down to the *rondavel* to close our windows. Janet was sleeping and it had started to hail. The wind was so strong you could hardly walk in it. Flattened banana trees and corn. I wonder if it was the tail end of a waterspout! The board has approved building a unit for the Bible School, so there's a lot of work to be done. Merlin and Vera's new house is cozy and they are nicely settled in. Merlin is to begin the Bible School in January. It's time to get supper. Sure wish we had a corner grocery store and could buy all sorts of food! It's more difficult to get things here than anywhere we've lived. Seems like nearly everything is scarce. We don't starve, but there are so many things you can't buy. Gets rather depressing sometimes. Janet's first sentence, "Where's the brush?" meaning toothbrush! Merry Christmas and Happy New Year.

December 28, 1965, We had a lovely Christmas. We ate a big chicken dinner at the single ladies' house, then we all went over to Orcutts' for our program and to open gifts. Julia and Jack Braddock were here from Mweya Mission. They are good people, from the Sylmar Free Methodist Church, in California. They have gone on a tour of Rwanda with Paul Orcutt this week. The kids sang "Silent Night" in German and "O Come all Ye Faithful" in Latin, and they had all memorized the Christmas story from Matthew and Luke, and said it in unison. It was nice. We were twenty-two altogether. Phil was given two sets of ping-pong nets and paddles! He is going to rig up a ping pong table, and we will all enjoy playing the game. Things still look bad in Burundi. We have heard of more executions of African leaders and enforced meetings of all pastors and missionaries in several areas. They were told by government officials that if they heard or observed anything that should be reported about any of their fellow workers that they must report to the government official! That is exactly the way the Reds operate! Do pray that those who have been so indoctrinated will no longer be in power there. We have been advised to keep our kids here in Rwanda.

January 17, 1966, Paul has gone back to Kenya again. We took him to the airport near Cyangugu Saturday early to catch the plane for Bujumbura. His plane took off at 9:45 a.m. He was scheduled to arrive in Nairobi, Kenya about 3:30 p.m., before we got back here at Kibogora Mission! Three kids from Congo were on the plane with him going back to Rift Valley Academy. Needless to say we were all sad to see him go.

He has turned out to be such a nice boy, it is a joy to have him home. We had a big taco supper the night before he left. Patty and I rolled out and fried all the tortillas, 48 of them! Paul said that wasn't enough, he only got three! There were twenty of us altogether, counting the little ones. The recipe we use is one Doris Moore made. Phil left at six this morning in the Land Rover to go to Kigali to purchase building supplies, get import permits for more building supplies from Burundi, and do some grocery shopping. He won't be back until Friday or Saturday. Really lonesome around here.

I suppose you hear more news about Burundi than we do. Things are worse again. There is fighting close to the border right now. The missionaries are just waiting tensely to see what will happen next. Gerald Bates told them all on the radio/telephone, "To sit loose in the saddle and keep an ear to the ground." "Yes, sit loose in the saddle, keep an ear to the ground, keep your nose to the grindstone, and your eye on the ball!" was Jim Kirkpatrick's response from Muyebe Mission! Dr. Hicks thought they had been sitting loose in the saddle, but said they would sit looser! Do ask people to continue to pray!

Estelle is going to Bukavu, Congo tomorrow to get her new glasses. She will take Jon to see about his glasses, Virginia to see the dentist, and Nancy to get her fillings polished. Paul Orcutt is recovering from a bout with malaria and flu. Had he been well, he would have gone to Kigali with Phil. Janet is talking more and more. She says, "Where's Daddy? I want more milk, Go away!" She's really an individual, and so independent now, will accept no help going down steps, goes down the steepest steps standing up! It's so nice to have the kids home so they can enjoy her too. Joe even likes her now. For a while he thought she was awful, too noisy! But she hugs his neck and kisses him and calls for him when he is up the hill. She really has him charmed. Well, I guess she has charmed us all! Nan is still asleep, and it is 5 o'clock! She is growing so fast she tires too easily. Doctor said she should have lots of rest until her heart muscle catches up with her bones! We are getting lovely tomatoes and cucumbers out of our garden now, also peas and beans, and lots of lettuce. We measured the kids while Paul was here. He is 5' 9 3/4," and Nancy is 5' 7 1/2"!

Jon, Estelle, Drusilla, Paul and Virginia Orcutt

Radio CORDAC goes off the air!

January 29, 1966, I guess I told you Phil had gone to Uganda to purchase and order building supplies. Merlin Adamson and Paul Orcutt were going to Nairobi for a big All-Africa Evangelicals meeting, in the Land Rover, taking two Africans along, so Phil decided to go as far as Kampala with them. They left last Monday. Sure a 'dead' place around here with no husbands! Janet keeps calling "Daddy!," and when you ask her where he is, she either waves and says, "bye-bye" or "all gom" which means all gone. Gerald Bates in Bujumbura was not on the radio/telephone net yesterday noon, and last night they said from Mweya Mission that Gerald had 'laryngitis', meaning that his transmitter had been confiscated. They also said that all Missions in Burundi were going to lose their transmitters. Early this morning I turned on Radio CORDAC, the Christian radio station in Bujumbura that our Mission cooperates with, and they were on! That was reassuring. When the English broadcast came on, they announced that this was their last broadcast! The governor in Bujumbura had ordered them to cease broadcasting! It was one of those horrible moments that you can hardly believe what you hear! But their broadcast was absolutely magnificent!

Tim Kirkpatrick does the English, and the whole program was full of assurance, encouragement and even victory in the face of seeming defeat. It was as thrilling as hearing about the Christians in Europe who defiantly sang, "A Mighty Fortress is our God," when under persecution. This noon Mweya and Muyebe Missions were both on the radio, and the American Ambassador in Kigali came on and announced that all missionaries in Burundi should listen as often as possible to the "Voice of America" radio station. Evidently they will give directions to the Missions in that manner in case it becomes necessary for them to evacuate. It's so heart-breaking, so immeasurably sad, to see this happen to Burundi. It makes your heart ache! Ask people to pray even more. It isn't too late yet for a miracle!

February 15, 1966, It's late, and I'm sure everyone on this hilltop is asleep, but me, and I should be. Phil got home on Wednesday, and left again yesterday. This time to Kigali to get import permits for the building materials, light plant and water system equipment he had ordered in Uganda. Poor man, I'm sure he is sick of all the red tape and forms to fill out in French already. He probably won't be home before Saturday. We are all well and happy. Janet is talking in clear, intelligible sentences now! "Where book go? Want me book." She knows all the kids' names and loves to call them. She's such a cute little one! There are still three Mission radio transmitters in operation in Burundi! They could be taken any day. Keep on praying! No further developments on the possible invasion of this country from the south. Pray that it won't happen!

We'll be taking up Myra Adamson's offer to trade houses with us soon. Adeline Fast is leaving to study for her Master's in French in Switzerland. So, we'll be living in a three bedroom house with all our family under one roof!

Invasion threatened!

March 1, 1966, Guess what? Radio CORDAC is back on the air! What a tremendous answer to prayer that is. We don't know the details, but it must have been miraculous! However, the Mission transmitters have not been returned and it certainly hampers and delays communication between Missions! Of course there are no telephones. Do pray that they will get their transmitters back. Also, we continue to hear rumors of thousands of *Batutsi* refugees preparing to invade Rwanda. One report said 17,000! What chaos and a mess that would make of this peaceful and calm corner of Africa. Pray that they will not invade, that something will happen to stop them, anything to keep such a terrible thing from happening! Gerald Bates writes from Bujumbura that he doesn't know of anything that can prevent an invasion. Only prayer can! My sinus infection is finally cleared up. Phil has it now. They are starting on the Bible School building today, leveling for the foundation. The site is ready for the generator house. They have torn down the out-house that we were using. They will build a new one farther down in the orchard for Myra, where it won't block Vera and Merlin's view of the lake!

Alert!

March 8, 1966, We've been hearing rumors for some time that an invasion was coming our way. Then last week the U.S. Embassy in Kigali called us by radio and told us to be ready to evacuate to Kigali, a 24 hour alert, with radio contact scheduled around the clock. So we packed our suitcases and were reminded several times a day that "the situation remains very serious! Keep on the alert!" Each time we listened, we expected they would say, "Get in your cars and come to Kigali." But each time the message was, "No change!" How thankful we were not to have to leave on Saturday! We were exhausted from moving all our things out of the *rondavel* to Orcutt's house so it could be ready for Myra to move into. It needs a fresh coat of whitewash. Then we had to pack our suitcases after all that! It's a terrible feeling to fear we might have to leave a Mission station unoccupied with all the unfinished work, Bible School in progress, buildings about to be built, a hospital full of sick people, Sunday School materials being prepared, and deacon's classes in progress before ordination at Conference next month. It would be awful if we had to evacuate now, so we are praying, and we know you and others at home have been praying also.

Then on Sunday, a U.S. official from the Embassy came around to all the American Missions in the Lake Kivu area and said if we had to evacuate it would be north to Kisenyi. That's on the very north end of the lake, next to Congo. They expected the Canadians from Butare and Belgians to flood Kigali, but that they expected no difficulty right here! How relieved we were! One group is expected to try to capture the Kamembe airport near Cyangugu that serves Bukavu, Congo, as well as this part of Rwanda. If it falls, we will be notified by radio, and told to evacuate, but it is well defended, so we expect to be able to stay right here and keep on working! We felt like singing the Doxology when we heard that. You see, Cyangugu is a good hour and a half from here by car, and we were relieved to hear that the invaders were on foot, so we are in NO real danger here. The Embassy is extremely cautious. They have orders that there are to be no more American hostages in Africa, so that's why they have the evacuation plans so carefully made. So, don't worry. Just continue to pray that the invasion will be stopped or prevented at or before the border. The U.S. Embassy wives and children have been flown to Nairobi to make room for people who might have to evacuate to Kigali. If you hear that on the news, don't be alarmed. It's just a precautionary measure! We are happy, relaxed, praising the Lord, and going about our business as usual. However, we are keeping our suitcases packed for the next few weeks and we continue to have three times a day radio contact with the Embassy. They expect an invasion south of Butare soon.

Janet is the cutest little mimic. If someone at the table asks for water to be passed, she reaches out and tries to pick up the water pitcher to pass it! Joyce Allmon sent her a sweet little red dress, so Janet wants that dress! Our catalog order came the other day with a pair of shoes for Janet, black nylon velvet, a little big yet, but she keeps climbing up, getting them out of the box and trying to put them on, and says "My shoes!" Phil says, "No doubt about it, she's a female!" Every time she does or says some cute new thing he shakes his head and very proudly says, "Did you ever see a child like that?"

March 15, 1966, We are still here, for which we are extremely thankful. Thanks to you and others for your continued prayers. Evidently they are being successful in persuading the *Tutsis* not to invade this time. However, the alert is still on. We still have radio contact with the U.S. Embassy and the daily message remains, "No change." Nice words to hear! After a while living under constant alert gets to be old stuff, and what was once something you laid awake nights and thought about with shudders, is now just the common place knowledge you live with. However, God's peace gives the assurance and joy to carry on as usual! The Lord has given me two verses in Psalms 5:11-12. "But let all those that put their trust in Thee rejoice; let them ever shout for joy, because thou defendest them; let them also that love Thy name be joyful in Thee. For thou, Lord, wilt bless the righteous; with favour wilt thou compass him as with a shield." And I took these thoughts to heart with the assurance that we were wrapped, sheltered and blanketed with God's love. He gave me **peace**. I made a notation of today's date in my Bible, and I praised and thanked Him!

I cut Janet's hair quite short. It makes her look so much older. She wakes up in the middle of the night and shouts for Joe, so he gets up and brings her to us! She says about everything now. It really seems strange to have such a talkative kid after our quiet Joe and Patty. Phil has finished the picture window in the *rondavel*. It really looks nice, and has a stupendous view of the lake. Phil's welder finally arrived. You should see him, just like a kid with a new toy! His sister, Jeanne, in McPherson, Kansas sent it to him. It was shipped about seven months ago! It's really nice. It generates its own electricity and can be used as a stand-by generator for electricity. It will also solder! Dr. Hicks' things arrived also. They had them sent here instead of to Burundi because the political situation here was more stable. You can never tell about these countries from one day to the next! Guess things are improving now in Burundi.

We move again!

March 22, 1966, Everything is fine here at Kibogora Mission. We are partly moved, and can't find anything! They still have another room to whitewash yet, so we wait. You get used to the slow pace. Everything in Africa goes in slow motion! Fortunately there's no rush, because Orcutts won't be coming back from Kumbya for another week. But I would like to get settled before Paul comes next Tuesday. Phil put the new engine on the washing machine and it really purrs! I had an absolutely huge wash, but it didn't rain until this evening, so most everything got dry. Phil is working on the plans for the new hospital unit he hopes to build next year. It will have an operating room and delivery room! The things Phil ordered from Kampala are due to arrive April 30. That includes light plant, materials for water system, bathroom fixtures, kitchen sinks.

March 23, 1966, It's a drippy, rainy day. The kitchen is full of soggy clothes, still dripping. The wood cook stove is blasting away, devouring wood like a starved monster! I've been teaching the third graders, Joe and Sharon, multiplication. I think they are beginning to understand! We are still in Orcutt's house and Orcutts are still over at Kumbya, teaching the deacons. Every time Patty puts on another dress, I see another hem to let down! That child is really growing. She is 10 1/2. We felt the earthquake the other morning that killed 100 people in Uganda, but here it was just a gentle rock-a-bye business that lasted rather long, but wasn't violent enough to scare you out of bed! We'll be moving into Myra's house next week. It's a duplex. Dr. Kuhn lives in the other half. They are patching and whitewashing the bedrooms for us now, and Phil is making the doorways high enough so he doesn't bump his head, poor tall man! Patty is sitting beside me doing geography. She is studying Holland. Nan is struggling with China. She is really doing well in piano, on the little pump organ. Her latest is "He Lives." Paul writes that he can pick out the melody of any song in the key of C and put the left hand with it. He is learning to improvise in his piano lessons at R.V.A. He'll be home April 5. The kids are counting the days! So are mom and dad! Nancy is learning to type. We don't have a book so I make up exercises for her. She is doing very well. She seems so much older than 12.

March 25, 1966, Dear Family, Surprise! Yes, it's really me, after such a long silence! We are still here in Rwanda despite the threat of invasion from the south. We hear the *Tutsis* who are hoping to invade are waiting for something, probably arms and ammunition coming from those who sponsor 'wars of liberation'! However, nothing could be more peaceful and lovely than Kibogora Mission now. Easter lilies are in full bloom down above the gardens, and there are also many lilies of the Nile. Lake Kivu is gorgeous, with its many islands and peninsulas that are green from all the rain we have been having. We are getting ready to plant more carrots and beets, and we have so many cabbages we are giving them away. Our lettuce is getting ready to head, and we have several rows of lima beans coming up. Wish you could see our kids. They grow so fast. Nancy is several inches taller than I. Paul is 5'10" already at 14! He will be coming home from high school in Kenya in two more weeks. We will drive to the airport near Cyangugu to meet him. He will be home for about five weeks before he goes back for the spring term. Paul writes that he is doing fine in his studies, especially piano. The main difficulty with his French is that he tries to say things just like you do in English! English is his least-liked subject. He is learning to play rugby, goes hiking in the nearby mountains along the Great Rift Valley, and helps the school maintenance man fix things, he is a chip off his father!

The 10th and lovely last house we lived in while we were in Africa

Patty has finally discovered that reading is fun. Janet can say just about everything now. We have just recently moved out of the little one-room round guest house where we have lived for a year. Myra Adamson has just moved down into the *rondavel*. Phil built a new picture window and door with a screen door even, for it. The old door let in mosquitoes. It will really seem strange to have all our kids sleeping in the same house with us. Our girls have been sleeping in a room at the single ladies' house, and Joe has been sleeping up in Orcutt's attic with Jon Orcutt. We will have three bedrooms! And we won't have to board with another family anymore. They have been really nice to us here, sharing their things and house with us, and we do appreciate it, but it will seem very nice to be by ourselves for a change. We think of you all so very often, even though we don't get many letters written. Your winter will soon be over. We don't have any here, except there has been snow on the volcanoes we can see at the north end of the lake, about 50 miles from here. They are about 16,000 feet high, but they don't look high because we are over a mile high ourselves! It never gets hot, stays about 70 the year round, day and night, however the sun can really feel hot if you are out in it for long. We are about 100 miles south of the equator. We try to take the kids over to the missionary rest camp at Kumbya about three miles from here every Saturday to go swimming. Of course, I like to swim too. We saw a waterspout about twenty miles up the lake today. It lasted about fifteen minutes after we first saw it! Phil has the hospital ward building finished, has the foundation started for the Bible School, and has the power house built for the generator when it arrives. Wow! We'll have electricity and water piped to our houses!

Myra Adamson in front of the remodeled *rondavel*

Janet is sick with malaria!

April 11, 1966, We are in our new house, nearly all settled. Only a few more boxes to unpack, but I've not made much progress the last few days. Janet has been very sick with malaria. She is feeling OK now, but we still can't give her solid food, nor let her run around. Needless to say we are all tired, but thankful she is so much better! We are so happy to have our son, Paul, home with us. He was chosen this term as the top Christian boy in his dorm! How thankful we are that he really loves the Lord and is determined to follow God's plan for his life! He has grown so much in so many ways. His voice has settled down. He can sing bass now, he loves playing rugby and runs a mile or two before breakfast every other day to keep in shape. Today he ran the three miles home from Kumbya! Don't I sound like a proud mama? April 12, Janet got so fussy last night I had to stop writing. By the time Phil got through fixing window screens, I was exhausted, and fell asleep before he finally succeeded in getting her to sleep. Another day and she should be almost back to normal and then the time will be up for her to get mumps! She really will be spoiled rotten by the time that is over! Wash day today, but it looks like rain. I guess I'd better wash anyway because the water is hot and our helper probably has the tubs and machine ready. Estelle is going to Cyangugu today to pick up Vic Macy at the airport. Conference starts in a couple days. Paul Orcutt and Merlin have gone to a meeting near Kigali. Phil took the kids swimming at Kumbya yesterday afternoon after it stopped raining. They enjoy it so much. Must get at my wash now.

April 20, 1966, We have mumps here too. Joe is in bed half swollen. The other kids are wishing they would hurry up and get them. All of Adamsons have them except Vera and she is about five months PG! Merlin is really sick and miserable. His mumps were practically without symptoms, so he didn't go to bed, but then he got worse. He had mumps when he was four, so you **can** get them twice! Phil and Paul are busy with electrical wiring. Paul is wiring the houses. Phil tells him where to put the fixtures and turns him loose! Phil is really thrilled that his son is such a big help! He seems so much older than fourteen! Phil has the complicated control panel finally figured out and wired. He used the big power plant to do some soldering on the wires with his new electric soldering iron! Vic Macy has left. He was here for conference. We got to see his new film, "Cheeza." It was made here at Kibogora Mission and at Kumbya. It won't be released until after Board meetings. He doesn't have the sound in it yet, but it is excellent. Sure hope you get to see it. It was filmed when they were just starting to build the ward unit and shows Phil and some of his workers building. It is the story of an African boy who is taken very sick with malaria while fishing and tells how he came to Kibogora Mission, gets well, and accepts the Lord as His Savior. There are some really good shots of Myra and Dr. Kuhn and the clinic. It's a really wonderful picture. Myra wrote the story for it. I made guava jelly yesterday. What a job! But the kids love it.

Unloading water system supplies from Kampala

Installing the power plant

April 25, 1966, What a beautiful day. I have beans coming up and cucumbers and carrots. The rainy season will soon be over, but by that time we should have water pumped up. Phil has the pump wiring done and they are taking lengths of pipe down the hill to the spring. Real progress these days, Paul has our house wired and is nearly through with Orcutts. He hopes to get all the houses wired before he leaves in about twelve days. Joe is better, but still in bed. He hasn't really been sick, but has been willing to stay in bed. Merlin is up, again, cautiously! (Tuesday) Phil left at 4:30 this morning to go to Kigali to buy cement. The last time he was there, there was none for sale! But they have since devalued their money, so there may be more things available, at a much higher price! The price of cement is nearly four times what it was a couple years ago! They have increased the duty charges a lot. Joe is still 'mumpy', but isn't sick. Patty thinks she is getting them!

African lady getting water from the spring way down the in the valley

May 2, 1966 (from Bujumbura) We are all done with our business here in Burundi, and will be leaving early in the morning for Kibogora Mission. We finished packing and sorting at Kibuye Mission, Tuesday, so came on down here Wednesday. We loaded the truck here this morning and did our shopping this afternoon. We were able to buy everything on our list! Really something to be back in civilization where you can buy things! Even cheese and luscious tangerines! We are taking back enough to pass around so everybody at Kibogora Mission can have some. Honestly, whenever I think of the States, I think of well-stocked shelves of food, all the many things you can't ever get here, especially in

Rwanda! Marlene has been getting quite a few packages from Women's Missionary Society ladies filled with all sorts of things that were needed. She is sending a boxful of stuff with us to Kibogora Mission, just like Christmas! We'll leave early in the morning. Phil has to clear the truck through customs at the border. It has a load of asbestos roofing, the rest of Adamson's things and some boxes of ours. Our little VW car is loaded with bedding, Jim Johnson's electric saw he is letting Phil use, and Paul's train set. After this trip, we'll be almost all 'moved' to Rwanda. The projects Phil has yet to do will probably keep him busy in Rwanda until furlough time. It is almost time to turn off the power plant, so goodnight.

Back at Kibogora Mission again

May 4, 1966, Another absolutely beautiful day. Bright sun after the daily downpour. Patty has the mumps now, and is quite swollen, but not too miserable. Nan is still wishing for her turn to stay in bed and get waited on! Jan gave us a scare last week. She fell off a bed and didn't try to get up. Just cried. She usually jumps up and says, "Fall down!" But this time she screamed and screamed. I finally got her quieted down and took her over to Dr. Kuhn. She said there were no broken bones, but for days she did nothing, but lie on her back. Then she started kicking her legs around and turning over on one side, but never onto her left side. I was so afraid she had injured her vertebra, but then one noon she said she wanted to sit in her chair. Phil very carefully sat her down and she ate and ate! We felt that was an answer to prayer. The next day she sat up by herself and that evening stood up in her bed! Then she began to walk and has gotten OK. Don't know what it was, but we are so thankful she is her lively, mischievous self again! Estelle said we all looked as though we had nearly had a funeral while Janet was flat on her back! Joe caught the weirdest looking praying mantis today. It is dark green and chartreuse with a bulls-eye on its back! It's really fabulous! Joe is sure it's rare. It even has ruffles on its sides! Phil is getting the pipes and underground electric cables to the houses. There are ditches everywhere!

CHAPTER 10

Building, Electricity, and Water at Kibogora Mission

May 9, 1966, Paul is back in school at Kijabe, Kenya already. What a short month that was! I didn't go in to Cyangugu when Paul left, because Patty was still sick and wanted me to stay home with her. She is still quite swollen, and is beginning to swell up now under her other ear. Nan came home Saturday sick, but she didn't want to be this sick! So all that remains to get the mumps yet are Janet and Drusilla! How wonderful to have electricity! They hurried up and finished connecting everything up the night before Paul had to leave so he could see the houses all lit up that he had worked so hard on! He was so excited, jumped up and down and ran around checking all the lights, and he turned off the main switch to fool everyone! Just like a kid at Christmas! When we finally sat down for supper he said, "You know, I've been so happy watching everyone be excited over getting electric lights, that I just now realized I don't have a light in my own room yet!" Joe is such a bird and nature lover. He and Steve Adamson try to identify every bird they see. Merlin has a good set of bird books.

You should have seen the excitement a couple days ago when they first pumped water up to the hilltop! The Africans just couldn't understand how electricity could make water come up the hill. They know how steep and far it is up from the spring! They were especially amazed that no one had to go down to the valley to start the pump! Everything starts with push buttons. How thankful everyone is to have lights and water! The plumbing in the houses still has to be done. Cement is available, finally for eighty dollars a ton!

And a miraculous thing has happened! After months of walking up and down the steep trail to the spring in the valley where the collecting tank has been built, day after day, several times a day, four hundred feet differential in elevation, Phil suddenly realized his legs no longer ached! After all these years of leg aches, and doctors trying to help him, and so many prayers for healing, the pain is gone! Praise the Lord! Rejoice with us!

Back to Burundi

May 20, 1966, (In Bujumbura) We had a very pleasant, but bumpy trip down from Kibogora Mission today. We'll go on up to Kibuye Mission tomorrow to begin the process of sorting out what remains of our things at Kibuye Mission. Betty Ellen Cox is moving into the house at Kibuye Mission where we were living in July. We'll have to pack up and put away all the things the Alexanders loaned to us too. Estelle offered to keep our kids, so we left them all with her. They felt we shouldn't bring Janet down here with us because she could come down with the mumps any day now! So we are alone. No kids. I'm really lost without my kids! We'll be going back in a week, probably accompanying the truck that will transport the asbestos roofing and the rest of Adamson's things that wouldn't go on the last truck! Things seem calm and quiet here. They are even working on the roads with graders! They really need it, too! Holes at least two feet deep, big ruts, rocks, deep sand and dust! Enough to jolt your liver! We heard a rumor that the thing we had been alerted about a few weeks ago was scheduled for this week! And now we are here and our kids are there! So, Phil and Gerald have gone downtown to check with 'Uncle Sam' to see what we should do! It's nearly dinner time, so they should be back any time, so we'll see! Do pray that this will all blow over again, and that all will remain as calm and peaceful as it is now. The thing that is really upsetting about this kind of thing is that so many innocent people suffer. These people never have enough of the basic human needs anyway. The men got back, and said that it must all be just another rumor, because 'Uncle' hadn't heard anything about it. So we'll go on up to Kibuye Mission and pack. But do pray and ask for continued prayer for all of these the countries in this area. Pray for stable political conditions, for relief for all the homeless, for peace and above all that more and more people will accept Jesus as their Saviour.

May 31, 1966, Back at Kibogora Mission in Rwanda. We had a pleasant trip back from Burundi. The trip took about nine hours, but we had to sit at the border an hour while they filled out all the customs papers for the load of asbestos roofing. We left the truck behind after Phil had paid the duty on it, and had it cleared. It arrived here about an hour after we did. The kids were thrilled to see us and to get the rest of their things from Mweya and Kibuye Missions. Janet still doesn't have the mumps! Nan and Pat are OK now and so is Estelle, but she is still weak. We had a big birthday party here last night for Janet, two years old, and Myra and Merlin. There were three cakes and supper for eighteen people! A lot of work, but lots of fun too. Janet's latest trick is to climb way up in the very tall loquat tree, and when you climb up to get her, she jumps from one branch to another and laughs at you! Just like a little monkey! She is a climber like Paul was. He was forever climbing up and over! Phil about has all his bookkeeping work caught up and is ready to start building again. He needs to finish the plumbing and start the construction of the Bible School and the house for Dr. Hicks and his family. They'll be coming up in September after the Ensigns get back from furlough to Kibuye. Orcutts will be moving over to Kumbya soon to supervise the grass cutting and getting ready for Kumbya Missionary Conference. There might be well over 100 people coming this year. It's our annual missionary family camp!

June 7, 1966, Nearly time for the lights to go out, but I'll hurry. Phil has the wiring done in the hospital ward unit and they have begun to level off for the foundation of the doctor's house. The water tank continues to go up, row by row. It's too high now to siphon water out by hose for the gardens, but Phil fixed taps at the bottom and one is already broken! Some of the people haven't learned yet how to use a water faucet! Phil has bursitis again. His shoulder bothers him a lot. The doctor has given him medicine and we hope it clears up.

Water tower being built

June 29, 1966, The water tank is up, about sixteen feet high. They are plastering the inside now. It will be great when we get all that water pressure! The walls are going up on the Bible school and the stones are rapidly filling the doctor's house foundation. We hope we can get some more cement before our few remaining sacks run out. A lot of cement has gone into building the walls of the water tank. It is double wall brick with cement and reinforcing iron fill.

In only two weeks all the people will be arriving for Kumbya Convention. Our kids can hardly wait! Orcutts, Dr. Kuhn and Myra all have been granted their furloughs, so maybe they will ask us to stay on. If they do, that will mean we won't be home until summer of 1968. We'll just have to wait and see. Paul likes R.V.A. so well, he would love to stay and graduate from there! Thank you for the four packages that just arrived. The kids are excited about the things you sent. For Christmas, the kids would like popcorn, candy bars, Tootsie roll suckers, chocolate chips and I would like vanilla, sage, cinnamon and nutmeg!

July 7, 1966, Another package arrived from you. It's fun having Christmas in July! The girls really look cute in their capri sets. You did a good job of fitting them. Thanks for making them. Also, please thank Mrs. Thrasher for the nice things she sent the kids. Vera had her baby today. Kathleen Ann. We saw her about an hour after she was born. Janet was absolutely entranced. Lorna said, "He's a girl!" Since Orcutts are living at Kumbya, Myra had set up a regular delivery room in Orcutt's bedroom. Really looks and smells like a hospital! Dr. Hicks and family came up from Burundi a couple days ago. They are temporarily staying at Kumbya. We may move over to Kumbya on Saturday. I wouldn't know what to do without Nancy! She really has a way with kids. Three more weeks and Paul will be home! Phil has been hauling bricks today in the Land Rover and trailer. All the trucks around are either broken down or hauling coffee. There are several coffee and tea plantations in the area. One has promised to haul bricks next week. Surely hope they do. It's hard to build without bricks! Phil's new tools and jointer arrived from Sears from the General Missionary Board. He is real happy with his new 'toys!'

Myra, Vera, Merlin
Lorna, Sharon and Steve Adamson

Dr. Floyd & Alice
Greg, Timmy & Tricia Hicks

Preparing for Kumbya Convention

July 11, 1966, Most things have doubled in price here, which makes it doubly difficult to stretch the money to build with! One tip you might pass on to anyone who mails clothing overseas. Pins rust and leave rust marks so it is better to remove them before mailing. Day after tomorrow we will move our beds over to Kumbya, so we will be all set up before the missionaries arrive from Burundi. The kids are looking forward to our convention. All their friends from Mweya Mission school will be here. Estelle says she is expecting about 120! With Estelle at Kumbya and Vera with a brand new baby, I'm station hostess, which means feeding lots of people.

The upper tank is finished and holds water! How marvelous to have hot and cold water piped into our houses! We don't realize how primitively we have been living until we get modern conveniences again! We get so used to doing without!

Paul finds it difficult to get home for vacation

August 5, 1966, The Kumbya Convention is over. The 100 people are gone, but we stayed on. Each day I relax and unwind a little bit more. We had a wonderful meeting, but it meant a lot of work for Estelle and me. We directed the work in the kitchen and with the help of other ladies, mixed the cakes, cookies, and salads, since our cook was usually busy making bread and Estelle's cook did the meat and vegetables. It was so nice seeing all the missionaries from Burundi again. They didn't have any trouble getting here, but the Burundi government has changed hands since, so they may be in for much trouble again. They have already gone through more than their share, so we hope and continue to pray for them.

1966 Kumbya Convention

August 9, 1966, Paul is home! Sam Vinton, in Bukavu found out that on Mondays there is a direct plane from Nairobi to Kamembe airport, in Rwanda, so he asked the American Embassy in Bukavu to contact the American Embassy in Nairobi to see if they could get Paul on. For good measure, he also sent a telegram for us to Kijabe and Phil went to Kigali on Monday to see if he could contact the school via radio-telephone. We had twice daily radio contact with Sam and last night he told us Paul had finally arrived! The border closed at 6 p.m., so we had to wait until today to go get Paul. Phil came back from Kigali late last night and drove out to Cyangugu, and Bukavu this morning to get Paul. He took Nan and Jon Orcutt with him. We were all thrilled at noon today to hear Dr. Hicks, at Kibuye Mission, back on the radio network! That is a real answer to prayer! The government gave Kibuye Mission back their transmitter. We hope and pray all the others will get theirs back too, especially Gerald Bates in Bujumbura. It is so difficult to carry on Mission business with no means of rapid communication. Keep on praying about conditions in Burundi.

August 16, 1966, We are about back to normal. The twenty-one people who came on the tour from the States came, but they could only stay here two hours! We had beds all made up for them, but we have no communication with Bujumbura, so they couldn't let us know. Can you imagine traveling thirty minutes by air, two hours by car, stay two hours, including a noon meal, get back in cars, drive two hours back to the airport over terrible roads, barely make it to the plane in time and fly back to Bujumbura? I'm sure they wouldn't have come here at all had they known how far it is! But we were glad to see them and hope they carry home a burden for the work and needs here. In the short time they were here, they toured the Mission station, had dinner and watched a program put on for them by the Youth directors who were here for a Sunday School Institute! When Paul Orcutt apologized for giving them such a bumpy ride, one lady said, "But we aren't any better than the missionaries. If they can take it, we can too." Without thinking, Paul Orcutt exclaimed, "But we have calluses!"

We are still enjoying having our son, Paul home with us. He is so big and grown-up and is crazy about playing rugby! Only three more weeks and he'll have to go back. Jon Orcutt will be going too. We helped Estelle print titles in *Kinyarwanda* on stacks of big pictures. We managed to get it all done in time for the Sunday School teachers to take them home. We kept Orcutts' kids for the weekend. Paul and Estelle went to a Youth Camp at an outstation. Paul, Jon and Joe are having fun sleeping in Merlin's tent! We had a heavy rain yesterday. How refreshing in the middle of the dustiest, driest dry season we've seen.

The herd boy's job is to keep the long horned cattle safe

A herd boy keeps dry with an 'umbrella'

August 23, 1966, It looks and feels as though rainy season has come already. The grass is green again and it rains nearly every day. You should see Paul's new toy! He made a little go-cart last vacation using wheels he brought home from school from an old power lawn mower. Today, he rigged up Merlin's gas engine on it with pulleys and V-belts, and even a switch and clutch and a steering wheel. It doesn't have enough power to carry Paul very far, but Joe drives it around! Even the men are getting a big kick out of it. The Africans think it is a real marvel.

Did I tell you what Janet said a couple weeks ago? She was praying, when all of a sudden she looked up and blurted out, "Patsy, you laughing at me!" She is the cutest, funniest little doll! Phil is building the fireplace now for the doctor's house. The walls are nearly up to the top of the windows. He has begun on the trusses for the Bible school roof. Our garden is doing nicely now. The tomatoes are big, but none are ripe yet. We had chili tonight with some of that good chili mix you sent. Yum! Thanks again. Do continue to pray. Revival is needed here.

Phil and Africans working on the house for Dr. Hicks' family

Morabafi and a helper building the chimney

School time

August 30, 1966, Another month gone and it's almost time for school again. Some of the kids' books have arrived. We are hoping they will all be here soon. Paul and Jon Orcutt leave for Kenya this Saturday. That's three days early, but there are only direct flights on Saturdays and he doesn't want to get there after school starts. Paul and Jon are doing the wiring in Adamson's house. Phil's bursitis is bothering him again. Sure wish he could get rid of it. Janet is fussy. She doesn't like to take naps, but is a mess when she goes without one. She is climbing up over the back of my chair and onto my back. What a monkey! Nan is just getting over another round with her tonsils. Guess we should have had them out. Surely looks like rainy season, and we can see the volcanoes now! Fabulously beautiful country! The kids have been having fun with an air-gun. Joe can shoot the birds he thinks are bullies, and I can get within an inch and a half of the bulls-eye! The doctor's house is ready for the concrete beam around the top of the walls. The Bible School building is ready for its roof! Good news, Muyebe Mission has their transmitter back and they were on the radio/phone network again today! Pray that Bujumbura Mission will get theirs back.

No school books!

September 13, 1966, We still haven't started school because our books are still not here. They come from Calvert Course in Maryland. We certainly hope they arrive soon! Phil made some really nice desks for the kids and a blackboard and bulletin board, so we're all set. I'll be teaching 2nd and 4th grades, Greg Hicks, Sharon Adamson, Virginia Orcutt and Joe. Estelle will have 5th, 7th and 8th, Nancy, Patty and Steve Adamson. I've just finished making a big department store order. Some things were stolen from our last order. Would you mind if I have them send this one to you, and then you can re-pack it all into small packets, sewn in cloth. Please fill the corners with popcorn, nuts, cinnamon, and candy.

Top row of our Kibogora Mission kids: Nancy &
Paul Kline, Jon Orcutt, Patsy Kline
Middle row: Steve & Sharon Adamson, David Kline, Virginia Orcutt
Bottom row: Drusilla Orcutt, Lorna Adamson, Janet Kline

September 20, 1966, Finally, we have started school. The kids are happy to be in school again. They were getting pretty bored. However, we still lack some of the books and materials. We hope and pray they arrive soon. Estelle gave me a big birthday supper last night, roast chicken. It was really nice. We received a letter from Paul written before school had started.

We planted cabbage, cauliflower, broccoli, cucumbers, celery, peppers and eggplant this afternoon. The rains continue, but not so heavy as they were. Phil's bursitis is finally not so painful. We are praying it will go away completely. It is so difficult for him to do nothing but stand and supervise the workers. The workers have to be shown again and again, so Phil has had to keep using his arm in spite of the pain. Patty wants me to thank you very much for the card and money you put in the bank for her. She was just as excited over that as she would have been over a package! Monday, All Phil's pain is gone! That's an answer to prayer!

September 26, 1966, (Letter from Mary's Mother) Dear Mary, Phil and Family, I had the nicest visit last night in a little corner of Africa, or should I say in the center of Africa. Victor Macy was here and showed one of his films, "Cheeza." The lake is beautiful. The whole picture was very good. We really enjoyed it. He did not have the sound track all worked out, but he did have background music. He narrated for it as we watched. I really felt like I had had a visit with you even though I could not see any of you but Phil. He looked good. Love, Mother

No furlough until 1968

October 11, 1966, Rain, and more rain, and most of the tomatoes are dead. We've got corn and beans, lettuce and cucumbers in now. We need the rain, but it is chilly, though. Phil is putting ceilings of corrugated iron to foil the termites in the doctor's house! (And someone told us that other missionaries, after hearing about Phil's ceilings, had decided that using corrugated iron for ceilings was a very good idea, instead of plastering with mud between and over wood poles.)

The Hicks family should be ready to move in sometime next week! Did I tell you that Gerald Bates flew down south to Baraka Mission in Congo? Things are pretty much of a mess there, he says. It looks more and more as if we won't be coming home until 1968 because the General Missionary Board has granted $6,000 for construction of a high school building for Africans here. Dr. Kirkpatrick will be here next month, so we'll talk with him then. Paul wants to go to Rift Valley Academy in Kenya again next year. He'd love to be able to graduate from R.V.A. If we do stay on, Nancy will go to school there in 1967 too. So, we'll see. We are praying for guidance. Phil is very tired. Hope it isn't malaria again. Our books still aren't here. Do pray that they will come soon. It's a lot of work to teach without books.

The school books arrive!

October 13, 1966, Such hilarious rejoicing you have never seen! Myra went to Cyangugu yesterday and when she returned last night she had packages. The rest of our Calvert School books had arrived! Soon our living room was swarming with excited kids and happy parents. All the books are here now. Only one package yet to come, papers and other supplies. Such nice books, really up-to-date, and even the new math! Nan's eighth grade spelling words are really something! The fourth graders are doing arithmetic. They have forgotten their times tables, again, so we have to start all over. It's so nice not to have to type all the lessons now. I'm even getting time for a little language study. We were relaxing last night, reading, when suddenly the lights went dim, and then out. Our new light plant has been so reliable, we've come to take it for granted! We lit the Aladdin lamps. Phil put on his shoes and socks and went to see what was wrong. It was just out of diesel fuel. Merlin usually sees about it, but he had gone to Kigali to take the two African men to the airport who are going to the Evangelical Conference in Berlin. The gauge was stuck and didn't register empty! Did I tell you Janet's latest cute saying? She was pretending she was feeding her dolls and said, "Eating curds and whey!" Nancy has been teaching her nursery rhymes! We do love our little doll!

November 1, 1966, Guess what arrived already? The airmail package of Janet's jeans and Phil's sander belt. I don't know who was the happiest, Janet or Phil! It came through right in the post box, not even any duty charged! So that was nice. I'm certainly glad to get Janet's jeans. It's so chilly and wet here now. I forgot to order undershirts and little girl panties, size three, for Janet. Also two black T-shirts for Paul, men's small size. He needs them for school, and the ones I had ordered before must have been stolen. Let me know how much, and I will send you another check. Rain, rain and more rain, but the gardens look nice and the strawberries I planted should bear soon. Phil has three rooms with floors poured in the doctor's new house. They are starting to paint one room and starting to plaster two more.

Phil's letter to members of his family

November 8, 1966, Dear Family, We have very little news from you, but our thoughts are so often of you, and we wonder how you are and what you are doing these days. Presently we are working on a house for Dr. Hicks' family. They are now staying at Kumbya, our missionary rest camp, which is about three miles from here while they are doing language study. We hope to have the house far enough along for them to move in by Christmas. We have stopped work on the Bible School until the house is completed. Joe has lots of fun studying and observing birds. All the kids enjoy catching and watching the chameleons eat flies, with their tongues popping out three or four inches to tack the fly on the end. Both Nan and Pat have the stamp collecting 'bug'. The kids have been having their ups and downs with flu, malaria, and some unknowns. Janet has just been sick for two days, and Pat for one, but both are playing now, so guess they are on the mend. Janet just went out to the living room singing, "The Lord is my shepherd." Nancy said, "I knew she could say it," and off they went to encourage her on. Janet is quite fond of her oldest sister. At 4 this morning, Janet was awake and crying, "I want Nancy." Before long, Nancy came. Real devotion. Paul is to come home about December 8 for over a month's school vacation. We are having him come to Kampala on the train, and someone from here will pick up Paul and Jon Orcutt. The plane service here is just so undependable these days! It is supper time this fine Sunday afternoon. Do write, so we will not be strangers when furlough time does come! Bye for now. Phil

Letter to Mary's parents in Los Angeles

November 23, 1966, Vic Macy and Dr. Kirkpatrick are about to leave for Bujumbura. We've had a very good visit with them, and they've learned a lot about the work in Rwanda. Since there is no personnel available for next year to start the high school, they agreed to let us use the money which was granted for it to begin to build the hospital surgical/maternity unit. Phil has agreed to stay on another year to get this built. So, that means we won't be home until August, 1968. We have made application for Nancy to attend Rift Valley Academy next year. I'll miss her terribly, but it will be good for her. There was another invasion attempt at our southern border a couple weeks ago. The border is closed again between the two countries. Three *Batutsi* groups tried at three different points to invade, but all three were driven back.

Air travel suspended in Burundi!

December 1, 1966, Only a week now until Paul comes home! I'm certainly glad he's not coming by plane. All flights through Burundi have been stopped! So that probably means no mail for us either! The borders are all sealed off because of renewed invasion attempts and now another change of government. What a mess! However, we heard today that all road barriers have now been removed in Burundi, so that probably means the airline flights may be resumed soon, too. The road south of us through the forest has been sealed off too because of the invasion attempts. There is still one box of school supplies that hasn't arrived yet! When it went through the Post Office in Bujumbura, paper was stolen. We got a letter about it from Kigali weeks ago, but still no package! The Hicks family plan to move to Kibogora Mission from Kumbya this week. Their bedrooms are finished and ready, and the electric wiring is done. Dr. Floyd did most of that. Phil is getting ready to have bricks made and burned for the new surgical unit. More work! Phil and I are in Bukavu. Phil brought me to the dentist. He filled one tooth, a small place in my rear tooth, but the upper one was too far gone. The nerve was exposed, so he pulled it out. It broke all to pieces. It was so grown to the bone that he had to hammer the three roots out separately! Quite a process! Leaves one rather shaky. But all the jarring should have shaken loose any gunk in my sinuses! He's from Haiti and is going to Chicago for a few months, and may not return, which leaves a huge area without even one dentist! Fortunately we all have pretty good teeth! The airplanes are again operating between here and Burundi. They were only stopped for one day. Well, we got everything done and are on our way home. Nancy took care of the kids today and taught the 4th graders and Greg for me. I would imagine she didn't get much of her own studying done.

December 20, 1966, School is out and we have our Christmas tree up, a small cedar we went out and chopped down. The kids have been having fun decorating it. Nan is making doll clothes and Pat wants me to help her make pot holders for all the 'aunties'. One of Joe's orchids is blooming in the big tree beside our house. The flowers are small, pale green, pretty. It is one that we brought from the rain forest. We may all go to Kampala to take the boys back to the train. I will get to go shopping! It's been ages since I've been in a store. More rain again, but it's good for our garden. We had our first corn today. It was good! Merry Christmas to all of you! We'll have our Christmas party all together Friday evening at Orcutts. We'll have our family Christmas Saturday evening. Hicks' kitchen is looking good. They have the kitchen cabinet uppers hung.

1967 – On the way to Kampala, Uganda

January 6, 1967, (In Kigali, Rwanda) We are in Kigali waiting for Phil to get through convincing the bank authorities they should give him an 'open' import permit so he won't have to fill out dozens of forms and yards of 'red tape'. Early tomorrow morning we are leaving for Kampala. We plan to stay three weeks, return the last of January, so Phil should get some rest in besides having lots of time to shop and order his building supplies for the year. We'll be staying at Lweza, Missionary Rest Home, which is also the favorite of Corrie Ten Boom. Beautiful place with huge lawn, flowers, forest paths, orchids and monkeys in trees, overlooking Lake Victoria. The boys' train to Kenya leaves on Sunday. It was such a hard trip today. Seven hours of bumping and bouncing and jolting to go not even 150 miles! Makes your bones ache! And most of the roads today were very narrow, mountainous, hardly wider than a driveway and in terrible condition. Tomorrow we'll have much better ones and in Uganda are asphalt roads! Oh joy! Civilization, here we come! And stores where you can really buy things! We'll also drive past Park Kagera, near the north eastern border of Rwanda, a game park!

We stopped at the equator marker when we took Paul and
Jon Orcutt to the train in Kampala, Uganda

Still in Kampala, Uganda

January 24, 1967, We went to Entebbe, about sixteen miles from
here. We took the kids to the zoo, geological museum, and botanical
gardens. They spent a good two hours at the Lake Victoria beach,
finding shells and rocks, beautiful place. We ate our lunch under
an enormously huge wild fig tree overlooking the beach. The fish
eagles, hornbills, anvil birds and starlings kept up a constant noisy
and interesting concert! We saw and identified a new bird, brilliantly
black and red. We are all bird crazy now. Phil takes pictures of them.
We are about ready to go to town to do our grocery shopping to take
back. We'll let the kids choose a few books and toys in the book shop.
Friday night we'll go to the circus, and Phil promised the kids a swim
in the hotel pool at Entebbe one day. We'll probably leave for Kigali on
Tuesday, but don't know when we'll get home. There will be quite a bit
of business to do in Kigali. We plan to go through the Kagera Game
Park on our way home too. It really seems strange to be having a real
vacation. We've really been relaxing!

January 31, 1967, (Still in Kampala) We've had a very nice vacation.
However, Phil hasn't gotten much rest. He's ordered about $8,000

worth of building materials that will be delivered from Kampala, on a truck. It has really taken a lot of his time to get all of that lined up. We're leaving in about three hours and I've not been asleep yet! I've a few more things to get organized before I can relax. We went swimming today in the pool at the Lake Victoria Hotel. The kids really had a good time. We're all sunburned. We went to the Royal Indian circus Friday night. It was very exciting. After the last trapeze act, Janet said she wanted to go up there and swing too! What a kid! We plan to stop at Park Kagera tomorrow night and spend Thursday in the Park to see the animals and to try to get some good pictures. Hope the tsetse flies leave us alone! We have some fly repellant, but they bite you through your clothes even! We hope to be home at Kibogora Mission by Saturday. We've been gone nearly a month. It won't be easy to go back to work again. We bought a beautiful butterfly book. I can just see all the kids starting to collect butterflies! Joe said tonight he was beginning to get excited about going home to Kibogora again, so he can see Steve Adamson and tell him about all the fantastic birds we've seen!

February, 1967, I'm sitting up in the church with the women's sewing class. You'd enjoy it, Mother. There are only ten women left to finish their projects. Most of them are making shirts for their husbands. I pin everything for them, they sew by hand. I check it and cut off another piece of thread for them if it is OK. Estelle is gone to the States, so I have both the women's and girls' classes to finish up. It's only Wednesday and Friday afternoons, but I try to pin everything in advance and that takes a long time at night. There are twenty girls left. But, unless I get a lot of pinning done before class, they line up and have to wait and wait! The women sew by hand so neatly you'd think it had been sewn on a machine! You may have heard Estelle left two weeks ago by plane with her two daughters for home. Her only sister, who is very sick, was asking for her. Paul Orcutt just got back late last night from Mombasa with the new Land Rover. He only had to pay ten percent duty instead of forty! Now we have adequate transportation for us all! Did I tell you we also have a new fridge? It took nearly a year to get here. It's really nice, stays cold, has a nice big freezing compartment, and doesn't use as much kerosene as the older types! The school kids are gone, blessed quiet! There is usually a first or second grade class in each wing of the church, no partitions. We meet in the middle, and when each class is singing a different song you really need ear plugs, and on Wednesdays there is a church membership preparation class besides, thirty kids repeating the catechism out loud after the preacher! The Kibogora Mission church is quite large, was built by Frank Adamson in 1960, and is usually full on Sundays.

Kibogora Mission Church, built by Frank Adamson

Bible School building at Kibogora Mission, built by Phil Kline

March 7, 1967, Seven packages arrived in four months time! That's amazing! They all arrived at the same time. Everything was in fine shape, nothing was broken open. Thanks for all your hard work. Thanks too for all the candy and popcorn you filled in the corners with and the spices and vanilla! How I enjoyed those Heath bars! Jan's jeans that you sent air mail have gotten lots of wear already. As soon as the new catalog arrives, I'll need to get off another order, since we're staying on another year. Do you mind repackaging it for me again? The jumper you made is cute and it fits nicely. Thanks. We've had no airmail for three weeks! They say the buses aren't running. Sure hope it comes through this week. The trucks arrived with building supplies and pipes from Kampala, twenty tons! Janet just came in near noon and said, "Mom, I'm sick and tired!" and when Nan put her down for her rest she said, "Cover me up properly!" What a vocabulary!

Drums call people to church

April 10, 1967, This is the Monday after the big weekend. We all feel pooped! Three to four thousand people here yesterday, for the big church Jubilee 25th year celebration. We fed about 150 guests at noon plus our families. Bishop Kendall leaves today for Bujumbura, Nairobi, London, and then home. We have so enjoyed having him. Good conference. Phil arrived back with Paul and Jon Orcutt on Friday from R.V.A., in Kenya. Phil took Dr. Kuhn clear to Mombasa, and made the trip back in **two** days! 1300 miles over these roads! His rear was so sore he could hardly sit down! They are through burning the first kiln of 40,000 bricks. The two VISA boys, John Van Valin and Don Hawkins, who are slated to go to Baraka Mission to do relief work have been here too. They are very nice fellows. We are all well. Janet just got over a little bout with malaria and has a cold now. It certainly is good to have Paul home again. Nancy was accepted at R.V.A. for next year, so we'll have to get her ready. Please send twelve dozen name tapes air mail for her, and twelve dozen for Paul, not air mail! Every item of clothing has to have a name tape on it.

We trek up north to see the volcanoes

May 2, 1967, Phil is in Kampala. He took Paul Orcutt to the train, so he could fly home from Nairobi for furlough. Our Paul and Jon Orcutt are on their way back to R.V.A. for the last term of school. It was so nice having Paul home. He's such a big help to Phil. Did I tell you about our volcanoes? We can see four of the chain of eight, the Virunga Mountains, north of Lake Kivu in Congo, Rwanda and Uganda. The two active volcanoes, Nyamulagira and Nyiragongo are both in Congo, and are puffing up clouds of smoke and if it's clear and the clouds are just right we can see the reflection of the fiery glow at night. They are about fifty miles north of here, it's terribly exciting! It's been many years since they last erupted. But we don't know if they are actually pouring out lava, or if it's just increased activity and smoke! They are pretty well covered with smoke most of the time now. Phil built a ping pong table and the kids are all busy learning to play. It's a good way for us to relax, too! Still lots of rain. Corn, tomatoes, and beans grow in our garden and a few strawberries too. Please add a roll of masking tape and some jean iron-on patches in the packages. I forgot to include them in our second Ward's order.

View of the volcanoes and Lake Kivu from our front door at Kibogora Mission
In clear weather four of the Virunga volcanoes north of Lake Kivu
can be seen from Kibogora Mission. Two are still active, Nyamulagira
and Nyiragongo. The other two, Mikeno and Karisimbi, are
dormant, and have been the home of mountain gorillas.

May 19, 1967, We received two letters from you last week! If someone wants to send me something, I need a plastic flannel backed table cloth, and four twin bed sheets. I have to send three with Nancy to school, which will leave us with not enough for when they come home on vacation. Please, only one to a package! Nancy is busy sewing pajamas to take to school. She is learning fast. She is such a nice daughter.

May, 1967, Janet's birthday! Looks as though dry season is here. It's ten degrees warmer than usual, 80 degrees! Don't need a sweater today. Nancy is taking tests today. Joe is finishing up today's arithmetic and Patty is putting away the wash. Nancy is taking time out to play with Janet. Phil is pouring the beam around the top of Dr. Hick's utility unit, and they are putting the roof on the shop building. Janet is three today, and is getting to be a little tease! Joe thinks she is terrible!

May 30, 1967, Another week and time again for the mail porter to come carrying the little tin trunk to Cyangugu. How he ever stands to walk 80 miles a week, I don't know! It seems I keep thinking of things that we need, rubber spatulas, Sears T-shirts for Phil. He brought twelve with him and they are falling to pieces. No rush, just the next time anyone goes to Sears, please. We are all counting the days of school left. Only one and a half months until Kumbya Convention. We hear they have secured J. Edwin Orr as speaker. He must be making an Africa tour. Thanks for your prayers.

June 13, 1967, No sooner had I started this than down came another rain. We ran out to rescue the sheets. Sure hope they get dry enough to use tonight! We hung them up in the warm kitchen. The wood stove keeps hot a long time. It's supposed to be the dry season, but that's the second heavy surprise rain today. They aren't making much building progress. Phil has knocked down the walls and took off the roof of the single ladies' apartment. The roof was all eaten by termites, so he decided to do some remodeling as well.

We hear about 150 are coming for Kumbya Convention. I'm in charge of cooking this year. I'll be glad when it's over. It's nice to see everybody, but oh the work! I must go over to Vera's soon to figure out beds. We've solved the housing problem, but need more beds. The people will have to bring camp cots. There will be fifty-seven Free Methodists, including kids, and we are responsible for arranging for their rooms. We'll have a grass hut this year and so will the new Congo VISA boys. There's been another battle over there so they are still unable to live at Baraka Mission! But we hear the rebels are pretty well cleaned out now. Bates plan to move to Bukavu, Congo before July, which is up near this end of Lake Kivu, not down where we were near Lake Tanganyika.

July 4, 1967, We are in the last stages of getting ready for the Kumbya Convention, our missionary family camp. We've heard we can buy carrots and potatoes in Bukavu, so that should help solve the food problem! We plan to move to Kumbya the last of this week, probably Saturday to help in the final getting ready there, and by moving, that's what I mean, even beds! Paul will be home in three weeks, and then only five weeks after that, Nancy will go with him to Kenya! The Nitzsches, both nurses, are scheduled to arrive Friday in Kigali from Belgium. Another rain today, but the green grass certainly looks nice! This time last year it was all brown and dry. If you have any packages left to send, please tuck in some sweet corn seed. We can't get any here.

More war!

July 11, 1967, We were planning on coming to Kumbya last Saturday to get ready for our annual missionary convention. We knew we had a lot of work to do because 150 had already sent in reservations, but we'll have 200 plus! On July 6 we heard the shocking news that Congo was having another civil war. The missionaries in Bukavu woke up July 5 to the sound of what sounded like firecrackers and then realized with horror that it was gunshots! As many as could were evacuated to Kibogora Mission and then to Kumbya by the American Consulate. He went back in several times to destroy papers, radios, rescue his decoding machine, and get more Americans and Europeans out. One group of missionaries was too late to meet up with the first group who had barely escaped. They were shot at! After having been held prisoners for a whole day, losing four cars and half their valuables and clothing, the American Consul finally got them across the border too! We all rejoiced when they came. None were injured, but several had been slapped and spit at. The local population in Bukavu was yelling, "Kill all the whites!" All the missionaries except the Swedes and Norwegians are safely out of Bukavu, and we are running a refugee camp! Many others are still out in the 'bush', unable to evacuate. Pray much for them. Bates had just moved to Bukavu, but had returned to Bujumbura to wind up their business there! Don and John, our VISA boys are here, safe. What a mess Congo is in!

August 8, 1967, Fighting is still going on now in Bukavu, Congo. The mercenaries have returned to retake the town, only it's a ghost town now. Everyone has left, except the soldiers! The Congo soldiers have been carting away white people's goods by the truck loads! One Baptist missionary family had only unpacked their shipment three days before they had to evacuate! Last week word came that their house had been completely emptied! More Norwegian families came to Kumbya today. Some are leaving to go back to Europe. It doesn't look as though any missionaries will be returning to Bukavu very soon. Some of the Congo missionaries are over here tonight listening to the radio, trying to eaves-drop on the battle radio talk in Bukavu! What a mess things are in. But our little country is still OK and is very pro-West, for which we are thankful. It's bad enough to be this close to all the trouble, it's only forty miles from here, but it won't cross the border.

August 14, 1967, (Letter from Nancy to Francie Langford, her cousin in California) Dear Francie, *Jambo, Habari gani*? Guess what that means? "Hello, how are things going down your way?" We have been having some excitement over here at Kibogora Mission. All the missionaries had to evacuate from Bukavu, about thirty-five miles from here, so we put them at Kumbya, the missions' rest camp close to here, and fed them for a week. After that we sold them food, so they could set up housekeeping for themselves. They have been there about a month and a half, and the *Prefect*, the local government official, came and told them they had to leave or they would be forced to go back where they came from. Anyway, they all left us yesterday, and this morning are on their way to Kigali. Some of them will probably go back to the States. This is the fourth time to evacuate for some of them! Janet is 3 1/2 and she is a little, or should I say a big doll. I will be fourteen in September, and I will be in ninth grade. On the 3rd of September Daddy is going to take Paul and me 1,000 miles to Rift Valley Academy in Kenya. Mommy is making my uniforms now. They are light gray. We have decided to stay here for another year. Paul wants to finish his senior year at R.V.A. Time sure does fly! We have already been out here 4 1/2 years and it only seems like one. It's so quiet and peaceful around here that it's hard to believe that there is war and trouble in other places. I wish you could be here and see beautiful Lake Kivu with all its islands and peninsulas. It is especially beautiful during rainy season when everything is all shades of green and the lake is deep blue and you can see the four volcanoes on the horizon. I think this is the prettiest place in the world. Well, it's about supper time, so I'd better say bye for now. Love, Nancy, P.S. Please write.

Nancy's school clothes arrive just in time!

September 2, 1967, It's very late and I finally have Paul and Nancy ready to go to school in Kenya. Dot Orcutt and Dale Nitzsche are going for dental appointments in Kampala. That's the nearest dentist now! We heard there were stacks of packages in at the post office, so Phil and Paul went to get them. They refused to let them out because the papers had not been filled out yet! Phil finally talked them into letting him have ours, after paying a $2.50 bribe! They were all from you, our catalog order! That's really timing it. All of Nan's school clothes arrived the day before she leaves! We've been sewing on name tapes, and pressing. How thankful we are they arrived! Everything she really needed! The war continues in Bukavu. Phil and Paul saw and heard the air battles. Phil said it reminded him of World War II in the South Pacific! All the Norwegian missionaries are out now and most have returned to Norway. There are still several American missionary families back in the northeast Congo Kivu rain forest. Pray for them. Thanks for sending the packages. Thanks too for all the goodies!

Nancy and Paul, ready to go to R.V.A., in Kenya

September 23, 1967, I've been taking some medicine for 'rheumatiz' and my aches are almost gone. Phil has gone to Kigali to dismantle an old V.W. bug. It is the same year as ours. He'll bring all but the frame! A letter came yesterday from Nancy. Sounds as though she is adjusting well. She's wishing for her coat, though, says it's cold! We are a mile high here and they are 2,000 feet above us, on the top of the Escarpment of the Great Rift Valley, so it's windy and cold! I expect the next order will arrive next month. We hear that more packages are in Cyangugu now. The dress you made is very nice, love the colors. Thanks. Rain and more rain, but the grass is beautifully green. Yes, the corn seed arrived in good shape. It is planted and should be sprouting soon. Our tomatoes are still beautiful. I've been canning lots of juice. Your letter finally arrived that you wrote at the beach. Took one month. Sounds like daddy likes being retired. School is well under way and the kids are doing good work. Patty has been doing a lot of reading, so her school work is greatly improved.

Low on cement

October 3, 1967, The dresses have arrived! Not even four months, and in lovely condition. Your prayers must have really speeded it on its way! Our second Ward's order is beginning to come through already too. Thanks for the chili mix, oregano, sage and the tablecloth. It's really nice. We'll be using it every day! Thanks again for getting them all packed and sent. Lots of work, I know, and we certainly appreciate it. Nancy's coat arrived, but not the liner yet. However, there are more packages waiting in Cyangugu for the papers to get written. Our corn is up three inches, looks really good. Phil's cement hasn't arrived yet! Pray that it will come soon! He managed to borrow a small amount from the Seventh Day Adventist Mission about two hours north of here. He went up to do some welding for them. So now he will be able to go ahead with the plastering on Adamson's house. Janet is getting more mischievous all the time!

October 17, 1967, More rain, but we need it now. We've had several days without any, but I don't appreciate having my wash rained on. I just sent off another catalog order. I hope you are game for another session of package packing and sending! I've written suggestions to a ladies group that wanted to send us something. The main item I suggested to them was sheets. We barely have enough sheets to go around, and several of them are almost worn out. Maybe if they send several, we won't have to wait until the wash is done to make beds again! One has arrived that you sent, and just in time. The others should arrive before Paul and Nancy do, so I'll have enough for them too. The Brock family has been ordered out of Burundi, so they will arrive here tomorrow night. She can help teach kids, and he can help Phil with the building, which will be a big help. Poor mission in Burundi. They were so counting on having the Brocks for this year. I feel sorry for them, but I'm glad for us. Pray for Burundi.

Janet's 'dump bed'

October 25, 1967, I forgot to order white socks for Janet. Merlin is going to Kigali, so this mail should get to you sooner than usual. Janet's bed was getting too small, so we brought a bunk bed over from Kumbya for her and Nancy when she comes. Jan calls it her 'dump' bed! The Brocks are fairly well settled in the *rondavel*. Feels like snow on Mt. Karisimbi today. Mt. Karisimbi is one of the mountains where the gorillas live.

November 21, 1967, Another rainy drizzling day. Brocks will eat supper with us tonight. I have spaghetti sauce simmering on the stove, smells good! Janet and her small friends are playing in her room. Paul and Nan come home the 8th or 9th. The Nitzsches and Dot Orcutt are taking a short vacation in Kampala and will meet the kids at the train on December 6 and then will bring them home. We plan to take our vacation in January, so we'll be taking them back to the train. We hope to make a trip to Murchison Falls in Uganda before they have to leave. The game park there is really fabulous. Finally the rest of the packages have arrived. They sat in Cyangugu for over a month while they tried to decide how much duty they dare charge us! Everything came through in perfect condition. Thanks! Janet loves her new sleeping panties. She says "Grandma Beenama sent them!" Beenama is what she calls bananas!

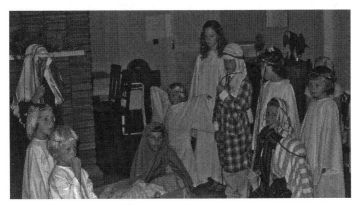

Kibogora missionary family children entertain parents with a Christmas program

1968, We vacation in Uganda

January 13, 1968, (from Kampala) Paul and Nancy have returned to school in Kenya. They went on the train from Kampala and the rest of us are staying on a couple more weeks to rest and shop. Before the kids had to catch the train, we took a trip to Murchison Falls Park on the Victoria Nile, up by Lake Albert in Uganda. We saw lots of hippos, crocodiles, and elephants, too many and too close to suit me! We took a boat tour up the Victoria Nile River so we could see the falls better. I held Janet tight and close, too many crocs in the river! The falls are 140 feet high and all that huge amount of water roars through a twenty foot opening in the rocky bluff, a really stupendous sight. There are 12,000 hippos in the park, 9,000 elephants, 20,000 Cape buffalo, innumerable crocodiles, and many different kinds of antelope. So we saw many animals, even one rhino. Have I told you about Janet's accomplishments? For our Christmas program she said all of John 3:16 by herself! Also she can sing the first verse of "Jesus Loves Me." She seems to have a very good memory. We plan to return to Kibogora Mission the last of this month and start work again. Phil has a lot to do before furlough time. Paul is hoping to stay on another year until he graduates from R.V.A., so if the Board approves, we'll leave him in Kenya while we go home!

February 13, 1968, The kids are all down at Brocks making valentine cookies for their party, so I get a little vacation this morning! It's chilly, we've a fire going in the fireplace. Rain again last night, but it's so clear you can see the volcanoes! Better not send any more packages. They probably wouldn't get here before we leave the last of July, unless you have some ready to go right away. The packages have been taking about four to five months to come. Nan writes that she is getting to take piano lessons now. At first, she was on the waiting list. Alice Hicks, the doctor's wife, teaches all the kids here piano lessons on the little pumpy organ. They are doing really good, especially Patty. She can play a few hymns. I injured my finger in some way and kept banging it, so Dr. Floyd says I can't use it for a month or he will put it in a cast! I thought at first it was arthritis. It looks like gout! But it is better. The swelling and most of the soreness is gone. But it means no typing and no playing the organ. Thanks for your prayers.

Changed lives at Rift Valley Academy

February 25, 1968, (Letter from Nancy to us from R.V.A.) I've got some wonderful news to tell you. There is an evangelistic team here in Kenya and they got them to speak here last week and today. Tuesday night Mr. Dawson was talking on consecration. When he gave the invitation to go forward, I went and gave my whole life to God. He's given me such peace and joy that I never knew was possible. My Christian life didn't mean much to me before, but now everything seems so different. I used to read my Bible before more or less out of a sense of duty, but now I can't seem to read it enough. I've been looking for something for about six months and I finally found it. I thank God that He has saved me and that He has taken all I can give Him, my life. I feel all the more now that God wants me to be a missionary, but I don't know where. Pray for me that I might find His will and stay in it. Monday night about 40 went up to accept Christ and about 100 of us on Tuesday. The attitude of the whole school seems changed. Please pray for the seniors, too. They were on safari during this week and seemed to see the change. I think that some of them need what we've been getting these last few days. The team is going down to Tanzania,

Uganda and Congo. We're having a science test this morning, and an algebra test tomorrow. This term has really flown by. Next Saturday our science class might climb Mount Longonot or go to Crater Lake. I hope we do. Our Sunday afternoon service was recorded and will be on the Word of Life broadcast in two weeks. Thousands of people listen to it. We just finished our science test. It wasn't really very hard. It's about time for the bell to ring. Lots of love, Nancy. P.S. Please pray that I'll be a witness to those here who aren't saved.

More bricks in the kiln!

March 4, 1968, Rain and more rain, but the atmosphere is crystal clear and the views around the lake are breathtakingly stupendous! I do think this must be the most beautiful place on earth! The lake level continues to rise. The water is so high now that when you dive off the diving board over at Kumbya, it dips right down into the water! But the air is a nice 70 again. For a couple weeks it was 60 and we were all chilly and kept fires going in our fireplaces. The men constructed and put up a new quad antenna for Merlin Adamson's ham radio. Two nights they were able to talk with Winona Lake, Indiana! We are well and are working hard. They have the foundation in and are starting up on the walls of the new surgical unit for the hospital. They also just sealed off a new kiln of bricks, almost 60,000 in one kiln. Costs only about $3 to make 1,000 bricks, but it really takes a terrific amount of trees to burn one! Phil is working on his bookkeeping. It's really a job to keep caught up on his accounts for all the projects he keeps going at once. The heat from the kerosene Aladdin lamps feels good. They have a mantle on them, something like a Coleman pressure lantern, but they burn without a noise.

Phil working on the quad antenna for talking to
mission headquarters in Indiana, U.S.A.

March 14, 1968, (Letter from Paul from R V A) Dear Mom and Dad, Well, it's 'raining cats and dogs', and I'm sick in bed. Yesterday I got hit in the head in rugby practice by Vic's knee. Then I tackled a guy and he ended up on top of my head; that finished me for that game. I had a real bad headache for the rest of the day and one this morning so I just stayed in bed. The choir's supposed to go into Nairobi tonight and make a TV program. I don't know whether or not I'll be able to go. I sure hope so.

On this going to the States business, I still want to stay here. What I think I'll do is, two of my roommates have asked me to come to their place for a vacation, so I'll go with them if the invitations hold. A couple days ago it rained so hard in Nairobi that Kenyatta Avenue was two feet deep in water. A feller stepped off the sidewalk onto the street and got whisked away to a drain; fell in and *kufad*, (died). He doesn't walk around Nairobi anymore. In typing all I can get is 42 words per minute. Nancy ends up with 43 and even 45 sometimes. That gets me discouraged, but Mrs. Coombs says that sisters can usually type faster than their brothers, so I guess I shouldn't feel bad. Well, it's only about 2 1/2 weeks until we come home. Tell all the peoples there *"Jambo,"* (hello) for me. Lots of love, Paul

March 19, 1968, We received a package from you mailed in June! Nine months to get here! That's some kind of a record! We've more in the post office waiting to be processed. More rain and a chilly 60! The surgical wing is up to the tops of the windows now. It will be nice. Our road to Kigali is blocked. The approach to a bridge is washed out, but they are working on it. Floyd Hicks smokes fish, hams and bacon for us after we have soaked the meat in salt water for several days. Really a delicious treat! We are all well. No more cases of infectious hepatitis. Please continue to pray that no one else here will get it! Two more weeks and Nan and Paul will be with us.

Kibogora Mission Hospital

Building the Kibogora Mission Hospital

1968 Kibogora Mission Hospital Staff

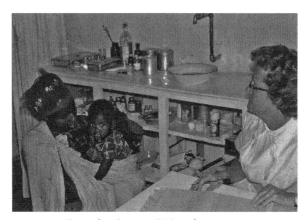

Dorothy Orcutt, RN with patients

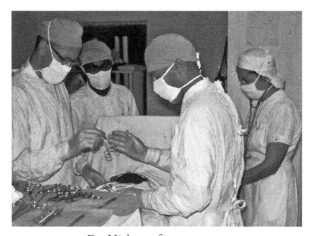

Dr. Hicks performs surgery

We go to the rain forest

April 16, 1968, Paul and Nancy are home and we've been having such a good time together. Today we drove up to the rain forest. We can see it on the mountains not too far from here, but to get there by car you have to drive about two hours. The kids had to stop every few minutes to catch some really beautiful butterflies. We brought back butterflies, rocks and plants. We also have four tree ferns, similar to the one you planted while we were home. We found a little road that went right down into the forest, with the tall trees over the road, just like you would imagine an equatorial forest to be. We found lots of orchids, both the tree and ground variety. We have most of them planted already. Joe tied the tree orchids up in a big tree in front of our house. They were on some big trees that had been cut down. Some of the trees were five to six feet in diameter. They were covered with orchids.

Brocks are taking Paul and Nan to the train in Kampala. They left at three this morning. Our whole family drove up to Kisenyi last weekend to see the volcanoes. We came back loaded with volcanic rocks. We took lots of pictures. Snow was on the highest one, Karisimbi! It's been wonderful having our family together again, and how we do miss them when they are in Kenya, but we know they are very happy at R.V.A. We received word yesterday from Dr. Kirkpatrick, approving Paul's staying at R.V.A. next year while we go home. So Paul is happy. I was really surprised at his answer. He said, "I would have been surprised had you been able to have gotten your son home during his senior year, and I am sure it will mean a great deal for him to be able to finish his work at Rift Valley Academy." He understands teenagers. He has two of his own!

Paul to vacation in Congo

May 2, 1968, A month is the usual time it takes airmail to arrive here! We suspect it comes by bus from Kigali, slowly! I think all the catalog order packages arrived, all at once! Paul has been invited to spend the next vacation at a Baptist mission in Congo, just north of the volcanoes. I'm so glad for him.

May 7, 1968, Phil's letter to Betty and Byron Lamson, from Kibogora Mission.

Dear Betty and Byron, Thanks for the run-down on cars. We have decided on the Olds 88 - 250 HP V8 4 door Sedan, with automatic transmission. Would it be possible for someone to do the temporary licensing, registering, and insurance for us, in order to save time after we get there?

Janet is four years old!

May, 1968, Big excitement around here today. It is Janet's birthday. She is about to burst her buttons at the importance of being four! This is very important to her because Timmy Hicks and Kathy Nitzsche have both been four for six months! We are all well. The kids are on their last month of school, and I've been sewing some summer clothes for Janet to take on our trip. Merlin talked with Winona Lake on the ham radio last night! The men built a good quad antenna for Merlin to use. We have been busy making jam and jelly out of guavas for Kumbya Convention. It will be held just the week before we leave. It's a lot of work, but it is fun, too. We will get to see everyone before we go. We are planning a birthday supper party for Janet tomorrow night. We are quite a crowd when we get together, five families, and Dorothy Orcutt. Between us we have fifteen kids!

June 6, 1968 (Excerpts from a letter from Betty and Byron Lamson.) We saw Krobers at Greenville last weekend. They are eager to see you and he said they had a job for you if you want it. I ordered your car yesterday from the local dealer, and he is selling it to us at the same price as what they would charge in Detroit. We will drive it for the first 1,000 miles, and get the 1,000 mile check-up done before you come here. Love, Betty

June 9, 1968, Phil's sister Jeanne Prevo from McPherson, Kansas, was wondering if we had decided where we would live in the fall. She said that Ed Pyle has a job for Phil, and that the church is acquiring things for us to set up housekeeping.

June 11, 1968, Friday night Alice Hicks plans a recital. She's been teaching all the kids music on the little pumpy organ. They are all doing nicely. Patty can play hymns. Nancy writes that she is the best hymn player in her dorm! She says, "So you know the musical ability of our dorm!" Paul is busy playing rugby. He is captain of the second team now. He could be on the first 15, but he'd rather be top man on second string than bottom man on first team! It's funny, when they write about the same game Paul tells about how they made points and all Nancy has to say is how dirty Paul's uniform got! She scrubs it clean for him after each game. What he ever did without her there, I'll never know! Dry season now, but we still get occasional showers. Only another week and a half of school. Then to pack! That's a job I don't enjoy!

June 23, 1968, (Letter to Mary's parents) Less than three weeks until we leave here! I hate the thoughts of leaving Africa! Please send your next letter in care of Betty Lamson. That will be our first stop. She has arranged for us to pick our car up at Fort Wayne or Warsaw, so we will be able to fly direct to Fort Wayne. Betty and Byron plan to meet us there. They have given us an air conditioner for our car so we won't perish in the heat! Phil has been talking to Betty on ham radio. Certainly a big improvement over our slow mail service! Our school is over, so I'm packing in earnest now. Our tentative schedule is to arrive at your place the evening of August 8, staying with you if you can put us up and can stand our noise that long, until the morning of August 15, when we plan to leave for Sue's. Do pray with us that the Lord will lead us to the place where He wants us! I'm sure He will! See you soon.

Almost ready to go, Janet is sick with malaria

July 17, 1968, Sunday night, and everyone else is asleep. We are getting near the end of our sorting and packing. We'll pack another drum this week and get our suitcases ready to go. I'm packing up all Myra's things she left for us to use. We're having no end of trouble over our plane reservations out of Kigali. We have heard that several other missionary families have had similar problems. Our Janet has been desperately ill with malaria. She began refusing to take her regular pills to prevent malaria attacks. We tried her on another kind, but they didn't help. So she got malaria. We called Dr. Floyd in the middle of the night. He gave her a shot of malaria medicine. She has had two more injections and is finally well again. We are so thankful! Now she is taking her pills because she doesn't like the shots! We are thankful we live in the days of modern miracle drugs! We are being careful to take extra Nivaquin these days of last busy work. By the time this reaches you, we'll be in Nairobi, waiting for our TWA plane! Do pray for a safe trip for us.

We are on our way to Kenya

July 20, 1968, (In the air over Kenya) At last we're on our way to Nairobi. Dale Brock drove us to Kigali yesterday. We hated to miss the rest of Kumbya Convention. We had learned that we had no reservations out of Kigali despite the fact that they had been confirmed long ago! This is Africa! So we had to charter a five-seater Piper Comanche to Entebbe and we had reservations out of there to Nairobi today, or so we thought! But our names weren't on the list! They finally found us places on the seventeen seater turbo-prop after Phil raised the roof! We should be in Nairobi in about an hour. We left Kigali at 8 this morning and took off from Entebbe, Uganda at 2. We are in clouds now and it's a bit rough. Joe loves it, but Patty doesn't feel so good. Tomorrow we plan to drive out to R.V.A. for the choir concert. Paul is in the choir. Commencement is on Monday.

Leaving Rwanda, heading for Nairobi, Kenya

In Nairobi

July 29, 1968, I'm in the most wonderful place in Africa! A **laundromat**! Can you imagine that in the wilds of Africa? Only you can't call the city of Nairobi a wild place! It's a big modern city. I've a huge wash, three tubs full. They have six new Speed Queens and two big driers! Phil has taken the kids to the airport to see one of Paul's friends off. Yes, we have Paul with us for this week! The Pelletier family, with whom he is spending the vacation in Congo went on ahead on Tuesday, taking the girl who was to go with a missionary lady next Monday. The lady is headed for the same Baptist Mission that Paul is going to! She was looking for a male rider! So everything is working out just right. We fully expected to have to say a goodbye to Paul this last Tuesday right after graduation, but the Lord answered our prayers in this marvelous way! Isn't He good to us? "Over and above all we could ask or think!" Ephesians 3:20. Yesterday we drove out to the Nairobi Game Park. We saw lots of different kinds of animals, zebra, giraffe, wart hogs, impala, hartebeests, wildebeests, waterbuck, bat-eared fox, and even a **lion**! We followed him around for about an hour and a half! Monday, July 29 - 5:30 a.m. Nearly time to get up, eat breakfast and get out to the airport. We've had a nice time in Nairobi, but it's really been chilly. Our plane leaves at 8:25. A Kombi is supposed to come pick us and our six suitcases and nine pieces of hand luggage up at 7:00. We eat on the plane. We are in the air again. This time in a 707 TWA. We've just passed Mt. Kenya sticking up above the clouds and we're still climbing. We will go up to 37,000 feet. Our only stop is Athens, but I'll mail this in New York. You might even get this one before the one I mailed in Nairobi.

We are at 5700 feet. Wish we could have flown near **Kilimanjaro**! We are waiting for breakfast to be served. Janet just said, "I wish we could stop and eat!" (Later) We just saw the Sudd, a marsh area that is covered with papyrus that the Nile River flows through. In the vast panorama of desert below, the Nile meanders all over, much more than one would imagine!

What lessons has God taught me?

1. God knows best. I need to be willing to be continually obedient to His Will. As we are continually surrendered to God's Will, He keeps us filled to overflowing with His Spirit.
2. God can use everything a person has learned, if we allow Him to.
3. God brings blessings to others through us as we keep yielded to Him.
4. I learned to hold loosely those I loved. The Mission Board asked us to go to Chikombedzi Mission in Southern Rhodesia to help the Embrees for a year. Some friends didn't think we should take our daughter, Patty, who was four, into such a bad malarial area since she had often been sick. The Lord led me to put her and our other children completely into His hands. Patty was the only member of our family who never had malaria!
5. During our second term, we lost almost everything we owned when we had to evacuate from Congo. I was tempted to become bitter and resentful. But God is faithful. He helped me learn that material possessions, even those things that seem precious to us aren't really what is important. Our family was protected, and our lives were spared. God abundantly supplied all our needs.
6. God lets us go through difficult times to help us grow spiritually.

Looking back after all these many years, I can see something I never realized until recently. God led us to follow in the footsteps of Frank and Hazel Adamson, who had met at Central College, and so did Phil and I. In 1947, the Adamsons, on furlough, from Ruanda, were our neighbors when Phil was attending Central College in McPherson, Kansas, and I was teaching there. They shared with us their love of working with the African people at Kibogora Mission in Ruanda.

In 1929, the Free Methodist Missionary Board had sent the Adamsons to South Africa, where Frank served as principal of the

Edwaleni School for African boys. We were sent to South Africa in 1953, and Phil was appointed principal of the same school, then named Edwaleni Technical College.

Frank and Hazel felt called to work in Urundi, in Central Africa, with the Haleys. They arrived in Urundi in 1936. We were given shelter and work in the same country, now called Burundi, after evacuating from Congo in 1964.

The Adamsons were pioneer Free Methodist missionaries in Ruanda, beginning in 1942, and established Kibogora Mission. Frank built a big church, mission houses, a shop and a garage, all with kiln burnt bricks. Hazel especially ministered to the needs of sick people and Ruandan orphans. They both were able to demonstrate how to live a victorious Christian life. Because of their example of sharing God's love, many people came to know Jesus as their Savior.

We felt so privileged to be led by the Lord to follow in the Adamson's footsteps to Kibogora Mission in Rwanda. Phil supervised the construction of a Bible School building, two hospital buildings, and two mission residences at Kibogora Mission. Phil also equipped the mission station with electric and water systems. I had the opportunity of teaching some of the missionary families' children at Kibogora, while the Mweya Mission school for the children of missionary families in Burundi was closed. What a wonderful privilege it was for us, to be able to work at Kibogora Mission, in Rwanda!

We arrive in the States

After a couple days of taking care of the required medical exams in New York, we flew to Fort Wayne, Indiana, where we were met by Betty and Byron Lamson, who had driven there in our brand new 1968 Oldsmobile 88, that they had ordered for us. We enjoyed our visit with them and others in Winona Lake. We stopped in Greenville, Illinois to visit friends there, drove on to Kansas to visit Lois and Johnny Bryan, Esther Kline, Jeanne and Glen Prevo, Joyce and Mitch Allmon and many other friends in McPherson, Kansas. We followed the route planned out for us by AAA, enjoyed our wonderful air conditioner, remembering those times years before when the only cooler we had for our car while crossing the desert was a water cooled dealie, mounted in a window, which blew cool air in on us! We were so thankful to be on smooth, paved highways, in a comfortable luxurious new car! What a difference from all those bumpy trips in Africa! We stopped in Phoenix, Arizona to visit with our good friends. We drove up to the South Rim of the Grand Canyon, stopping to see more as often as we could convince Phil to stop! And then we were in Los Angeles with Mary's parents, visiting with them, Orlean and Bill and family, Harland and Lois and family, P.D. and Norma Kline in Sierra Madre, and Ray and Ro Kline in Alhambra. Then up to Burlingame to visit Sue and her family.

Chapter 11

God Leads us to Modesto, California

We wrote the following letter to Paul at R.V.A: August, 1968, Dear Paul, We are at the airport, waiting for Daddy's plane to leave to take him to Winona Lake, Indiana for the deputation seminar. We love our car. It rides like a dream. Smooth, quiet and cool with that marvelous air conditioner. Does it ever have power! While we were at my folks' in Los Angeles, we received a letter from Esther Embree asking us to visit them in Modesto. We decided we could only have dinner with them because of our tight schedule. But at Sue's, Grace called and said she thought her kids had mumps. Since we couldn't go to see them at Oroville, we decided to spend the night with Embrees instead.

Daddy got to talking with Al Flory, who builds houses. Al and Gertrude live near Embrees. Dr. Paul had been trying to persuade us we should live in Modesto. Al offered Daddy a job as supervisor on the job, and so here we are, living in Modesto, California, and it is all in God's plan! We have a beautiful brand new home, just built this year. It has four bedrooms, fully carpeted, two bathrooms, air conditioning, forced air heat, dishwasher, built-in electric stove, everything! Washer and dryer are to be delivered Tuesday. It's a dream house and we all love it. The church people have loaned or given us a houseful of nice furniture. And the Embree family lives just down the street! All of us will enjoy living close to them again! The local junior college offers courses in carpentry, cabinet-making and mechanics. I'll have them send you a catalog, and you can see if you'd like it. It's only a couple miles from our house. Esther Embree did her first two years of college there. Isn't all this amazing? But this is unmistakably where God wants us for now! Did you have a good vacation? Be good. Study hard.

Love, Mom and Dad.

The Modesto Church gave our family a shower

The Lord provides us with a house of our own!

We returned to Modesto after visiting relatives, cancelled the rest of our trip, apologized to our good, generous friends in McPherson, Kansas, and moved into our beautiful brand new house. It was just right for us, the place God had prepared for us, and where I still live to this day! God marvelously again supplied **all** our needs. Phil had to do some deputation for a few months, and then went to work for Al Flory. Al arranged for us to pay rent until we had lived here long enough to qualify for an F.H.A. loan, and said he would apply the rent money on the down payment.

Our new home in Modesto, California

In 1972, Phil injured his back on a fishing trip in the Sierras. That was the beginning of a long series of back surgeries, hepatitis C, atrial fibrillation, cardioversions, bypass surgeries, aortic valve replacement, pacemakers, Non-Hodgkins Lymphoma, chemo, pneumonia and finally, advanced senile dementia. Through all of that, and even when Phil died in 2006, a few days after our 60th anniversary, God graciously continued to supply all our needs. We knew God would keep His promise to never leave us alone, and we continue to praise and thank Him.

I am 91, have stopped driving, and have finally retired from teaching an adult Sunday School class. I miss, a whole lot, my wonderful, sweet husband of sixty years, Phillip. I am filled with thanksgiving and praise to God as He has marvelously supplied all our needs for these many years. Our family has been very blessed! I am so thankful that God gave us such loving, kind, helpful, and considerate children. I am thankful that I do not have to live alone. Patty and her family live with me and help me in many ways. My two sons, Paul and David also live in Modesto with their wives. Nancy and her husband recently moved to Arroyo Grande, after living in Modesto for many years. I enjoy spending summers with my youngest daughter Janet, and her family. I love that Oregon mild weather, and living way out in the tall tree and hill country so close to the Siskiyou Mountains!

One Sunday, a few years ago, I had urged the members of my adult Sunday School class to pray that God would search each of our hearts and help us to see ourselves as He sees us. As I was walking to our car after class was over, the thought came to me, "Mary, you have never forgiven those who were responsible for the loss of your possessions when your family had to evacuate from Baraka Mission, Congo, during the *Simba* Rebellion in 1964!" A shocking thought! "Lord, I **do** forgive them. Through that experience You taught me that I was too attached to 'things'. You have miraculously supplied **all** our needs, and You have continued to bless us. Thank You for forgiving my resentment, and for **continuing to teach us to rejoice in the middle of whatever!"**

My prayer is that each of us will learn the secret of living a contented life, as taught by the Apostle Paul, " ...Rejoice in the Lord always, and again I say rejoice." and "I have learned, in whatsoever state I am, therewith to be content." Philippians 4:4 -11. I pray that my personal goal will always be to agree with the Psalmist David, "Let the words of my mouth and the meditation of my heart, be acceptable in thy sight, Oh Lord ..." Psalm 19:14.

I try to remember to take advantage of every opportunity to advise our grandchildren to pray for wisdom to always make good decisions. God allows us to suffer the consequences of our wrong choices.

I pray, "Oh Lord, may everything I do, say, or allow myself to think about, bring praise, honor, and glory to the name of our precious Lord and Savior, Jesus Christ." I also pray that God will enable all of us to be continually surrendered to His will.

RICK
Roberts

-907-
98
866 REDEYE Radio
www.Redeye.com
866-90-RED EYE

HONEY on google Chrome Store

Edwards Brothers Malloy
Oxnard, CA USA
April 1, 2016